Behavioural and Mental
Health Research

Behavioural and Mental Health Research

A Handbook of Skills and Methods

Second Edition

Edited by

Glenys Parry
Sheffield Consulting and Clinical Psychologists,
Community Health Sheffield

and

Fraser N. Watts
Faculty of Divinity, University of Cambridge

Erlbaum (UK) Taylor &Francis

Erlbaum (UK) Taylor & Francis
27 Church Road
Hove
East Sussex, BN3 2FA
UK

British Library Cataloguing in Publication Data

A catalogue record for this book is available from the British Library

  ISBN 0-86377-387-7 (Hbk)
  ISBN 0-86377-388-5 (Pbk)

Printed and bound by Redwood Books, Trowbridge, Wiltshire

Contents

List of Contributors

Paul Alexander Consultant Clinical Psychologist, District Psychology Services, Gregory House, St Martin's Hospital, Littlebourne Road, Canterbury, Kent CT1 1TD

Neil Brooks Director, Case Management Services, 14 Greenfield Road, Spinney Hill, Northampton NN3 2LH

Christopher J. Colbourn Department of Psychology, University of Southampton, Highfield, Southampton SO17 1BJ

Robert J. Edelmann Department of Psychology, University of Surrey, Guildford, Surrey GU2 5XH

Dorothy Margaret Fielding Consultant Clinical Psychologist, Head of Psychological Services, Department of Clinical Psychology, St James University Hospital, Beckett Street, Leeds LS9 7TF

David A. Good Social and Political Sciences, Free School Lane, Cambridge CB2 3RQ

Ray J. Hodgson Consultant Psychologist, Cardiff Community Health Care NHS Trust, Whitchurch Hospital, Whitchurch, Cardiff CF4 7XB

Paul Jackson MRC/ESRC Social and Applied Psychology Unit, Department of Psychology, University of Sheffield, Sheffield S10 2TN

Edgar Miller Department of Psychology (Clinical Section), University of Leicester, Leicester LE1 7RH

Stephen Morley Division of Psychiatry and Behavioural Sciences, School of Medicine, University of Leeds, Leeds LS2 9JT

Jim Orford Professor of Clinical and Community Psychology, School of Psychology, Univ ersity of Birmingham, Edgbaston, Birmingham B15 2TT

R. Glynn Owens Division of Science and Technology, University of Auckland, Private Bag 92019, Auckland, New Zealand

Glenys Parry Director of Psychology Services, Argyll House, 9 Williamson Road, Sheffield S11 9AR

Graham Powell The Psychology Service, 9 Devonshire Place, London W1N 1PB

Stephen Rollnick Consultant Psychologist, Cardiff Community Health Care NHS Trust, Whitchurch Hospital, Whitchurch, Cardiff CF4 7XB

David A. Shapiro .Director, Psychological Therapies Research Centre, Department of Psychology, University of Leeds, Leeds LS2 9JT

Geoff Shepherd Head of Research, The Sainsbury Centre, 134–138 Borough High Street, London SE12 1LB

Peter Slade Department of Clinical Psychology, Whelan Building, University of Liverpool, PO Box 147, Liverpool L69 3BX

Fraser N. Watts Faculty of Divinity, University of Cambridge, St John's Street, Cambridge CB2 1TW

Preface to the first edition

We are frequently consulted by colleagues and students for advice about research, as are all the contributors to this book. Although a number of excellent texts are available on research design and analysis, we continue to find a need for something rather different. Most of the people who consult us are psychologists, psychiatrists, social workers or graduates training in these disciplines. Their need for guidance arises in two main contexts—they are either conducting research or reading about someone else's. We wanted to provide a book which would be helpful in both enterprises. As behavioural scientists working in the mental health field, we were also aware of how many social and applied psychologists would find such a book useful.

Mental health professionals who are conducting research need information about the practicalities of how to do it, at least as much as advice about an appropriate research design. Most books on research methods do not give much insight into research skills. Our coverage of skills includes the basics: how to prepare a project, how to choose or develop measures, how to use computers, how to analyse data, how to write a research report. We have also included less obvious topics which we find are just as important: how to enjoy the research and so avoid a stressful research experience, and how to apply for funding. Each of these chapters is written with an honest appreciation of the realities of the research enterprise. These *tricks of the trade* are seldom written down. Sometimes they are handed on from supervisor to student during research training, but many of our readers may not have had the opportunity to learn them at first hand.

Many health professionals, when faced with a research problem, will consider only a narrow range of possible methods to explore it. All too often, the research question seems to be determined by knowledge of a particular method (e.g. experimental group comparisons). We would prefer the research problem to dictate the choice of method. Research should be like detective work, starting with a question and working towards an answer; the report of the research should be the story of how the question was answered. The *rules* of research methodology are really just tips about how to arrive safely and securely at a solution to the problem. We have tried to make sure that guidance on research is presented here, not as a set of arbitrary requirements, but as practical help in doing successful research.

A recurrent problem with psychological research is that it can too easily become trapped in particular paradigms. The range of research approaches available is actually very broad. Unfortunately, most *research methods* textbooks confine themselves to quantitative methods using group designs, and they also assume quite an advanced level of statistical knowledge. A particular research problem in the mental health field may be best explored by using a qualitative, language-based method rather than a quantitative, statistical one. Alternatively, the study of single cases or using one of a related family of intensive designs may be called for. Quite often, a method is needed which can be successfully used in a clinical situation to yield results directly applicable to clinical practice, for example, evaluating clinical services or investigating a patient series. Behavioural researchers will be able to recognise the relevance of these clinical examples to work in their own fields.

Although separate volumes about qualitative methods, epidemiology, single case research or service evaluation are available, they are often inaccessible to the beginner. We have found a need for one volume which covers a range of available research approaches to mental health problems. Each of our contributors is an established researcher in his or her field. In this way we hope to bring a breadth of experience to the reader and a deeper knowledge of each particular skill or method than could be achieved by a single author.

For every mental health worker engaged in research, there are several who are not. This is particularly true in those fields which require extensive resources, such as outcome research and epidemiology. However, everyone in the field of mental health needs to be an intelligent consumer of research findings. Making sense of other people's research is a skill in itself, and we know it is one which many find difficult. The present book should be helpful. It is much easier to evaluate a research report when one understands the basics of research design, measurement, analysis and interpretation.

Finally, many books are written in technical language which is daunting to the would-be researcher. We believe it is possible to explain most basic research skills and methods using ordinary language, and that where technical terms are unavoidable, they can be explained. We wanted a book which was *user-friendly*—accessible to the beginner, yet valuable to the more experienced.

We were quite clear what kind of a book was needed: a handbook rather than a textbook, a book for the desktop rather than the bookshelf. Whether we have achieved it, we shall leave the reader to judge.

Preface to the second edition

We have been encouraged by the positive response to the first edition of this book to prepare a revised and expanded edition. Research skills remain a fundamental part of the contribution of clinical psychologists to the Health Services and, given the renewed emphasis on Research and Development in Health Services, are increasingly important to all mental health professionals. However, many of those training in clinical psychology, psychiatry and nursing can feel intimidated by the complexity of research methods. We hope that they will find here a reliable, authoritative and user-friendly guide.

Research methods have not changed enormously in the five or six years since the first edition of this book was published. All the chapters have been carefully reviewed, but in most cases we found that the chapters have stood the test of time and have not needed massive reworking. However, we have become aware of several areas in which the previous book seems somewhat incomplete, and to remedy this we have added three new chapters in this expanded edition.

One, by Robert J. Edelmann, deals with the range of measures available to clinical psychologists; questionnaires, behavioural observation, psychophysiological measures etc. This complements the chapter in the previous edition by Graham E. Powell on the general principles involved in selecting and developing measures.

Secondly, there has been a growing tendency for psychologists to work in social or group settings, or in health-delivery systems. This development in the provision of services has been accompanied by similar development in research methods suitable for use in social settings. These methods are being reviewed in a new chapter by Jim Orford.

Finally, Health Services everywhere have placed an increasing emphasis on the careful monitoring and evaluation of the services that are provided. Mental health professionals are increasingly required to monitor their own effectiveness, and psychologists can make a significant research contribution to the monitoring of a broad range of health services. This change in the management climate of Health Services has led to the rapid development of expertise in the monitoring of services and the research methods used for this purpose are reviewed in a final new chapter, by Glenys Parry.

We hope that this revised edition will prove as useful as the previous one, and in particular that the new chapters will encourage clinical psychologists and others to extend their research competence.

Glenys Parry and Fraser Watts

About the editors

Glenys Parry is Director of Sheffield Consulting and Clinical Psychologists (an agency of Community Health Sheffield NHS Trust), and Senior Psychological Officer at the Department of Health in London. She has previously worked as a scientist at the Medical Research Council Social & Applied psychology Unit in Sheffield and was an Academic Director of the Wessex Regional training Course in Clinical Psychology.

Fraser Watts, a former scientist at the Medical Research Council Applied Psychology Unit in Cambridge, and former President of the British Psychological Society, is now Starbridge Lecturer in Theology and Natural Science in the University of Cambridge, and a fellow of Queen's College Cambridge.

PART ONE
Skills

CHAPTER ONE

More fun, less stress: How to survive in research

Ray Hodgson and Stephen Rollnick
Cardiff Community Healthcare, Whitchurch
Hospital, Cardiff

It is often said that stress is a feature of modern life. Therefore, stress management unsurprisingly is a bandwagon which is rapidly gaining momentum. Most airports and supermarkets display numerous books and articles on how to cope and how to succeed. It is very easy to find a self-help book which provides very practical advice on how to overcome stress, marital problems, alcoholism or all of these together. There are shelves full of paperbacks on how to succeed in management and how to delegate, with a strong emphasis on how to succeed without stress and without really trying. This is all well and good; but what has been published that will help the young, lively, questioning researcher who has great expectations but a lack of practical experience? As far as we know the answer is very little. The avowed aim of this chapter is therefore to provide what has come to be known as a 'brief intervention' which might help to prevent learned helplessness.

In the style of the non-conformist minister, John Wesley, we will begin by preaching doom and gloom, hellfire and damnation. Trouble awaits those unwary souls who believe that research flows smoothly and naturally from questions to answers via a well-organised data collection system. This is certainly not the case. Even the most experienced, systematic and hard-working research worker will have to face trials and tribulations before a project is successfully concluded. Hence to prevent relapse into more comfortable lifestyles, the problems encountered in carrying out a research investigation must be clearly anticipated. The following may appear to be simply a list of aphorisms but actually they are laws of nature. Ignore them at your peril!

1. GETTING STARTED WILL TAKE AT LEAST AS LONG AS THE DATA COLLECTION

This is not a problem provided that everybody is aware that this is the case and forward planning takes this law into account. Settling upon a key question, choosing a population or client group, devising questionnaires and a research design, guiding the proposal through the appropriate ethical committees and obtaining the co-operation of others are just a few of the time-consuming activities that seem to continue until somebody says that's enough. There may be a PhD at stake, and so one member of the team keeps adding extra conditions or novel questionnaires to make sure that his/her PhD has a strong base. The questions to be asked and the methods of answering them will repeatedly change. Complicated subsidiary projects will be grafted on until everybody is happy. We know of one study that took over 4 years to get started and about 3 years to collect the data. Although we were not closely involved we do know that the team members began to imagine that the project would never get off the ground and yet, when finally published, the study turned out to be very influential. The job satisfaction of the research team would have been much greater had they known about rule number one.

2. THE NUMBER OF AVAILABLE SUBJECTS WILL BE ONE-TENTH OF YOUR FIRST ESTIMATE

It is well known that if a particular disorder is being researched then people suffering from that problem seem to leave the district. The wider the net is spread the further they go. Recently, a trainee clinical psychologist in South Glamorgan decided that obese subjects would be very easy to obtain, and so obesity was chosen as the topic of his dissertation. You would imagine, as he did, that many people suffering from obesity would welcome the opportunity to discuss their problem with a psychologist and to obtain some advice on changing habits and self-management. Discussions with GPs indicated that at least forty subjects would be referred within a couple of months and the trainee was almost overcome by a sense of joyful anticipation. Six months later a desperate situation arose when the deadline for data collection had passed and still only three suitable clients had been referred.

Obtaining subjects is like betting on a horse. The most realistic assumption to make is that your expectations will turn out to be wrong.

3. COMPLETION OF A RESEARCH PROJECT WILL TAKE TWICE AS LONG AS YOUR LAST ESTIMATE AND THREE TIMES AS LONG AS YOUR FIRST ESTIMATE

A piece of research will almost never take less than the first estimate unless it is drastically cut down to size. Of course it should be recognized that the first estimate will be a function of personality and cognitive style. Pessimists will tend to over-estimate the time needed to carry out a variety of research tasks. Our deliberations have taken this into account but it is a very minor factor since only optimists get involved in research. Very often a project takes so long that it is never completed, but we have left these failures out of the calculation when formulating our equations.

4. A RESEARCH PROJECT WILL CHANGE TWICE IN THE MIDDLE

One common misconception of the research process is responsible for a great deal of frustration. It is a popular view that a research worker progresses as smoothly as Sherlock Holmes from questions to answers via the systematic gathering of evidence. This is not the case, as the following typical example demonstrates. A few years ago, we decided to test out the effectiveness of Drinkwatchers groups for problem drinkers attempting to control their drinking. We obtained a small grant from the Medical Research Council and started to advertise. All we needed were thirty subjects from amongst the estimated 10,000 problem drinkers in South Glamorgan. One hundred and sixty problem drinkers answered the advertisement which deliberately did not provide details of the type of help that we were intending to provide. Of these only eight volunteered to join a Drinkwatchers group, three turned up to the first meeting and one of these came to the second. There was no choice but to abandon our original plans. Since one of us had been appointed for a year to carry out a small-scale study our only option was to change the project. Our first change of direction focused upon our advertising and the general messages that we were communicating (e.g. alcoholism, alcohol and health, or alcohol and fitness). Such an investigation turned out to be unrealistic and the project ended up answering the question: what sort of help do problem drinkers really want?

Unlike some politicians, research workers have to respond flexibly when their cherished models begin to break up and well-laid plans go haywire. Funding bodies as well as apprentice researchers should be made aware that even the most experienced research workers have to do U-turns and S-bends in the middle of a project.

5. THE HELP PROVIDED BY OTHER PEOPLE HAS A HALF-LIFE OF TWO WEEKS

It is very difficult to say No when an enthusiastic and earnest research worker accosts you in the corridor. On the other hand, it is very easy to forget a promise to help. Most research projects rely upon some cooperation from others but it is wise to assume that actions won't speak as loud as words. If you are relying on ratings from nurses, spouses or GPs then you will have to set up a regular monitoring system to ensure that these tasks are carried out to your satisfaction.

6. THE TEDIUM OF RESEARCH IS DIRECTLY PROPORTIONAL TO ITS OBJECTIVITY

Some research workers manage to make use of interesting and productive research strategies such as the semi-structured interview and naturalistic observation of social interactions. Unfortunately, some questions are not amenable to this sort of methodology but have to be answered by devising experimental investigations involving very specific objective and tedious measurements. It is not easy to sustain 6 months of research activity which comprises giving a battery of reaction-time tests to 100 subjects or observing speed of drinking in alcoholics. Most research involves some activities that are repetitive and boring, but then so do most jobs. Cabinet makers, space explorers and circus clowns all have to put up with a great deal of tedium if they are going to succeed in their chosen profession. This must be recognised so that ways of coping with the boredom can be devised.

7. THE EFFORT OF WRITING UP IS AN EXPONENTIAL FUNCTION OF THE TIME SINCE THE DATA WERE COLLECTED

Not everybody writes up as soon as, or even before, the data have been collected. If the raw data lie in a filing cabinet for a year then they are likely to stay there for 2 years. If they lie there for 4 years they will never escape and will certainly never be written up. One of us has a folder entitled 'The inhibitory effects of mental set' which contains data collected a quarter of a century ago and never written up. It is difficult to understand why these data were not thrown away 20 years ago.

8. EVIDENCE IS NEVER ENOUGH

Although research is beset with difficulties the rewards justify the effort. Good strong evidence from good solid research is the best way to change conceptual frameworks as well as the behaviour of policy makers and practitioners. Or is it? Unfortunately, rigid views are not susceptible to change even when the evidence is overwhelming. One very good example of this phenomenon is provided by the debate between Priestley, Lavoisier and other eighteenth-century chemists, about the existence of phlogiston. When metals are burned or calcinated the modern view is that they are turned into oxides as they combine with oxygen in the air. According to the phlogiston theory a totally different process occurs since a metal is not an element but a compound which gives out phlogiston when heated. Now a crucial test would be to weigh the metal before and after calcination. The phlogiston theory would be falsified if the metal actually gains weight when it is burned. This experiment was carried out and the phlogiston theory was certainly not supported. Calcination of a metal leads to an increase in weight. It turned out that such apparently conclusive evidence did not convince the phlogiston supporters since they responded by suggesting that phlogiston must be a substance having a negative weight or that the departure of phlogiston increased the density, and therefore the weight, of the substance which held it.

One piece of evidence is never enough and an important research finding could well be ignored if it conflicts with the prevailing view. The heated debate about controlled drinking for alcoholics is a good example which should make a fascinating field of study for future philosophers of science.

There are many other laws which should be taken into account. For example, every research worker will have regrets: they will regret that they didn't include a particular measure or a particular intervention. Research workers will spend too long squeezing every last pip out of a data set. On the other hand, most of them will spend too little time plotting graphs and getting to know their data. We must now remember, however, another law of nature which we have recently uncovered: those people who teach research methods and those who write chapters about research spend too much time concentrating on problems and not enough time on solutions. Bearing this law in mind we will now change the focus of our attention.

Our views have been coloured by our own interest in relapse and particularly the work of Alcoholics Anonymous. Every year thousands of research workers start off with good intentions and high ideals. They want to push forward the frontiers of science and to help their fellow human beings. Unfortunately, most of them give up the ghost before the year is out and relapse into a more settled way of life. There are a few simple ways of preventing such a relapse process, and most of them have been adopted by AA. The first is the most important.

A. FORM A TEAM

It is almost impossible to carry out research when working alone, especially if there are strong pressures to do everything but research, as there are in the UK National Health Service for example. In the summer of 1935 Bill Wilson, a New York stockbroker, and Robert Holbrook Smith, a doctor in Akron, Ohio, worked together to overcome their drinking problems and were able, together, to achieve and maintain the sobriety that had been so elusive while each battled alone. The subsequent evolution of Alcoholics Anonymous is a remarkable success story. From its inception in 1935 AA has grown into a worldwide organisation claiming well over one-million active members. Most members of AA attend one or two groups every week and rely upon the support of like-minded people with similar problems. We believe that the best way of getting research completed is to form a team of three or four people who are interested in answering similar questions. They should meet once a week to set specific objectives and solve specific problems. Such a team can work very efficiently. They can share out a variety of tasks such as identifying appropriate measures, reading the relevant literature and speaking with key people. More importantly, such a team develops a sense of cohesion and enthusiasm. Where two or three are gathered together a sense of purpose develops which can resist the strong personal and social pressures to relapse.

If a team is formed then it is important to discuss and clarify the aspirations of team members. An open and honest approach is particularly important for a research team. One issue that must be addressed from the start is the ordering of authors and how problems relating to publications can be solved.

The next best alternative is to form a support group: a network of people working in the same locality but researching different areas and asking different questions. Ideally, a small research team would also be members of a larger support group. This larger group would make sure that they keep up with developments in computing, statistics, measurement and methodology; and this larger support group might link up with other groups in different locations. Both of us have worked alone and also in a team. The experiences are totally different, and it is our contention that most research, and certainly most PhD research, flounders simply because of the lack of adequate social support.

B. ONE DAY AT A TIME

This famous AA catch-phrase economically captures a basic element of self-control or self-management. It is easy to be overwhelmed by the size of the task, and focusing upon smaller goals has a number of important consequences. As Weick (1984) observes:

> Deliberate cultivation of a strategy of small wins infuses situations with comprehensible and specific meaning (commitment), reinforces the perception that people can exert some influence over what happens to them (control), and produces changes of manageable size that serve as incentives to expand the repertoire of skills (challenge). Continued pursuit of small wins could build increasing resistance to stress in people not originally predisposed toward hardiness.

One of the examples given by Weick is the success of the US Environmental Protection Agency in the early 1970s. The first administrator, William Ruckelshaus, decided not to draw up policies and plans to clean up all aspects of the environment but went instead for a relatively small win. Prior to the formal opening of the agency he discovered an obscure 80-year-old law relating to water pollution which permitted him to take a number of cities to court. On the first day of the Agency's formal existence he announced five law suits against major

American cities. There then followed a long series of successes that resulted in the strengthening of the Agency and additional resources as well as the increased enthusiasm to take on slightly larger goals.

The fact that going for small wins increases commitment, control and hardiness is sometimes difficult to translate into the field of research but the following guidelines are suggested:

1. Unless you are sure of your ground avoid the massive multicentred study. If an error of judgement is made early on there will be an enormous waste of resources.
2. Always try to cut a study down to size and go for relatively quick results. It is better to have six people working on a 1-year project than one person working on a 6-year project.
3. Don't imagine that you have to follow the tradition of writing a large and comprehensive literature review before starting work on a study.
4. A small win that does not shake the world could lead to a big win. In any case, it is better than a large flop.
5. Don't try to ask too many questions.

Of course, large-scale research has to be done but only after carrying out enough small-scale work to be almost certain that the large-scale study will be a success.

C. KEEP IN MIND THE PAYOFFS

It is very easy to sink into a routine of collecting data and coping with the day-to-day problems of research whilst forgetting the reasons for starting the project in the first place. Such a state of mindless persistence is a recipe for relapse. One basic process in self-control is to bear in mind the future consequences of today's activities (Horan, 1971). What are the positive outcomes that might reasonably be expected if the research project is completed? Of course the basic reason for carrying out a piece of research is to answer a question or solve a puzzle. The more important the question is considered to be, the greater will be the motivation to complete the study, so it is important to focus upon a burning issue when planning a project. Discovering something new is certainly the biggest reward of research. Nevertheless, research is also associated with a wide range of pleasurable experiences over and above the intellectual stimulation of solving puzzles and these should be kept in mind especially when the burning question begins to look more like a dying ember.

Consider the example of Heartbeat Wales, which is a community programme designed to reduce high levels of heart disease throughout the principality. When this project had been in existence for about a year and had not yet uncovered any world-shaking facts about changing human behaviour, the project team had still been rewarded in a large number of ways.

First, they had increased the level of awareness about healthy lifestyles throughout Wales. For example, Heartbeat Wales' health surveys had produced local information which communities considered very seriously. Second, they had written a great deal for professional journals and the mass media. Third, they were recognised experts in the field and were asked to lecture and to advise other programmes (e.g. the English Heart Programme). Of course Heartbeat Wales is not representative of other research projects since it is also a campaign. Nevertheless, many other projects lead on to a wide range of benefits. Often they can raise awareness and research workers do become the 'experts' who are frequently consulted. Furthermore, research involves thinking. Thinking sometimes produces ideas, and ideas can lead to publications, lectures and new research projects.

One Medical Director of the World Health Organisation insists that research workers affiliated with the WHO should be considering the 'products' that can result from their research over and above the final research publication. These products could be questionnaires, self-help manuals, guidelines for treatment, speculative articles, review articles, guidelines for community projects and proposals for further research. He recognises that a 5-year wait for a definitive article is not the best way of maintaining enthusiasm for a study. Rewards have to be built in along the way.

There are many benefits associated with research, and all research projects have a range of spin-offs. We are proposing that one way of preventing relapse is to regularly bring them to mind.

D. AVOIDING HELPLESSNESS

Many skills are needed in carrying out research and they have to be learned if a feeling of helplessness is to be avoided. It helps to know a good deal about experimental designs and methodology. Basic principles of reliability and validity will have to be considered. Data will have to be analysed possibly using a computer program. In our experience many researchers fall by the wayside because they feel that they lack knowledge and experience in these areas. Other chapters in this book are intended to provide this type of knowledge, and we suggest that the best way to ensure that some of these skills are well learned is to offer to give a course of lectures, in 6 months' time, on basic statistics and methodology. Some of the advice that we have given in this chapter has been tongue in cheek but we make this suggestion in all seriousness, bearing in mind that your audience will have to be carefully chosen.

E. DOUBTING AND QUESTIONING

Our final piece of advice is very simple. Research is all about doubting, questioning and enquiring. Even the laws described earlier in this chapter can be questioned, and a good research worker is someone who is always asking questions and coming up with ideas that fly in the face of prevailing views. Sometimes the questioning leads to radically different approaches and models. For the past 50 years it has been held that alcoholics must be abstinent for life but now this view is being questioned. Early behaviour therapists questioned the prevailing view that curing a phobia by desensitisation or exposure would only cure the symptom and subsequently result in catastrophic consequences. The traditional response to mental illness has been hospitalisation, but the wisdom of institutionalisation is now being questioned.

It follows that one of the most basic methods of maintaining motivation and enthusiasm for research is to develop attitudes which take into account the possibility that research will lead to radical approaches in the future. To take one example, in 50 years' time the National Health Service will be very different. Unless our own views are very wide of the mark there will be more work carried out in the community, with a wider range of professionals being responsible for services and greater emphasis on prevention. Changes in our traditional systems will occur more speedily if a large number of health workers are repeatedly questioning current practices, researching ways of making changes and developing an attitude of mind that welcomes a questioning spirit and welcomes appropriate changes. Maintaining a sense of wonder about human behaviour and human institutions as well as a vision of the continuous process of change that can and should be influenced by good evidence is perhaps the best way of maintaining enthusiasm for research.

THE RESEARCH GAME

Before concluding this chapter we would just like to provide one very simple method of surviving in the research field without really trying. Table 1.1 shows young researchers everything that is needed to make a name for themselves if they are researching psychological phenomena. In all fields of exploration and discovery those lucky individuals who are able to put a catch-phrase or title to a new phenomenon will not only survive but will be put on a pedestal by their colleagues. We will now reveal how this can be accomplished. It is often thought that research workers discover a phenomenon and then put a name to it, but actually the reverse is true. We have discovered that impressive-sounding labels are first of all generated and then a search is mounted for a phenomenon that fits the label. This is how many psychological phenomena were originally discovered including cognitive dissonance, erogenous zones, the inverted Oedipus complex, the reinforcement retroaction paradox, waxy flexibility, dementia infantalis, critical fusion frequency and the abstinence violation effect. Now, for the first time, we are publishing the buzz-word generator that was used to produce these and many other labels within the field of psychology. The words displayed in Table 1.1 can be put together in over 2000 ways and only 55 combinations have so far been used to label psychological phenomena. If you play around with this buzz-word generator your perceived self-efficacy will be enhanced and from an instrumental relativist orientation your future functionally autonomous self-actualisation will be guaranteed.

TABLE 1.1
Buzz-word generator

1.	Dementia	Retroaction	Complex
2.	Abstinence	Self-	Therapy
3.	Perceived	Restructuring	Fixation
4.	Oral	Violation	Efficacy
5.	Learned	Dependence	Questionnaire
6.	Anal	Helplessness	Syndrome
7.	Instrumental	Dissonance	Effect
8.	Cognitive	Autonomous	Paradox
9.	Reinforcement	Oedipus	Frequency
10.	Inverted	Infantalis	Self-actualisation
11.	Critical	Relativist	Construct
12.	Functional(ly)	Flicker	Orientation

To form acceptable and influential psychological terminology randomly choose one number from each of the three columns. For example, 4 3 2 = Oral Restructuring Therapy; 6 1 8 = Anal Retroaction Paradox; 8 6 5 = Cognitive Helplessness Questionaire.

REFERENCES

Horan, J.J. (1971). Coverant conditioning through a self-management application of the Premack Principle: its effects on weight reduction. *Journal of Behaviour Therapy and Experimental Psychiatry, 2*, 243-249.

Weick, K.E. (1984). Small wins: Redefining the scale of social problems. *American Psychologist, 39*, 40-49.

CHAPTER TWO

Preparing a research project

Edgar Miller   *Department of Psychology (Clinical Section), University of Leicester*

For those setting out on clinical research for the first time the biggest difficulty is often that of identifying a suitable problem that is both researchable in practical terms and that is likely to lead to worthwhile results. There are no rules for doing this that are guaranteed to lead to a high-quality end result. So far it has not proved possible to operationalise the processes that lie behind inspiration and this chapter will not attempt to do so. What it aims to do is much more modest. This is to set out some general principles which it is hoped will help those inexperienced in clinical research to achieve better results than they might otherwise have done.

Encountering research in its final form as an impressive paper in a prestigious journal gives a certain indication as to how research develops. The published paper starts with a review of the literature which then leads logically into an elegant hypothesis derived from that review. A well designed experiment or investigation to examine the hypothesis then follows. The results are then analysed with confidence and lead on to conclusions concerning the question that prompted the investigation. This is a nice, neat and logical progression. Needless to say this is a very formalised account of what typically goes on. The researcher may have thought of the hypothesis first with only the vaguest knowledge of the literature. The experiment may originally have been much bigger in scope, with what is reported being only those aspects of the data that seem to be interpretable. The execution of the project may have included a great many vicissitudes that the final account fails to describe.

Although the course of research generally rivals true love in not running smoothly, it is usually sensible to try to follow a certain logical progression. This is despite the fact that some good clinical research obviously does not follow this sequence. For example, it is generally advisable to have a reasonable background knowledge of the relevant literature before embarking on the details of any investigation. This is not always possible. Sometimes opportunities arise suddenly and the investigator has to do something quickly or miss the opportunity altogether (e.g. when a patient with a very rare and exotic condition turns up out of the blue and something has to be done immediately). This happened to the writer when a case of transient global amnesia was admitted one lunchtime still in a profoundly amnesic state. This condition is very rare, and the patient's amnesia was expected to recover within a few hours at most.

Putting aside instances like this, the sequence may run more or less along the following lines. First, the researcher identifies a particular problem to investigate in very general terms, e.g. the effects of contrary evidence in modifying delusional beliefs or incontinence in psychogeriatric patients. Secondly, background information is acquired about the topic, most commonly from the literature, including what has been discovered (or not discovered) so far. Next a specific question or hypothesis needs to be formulated and, finally, the investigation or experiment is designed in such a way that it will offer a reasonable attempt to answer the question chosen. These last two stages really need to be seen as the two sides of the same coin. The experimental design is very much determined by the hypothesis under consideration and a good hypothesis is, amongst other things, one that will lead to a suitable research design. With the reservations already alluded to, these four stages form a convenient base around which to organise subsequent discussion.

SELECTING A PROBLEM AREA

This is the crucial first step, but is also the aspect about which it is most difficult to offer advice. Researchers select problems on which to work for a variety of different reasons, and not all of these are particularly logical. That the researcher actually identifies a suitable problem area is of greater importance than the means by which that area is chosen in the first place.

A common basis for selecting a problem area is the inherent interest that it holds for the individual. Providing it can lead to a useful outcome, interest is certainly not a bad basis for selecting a research topic. It is very difficult to research a topic that appears tedious and dull. Nevertheless, the initial attractiveness of an area may lead to unfortunate decisions when used as the sole criterion for determining the topic. To take a rather extreme example, just why some men should develop couvade (the husband having symptoms such as morning sickness and pains like labour pains whilst the wife is pregnant and giving birth) may be a fascinating question. Despite this it has severe limitations as an area for clinical research. Instances of couvade are only rarely encountered in clinical practice and even more rarely still is it a problem of such magnitude as to warrant intervention.

It is often advisable to consider research topics other than those of initial attraction. A very useful approach is to consider problems that are frequently encountered in clinical practice. These are not only likely to be of immediate practical importance but will also provide a flow of suitable subjects on which to carry out research. Monitoring one's own clinical practice carefully can provide a fund of ideas. For example, the writer once had a period in which a series of referrals arose requiring advice as to whether a brain-damaged individual was safe to drive again. In general there is very little established knowledge on which a decision of this kind might be based and it is a problem not infrequently encountered by clinical psychologists working in neurological/physical rehabilitation settings as well as by other professionals (e.g. physicians) working in the same fields. Any further information that might help decision making would therefore be of real practical value.

Not only may relatively underinvestigated problems be encountered but clinical practice can also identify important but little understood features of otherwise well-researched topics. For example, it might be noted that one particular type of patient under treatment by cognitive or behavioural methods seems to be especially poor at carrying out 'homework' assignments. Trying to determine just why this should be the case might result in knowledge that could be used to enhance the efficacy of future therapeutic interventions.

A topic identified from clinical practice, like that of assessing the suitability of patients to drive, may at first sight be of little intrinsic interest. However, some careful consideration of the problem as well as background reading can produce an interest in the most unlikely things. Something like incontinence in psychogeriatric patients may have very low initial appeal but, as this writer once found, external pressure to look at this problem did reveal features of interest even in this most unlikely of topics. Even if the first topic identified from routine practice is rejected further monitoring will always throw up additional problems.

Research topics can be suggested in a number of other ways. The scientific and professional literature is continually throwing up ideas. An example here is a review paper by Barraco and Stettner (1976) which indicated that memory/learning may be adversely affected by the administration of antibiotics in experimental animals. Similar effects in humans could be of considerable significance. Such effects are most likely to occur where antibiotics are prescribed on a long-term basis. This sometimes happens to dermatological patients with severe and unremitting acne. Such patients are often teenagers and many will be in the later stages of schooling where cognitive functioning needs to be at its best.

A further example of ideas that can be derived from the literature is the steadily burgeoning work by social psychologists on 'social cognition' (e.g. Fiske & Taylor, 1991). Social cognition is concerned with how people understand and make sense of others. This is also an important aspect of clinical practice since this involves trying to understand and make sense of clients and their problems. Social cognition is therefore an area of research that can be carried over into investigating crucial aspects of clinical practice.

Yet another source of ideas for research can come from new service developments. Most services change from time to time as new ideas for service provision are developed and incorporated into practice. These changes are rarely evaluated properly. The provision of a newly con-stituted clinical team within a learning disabilities service specialising in dealing with challenging behaviour is something that cries out for evaluation. Does this team increase the effective management of such problems and to a degree that justifies the additional investment of resources?

One word of caution needs to be entered here. Many researchers end up by studying problems that are essentially trivial. Just because an anomalous result can be found in the literature does not mean that further investigation of that problem will necessarily lead to findings of any practical value. Similarly, the ready availability of certain clinical techniques does not mean that further exploration of their application is called for. To take but one instance, the presence of neuropsychological test batteries has resulted in these being applied to almost any clinical population that comes to hand, ranging from depressed psychiatric patients to subjects with diabetes mellitus. That the resultant pattern of scores may show some superficial features in common with some neuropsychological groups often has no practical significance and, in any case, the finding may defy satisfactory interpretation (Miller, 1983).

Just where the initial ideas for research come from is not really important as long as the idea is suitable, in that it leads to research that can be carried out within the confines of the clinical setting and which will lead to worthwhile results. Nevertheless, the best ideas for clinical research often follow from taking an enquiring and critical attitude towards everyday clinical practice. By its very nature clinical practice requires the practitioner to go beyond what is known and make assumptions about the nature of problems, the mechanisms that underlie them, and the means by which they can be resolved. Examining these assumptions, at least where this is practicable, leads to useful research with direct implications for practice and which can be carried out on subjects that are immediately to hand.

Before leaving the issue of selecting a research topic, one practical limitation needs to be mentioned. Quite frequently clinical research requires some cooperation or assistance from colleagues or key members of local services. Nursing staff may be asked to fill in ratings on patients in the ward or GPs may be encouraged to refer certain types of case to the service. This assistance or cooperation may be crucial for the effective execution of the project and is much more likely to be forthcoming if these key individuals also see the work as being worthwhile rather than some 'bee in the bonnet' of the researcher. The likely reactions of such key people therefore need to be taken into account in both selecting and planning the project.

THE BACKGROUND

Having identified a general topic it is advisable to gather background information. This usually comes from the scientific literature, especially other reported studies of the same or similar topics, but it can also be derived from discussing the problems with others who share an interest in the same general area. In this search for background information certain things are of particular significance. Obviously, it is sensible to know what has been established, or not established, so far. Previous investigations in the same general area will also give some idea of the kinds of methodology that might be useful, the pitfalls that may need to be avoided, and the sorts of measures that might be used.

Most of this depends upon a literature search. Again there are no really hard and fast rules about this, but certain things are worth bearing in mind. Getting started may be difficult, especially if the problem is a little unusual and rather circumscribed, with relevant papers and books not coming to hand very readily. After a while the problem more commonly becomes one of coping with the vast amount of relevant, or potentially relevant, information. Once a start is made and some access to the relevant literature is achieved, the question then typically becomes one of when to stop chasing further background information.

Initially the abstracting journals are often very useful. As well as *Psychological Abstracts* there are the medical abstracting journals which can often be at least as useful for clinical psychologists. The main ones are *Exerpta Medica* and *Index Medicus*. Many libraries can also obtain computer searches which are based on the abstracting journals. These searches are based on keywords to identify material of potential relevance. It is important to realise that some material of interest is inevitably missed because it does not have the relevant keyword(s) assigned to it. Looking through the index of one or more of these abstracting journals over a year or two will usually turn up something on even the most obscure topic. This source will itself cite references which will in turn often be useful.

Once some idea of the basic key references has been obtained the *Science Citation Index* may be of value. This starts from specific references and then lists the current sources citing this reference. Thus someone wanting to consider the impact of the family on discharged schizophrenics may identify the by now well-known paper by Vaughn and Leff (1976) on expressed emotion. Looking up this reference in the *Science Citation Index* would then show which authors had cited this paper and who, therefore, might also be dealing with the same general problem.

The real need is then to develop a picture of the state of knowledge in the relevant field including what seems to be well established, what is not so well established, what controversies exist and where the main gaps in useful knowledge lie. Eventually the search for additional background information will reach a stage where newly identified material will be adding little of consequence to this overall picture. This is the point at which it then becomes safe to start formulating questions or hypotheses for further investigation. On the other hand, if this search has by itself led the enquirer to a new and much enhanced under-standing of the nature of the problem area that prompted the search, then writing a review article may be a useful preliminary outcome. Not all research includes the collection of new data (a literature search is itself a form of research) and the ability to present and systematically summarise a complex and varied literature so as to be able to draw out implications for clinical practice can be a very useful achievement on its own.

In considering the literature it should be remembered that authors' conclusions about their own data are not necessarily correct and can sometimes fail to take into account other possibilities or even be totally misleading. Sometimes there is a good case for re-analysing data to check how well the conclusions can be substantiated. Furthermore, the development of meta-analysis (see Chapter 10) has created new scope for collating the results of separate investigations statistically. Again, this may be a useful preliminary before trying to gather new data.

FORMULATING A QUESTION OR HYPOTHESIS

The next stage is to select a specific question or hypothesis for investigation. Essentially the ideal question is one which, if answered properly, would lead to new information of clinical value and that would add to existing knowledge. There are no firm rules for achieving this but a useful guide is provided by the 'so what?' test. Even if the question proposed for investigation could be answered definitely, then 'so what'? Would the clinician actually be better placed to deal with a certain kind of problem or, at least, would the clinician be a step nearer to being better placed? Trying to determine whether one suggested subtest pattern on the WAIS-R is better at distinguishing people with dementia than another is a researchable question. If there are reasons to believe that no WAIS-R subtest pattern is likely to achieve a good enough level of reliability in distinguishing early dementia to be of any clinical value (Miller, 1980) then is the answer to this question worth obtaining?

To answer the question posed usually means devising an investigation. A researchable question is also one that can be investigated given the limitations under which the investigator has to work whether these be physical, ethical, financial or whatever. The limitations that are most important in practice typically centre around the availability of suitable subjects and the ability to carry out the necessary manipulations or procedures. Investigating commonly encountered problems can help ensure a supply of subjects, but practical or ethical considerations usually greatly reduce the things that can be done as part of the investigation. Such things as the inability to have an ideal control group or to carry out an adequate follow-up may limit what can be done and therefore what questions can be adequately answered. Other methodological constraints may be of significance. For example, it may not be possible to obtain or devise a suitable measure to meet the purpose of the investigation. Some of these problems are much less tractable than others in that practical limitations can sometimes be circumvented by using an alternative research design whilst an inability to measure the key variable in a satisfactory way may be insurmountable.

It has been suggested earlier that to be of value the question chosen should yield new information or break new ground. This is so eventually, but if the question that the investigator would like to answer means building directly on to a finding in the literature that is not well replicated then it can sometimes be a good thing to start by trying to replicate the finding in the investigator's own setting. This can achieve a number of things. If the original finding is important enough to lead on to other things then a replication may well be useful in itself. Secondly, the replication establishes that the investigator can obtain the effect that is being depended upon. A replication, or near-replication, also gives the experimenter experience in working in the general problem area, use of a possible methodology, etc. This can itself help to suggest better questions for further investigation. Starting with a replication, or near replication, can be of particular value to new researchers starting to feel their way.

Finally, it is probably important for inexperienced researchers to remember that usually any one investigation can only produce a very small step forward. It is often tempting to try to hit the jackpot first time and try to produce a result of appreciable significance. Since experienced and distinguished research workers only very rarely do this, novices are well advised to set modest goals that might be within their grasp. Establishing the cause of schizophrenia or the ideal treatment for anorexia nervosa at the first attempt is highly unlikely!

DESIGNING THE INVESTIGATION

Having decided upon a hypothesis to test or a question to answer, there now comes the critical problem of designing the actual experiment or investigation. Most psychologists will have been through under-graduate and even postgraduate courses with titles like 'statistics and experimental design'. These courses generally say a lot about statistics and very little about design. They thus often give the erroneous impression that the design of investigations is little more than the problem of selecting a suitable statistical model with the best experiments using a sophisticated form of analysis of variance. This may be a caricature of what is taught but it is much less of a caricature of the beliefs many students derive from such courses.

In fact the problem of designing an experiment is primarily one of logic rather than statistics. The statistical model employed, if such is required, is selected because it matches the logic of the investigation. To go straight for the statistical model implies that the experimental logic implicit in the statistical model is suitable for the question which it is hoped to answer. If the logic has not been thought out first then it will be impossible to say whether the logic implicit in the statistical model is or is not appropriate.

This is not in any way to decry statistics which are an essential tool in many investigations. The aim is merely to set them in their proper context as tools of analysis rather than as a factor determining how the experiment should be designed in the first place.

It is only possible to design a sound and logical investigation if the researcher is clear about the nature of the question being asked, or hypothesis to be tested, and can see what kind of information needs to be collected and in what way in order to offer a satisfactory answer to the question. In this respect it is often helpful to test out possible designs by imagining that the investigation has been completed and the expected results obtained. Are these results really interpretable and can they be interpreted relatively unambiguously having been subjected, if necessary, to appropriate statistical analyses?

The key concept here is 'control'. Essentially, control refers to the ability to relate the outcome of the investigation (i.e. changes in the dependent variable) to the factors that are of particular interest to the investigator. Thus if the aim is to show that changing the environment on a psychogeriatric ward has an effect on the behavioural competence of residents, then the investigator needs to be reasonably sure that any effects produced really are the consequence of altering the environment and not to some other extraneous and unwanted factor (e.g. a change in nursing staff on the ward that happened at about the time the general environmental change was introduced). This ability to relate one set of factors to another is referred to as 'internal validity' by Cook and Campbell (1979).

Another important aspect of any investigation is what Cook and Campbell (1979) refer to as 'external validity'. Except under very rare circumstances investigators are not just concerned with those particular subjects in the particular setting in which the study is carried out. The hope is to draw some sort of conclusion applicable to, say, other psychogeriatric patients in other residential units. For the most part this ability to generalise from the results is dependent upon using subjects that are as far as possible typical examples of their kind and studied under typical circumstances.

A problem arises because there can be advantages in having very clearly defined groups of subjects. Rather than studying chronic schizophrenics in general the investigator may opt for chronic schizophrenics within a certain age range, having been resident in hospital for a certain length of time, who clearly meet certain diagnostic criteria, who have never had any other psychiatric label applied to them, etc. This makes it clearer to others exactly what the population studied happens to be and so allows easier replication of the investigation. In addition, using a homogeneous group of subjects reduces the within-group variance, thus enhancing the statistical power of the experiment. The question then arises as to how typical of long-stay patients generally labelled as 'chronic schizophrenics' such a narrowly defined sample would be.

The extreme of this situation arises when studies (often single case or using very small numbers of subjects) are carried out on very 'pure' examples of a particular problem. For example, if the interest is in what mechanisms underlie compulsive checking behaviour then many cases encountered in clinical practice will have other features, such as some degree of depression. A pure case with only checking may then be of particular interest for study since the results will not run the risk of being contaminated by these other factors. However, generalisation to more typical cases must take into account the possible confounding effects of factors like depression. In general terms the study of relatively pure cases is useful for teasing out the mechanisms controlling some form of abnormal behaviour, but this is at the price of weak generalisation to more typical examples with regard to such things as the ease and extent to which the identified mechanisms can be manipulated as part of a therapeutic intervention.

Another important consideration is the 'power' of any experimental design in the sense of its ability to detect an effect if the looked-for effect really does exist. This is called 'statistical conclusion validity' by Cook and Campbell (1979) but this term can be misleading because the general issue of the power of the investigation to detect the effects sought is still present even if no formal statistical procedures are being used. Thus if it is intended to increase detection of post-natal depression in the 6 months after birth from a current level of 6% to nearer the real rate of, say, 10-15% (e.g. Cox, Connor and Kendell, 1982) then introducing an experimental screening procedure that might improve detection by about a further 2% at best, and expecting to get a definite indication of improvement after screening 40 consecutive cases, would be extremely hopeful to say the least. In general power can be achieved by improving the sensitivity of the measures and by either increasing the number of subjects or by increasing the number of observations/data recorded from each subject in single-case or small N designs (see Cohen, 1988, for a full discussion of power analysis).

A final general consideration is that of the measures used. Do these really reflect the things that they are supposed to reflect? For example, in looking at anxiety is the investigator really concerned with state or trait anxiety and is the measure of anxiety being used of the right kind? Different measures tend to be useful in different contexts. Thus the considerable stability of IQs derived from the major intelligence tests can be of value under some circumstances. This stability, however, makes them relatively insensitive to change and therefore not good as dependent variables where the aim is to detect some small change. Given the considerable problems of measurement in psychological research it is often sensible to avoid having to rely on single measures, and including an alternative measure of the same function can act as a useful insurance against problems with the first.

Besides these questions of logic, practical limitations also have to be taken carefully into account in planning clinical research. Two commonly encountered problems are a shortage of suitable subjects and the fact that it is not always possible to use what might be considered the ideal type of experimental design because of either practical or ethical reasons. Examples of the latter are where in looking at the effect of changing a ward environment it is not practically possible to get an adequately matched control ward and it is not considered either practical or ethical to return the experimental ward to its pre-intervention state to see if an obtained effect is reversed.

As has already been stated earlier in the chapter, selecting problems commonly encountered in clinical practice is one way of trying to ensure an adequate flow of subjects. Where an adequate number of subjects are not available researchers can adopt two strategies. One is to use 'analogue research' as when college students reporting a fear of spiders are used to study ways of treating phobias. Analogue research of this kind does have its limitations (Miller and Morley, 1986; see also Chapter 9) but will not be considered any further because it is not really clinical research as conceived here.

The other strategy is to rely on small N or even single-case designs. These intensive designs usually rely on obtaining a large amount of data from subjects over a prolonged period of time and demand the use of suitable measures (e.g. measures that do not have large practice effects where the subject obtains the maximum level of performance after a few administrations). The fact that single-case studies typically go on over long periods of time makes them susceptible to interference from uncontrolled changes in the environment (i.e. the longer an experiment goes on the more chance there is that something will happen that can upset the experiment, especially if it is being carried out in a natural setting). As indicated earlier, these designs are best for examining underlying mechanisms but they are weak at indicating what the typical patient's response to some form of intervention might be. For a more detailed discussion of such designs see Chapter 13.

The other major practical problem in clinical research is that it is not always possible to carry out what would be the ideal experimental design. For example, if a ward-based intervention is being used then it may not be possible to find a similar ward containing identical patients. The logic of experimental design might suggest pooling the patients from two wards and reassigning them to the wards at random. There are usually strong practical and ethical objections to such a procedure. Thus it may be necessary to work with a control that differs in a potentially relevant way from the experimental ward/subjects (e.g. in having different levels of severity of disorder or different lengths of time resident in the institution). This then necessitates working with quasi-experimental designs (Cook and Campbell, 1979; see also Chapter 11). In general quasi-experimental designs tend to have good external validity. Because they are typically carried out in the 'real life' setting and with typical subjects, generalisation to other clinical samples is good. (It is indeed usually the restrictions imposed by working in 'real life' settings with typical subjects that force the investigator to opt for a quasi-experimental design in the first place.) The most serious limitation for quasi-experimental designs relates to internal validity. In other words it is less possible to be sure that changes observed really are the consequence of the manipulations that were applied. Quasi-experimental designs are discussed in Chapter 11.

ETHICAL ISSUES

Ethical issues should be considered at an early stage of planning research. Researchers need to ensure that the research they are planning is ethical in essence, as well as that detailed aspects of the procedure do not raise any specific ethical problems. Researchers should be familiar with an accepted set of ethical guidelines, such as those produced by the British Psychological Society and the American Psychological Association. Such guidelines tend to be updated from time-to-time in line with developing experience and so getting hold of the latest version is important. Where any doubts arise, the comments of an independent colleague should be sought at an early stage. The role of obtaining ethical approval in preparing a grant application is referred to in Chapter 8.

Each field of psychological research raises its own characteristic ethical problems. For example, animal research raises particularly distinctive problems that have recently been much discussed. Research in social psychology raises the issue of deception more commonly than other areas of psychology. In clinical research, there are two particular problems that recur regularly. One relates to the ability of particular groups of clinical participants to give free and informed consent. There is quite an extensive literature on specific populations, of which Kinard's (1985) discussion of the ethics of research with abused children is a good example. Another recurrent ethical problem in the clinical field concerns providing or withholding treatment in the course of research and this is well covered in Garfield's (1987) discussion of ethical issues in psychotherapy research.

FINAL COMMENTS

Fundamentally research is an intellectual exercise. No matter how elegant or sophisticated the procedures adopted or the form of the statistical analysis, what emerges will be trivial or worthless, unless the investigator has phenomenal luck, if the whole business has not been carefully and logically thought through beforehand. Much of the best clinical research emerges from a critical and questioning attitude to clinical practice and the problems that emerge in practice. It also relies on the investigator's familiarity with the current state of knowledge in the relevant field, an ability to generate sensible and researchable questions as well as a keen appreciation of the logic used in trying to answer these questions. If this admittedly tall order can be achieved the rest tends to fall into place. Even if some technical problems remain it leaves the investigator properly equipped to approach other experts, such as statisticians, with a reasonable hope of getting appropriate and helpful advice which will resolve them.

REFERENCES

American Psychological Association (1981). Ethical principles of psychologists. *American Psychologist, 36*, 631-638.
Barraco, R.A. & Stettner, L.J. (1976). Antibiotics and memory. *Psychological Bulletin, 83*, 242-302.
Cohen,. J. (1988). *Statistical Power Analysis for the Behavioral Sciences*, 2nd Ed. Hillsdale, NJ: Lawrence Erlbaum Associates Inc.
Cook, T.D. & Campbell, D.T. (1979). *Quasi-Experimentation: Design and Analysis Issues for Field Settings*. Chicago: Rand McNally.
Cox, J.L., Connor, Y., & Kendell, R.E. (1982). Prospective study of the psychiatric disorders of childbirth. *British Journal of Psychiatry, 140*, 111–117.
Fiske, S.T. & Taylor, S.E. (1991). *Social Cognition*, 2nd Ed. New York: McGraw-Hill.
Garfield, S.L. (1987). Ethical issues in research on psychotherapy. *Counselling & Values, 31*, 115-125.

Kinard, E.M. (1985). Ethical issues in research with abused children. *Child Abuse & Neglect, 9,* 301–311.

Miller, E. (1980). Cognitive assessment of the older adult. In J.E. Birren and R.B. Sloane (Eds.), *Handbook of Mental Health and Aging.* Englewood Cliffs, NJ: Prentice Hall.

Miller, E. (1983). A note on the interpretation of data derived from neuropsychological tests. *Cortex, 19,* 131–132.

Miller, E. & Morley, S. (1986). *Investigating abnormal behaviour.* London: Weidenfeld & Nicolson.

Vaughn, C.E. & Leff, J.P. (1976). The influence of family and social factors on the course of psychiatric illness. *British Journal of Psychiatry, 129,* 125–137.

CHAPTER THREE

The selection and development of measures

Graham E. Powell *The Psychology Service,*
London

WHAT IS MEASUREMENT?

Psychological measurement is most commonly encountered in the form
of psychological *testing* or *assessment*.

This branch of science and psychology has a fascinating history,
dating back at least to the early Chinese some 22 centuries BC (Du Bois,
1966; 1970). They formally attempted to assess the capabilities of their
civil servants and developed a system that lasted for 3000 years. In more
recent history, the late nineteenth century saw the emergence of an
interest in individual differences and how to test them. For example,
Galton in 1879 published the results of 'psychometric experiments' in
one of the first volumes of *Brain*, James Cattell opened his laboratory
in Pennsylvania, and Alfred Binet began work on his famous intelligence
scale. Early in the twentieth century several factors combined to create
an urgent interest in their work. In particular, it became crucial to assess
persons for military, industrial and educational purposes for both
economic and social reasons. Psychological testing, then, has its roots
in the need to make decisions about people. 'Standardised' tests were
developed which had a manual describing the exact way to administer
the test, defined the precise materials to use, had an objective scoring
system, and which could be shown through controlled studies to
contribute to better decision making.

Psychological *measurement*, on the other hand, is a broader topic relating to a more general interest in how to describe and ultimately understand the way that a person functions. Psychologists as experimental scientists are called upon to measure an ever-increasing diversity of behavioural, social, cognitive, biological and environmental parameters. In the social sphere, for example, even a cursory glance at the published literature is revealing; there are attempts to measure such disparate things as facial expression, speed of eye movements, embarrassability, stressfulness of a situation, reciprocity in dyadic behaviour patterns, marital satisfaction, availability of social contacts, consensus in social stereotyping, social conscience and social adjustment. The development of published, standardised tests cannot possibly keep pace with these demands, therefore the mental health researcher must acquire two fundamental skills:

1.   How to locate, compare and select measures from the published literature.
2.   How to develop proper measures unique to the study at hand.

These two skills are addressed by this chapter, but there is one axiomatic statement to make at the outset; the basic principles of psychological testing are applicable to all forms of measurement without exception. It is all too convenient to forget this. For example, tens of thousands of research studies used psychiatric diagnosis as a measure before the major problems of reliability and validity were attended to, as described elegantly in an influential and scholarly book by Kendell (1975).

The basic principles of psychological testing just alluded to are discussed in the following sections. Why it is convenient to forget them will become obvious, as to acknowledge them can significantly add to the complexity of research and to the time and resource necessary to allocate to a good study.

TYPES OF MEASURE: SCALING

At the simplest level, to measure is to assign a number to the properties or qualities of people (situations, objects or whatever) for the dual purposes of *description* and *analysis*.

Some description is fairly crude and merely indicates the presence of a quality or feature. This comprises assigning people to categories such as paranoid versus non-paranoid schizophrenia, those who believe they have control over their lives versus those who feel they are merely blown by the winds of fate, or those children who are behind at reading versus those whose achievements are within normal limits. More refined description comprises assigning a number on some scale which enables or implies a comparison between the subject and all other persons, such as degree of extroversion, level of intelligence or strength of fear of spiders.

Measurements are usually expressed as numbers to allow for computer coding and statistical analysis—but beware! These numbers do not necessarily have the same properties from one scale to the next since the relationship between any two numbers on a scale varies according to the *type of scale*, thus influencing the type of numerical analysis that can be legitimately undertaken.

A *nominal* scale is where numbers are used merely to name or label categories rather than to indicate order or magnitude. These are not numbers in the real sense as they are entirely arbitrary. For example, if marital status were a scale or variable in our study we might have the categories 'married' 'separated' 'divorced' 'widowed' 'co-habiting' and 'single' as the scale points. For computer coding purposes these might be translated into 0, 1, 2, 3, 4, 5, or 5, 4, 3, 2, 1, 0 or 77, 9, -4, 6½, 1000, 2, or any other set of six different numbers. It would not make any sense, therefore, to perform statistical manipulations on these 'scores', such as computing the average 'score' for the subjects in the study (though this fact does not stop some people mistakenly trying to do so).

Nominal scales are most often seen as independent variables, used as ways of splitting a population into subgroups to be compared on another scale. Hence one might divide a group of children into those that are brain damaged and those that are not (the independent variable) and compare their progress in reading (the dependent variable). This is not to imply that no statistical analysis can be undertaken when all the information is in the form of nominal scales, because it is a relatively simple matter to compute relationships or associations between them by drawing up frequency tables of how many subjects fall into which categories and undertaking a χ^2 analysis. This is described in any basic statistics book that covers the analysis of qualitative or non-parametric data such as Maxwell (1961) or Siegel (1956). A fine example of the approach and worth looking at in this light is given by Rutter, Graham and Yule (1970) who in a very large-scale study teased out some of the complex relationships between childhood handicap, intellectual and academic performance and various measures of psychological and behavioural adjustment using almost exclusively nominal scales and variants of frequency analysis.

An *ordinal* scale is one in which larger numbers indicate greater possession of the property in question. There is therefore a logical relationship between numbers, which allows subjects to be *rank-ordered*. However, no assumptions are made about the *magnitude* of the difference between any two scale points. Suppose there were ten people in a room. Their height could be recorded using an ordinal scale by assigning 1 to the shortest, 2 to the next shortest, up to 10 for the tallest, but in absolute terms the two shortest may differ by one inch and the two tallest by three inches. For this reason, one must be careful of interpreting ordinal data. For example, returning to the people in the room, half are Finnish and half are Venezuelan. The mean rank of Finns is 5.4 and for Venezuelans it is 5.6. Can one conclude that the mean height of the Venezuelans is also greater than that of the Finns? Not necessarily.

The data presented in Table 3.1 show an example of how the reverse can be true, by a matter of more than three inches, with the ordinal scale being unable to take into account that the two tallest Finns are very tall indeed. The 'power' of ordinal scales (the amount of information they contain) is therefore less than it might be. There are other problems. In the next room there are five more Finns and five more Venezuelans, and these are also ranked. The mean rank of the Finns is the same as in this room, 5.4. Can we conclude that the Finns in the two rooms are of the same height? No, because all those in the second room are the young offspring of those in the first room. A mean rank on a scale is completely different to the absolute value on that scale, and one therefore cannot generalise ranks across populations unless one can guarantee that the

TABLE 3.1
Height of two subgroups expressed as mean rank
(1 = shortest, 10 = tallest) and mean

Nationality	Rank	Mean rank	Actual height	Mean
Finnish	10		6'6"	
Finnish	9		6'3"	
Finnish	5	5.4	5'4"	5'7.6"
Finnish	2		5'1"	
Finnish	1		5'0"	
Venezuelan	8		5'7"	
Venezuelan	7		5'6"	
Venezuelan	6	5.6	5'5"	5'4.6"
Venezuelan	4		5'3"	
Venezuelan	3		5'2"	

two populations are perfectly matched. Another problem is that the distribution of scores on an ordinal scale can be arbitrary, depending upon the scale intervals that the experimenter chooses. Suppose that all the people in the first room are rated on a three-point scale as follows: 1 = less than 5', 2 = 5' to 5'11" and 3 = 6' or more, giving a distribution of 0, 8, 2. A three-point scale but with different intervals (1 = less than 5'6", 2 = 5'6" to 5'11", 3 = 6' or more) will yield a distribution of 5, 3, 2, which looks quite different to the first and neither is a nice smooth curve of known mathematical properties.

For these reasons and others, ordinal data can only be subjected to *non-parametric* statistical analysis, which makes the absolute minimum of assumption about intervals and distributions (Leach, 1979). Although as mentioned these analyses are less powerful than they might be, the loss of power has a *conservative* effect, i.e. a non- parametric analysis may fail to find the significant differences in means or significant correlations that actually exist. Further, non-parametric analysis has progressed a great deal over recent years and offers a very wide range of techniques; it is no longer a second-class citizen and is frequently not just the only way but the *best* way both to obtain and to analyse data.

Finally, we have the *interval* scale, in which each scale point is a fixed distance from the next; height, speed, temperature, age and so on. Many tests and measures in psychology are taken to be interval scales, such as Neuroticism scores on the Eysenck Personality Questionnaire or on the Beck Depression Inventory, or ratings on a 'Fear Thermometer' during exposure to snakes in studies of phobias, or ratings of relaxation during certain therapies. In fact, this is often just an assumption: no one has ever shown, for example, that a change of one unit on a relaxation scale, whether it occurs at the 'relaxed' end or 'panic' end, always equals a certain change in heart rate or GSR or power in the alpha band of the EEG; and does it make any psychological sense to say that someone who scores 20 on Extroversion is 'twice' as Extroverted as someone who scores 10? If I ask teachers to rate the children in their class on a scale of naughtiness from 1 to 10, am I entitled to treat it as equal-interval data without further investigation? Not at all.

There are three points to make. First, interval scales have to be designed and their interval properties empirically evaluated using special scaling techniques as developed, for example, by Lickert, Thurstone and Guttman (Aiken, 1985). Ad hoc, superficially appealing methods such as the mere use of whole integers does not constitute interval scaling. Second, it is debatable whether the concept of the equal interval scale is fully applicable to all psychological dimensions. Third, psychologists outside of the field of psychometrics and specialist scale construction (e.g. Aiken, 1980) have largely ignored these problems.

Fourth, this is the right decision—although by choice one would always employ the most adequately scaled measure available, for pure practical reasons reasonable or sensible approximations to equal interval scaling will usually have to suffice unless the proof of perfect scaling is absolutely essential to or integral with the validity of the findings. Interval scales allow the most sophisticated of *parametric* statistical analyses, which require one to be able to make certain assumptions about interval and distribution.

To conclude this brief discussion of the meaning of numbers in measurement, one might recommend that the researcher aspires to interval measurement because of the statistical power it affords, but falls back graciously to ordinal measurement and non-parametric statistics if one cannot reasonably support the claim that one's measure is truly an interval scale or if one cannot devise a method to construct such a scale. To pose a concrete problem, one of the most widely used measures of the long-term effects of cerebral trauma is the Glasgow Outcome Scale. It has four points: 'Vegetative State' 'Severe disability' 'Moderate disability' and 'Good recovery'. In the absence of any scaling data (there is none) would you treat it as an ordinal or interval measure? The published literature reports it both ways, but one might feel that those taking an interval stance were being somewhat liberal.

TYPES OF MEASURE: TECHNIQUES

Thus far we have covered the nature of a scale without defining how one actually obtains the number pertaining to the subject. Here we are concerned with measures as techniques rather than abstractions. Each type of technique has a different range of convenience (i.e. is capable of measuring only certain properties) and each has various advantages and limitations.

The *rating scale* in its numerous guises is the commonest form of psychological measurement. The subject may rate him- or herself on the scale (self-report) or be rated on it by someone else (observer report). The scale always has a number of points; too few and it may lack sensitivity; too many and it may become arbitrary as to which of two or three points is indicated. Let us suppose that a five-point scale is used to measure current anxiety. The scale can come in various forms. The scale may be unipolar using a numbering system:

Place a number in the box from 1 to 5 according to how anxious you feel at this moment, where 1 is not anxious and 5 is very anxious.

ANXIOUS [4]

or unipolar using a horizontal scale:

> Place a cross in one of the five spaces to indicate how anxious
> you feel at this moment

NOT ANXIOUS _ _ _ _ X _ ANXIOUS

or bipolar using one of these scales:

> Place a cross in one of the five spaces to indicate how you feel
> at this moment

RELAXED _ _ _ _ X _ ANXIOUS

or may have each point explicitly described (or 'anchored'):

> Put a circle around the statement which most applies to you
> at this moment:
>
> 1. I feel very relaxed.
> 2. I feel relaxed.
> 3. I feel neither relaxed nor tense.
> 4. I feel anxious.
> 5. I feel very anxious.

or may do away with all points and simply have a straight line for a
mark which will later be measured by the experimenter:

> Place a cross on the line to indicate how anxious you feel at
> this moment

NOT ANXIOUS _____ X_ ANXIOUS

These scales have the advantage of great flexibility, wide range of
convenience and ease of administration but they are subject to various
biases. The *halo effect* is when the score on a previous scale influences
scores on a subsequent scale ('I rated myself as "CONFIDENT" on the
last scale so shouldn't rate myself as "ANXIOUS" on this one'). The
experimenter effect is when the subject consciously or unconsciously tries
to please the test administrator ('He's trying so hard to put me at my
ease I can't let him know he's making me quite anxious with all these

questions'). The *leniency error* is shown by many subjects who resist assigning negative qualities to themselves or others. *Central tendency* is shown by some subjects who over-use the neutral category, which can be contrasted with *extreme responding*, a tendency to use just the extreme points of a scale in an all-or-none fashion.

There are many techniques related to the basic rating scale. There are *check lists*, for example, in which the subject is given a list of feelings (CONFIDENT, ANXIOUS, SLEEPY ...) and requested to tick those that apply (which is really a series of two-point unipolar rating scales). There are also *card sorts* where the subject may have a pack of cards on each of which is a statement (e.g. 'I feel anxious')—each card in turn is placed on one of five piles or into one of five boxes labelled in terms of applicability ('I strongly agree with this statement', 'I slightly agree with this statement', etc.). *Grid* measures can also be mentioned here (see Chapter 14). The subject rates a number of people ('My sister', 'a famous sporting figure', 'the person I most dislike', etc.) on a series of scales ('confident', 'anxious', 'energetic', 'like myself', 'like I want to be', etc.). Here, the correlation between ratings on 'anxious' with ratings on 'like myself' becomes the measure of anxiety.

The *questionnaire* (measuring personality, attitudes, interests, etc.) is also in many cases just a thinly disguised collection of two or three point rating scales, and their verbal equivalent is the *interview*, although the interview does have an extra dimension, in that often information is elicited from the subject but interpreted in relation to points on various scales by a 'judge', usually the interviewer.

Alternatively, the subjective element can be largely removed and the data collected straight from the subject without interpretation either by the subject or the judge. Here we have *direct observation* (See Chapter 14) of behaviour, *performance measures* such as cognitive tests (See Chapter 10), and *psychophysiological tests* such as skin conductance (Martin and Venables, 1980).

But before we move on from techniques, let us preface the following sections by assuming that all of these tests aim to measure a real quantity—a person's real height, real intelligence or real social anxiety. This fabrication (i.e. real quantity) is known in Classical Test Theory as the 'true score'. This theory assumes that the score obtained on a measure (the 'observed score') comprises two portions, that is the true score plus an error score. If a test were ideal there would be no error component and the observed score would in fact be the true score. But no test is ideal and the problems posed by this error component have to be squarely faced.

PROPERTIES OF MEASURES: RELIABILITY

Reliability is to do with whether one gets the same answer if two measurements are taken of the same thing. For example, a wooden ruler marked out in inches would give a pretty reliable measure of the width of this page. I could measure it on two occasions and get the same answer, or my colleague from the next office could also take the measurement and get an answer very close to my own. But the same scale marked out on something slightly stretchy, let's say a length of elastic to use an extreme example, would not necessarily always give the same results across either time or persons; the answer obtained would crucially depend upon the exact tension placed on the elastic ruler as it was drawn across the page. In research, then, it is important to be sure that the measures we use are as stable as the wooden ruler. There is little point in putting a lot of effort into a research study if inaccuracies in measurement are likely to obscure the findings by generating a lot of 'noise' in the data. This analogy to radio reception is quite apt—because if the effects we are looking for are delicate (i.e. a weak signal) then it is even more important that noise and crackle be kept to a minimum, or we will miss them altogether.

Reliability is succinctly described by Aiken (1985, p. 84) as a test's 'relative freedom from unsystematic errors of measurement'. Under specified conditions the test should always yield the same results; they should not vary randomly or unpredictably. There are several ways of assessing reliability and these will be described in turn.

Test-retest reliability is when the same test is administered to the same group of subjects on two different occasions separated by a specified time interval. Scores on the first occasion are then correlated with scores on the second. If there were no errors in the measurement subjects would maintain exactly the same distance from each other (or rank order if we were using non-parametric statistics) which would result in a correlation (now called a reliability coefficient) of exactly 1.0. If the test measured nothing but error then the correlation would be zero. The reliability of psychological measures in practice never reaches 1.0 because of fluctuations in many variables such as a subject's mood or level of fatigue.

Note, though, that the *mean* score might well change because of practice effects on the specific test items. This change in means does not affect the computation of the correlation coefficient which is independent of the mean score. *Systematic* errors then, such as practice effects, do not affect reliability.

Parallel form reliability takes into account the fact that the state of subjects varies unpredictably from the first to second testing, and assesses reliability during a single test session by giving all subjects two versions of the test. These should be equivalent or parallel, and usually the order of test-taking is organised such that half of the subjects take version A first and a half take version B first. The reliability coefficient will fall short of 1.0, depending upon short-term fluctuations in the subjects' state and upon the degree to which the forms are truly identical.

Often one can neither arrange to see subjects on two occasions nor obtain two parallel forms, in which case one can resort to *split-half* reliability. The test is split into two (e.g. odd versus even items) and the scores on the halves are correlated. A slight adjustment is made to the obtained correlation to take into account the fact that a shorter test is less reliable; this is called the Spearman-Brown formula. For obvious reasons this type of reliability coefficient is often called a coefficient of Internal Consistency. In fact there are many ways of dividing a test into two halves which would give a whole range of reliability coefficients; therefore, the natural thing to do is to compute the mean of all possible split-half coefficients using the Kuder-Richardson formula 20 (Aiken, 1985, p. 87; Anastasi, 1976, p. 114). This formula itself is only a specific instance of the general Alpha Coefficient (Cronbach, 1951) which considers the relationship of each item to every other item.

Scorer reliability must be estimated whenever scoring is fallible. At a basic level scorer mistakes can be made when entering or adding up numbers on an IQ test, say, but at a more general and subtle level most tests demand that the scorer make judgements during both administration and scoring which are subject to personal biases. Degree of judgement is least on those tests with an extensive and explicit administration manual and with similarly explicit scoring criteria. Such is the case with most of the commonly used intelligence tests. The degree of judgement that has to be exercised is greatest when questions are allowed to be asked in slightly different ways and when only broad guidelines can be given for scoring—this is the case in regard to interviewing. To obtain an estimate of scorer reliability two or more judges score the same subjects. The correlation (or alpha coefficient if there are more than two scores) should approach 1.0. If not, the administration and scoring criteria have to be tightened up and/or the training of the judges improved.

Having described reliability, we must be clear as to why it is important and should in general be maximised. Because every test has an error component the observed score is only an estimate of the true score. If a test were repeated many times a distribution of scores would be obtained that would cluster around the true score. Like the distribution of any variable, the distribution of observed scores would have a mean and standard deviation. The mean, as stated, would be the true score and the standard deviation (SD) is known as the *standard error of measurement*, or SEM. There is a relationship between SEM and reliability (r_{11}) as follows:

$$SEM = SD \sqrt{1 - r_{11}}$$

This simple formula tells us why reliability is so important. If reliability is perfect (r_{11} = 1.0) then the SEM will be zero (i.e. $SEM = SD \sqrt{1-1} = 0$). This would mean one had a perfect test in which repeat measures on the same subject would always be the same (because as just shown their distribution would have zero standard deviation) and would all equal the true score. Conversely, if reliability were zero ($r_{11} = 0$) then the SEM will be equal to the standard deviation of observed scores (i.e. $SEM = SD \sqrt{1 - 0} = SD$). This would mean that all the variation in observed scores across different subjects would be due to unsystematic error and nothing whatever to do with qualities purported to be measured by the test. The test, then, would be perfectly useless. However, a test invariably does contain error, and so one must try to define an acceptable reliability. Acceptability in this instance is more than just the statistical significance of the particular reliability coefficient. It would be very easy, especially with a large group of subjects, to obtain a significant test-retest correlation of, say, 0.3. But if one worked through the mathematics one could show that this meant that only 30% of the variance in test scores was due to the subjects and 70% would be error variance. Broadly speaking, a reliability much less than 0.9 would be disappointing and call into question the point of using the test.

But having said this, one must also say that the search for high reliability is not the be-all-and-end-all of the exercises for it must be tempered with thoughtful commonsense. There are many examples of this. If the alpha of a test were unity, with all items correlating perfectly with each other, then it would mean that all items measured exactly the same thing so that all except one could be dropped. If the test-retest reliability of a trait were unity, then would this not inhibit the measure from detecting genuine changes on that trait? If one tries to improve the reliability of a test one can drop individual items with the lowest reliability; but would one not reach the point where the gain in test reliability resulting from dropping an unreliable item is matched or outstripped by a loss in reliability caused by having a shorter test?

Further, we can drop items to make a test more reliable but we must also take into account what we want the test to measure. Suppose we want a test of Extraversion (E) and that E is a trait combining elements of two things, impulsivity (I) and sociability (S). Our test of E therefore comprises I items and S items. But suppose I items were less reliable. If, in an effort to increase reliability we rejected the lowest reliability items we would in effect be rejecting I items so that our test would no longer be measuring Extraversion but only one component of it, namely sociability. Some of these issues and many others are well discussed by Levy (1973).

PROPERTIES OF MEASURES: VALIDITY

Should a measure prove to have acceptable reliability of the type needed, then it is worth pursuing its psychometric properties to see if it is also a valid measure of that which it is supposed to be measuring.

To return to the example of the wooden ruler marked out in inches, we can be sure that it will give the same answer twice, but is the inch as marked out on the ruler precisely what we think it is? Not necessarily. This is why, in England, we have Trading Standards Authorities checking all measures of length, weight and volume used in commercial dealing, to make sure that customers are not taken advantage of through deliberate or accidental tampering with the measuring devices, making sure that scales are accurate, that pint glasses in pubs indeed contain one pint, and so on. Our ruler, then, might be compared with some accepted criterion. Further, thinking of the elastic ruler this time, we can say exactly why it is potentially not a valid measure of length, because any one reading is in fact the product of *two* constructs, both length and tension.

Validity is affected by both systematic and unsystematic error, unlike reliability which is only attenuated by unsystematic error. Consider the test-retest reliability of an IQ test. It was noted earlier that practice effects would cause scores to increase across the two occasions but that this would not affect reliability. However, the second test is clearly in some sense a less valid measure of IQ as it will be an over-estimate. There are several types of validity to consider.

Face validity
Face validity concerns the fact that when confronted with a new test one automatically makes a subjective judgement as to whether it *appears* to be measuring what it is meant to. If a test of extraversion consists of

questions about going to parties and cracking jokes it has 'face validity'. But if a test of extraversion comprises looking at a black spiral spinning on its axis and measuring the length of an after effect it might seem a 'stupid' test, even though both the sensible and 'ridiculous' test might both predict certain features of extraversion quite well and correlate with each other to a significant degree. Face validity is not then a statistical concept but merely a subjective evaluation and as such is not a true measure of validity, although lack of face validity is not something to ignore as it can foster a negative attitude in the subject.

Content validity

Content validity concerns whether a test samples from the entire domain of that which is to be measured. Suppose one wanted to measure the amount of friction in a marriage. It would not be sufficient, say, to enquire about arguments over money. One would also have to examine for conflict over child-rearing, habits, lifestyle, plans for the future and so on. Once again, it can be seen that this is not a statistical concept but a question of 'expert judgement' (Aiken, 1985, p. 94).

Criterion-related validity

Criterion-related validity is achieved when a test yields the same result as another test that is already known to be valid (this second test is known as the *criterion measure*). The circularity of this definition is obvious and can cause problems, particularly when at a later date the validity of a criterion measure is called into question. A second feature of this definition is that it suggests a 'parallel' with reliability, in that a new test in order to be valid must have parallel form reliability with a test of proven validity.

Criterion measures can take many forms, but there is one supraordinate division that is usually made depending upon the time at which the result of the criterion measure becomes available. *Concurrent* validity is when results on the criterion measure are available simultaneously (e.g. those people with a neurotic psychiatric disorder, the criterion measure, are found to be higher on a new test of neuroticism). *Predictive* validity, on the other hand, is when scores on a new test are used to predict scores on a subsequent measure (e.g. 'A' level results can be validated as a measure of suitability for a university education by correlating them with final class of degree, the criterion measure). Predictive validity seldom rises above 0.6 (thereby leaving 64% of variance unexplained) because many factors will ultimately influence final outcome.

Construct validity

Construct validity, the most important but elusive type, is concerned with the psychological meaning of test scores. With criterion validity the concept of validity can be hedged by saying that the test measures what the criterion measure does. But in construct validity a genuine attempt is made to define the 'thing' or construct that one is interested in. Aiken (1985) manages to capture this elusiveness in a few well-chosen lines: 'The construct validity of a test is not established by one successful prediction; it consists of the slow, laborious process of gathering evidence from many experiments and observations on how the test is functioning.' Among the sources of evidence that can be cited are:

1. Expert judgement that test content pertains to the construct.
2. The demonstration of internal consistency of the test (if it can be broken down into two or more unrelated groups of items it can hardly be measuring a single construct).
3. High correlations with other measures of the construct (*convergent validity*).
4. Low correlations with measures of different constructs (*divergent validity*).
5. The thoughts and comments of subjects as they undertake the test.
6. Studies of group differences.
7. Successful prediction of task performance when one would expect such task performance to relate to the construct.

The Wechsler Adult Intelligence Scale

Some of the points listed here will be discussed with respect to an actual test, the Wechsler Adult Intelligence Scale (WAIS), and implicit reference made to much of the work on this test reported by Matarazzo (1972).

First, the WAIS does indeed on inspection contain subtests or individual items that most would judge as pertaining to the construct of intelligence—there are tests of conceptual thought, mathematical reasoning, speed of problem solving, etc.—although critics might say that the test is not culture fair (i.e. measures a white middle-class definition of intelligence) and fails to tap other aspects of intellectual performance such as persistence.

Next, the WAIS does have internal consistency because the manual shows that all subtests intercorrelate positively as to the two main subfactors of verbal and performance IQ.

As for convergent and divergent validity, performance on the WAIS does indeed correlate with other measures of intelligence, such as its forerunner, the Wechsler-Bellevue scale, and with less formal measures of intelligence such as gaining admission to university; whereas conversely, in regard to divergent validity, although WAIS scores do correlate with some other psychological traits none of the correlations is high enough to suggest that the test measures something other than intelligence. For example, if WAIS scores were to correlate very highly with measures of, say, fear of failure, state anxiety, neuroticism and fear of negative evaluation, then one might say that it measured not intelligence but test-taking anxiety.

More detailed statements concerning construct validation can be made using a 'psychological decomposition' approach. Levy (1973) points out that when validating a test there is a great tendency to correlate it with everything else in sight in the hope that a 'meaning' emerges. The problem is that we often know even less about the tests dragged in, so that 'what starts as a problem of understanding something about one test becomes a multiple act of construct validation'.

Alternatively, using psychological decomposition, the one test is systematically varied, changing one aspect each time, and performance on these slightly different versions correlated. Levy cites Hopkins (1971), who studied the Digit-Symbol subtest of the WAIS. Holding test format, timing, scoring and so forth constant, he developed one test that measured only writing speed (i.e. only one symbol was used which was written repeatedly); one test of eye-movement (twenty five digits were used rather than the normal nine so that Ss could not simply learn digit-symbol relationships) and so on. He found that the speed of eye movement version correlated rather well (0.68) with the original version, as did the writing speed version (0.47). Therefore, one can say that the Digit Symbol subtest of the WAIS in part measures speed of eye movement and speed of writing.

PROPERTIES OF MEASURES: GENERALISABILITY

A bridge between the concepts of reliability and validity is generalisability theory (Cronbach, Gleser, Nanda & Rajaratnam, 1972; Levy, 1974; Shavelson and Webb, 1981). This concerns the broader problem of how to make a general statement from a specific test score: that is, how to generalise from one observation to other classes of observation, often known as the *dependability* of a score or test. One might wish to generalise from:

1. Scores obtained from one judge to those derived from other judges.
2. Scores on one test of, say, depression, to scores on other tests of depression.

3. Scores at this particular moment to scores at some time in the future.
4. Scores from one sample of possible items to scores from other samples.
5. Scores obtained under one set of motivational conditions to those obtained under others.

In looking at these examples it can readily be seen that the traditional division between reliability and validity becomes quite deliberately blurred. In fact the concept of there being *one* true score is swept away as described by Wiggins (1973) to be replaced by the notion of the universe score, the mean of all possible observations under all 'conditions'. (The assumptions this definition requires are listed in Wiggins, 1973, p. 286.)

Cronbach, Gleser, Nanda and Rajaratnam (1972) state the problem thus:

> The score on which the decision is to be based is only one of many scores that might serve the same purpose. The decision maker is almost never interested in the response given to the particular stimulus objects or questions, to the particular tester, at the particular moment of testing. Some, at least, of these conditions of measurement could be altered without making the score any less acceptable to the decision maker. This is to say, there is a universe of observations, any of which would have yielded a usable basis for the decision. The ideal datum on which to base the decision would be something like the person's mean score over all acceptable observations, which we shall call his 'universe score'. The investigator uses the observed score or some function of it as if it were the universe score. That is, he generalizes from sample to universe.

In a generalisability study a whole range of observations is made under the different conditions that interest the experimenter. The basic data matrix for a generalisability design is given in Table 3.2, taken from Wiggins (1973). Here, conditions is a loose term that could relate to 'particular test items, test formats, stimuli, observers, occasions or situations of observation' and more. The observed score for a person in one condition is x_{pi} and the universe score is the mean of all x_{pi} over all conditions. An analysis of variance of the data will apportion the variance to persons, conditions and residual (or error). This ANOVA replaces traditional coefficients and becomes more complex as more

TABLE 3.2
Basic data matrix for a generalisability design (based on Wiggins, 1973)

		\multicolumn{5}{c}{Conditions}
		1	*2*	*3*	. . . .	n_i
	1	X_{11}	X_{12}	X_{13}	. . . .	X_{1ni}
Persons	2		X_{22}	X_{23}	. . . .	X_{2ni}
	3			X_{33}	. . . .	X_{3ni}
	:			:		:
	np			X_{np3}	. . . .	X_{npni}

than one set of conditions (more than one facet) is considered simultaneously.

One might measure the sociability of persons under two sets of conditions: Facet I might be different judges and Facet II different settings. Hence the study might comprise four judges rating the subjects at work, at a social gathering, with the family and with one close friend. How does one choose the range of conditions? This is a judgemental and not a statistical concept. It depends upon the type of generalisations that the experimenter sees as being demanded of the test: if different judges will be using it then it is necessary to gauge variance due to judges; if observations are made in a psychiatric ward but will be used in practice in hostels and outpatient departments as well, then having specified the universe to which observations must generalise the researcher must 'provide empirical evidence of such generalisability in the form of generalisability coefficients or estimates of the components of variants involved' (Wiggins, 1973, p. 295). Those coefficients are often in the form of inter-class correlations (somewhat like the alpha coefficient) for the universe specified.

An example of a generalisability study can be found in the work of Mariotto and Farrell (1979) who focused upon the Inpatient Multi-dimensional Psychiatric Scale (IMPS). This is used as a standardised instrument for measuring change in the level of functioning of psychiatric patients. It has 75 items that are scored for (a) intensity (b) frequency and (c) presence, by a trained interviewer and observer after a 40 minute interview. It can be scored for ten 'syndrome' scores and also for some higher level factor scores. Several previous studies had shown that raters could order patients comparably on both syndrome and higher level scores (i.e. good inter-rater reliability of around 0.90) but the comparability between raters of absolute level of scores was at issue. Indeed, other studies had indicated that the absolute level of scores given by a particular rater might vary with such variables as increased professional training, years of experience and age. The suggestion is, then, that non-patient factors affect judgements on the IMPS so that 'the scale may not validly reflect patient behaviour over differing times, situations, patient groups or raters'. Mariotto and Farrell took 10 chronic schizophrenics (mean age 43 years; mean hospitalisation 7 years 5 months) in a large state psychiatric hospital and gave each one the semistructured interview developed for the IMPs. Observing the interview on a video monitor in an adjacent room were 11 graduate raters. They had received 7 hours of training. Inter-rater correlations between the 11 raters for the 10 syndrome scores were calculated, and the 4 'worst' raters dropped. The next analyses therefore took place on only the 7 'best' raters.

In the first place it was found that, as in previous studies, generalisability coefficients (intra-class correlations) for the scales were generally high. On only two scales, grandiosity and retardation, did the raters fail to order subjects consistently.

Next, to assess level differences, two-way analyses of variance (raters × patients) were undertaken for each IMPS score. The main effect for raters particularly concerns us. The effect was significant on an F test on all bar two of the 14 syndrome and higher level scores. Therefore, the absolute level of ratings was significantly different between raters. Indeed, the rater effect accounted for as much as 20% and 23% of the variance on the scales Cognitive Distortion and Paranoid respectively, and for 18% of the variance of the IMPS total score. Further, with Wilk's λ multivariate analysis it was shown that different raters had different biases on different scales, so that the profiles obtained from each rater across the 10 syndrome scales were not parallel.

The contribution of rater bias to IMPS scores is therefore high, especially when one takes into account that the raters were especially selected so as to be homogeneous. Mariotto and Farrell were able to conclude that IMPS cannot be used when absolute level differences are required, as in outcome studies and normative comparisons across patient groups. Further, because of the contribution of rater bias to the patient profile, IMPS profiles could not be recommended for diagnostic usage.

Generalisability theory, though widely regarded as a conceptual leap, has not caught on. An excellent book on psychological testing (Kaplan & Saccuzzo, 1982) does not mention it at all. There are two reasons. First, to estimate universe scores requires a generalisability study that is complicated to design, time consuming to carry out and awkward to analyse. Second, traditional reliability and validity are not 'wrong'—rather, they are just limited aspects of generalisability (Sechrest, 1984). As long as the researcher does not abuse reliability and validity coefficients (particularly by using reliability coefficients as interchangeable) and thoughtfully and deliberately specifies the *type* of reliability and *type* of validity that is needed, they remain a credible backbone of measurement.

The reader who does not wish to pursue generalisability theory is referred to an excellent recent book by Shardson and Webb (1991) written for people with limited psychometric knowledge and skills, and describing different kinds of design for generalisability studies.

A PRACTITIONER APPROACH TO MEASUREMENT

Measurement within a clinical context relates to the model of the therapist as a 'scientist practitioner' (Barlow, Hayes & Nelson, 1984). The scientific practitioner takes measures mainly because it improves treatment; by measuring problems one gets feedback on progress and by measuring treatment one can ensure treatment integrity (i.e. that the client receives the treatment intended). A second reason is that interesting results can be published as single case studies to enhance clinical science in general. Third, measures provide for accountability— they can be used as indicators of the effectiveness of a service.

Barlow and his colleagues offer excellent advice about how to go about measuring with the individual client:

1. State client problems in specific terms.
2. Specify several problem areas.
3. Obtain multiple measures for each problem behaviour.
4. Select measures that are both sensitive and meaningful.
5. Collect measures early in the course of treatment.
6. Take the same measures repeatedly, at least before, during and after treatment.
7. Make comparisons within measures only if data are collected under similar conditions.
8. Graph the data.
9. Record inconvenient measures less frequently than convenient ones.
10. Select measures with appropriate psychometric properties, looking for certain types of reliability such as inter-judge agreement, and noting that some types of reliability are less appropriate. For example, test-retest reliability presupposes consistency, but usually the therapist needs a measure of change.
11. Obtain client consent and co-operation.

These suggestions are developed and extended in a further book by Barlow which shows how the gap between individual therapy and research study can be bridged (Barlow & Hersen, 1984).

A RESEARCH APPROACH TO MEASUREMENT

In terms of research method, the aim of measurement is to achieve an acceptable operational definition of the aims and/or hypotheses of the study. The process used to achieve this is described here step by step, using an actual study as an example to illustrate some of the operations used.

Step 1: State the aims and/or hypotheses

This must be done decisively, almost boldly; avoiding excessively general statements on the one hand and obsessionally elaborate detail on the other. The over-broad aim does not describe the study well, and detail can for the most part be left to the Method section. The aims must flow naturally from the introduction and the method must flow naturally from the aims.

The example considered is that of a study performed by Kaiser and Pfenninger (1984). They state the aims of their investigation as follows. 'The objective of this report is to examine if the outcome of the severely head injured child is better following a neurointensive care than without it.'

This is a pretty clear statement of intent. The outcome could have been defined a little more precisely, although in the context of the introduction the reader would have readily understood that the study was concerned with 'long-range' outcome which implies consideration of many outcome variables other than just survival rate.

Step 2: Content analysis of aims/hypotheses

The measures must flow from the aims, so one must define the content of each aspect of the aims. The facets to be defined and measured are:

1.   The subjects ('the child').
2.   Severe head injury.
3.   Neurointensive care.
4.   Outcome.

1. The subjects.   Putting 'outcome' and 'severe head injury' to one side for the moment, 'the subject' has to be defined and measured for two reasons: (a) to ensure they meet inclusion criteria; and (b) to provide independent variables that may be associated with outcome (dependent) variables. The inclusion criteria chosen by the authors were:

a) Dates of hospitalisation (March 1978-August 1981).
b) Place of hospitalisation (Department of Paediatric Surgery, Barn).
c) Age (0-14 years, although this was not explicitly stated).

None of these simple inclusion criteria poses any measurement problem, although others would have, such as 'premorbid IQ' or 'able to comprehend testing instructions'.

The independent variables identified were:

(a)   Age.
(b)   Cause of accident (e.g. falls, road accidents).
(c)   Clinical signs on admission (e.g. vital functions, extracranial injury, neurological signs, Glasgow Coma scale score).
(d)   CT findings (e.g. haematoma, contusion, CSF bleeding).

Again, none of these poses particular measurement problems although it cannot be supposed that either a neurological exam or interpretation of a CT scan are perfectly reliable. Other independent variables could have been chosen, such as 'premorbid behaviour adjustment' which *would* have been awkward.

2. *Severe head injury.*   Severe head injury is not a technical term as such and needs an operational definition, in this case having a Glasgow Coma scale (GCS) score of 7 or less. The GCS is an extremely well-known behavioural measure of depth of coma (Teasdale & Jennett, 1974, 1976; Teasdale & Mendelow, 1984) that measures three things: conditions under which the eyes open, best verbal response and best motor response, summing observations to produce a single score. Score reliability is higher than other possible measures of severity such as length of post-traumatic amnesia, which is assessed retrospectively and depends upon often patchy observations in the notes or upon the subjective report of the patient.

One must mention one more inclusion criterion here in that only 'blunt' or 'non-penetration' injuries were accepted into the trial, as penetration injuries usually require different management.

3. *Neurointensive care.*   As in any experiment the treatment must be explicitly defined, usually by way of a statement of principles or strategies, since treatment can rarely be specified to the level of detailed action. Neurointensive care was defined as the use of a series of medical procedures:

(a)   Continuous intracranial and arterial pressure monitoring.
(b)   Normalisation of intracranial pressure and cerebral perfusion pressure.
(c)   Intubation.
(d)   Hyperventilation.
(e)   Control of body temperature.
(f)   Dexamethasone.
(g)   Barbiturates.
(h)   Osmotic agents.

These procedures were described in detail and present no measurement problems.

4. Outcome.   This is the tricky one, as shown by the outline of a content analysis of outcome in Table 3.3. This breakdown could be elaborated almost indefinitely to include almost everything we could possibly measure about someone. For instance, intelligence could be broken down into speed, persistence, verbal skill, non-verbal skill, reasoning, abstract thinking, judgement; personality could be subdivided into traits, interests, hobbies, self-concept, self-esteem, flexibility, ego-centrism, adjustment etc.

The impossibility of measuring everything in detail is self-evident. Therefore, the next difficult decision the researcher must make is how to limit the size of the task. At this point the accumulated experience of other researchers needs to be sought. This is what the published literature is for.

Step 3: Selecting from the content analysis and undertaking a literature search

These two steps are logically distinct but in practice go hand in hand, for the following reason. Choice of measure is a complex juggling act based on knowledge of the following factors:

1.   Content analysis of aims.
2.   Priority areas of content.
3.   Financial resources of the study.
4.   Time-scale of the study.
5.   Administration time of each test.
6.   The length of time that subjects can tolerate testing.
7.   Available tests of priority areas.
8.   The adequacy of such tests.
9.   The need for the study to relate to a larger body of research.

TABLE 3.3
Content analysis of outcome

Outcome
- Dead
- Survived
  - Physical outcome
    - Complications (e.g. epilepsy, headaches)
    - Sensory impairment (vision, hearing, touch, etc.)
    - Motor impairment (spasticity, ataxia, etc.)
    - Need for further medical attention
  - Psychological outcome
    - Cognitive performance
      - Intelligence
      - Language
      - Motor skill
      - Memory
      - Attention
    - Behaviour
      - Personality
      - Psychiatric state
      - Interpersonal skills
      - Disruptive behaviours
    - Affective state
      - Mood
      - Impulsivity
      - Aggression
      - Tolerance of frustration
      - Insight
      - Motivation
      - Activity level
      - Libido
    - Social integration
      - Work performance
      - School performance
      - Criminality
      - Family adjustment
      - Alcohol/drug abuse
      - Patterns of friendship
    - Psycho-physiology
      - Regional EEG
      - Expectancy waves
      - Event related potentials
      - Evoked potentials
      - 'Arousal'

It can be seen that there are interactions between some of these: in particular, what one finally selects from the content analysis in part depends upon the analysis of alternatives available, and which alternatives one examines in turn depends upon priorities in the content analysis.

Therefore, the examination of alternative measures through a detailed literature search is always a compromise. One cannot possibly read around all of the topics listed at the end of Table 3.3, therefore one rejects from the literature search:

1. All aspects that one definitely cannot measure through lack of facilities (let us suppose this takes out the psychophysiological branch of Table 3.3).
2. All aspects in which one is confident of one's knowledge or expertise (in Kaiser and Pfennigger's case this takes out the physical outcome branch).
3. All aspects that are low in one's hierarchy of priorities (let us suppose that this removes the cognitive performance branch).

This leaves the general area of psychosocial recovery; so a computer search was made on MEDLINE in March, 1986 requesting all references dating back to 1st January, 1980 which had the keyword HEAD INJUR? in combination with RECOVER? or OUTCOME? or PERSONALITY? or PSYCHOSOCIAL? (Note that a question mark indicates that the term may be followed by different endings or a second word.) An identical search was also undertaken on PSYCINFO. Together with other searches using slightly different keywords (such as BRAIN DAMAGE for HEAD INJUR?) and with a search by hand working backwards in time from the most recent issues of the relevant journals and books, 41 articles were identified, mainly 1980 or later, but including a few important articles that appeared earlier.

Step 4: Evaluation of the measures that have been used in the literature

In evaluating the adequacy and usefulness of the specific measures employed in these 41 studies, one must keep several questions in mind that constitute broad judgemental criteria for eventual selection:

1. Are the basic psychometric properties of the measures known?
2. If known, are they adequate?
3. Are the measures generalisable to my subject population (in relation to our example, can the measure be used with children)?

4. If the measure is to be adapted (e.g. for use with children; to make it suitable for a British rather than American population; needing translation from a foreign language) then will it need re-standardising?
5. In what areas do I need only broad summary measures or first approximations?
6. In what areas do I need fine measurements that might relate to process as well as outcome?
7. Are there some papers so germane to mine that I should use some of their measures to establish a bridge for easy comparison of data and findings?
8. What resources does the study need to undertake particular measurement, such as expensive test material, equipment, access to relatives and many others?
9. What resources does the subject need in order to take the test (e.g. facility with language, demands upon concentration, motor ability required)?
10. Are there ethical problems (e.g. confidentiality of test data, the stressfulness of the test)?

To return to our example, of the studies reviewed, a large percentage (37%) just used interviews and/or simple rating scales to provide broad descriptions of psychosocial outcome, without any knowledge whatsoever of their psychometric properties. For example, Eggleston and Cruvant (1983) examined recovery from intracerebral haematoma in children and adults and developed, or rather invented, a 'Patient Data Scale' which included 4-point ratings of 'Activities of daily living' 'Psychosocial Adjustment' 'Work/school adjustment; developmental progress' and 'Speech function'. Sometimes these studies also included a simple checklist of symptoms, also invariably of unknown reliability and validity, such as the 'Head injury symptom checklist' of McLean, Temkin, Dikman and Wyler (1983).

In fact only three studies (7%) ascertained the reliability of their rating or interview measures. One study in particular (Rappaport et al. 1982) was especially concerned with reliability and made it a focus of the study. They developed the Rappaport Disability Rating Scale and computed the inter-rater reliabilities for trained raters. These were very high at between 0.97 and 0.98, but reliability for untrained raters (of the type who would in practice be using the scale) was not computed.

Similarly, only three studies (7%) tried to ascertain the validity of their measures. One was the study of Rappaport cited earlier, one is as yet unpublished, and one was an older study by Shaffer, Chadwick and Rutter (1975), who validated a rating of psychiatric handicap in brain injured children against detailed questioning of the parents. They also used questionnaires of known validity such as the Teachers' Questionnaire (Rutter, Tizard & Whitmore, 1970).

Finally, 29% of the studies used ad hoc interviews and scales mixed with a few well-known, standardised tests such as the Katz Adjustment Scale (Katz & Lyerly, 1963).

This brief review makes somewhat chilling reading, especially in an area like neuropsychology which is renowned for its experimental rigour. It would be usual at this stage to draw a few conclusions about measurement within the field of interest. In this case:

1. Most of the measures in the studies reviewed provided data of dubious credibility since psychometric properties were ignored.
2. Where psychometric properties were known they were on well-known psychiatric scales not intended for use with the head injured and as such they may well have missed important features of this population.
3. Description of behaviour and cognitions were extremely broad—not to say gross, in more senses than one.
4. Data collection was never theory driven. The studies mainly aimed at obtaining a description, even then without a proper content analysis.

Clearly, if Kaiser and Pfenninger had had access to these searches, they would not have found a body of tried and trusted outcome measures upon which they could draw as needed. On presumably limited resources (i.e. within the context of an on-going clinical service with no special research grant) they sensibly used measures that are readily applied to children and are widely used in other studies, notably the Glasgow Outcome Scale. It is a crude scale admittedly, compressing all features of recovery onto a 4-point scale:

Vegetative state.
Severe disability.
Moderate disability.
Good recovery.

But direct comparisons can be made with many other studies, the measure usefully relates to actual performance, and it is probably sensitive enough to offer a first approximation to the question of whether intensive care is worthwhile. On the other hand, it certainly can never have construct validity since outcome is multi-faceted, and as it does not relate directly to the detail of the content analysis in

Table 3.3 it can never obtain information about specific patterns of mechanisms of recovery.

In general terms, what might have been done? General principles are considered here, as many researchers will find themselves in this position:

1. Select from previous work measures of known psychometric properties, so as to form a solid bridge with the corpus of knowledge.
2. Select from previous work interesting measures of unknown psychometric properties, but design the new study so as to assess these properties. This also forms a bridge with the corpus of knowledge, but in addition improves our understanding of the dependability of that knowledge.
3. Undertake a content analysis of areas of interest to define what other variables one needs to measure, and develop them psychometrically in the new study.
4. Be reasonable; accept that no study is perfect and that the inclusion of one or two measures of unknown properties is 'allowed'.

SUMMARY

The principles of psychometric testing should also underpin all forms of measurement whatever the metric or technique used. Therefore for every measure employed, one should be able to state the type of reliability that it should and does have, the type of validity that is required and demonstrated. and the universe of conditions to which test scores can generalise. Good measurement is a prerequisite for the scientific approach to both treatment and research. It is facilitated by a clear statement of aims, by a content analysis of these aims, and by a critical appraisal of measurement within the relevant literature. Good measurement usually demands that a portion of research resources is allocated to the development of measures.

REFERENCES

Aiken, L.R. (1980). Problems in testing the elderly. *Educational Gerontology, 5,* 119-124.
Aiken, L.R. (1985). *Psychological Testing and Assessment* (5th edition). Boston: Allyn & Bacon.

Anastasi, A. (1976). *Psychological Testing.* 4th edn. New York: Macmillan.

Barlow, D.H., Hayes, S.C. & Nelson, R.O. (1984). *The Scientist Practitioner: Research and Accountability in Clinical and Educational Settings.* New York: Pergamon.

Barlow, D.H. & Hersen, M. (1984). *Single Case Experimental Designs: Strategies for Studying Behavior Change.* New York: Pergamon.

Cronbach, L.J. (1951). Coefficient alpha and the internal structure of tests. *Psychometrika, 16,* 296-334.

Cronbach, L.J., Gleser, G.C., Nanda, H. & Rajaratnam, N. (1972). *The Dependability of Behavioural Measurements.* New York: Wiley.

Du Bois, P.H. (1966). A test-dominated society: China 1115 BC-1905 AD. In A. Anastasia (ed.) *Testing Problems in Perspective.* Washington: American Council on Education.

Du Bois, P.H. (1970). *A History of Psychological Testing.* Boston: Allyn & Bacon.

Eggleston, C. & Cruvant, D. (1983). Review of recovery from intracerebral hematoma in children and adults. *Journal of Neurological Nursing, 15,* 128-135.

Galton, F. (1879). Psychometric experiments. *Brain, 2,* 149-162.

Hopkins, N. (1971). *Unpublished observations.* cited in Levy (1973).

Kaiser, G. & Pfenninger, J. (1984). Effect of neurointensive care upon outcome following severe head injuries in childhood—a preliminary report. *Neuropediatrics, 15,* 68-75.

Kaplan, R.M. & Saccuzzo, D.P. (1982). *Psychological Testing: Principles, Applications and Issues.* Monterey: Brooks/Cole.

Katz, M.M. & Lyerly, S.B. (1963). Methods for measuring adjustment and social behaviour in the community I Rationale, description, discriminative validity and scale development. *Psychological Reports, 13,* 503-535.

Kendell, R.E. (1975). *The Role of Diagnosis in Psychiatry.* Oxford: Blackwell.

Leach, C. (1979). *Introduction to Statistics: A Non-parametric Approach for the Social Sciences.* Chichester: Wiley.

Levy, P. (1973). On the relation between test theory and psychology. In P. Kline (ed.) *New Approaches in Psychological Measurement.* London: John Wiley & Sons.

Levy, P. (1974). Generalizability studies in clinical settings. *British Journal of Social and Clinical Psychology, 13,* 161-172.

Mariotto, M.J. & Farrell, A.D. (1979). Comparability of the absolute level of ratings on the Inpatient Multidimensional Psychiatric Scale within a homogeneous group of raters. *Journal of Consulting and Clinical Psychology, 47,* 59-64.

Martin, I. & Venables, P.H. (1980). *Techniques in Psychophysiology.* Chichester: Wiley.

Matarazzo, J.D. (1972). *Wechsler's Measurement and Appraisal of Adult Intelligence.* 5th edn. Baltimore: Williams & Wilkins.

Maxwell, A.E. (1961). *Analysing Qualitative Data.* London: Methuen.

McLean, A., Temkin, N.R., Dikmen, S. & Wyler, A.R. (1983). The behavioral sequelae of head injury. *Journal of Clinical Neuropsychology, 5,* 361-376.

Rappaport, M., Hail, K.M., Hopkins, K., Belleza, T. & Cope, D.N.N. (1982). Disability rating scale for severe head trauma: coma to community. *Archives of Physical Medicine and Rehabilitation, 63,* 118-123.

Rutter, B.M., Graham, P. & Yule, W. (1970). *A Neuropsychiatric Study of Childhood. Clinics in Developmental Medicine.* London: Heinemann.

Rutter, M., Tizard, J. & Whitmore, K. (eds) (1970.) *Education, Health and Behaviour.* London: Longman.

Sechrest, L. (1984). Reliability and validity. In A.S. Bellack & M. Hersen (eds.) *Research Methods in Clinical Psychology.* New York: Pergamon.

Shaffer, D., Chadwick, O. & Rutter, M. (1975). Psychiatric outcome of localised head injury in children. In *CIBA, Outcome of severe damage to the central nervous system.* Amsterdam: Elsevier.

Shavelson, R.J. & Webb, N.B. (1981). Generalizability theory: 1973-1980. *British Journal of Mathematical and Statistical Psychology, 34,* 133-166.

Shardson, R.J. & Webb, N.M. (1991). *Generalizability theory: a primer.* Newbury Park: Sage.

Siegel, S. (1956). *Nonparametric Statistics for the Behavioural Sciences.* New York: McGraw-Hill.

Teasdale, G. & Jennett, B. (1974). Assessment of coma and impaired consciousness. *Lancet, ii,* 81-84.

Teasdale, G. & Jennett, B. (1976). Assessment and prognosis of coma after head injury. *Acta Neurochirurgica, 34,* 45-55.

Teasdale, G. & Mendelow, D. (1984). Pathophysiology of head injuries. In N. Brooks (ed.) *Closed Head Injury: Psychological, Social and Family Consequences.* Oxford University Press.

Wiggins, J.S. (1973). *Personality and Prediction: Principles of Personality Assessment.* Reading. MA :Addison-Wesley.

CHAPTER FOUR

Domains of assessment

Robert J. Edelmann *Department of Psychology,*
University of Surrey, Guildford

INTRODUCTION

The aim of this chapter is to provide a brief overview of different methods used by clinical psychologists and other mental health professionals in both practice and research for the assessment of common problems. For more detailed discussion of both the principles of assessment and the psychometric properties of some of the instruments referred to, the reader should consult more general texts such as Barlow (1981), Ciminero, Calhoun, and Adams (1986), Bellack and Hersen (1988) or Peck and Shapiro (1990). In the broadest sense, there are four primary purposes of assessment in a clinical context: (i) to determine whether the service offered is likely to be of benefit to the person; (ii) to provide a description of the problem; (iii) to facilitate treatment selection; and (iv) to provide a means for treatment evaluation (Barrios, 1988). If the referral is indeed appropriate then further analysis of the problem will be required. Key aims of problem identification are (i) to identify those areas that are most problematic to the client; (ii) the order in which these problems should be addressed; and (iii) the variables maintaining each problem. The treatment can then be selected accordingly and its efficacy in helping the client to overcome their problem monitored. Assessment should thus be directly related to and continuous with treatment.

Assessment can be related to one of three levels: the symptom, syndrome, or system. Symptom is not used here in the medical sense to give information about underlying disease or pathology but rather to indicate the particular manifestation of the person's difficulties. Thus, symptom assessment involves the evaluation of an isolated behaviour, feeling or reaction, such as number of binge episodes, pain rating, or extent of blushing. Whether the target selected is representative of the client's difficulties is an inevitable problem. For example, quality of life or mobility may be more important then pain per se; social avoidance or communication difficulties as important as blushing. It is thus questionable whether the assessment of just one particular behaviour or reaction provides sufficient information. Assessment at the level of the syndrome reflects the assumption that a set of symptoms covary, necessitating assessment of each related symptom. Clearly if symptoms covaried as predicted then assessment of the syndrome would hold many advantages both for selecting appropriate treatments and evaluating treatment outcome. Unfortunately, symptoms may be expressed differently and are frequently evident in variant combinations. Assessment at the level of the system is based on the assumption that cognitive, behavioural, affective, and biological aspects are inextricably linked so that a change in one component is related to a change in another. This inevitably necessitates a broader focus to assessment which is generally the aim of assessment in clinical psychology, although assessment of different parameters may not always be feasible in practice. In addition, the underlying assumption that each component functions concordantly with another is not necessarily evident in reality.

TRIPLE-RESPONSE APPROACH

Since Lang's (1968) classic article emphasising the tripartite model of behaviour—measurement of verbal-subjective components (more recently expanded to include cognitive elements), physiological activity and overt behaviour—has become standard practice for many studies investigating the nature of psychological problems and the efficacy of therapy. The verbal-subjective component typically refers to verbal reports of thoughts associated with an event or behaviour but may also include reports of distress, arousal, or behaviour. Typical measures of physiological activity include heart rate, respiration, perspiration, and muscle tension. Overt behaviour typically refers to observable aspects of the particular problem such as amount of food consumed or distance travelled from home.

The wide acceptance of the tripartite model of behaviour, particularly in relation to anxiety-related problems, has not only led to more comprehensive assessments but also to investigations of interrelationships between measures and variations in reactions across individuals. Numerous instruments have been developed for the measurement of each type of response (see Hersen & Bellack, 1988). One positive outcome of this work is more carefully targeted interventions. In addition, the inclusion of measures other than just self-reports has improved the clinical validity of both intake and outcome assessments.

However, as noted previously, when all three response systems are assessed, a number of studies have found low, statistically non-significant correlations between them (e.g. Borkovec, Weerts & Bernstein, 1977). This low correlation between response systems at a particular point in time has been referred to as discordance. It has also been noted that the three systems can covary over time in relation to intervention, a phenomenon termed desynchrony (Rachman & Hodgson, 1974). If this is taken to imply that the three systems are partially or functionally independent then not only will a thorough assessment within each response system be necessary, but a multimodal intervention will be required.

It is also possible. however, that variations in response systems, rather than indicating functional independence, might be explained by measurement error. Thus, variations have been found among measurements of different aspects within the same system. This is particularly evident in the assessment of physiological activity such as heart rate, muscle tension, and galvanic skin response (e.g. Abelson & Curtis, 1989). In addition, evaluations of interrelationships commonly vary both measurement methods (e.g. self-reports, direct observation) and response mode (cognitive, physiological, and behavioural), thus confounding the two (Cone, 1979). A particular problem exists with the verbal-subjective mode which seems to encompass all measures involving some form of self-report including self-observed physiological activity (e.g. my heart pounds) and behavioural activity (e.g. I avoid social events). Low relationships may thus be an artefact of using different measurement strategies rather than a reflection of the actual relationship between response systems. Conversely, positive relationships between, say, self-reports of perception of autonomic arousal and self-reports of a problem domain such as anxiety may either reflect a real relationship between different parameters of a problem or may simply reflect the common methodology used.

In view of the growing interest in cognitive measures, Eifert and Wilson (1991) have recently proposed four rather than three content areas for assessment: i.e. behavioural, physiological, cognitive, and affective. They further suggest that each area can be assessed in three different ways: i.e. by self-report, or observation and instruments, or technical equipment. Behaviour can thus be assessed by self-report inventories, or direct observation, or instruments such as pedometers. Physiological activity can similarly be assessed by self-report, or by direct observation of reactions such as blushing and perspiration, as well as by the usual psychophysiological recording instrumentation. Cognitions can be assessed by self-report and thought-sampling procedures, observations of behaviour such as delayed recall on tasks, or via technical equipment using methods derived from experimental cognitive psychology such as the STROOP test (see Williams, Watts, Macleod, & Mathews, 1988). Finally, affective responses can be assessed via self-report instruments such as mood adjective checklists, by observation of behaviour such as facial expressions and body posture and by some, as yet to be determined, instrumentation.

As Eifert and Wilson note (pp. 290-291):

> ... the potentially positive contributions of the triplereponse-mode conception of assessment has been obscured by the frequent confounding of content and method of assessment ... vague and inconsistent definitions of the verbal-cognitive content area and the failure to take account of affective responses as a separate class.

Given the multifaceted nature of psychological problems then any assessment will only have genuine clinical utility if at least one measure of each content area is included, preferably with each content area assessed by more than one method. As Eifert and Wilson further note (p.288), "this would enable variance related the method to be distinguished from variance related to the content". Although such assessment may be desirable it may not be feasible in clinical practice. While the remainder of this chapter examines methods available for assessing different components, each of which has its advantages and disadvantages, the need for a comprehensive assessment should be borne in mind.

INFORMATION DERIVED FROM SELF-REPORTS: INTERVIEWING

The interview is the most common procedure for assessing psychological problems and yet it is not without its difficulties. In relation to assessment in general, a distinction is often made between the method and the process of synthesising the information obtained (Marsh, 1985). The methods are frequently characterised as objective, structured, reliable, and valid, whereas the process has been assumed to be clinical, subjective, flexible, and changing (Marsh, 1985). The interview is expected to be both reliable and valid as well as flexible and sensitive enough for subtle information to be obtained. Some have argued that the former can only be achieved with structured interview formats whose primary purpose is diagnosis. More open, process-oriented interviews, whose aim is to enable the clinician to define and fully understand the nature and context of an individual's problematic behaviour(s) will inevitably have a more subjective bias (O'Leary & Wilson, 1975). The former is thus more useful as an index of whether or not the person meets diagnostic criteria and/or inclusion criteria for research studies, the latter is more useful for providing essential data for structuring therapeutic intervention,

The clinical interview

A properly conducted interview will allow the clinician to assess as many functional or controlling elements of the problem as possible. A great deal has been written about skilful interviewing (see review chapters by Morganstern, 1988 and Turkat, 1986). Skills discussed include an ability to listen in order to understand what the client is saying and experiencing, and communication skills, including an ability to express empathy and support. Process variables addressed include how to start an interview, how to prepare the client for the assessment process, specifying target behaviours, redefining problems, and, finally, closing the interview. Clearly the interview will vary somewhat according to the presenting problem; the person's initial account of his or her problem will alert the interviewer to particular aspects to be emphasised in the remainder of the interview (see Wilson, Spence, & Kavanagh, 1989 for variations in interview content in relation to presenting problem). The importance of having a structure that underlies the interview is, however, of paramount importance. The SORC approach (stimulus organism—response—consequences) suggested by Goldfried and Sprafkin (1976) is a conceptual model traditionally drawn on by behavioural psychologists in the assessment of an identified problem. The stimulus variable is the environmental event that elicits or evokes the problem behaviour, the response refers to the elements that constitute the problem, the organism variable refers to the physical and hypothetical states of the person that mediate the problem behaviour, and the consequence variable refers to the events that follow the problem behaviour. The general content of an interview is likely to include the following elements (see Wilson et al., 1989):

(i) What is the person's chief presenting problem, including severity (frequency, intensity, duration) and reported cognitive, behavioural, and physiological aspects?

(ii) What is the aetiology of the problem, including antecedents and consequences and any current precipitating factors?

(iii) What is the history of the problem, including duration, changes in severity, nature of onset, and development?

(iv) Are there any maintaining factors such as positive reinforcers for occurrence or avoidance?

Structured diagnostic interviews

The emergence of DSM-III (APA, 1980) led to the development of standardised interview schedules for a widening variety of disorders, while DSM-III-R (APA, 1987) led to the development of its associated structured clinical interview (SCID; Spitzer, Williams, & Gibbon, 1987). Of the many structured interview schedules available to assist in the process of diagnosis the most widely used include the Anxiety Disorders Interview Schedule Revised (ADIS-R; DiNardo et al., 1985), Schedule for Affective Disorders and Schizophrenia (SADS; Endicot & Spitzer, 1978) and the Diagnostic Interview Schedule (DIS; Robins et al., 1981). The ADIS-R is designed to provide differential diagnosis among the anxiety disorders, and includes detailed symptom ratings, particularly of symptoms of panic and generalised anxiety, and of phobic avoidance and interference of functioning. Studies by DiNardo, Barlow and their colleagues indicate variable reliability for the ADIS-R across anxiety disorders with excellent reliability reported for current principle diagnosis of simple phobia, social phobia, and obsessive-compulsive disorder, good reliability for panic, and fair reliability for generalised anxiety (DiNardo et al., 1993). A number of questions within the schedule require elaboration by the client and hence evaluation of these responses necessitates some element of clinical judgement. The SADS has been widely adopted by the research community although there is surprisingly little psychometric data on the schedule particularly relating to the reliability of the eight subscales suggested by Endicott and Spitzer (1978). It is likely that the SCID will replace the SADS in clinical research (Gotlib & Hamman, 1992).

The SCID also contains a section for diagnosis of DSM-III-R personality disorders (SCID-II) which are often manifest by social dysfunction. For a discussion of the many scales and interviews schedules for assessing personality disorders and social functioning see Tyrer (1990). The DIS, a highly structured interview schedule developed for epidemiological research, has also been widely used. However, there is surprisingly little psychometric data relating to the schedule, and the reliability of DIS diagnoses has been questioned (Anthony et al., 1985).

Commentary on interviews

Among the values of the interview method are the opportunity it provides for the client to give, in their own words, a detailed commentary of their circumstances, the problem, and so on, while the therapist is able to observe their behaviour. As noted earlier, in moving from structured interviews to rather more subjective, open, process-oriented interviews one inevitably sacrifices a degree of reliability. In the latter case the ultimate usefulness of the interview will depend not only on the accuracy of the information the therapist is able to elicit but also the accuracy of the inferences or predictions made by the therapist. In addition, any self-report method inevitably provides only an indirect measure of a problem and may thus be biased by the respondent's inclination to give a socially desirable response. This is likely to result in the under-reporting of negative behaviours and the over-reporting of positive behaviours. People with certain difficulties may be more likely than others to provide inaccurate information. Demand characteristics of the situation may also influence respondents to under- or over-report symptoms. Those referred for compensation claims may be motivated to over-report symptoms whereas those whose work or relationship might suffer as a result of symptom reporting may be motivated to under report. The aim of an interview is to gain accurate information in an efficient and systematic manner, hence the emphasis on interviewing skills and clinical judgement. The former in particular have been widely documented (see Wilson, Spence, & Kavanagh, 1989) with variables such as empathy, warmth, genuineness, and honesty assumed to be important therapist qualities. However, an assumption is often made that "experienced" clinicians are more adept at conducting effective evaluative interviews; but the process of change from "inexperienced" to "experienced" clinician is poorly defined. As well as input from both client and therapist, the nature of the interaction between them is likely to influence both the extent and accuracy of information provided. Although the importance placed on the therapist-client relationship varies as a function of therapeutic orientation few would deny that a "good" therapeutic relationship is essential to the assessment and treatment process. Perhaps more than other assessment techniques the usefulness of the interview will depend on the skill and perceptiveness of the therapist.

QUESTIONNAIRES

As Morrison (1988, p.267) comments, "it would be a trite understatement to report that there are numerous rating scales in existence for the evaluation of psychopathology and related behaviours". The aim of many of these is to gain some indication of symptom severity, although some measures focus more specifically on the thought processes associated with a particular problem area. It is beyond the scope of this chapter to refer to more than a few of the more widely used instruments for assessing a range of symptoms, and anxiety and depression in particular. The interested reader is referred to reviews of questionnaires available for assessing a range of other problems (see Hersen & Bellack, 1988).

Two of the most widely used general-purpose questionnaires are the General Health Questionnaire (GHQ; Goldberg, 1972) and the Hopkins Symptom Checklist (SCL-90: Derogatis, 1977). The GHQ is a 60-, 30-, 28-, or 20-item self-report questionnaire designed to detect psychiatric morbidity in community samples. It has been widely used in a variety of settings, although it has been suggested that it is unsuitable as a screening instrument as it tends to miss chronic cases (Benjamin, Decalmer, & Haran, 1982). The SCL-90 taps nine dimensions including depression and anxiety, and appears to be psychometrically sound.

Anxiety

There are a range of inventories which assess either general fears or phobias, or which relate to specific anxiety disorders (see Edelmann, 1992; Nietzel, Bernstein, & Russell, 1988). The Fear Survey Schedule (FSS; Wolpe & Lang, 1964) and Fear Questionnaire (FQ; Marks & Mathews, 1979) are perhaps the most widely used general phobia measures both for screening clinical populations and for monitoring clinical progress. Although the FSS has been used by clinicians for almost three decades it is only within the last decade that reliability of the instrument has been systematically investigated within clinical populations. These studies suggest that the factor structure of the FSS is generally invariant across samples (Arrindell, Emmelkamp, & van der Ende, 1984) and that it is a robust and valid measure of fear in anxiety disorder patients. The FQ consists of three factor-analytically derived scales (agoraphobia, social phobia, and blood-injury phobia), each consisting of five items rated on an 8-point scale of severity. It possesses good test–retest reliability (Marks & Mathews, 1979) and is a valid discriminator of improvement in treated agoraphobics (Mavissakalian, 1986), with whom it has been most widely used.

Of the wide variety of measures of subjective anxiety used for clinical assessment and research perhaps the most widely employed are the State-Trait Anxiety Inventory (STAI; Speilberger, Gorsuch, & Lushene, 1970) and the more recently developed Beck Anxiety Inventory (BAI; Beck, Epstein, Brown, & Steer, 1988). The focus of the BAI on physiological sequelae of anxiety and the originators' emphasis on its use with clinical populations tends to distinguish it from the STAI.

A variety of measures have also been developed to assess anxiety relating to specific objects or themes, or types of anxiety. The most widely used measures of social anxiety/phobia include the Social Avoidance and Distress Scale (SADS; Watson & Friend, 1969) and the Social Phobia and Anxiety Inventory (SPAI; Beidel, Turner, Stanley, & Dancu, 1989). Although the SADS has been used in numerous clinical studies, it was standardised on a population of undergraduates and does not necessarily distinguish social phobics from other anxiety conditions (Turner, McCann, & Beidel, 1987). The SPAI has thus recently been developed as an alternative measure. With regard to cognitive aspects of social anxiety the Social Interaction Self Statement Test (SISST; Glass, Merluzzi, Biever, & Larsen, 1982) has become one of the most widely used self-statement measures in social anxiety research. The scale consists of 30 items assessing the frequency of positive and negative self-statements in heterosexual social situations. Subjects use a 5-point scale to rate how frequently they experience each thought during an immediately preceding role-played interaction.

Measures of agoraphobic avoidance and panic symptomatology include the Mobility Inventory (MI; Chambless et al., 1985) the Body Sensations Questionnaire (BSQ) and the Agoraphobic Cognitions Questionnaire (ACQ; Chambless, Caputo, Bright, & Gallagher, 1984). All three measures have high internal consistency and reliability, the MI reliably discriminating agoraphobic patients from others with anxiety disorders. A number of standardised scales have been developed to assess obsessive-compulsive disorder, of which the Maudsley Obsessive-Compulsive Inventory (MOCI; Hodgson & Rachman, 1977) is probably the most widely used. A more recently developed measure, the Padua Inventory (PI; Sanavio, 1988), shows a close relationship with the MOCI and reliably distinguishes between outpatients with OCD and other anxiety disorder outpatients. Examples of anxiety measures relating to specific objects or situations include the Spider Phobia Questionnaire (Watts & Sharrock, 1984) and the Dental Fear Survey (Kleinknecht, Klepac, & Alexander, 1973).

Depression

The Beck Depression Inventory (BDI; Beck et al., 1961) is probably the most frequently used self-report measure of depression. Its 21 items each consist of four alternative statements graded in severity from 0 to 3 from which the person selects the one most accurately reflecting their current status. The items reflect affective (2 items), cognitive (11 items), overt behavioural (2 items), somatic (5 items), and interpersonal (1 item) symptoms of depression. Considerable psychometric data on the BDI has accumulated (Beck, Steer, & Garbin, 1988) which suggests that it is a reliable and valid measure. It is important to note, however, that the BDI was not designed to yield a discrete diagnosis of depression but to measure depression as a dimension of psychopathology cutting across other psychological problems. Its major focus, therefore, is on the depth of depressive symptomatology rather than diagnostic status and indeed nonspecific distress, rather than depression as such, may be captured by the BDI (Gotlib & Hammen, 1992).

Although there are numerous other depression measures these tend to be less widely used than the BDI. One of the most widely cited alternative measures is the Zung Self-Rating Depression Scale (SDS; Zung, 1965) although this scale's sensitivity and specificity to depression has been questioned (Carroll, Fielding, & Blashki, 1973). A further measure, the Centre for Epidemiologic Studies Depression Scale (CES-D; Radloff, 1977), which has been widely used in the US rather than the UK, is derived in part from both the Beck and Zung. This was designed to measure depressive symptoms in the community although a number of studies suggest that the ability of the CES-D to predict clinically diagnosed depression is unacceptably low (Myers & Weissman, 1980). Although not widely used, a measure that seems to map more closely to a clinical diagnosis of depression, is the Levine-Pilowsky Questionnaire (LPQ; Pilowsky, Levine, & Boulton, 1969). Carr and Smith (1985), for example, found a significant relationship between the LDP category of endogenous depression and DSMIII-diagnosed major depressive disorder. Although a range of instruments thus exists, it is of interest to note that Rehm (1988, p.329) commenting on a variety of depression measures states that "the psychometric properties of the instruments offer relatively little superiority from one to the next".

In addition to scales of depression severity there are a number of instruments designed to assess cognition in depression. Perhaps the most widely used of these is the Attributional Style Questionnaire (ASQ; Seligman, Abramson, Semmel, & von Baeyer, 1979) derived from the attributional reformulation of the learned helplessness theory of depression (Abramson, Seligman, & Teasdale, 1978). The ASQ consists of 12 vignettes, 6 describing generally positive outcomes and 6 describing generally negative outcomes with further subdivisions into interpersonal and achievement related themes. Respondents are asked to identify one major cause for each vignette and then to rate this cause on four 7-point dimensions of internality–externality, globality–specificity, stability–instability, and importance. In spite of its relative complexity the ASQ does seem to distinguish depressed from nondepressed people with few nondepressed showing the supposedly depressogenic attributional style.

Commentary on questionnaires

One of the obvious advantages of self-report instruments is that they are easy, relatively quick, and inexpensive to administer. In addition, as they are subject to objective scoring they minimise the degree of subjective inference. Assuming the instrument used is reliable and valid it is a useful means of specifying the nature and extent of the presenting problem. There are, however, a number of sources of error inherent in many instruments, including the instructions provided, response format, and the item wording. The number of instruments administered and their timing within the session, particularly in relation to other information elicited, can all effect the validity of information derived from questionnaires. In addition, as noted earlier, any self-report method inevitably provides only an indirect measure of a problem and thus may be biased by the respondent's inclination to give a socially desirable response or by the demand characteristics of the assessment situation. For example, the client has expectations of therapy and may not want to let their therapist down, hence they may respond so as to appear to be particularly bad ("faking bad") prior to therapy and to be particularly good ("faking good") following treatment. As noted later, however, this is not a problem peculiar to questionnaires; behaviour and physiological responses also being subject to demand characteristics.

SELF-MONITORING

Self-monitoring, sometimes in the form of systematised diary records, is often recorded as a matter of course during therapy, and frequently reported in outcome studies. A range of parameters can be recorded. When the target is discrete a frequency count is appropriate; for example, the frequency of obsessive thoughts or compulsive rituals, number of headaches each day, daily panic attacks, or episodes of self-induced vomiting. When the duration of a behaviour shows considerable variation on each occurrence then this should also be assessed. For example, Foa et al. (1984) obtained details of the average daily time spent washing and cleaning. In addition, clients can be asked to rate their subjective state, such as the severity of a headache, or intensity of a panic attack. For example, Foa et al. (1984) obtained details of severity of rituals and urge to ritualise. In a further study Lindsay et al. (1987) asked subjects to rate how anxious they were each day by marking a 15cm line ranging from no anxiety at the left of the line through three gradings of anxiety to extremely anxious at the right of the line. Subjects were also asked to record on a daily basis "how much time they spent worrying and thinking about their problem" on a 15cm scale separated into four points from no time on the left to all the time on the right.

It may also be appropriate to monitor other parameters and numerous diary forms have been developed for such a purpose. For example, Barlow (1988) describes a self-monitoring form for panic attacks which includes an anxiety rating, sensations experienced, time of onset and offset, whether anyone was present, and whether the panic is associated with a stressful event or not.

Self-monitoring has been widely used in relation to a range of problems including anxiety disorders, depression, substance misuse (Wilson et al., 1989) and eating disorders. Agras (1987), for example, describes self-monitoring forms for use with obese and bulimic patients recording intake, time of day, and also type of food, quantity of food, binging, purging, and use of laxatives. In relation to depression Rehm (1984), for example, asked clients to record activity and mood on a daily basis.

Commentary on self-monitoring

The main values of self-monitoring lie in the fact that it is relatively inexpensive and easy to administer, can be used with both a variety of problems and a wide range of clients, for assessing both cognitive or covert aspects as well as observable aspects of a problem, and because it provides the only possible way of sampling the entire behavioural repertoire of the client; they are the only ones who are always there when the particular behaviour or thought occurs! However, the information obtained from daily self-monitoring will only be as useful as the information requested on the form. As noted, there are several standard forms available, or the therapist may prefer to construct an individual form for each client to elicit specific information about feelings and thoughts. The record can be kept as often as the therapist and client wish, although it is clearly important not to place unrealistic demands on the client. Accuracy is generally higher when one rather than two or three behaviours are self-monitored. Because regular monitoring of activity may be a novel experience for many clients one potential difficulty is poor adherence. Adherence can be increased by reviewing the forms during sessions and hence stressing the importance of the procedure. Self-monitoring clearly requires accurate and unbiased self-reporting; unfortunately a range of factors including demand characteristics militate against such accuracy. A further problem is reactivity; the extent to which the act of self-monitoring affects the behaviour being monitored. It is assumed that reactivity occurs because the act of recording the behaviour cues the negative environmental consequences associated with the event. Because recording serves as a reminder of the consequences of the event, the likelihood of performing the target behaviour in the future decreases. If self-monitoring itself serves as a therapeutic tool it cannot also be regarded as an accurate assessment of another therapeutic intervention. Any effects of self-monitoring alone can be revealed by adequate baseline assessment.

SELF-REPORTS OF COGNITIVE FUNCTIONING

Within recent years a range of self-report strategies have been used to assess pathology-related cognitions (Martzke, Anderson & Cacioppo, 1987; Parks & Hollon, 1988). The term *cognition* in this context refers to the person's thoughts and ideas, in contrast to the term *cognitive process* which refers to the operations or events underlying the elicitation or generation of cognitions. Cognitions can thus be viewed as products or markers of cognitive processes. It is beyond the scope of this chapter to provide more than a few illustrative examples of strategies for collecting cognitive data.

One of the most widely used methods is thought-listing (Cacioppo & Petty, 1981). The person is typically asked to spend two to three minutes recording everything they have been thinking about prior to exposure to a specified stimulus (for example, with socially anxious clients prior to an anticipated conversation). Subsequently thoughts can be rated as either favourable towards themselves, unfavourable towards themselves, or neutral. A variation of the procedure is to employ a videotaped reconstruction. This involves videotaping individuals engaging in some target behaviour, with the person subsequently attempting to reconstruct their thoughts and feelings while reviewing the videotaped behaviour.

An alternative strategy, referred to as the think-aloud technique, is to ask the client to verbalise all thoughts and feelings experienced while completing a task, or during a defined time period. Reported thoughts and feelings are transcribed and content-analysed in a similar manner to that used for thought-listing. Another method for eliciting concurrent reports is thought sampling (Hulbert, Lech, & Saltman, 1984). In this instance the client is interrupted at random intervals and makes a record of what they were thinking immediately prior to the interruption.

Commentary on self-reports of cognitive functioning

Given the inevitability of selective recall or reporting of thoughts, the possibility that respondents may be prompted to provide socially desirable responses, or that they may be subject to demand characteristics of the assessment situation, is perhaps more pertinent for assessments of cognitive functioning than other self-report methods. This is exacerbated by the fact that recalling thoughts may be a difficult task for many clients to perform. In addition, the interpretation of data yielded from cognitive assessment techniques often requires inferential judgments on the part of the therapist. There are also special problems inherent in the specific technique used. First, research comparing retrospective thought-listing to concurrent think-aloud techniques suggest that these procedures elicit quantitatively and qualitatively different reports (Blackwell, Galassi, Galassi, & Watson, 1985). Think-aloud techniques seem to be less vulnerable to post hoc rationalisation or reconstruction by the client and are less dependent on memory. Second, the process of eliciting thoughts concurrent with performance may actually interfere with that performance. Third, given that thoughts occur more rapidly than speech, think-aloud procedures are at best a selective sample of thoughts and feelings. Given that techniques differ in the cognitive content they most appropriately assess and the contexts to which they are most suited, thought needs to be given to the technique to be used. Certainly, in combination with assessment of other domains, assessment of cognitions can provide valuable additional information.

BEHAVIOURAL OBSERVATION

Direct observation of behaviour, either in the natural environment or in laboratory or clinical contexts, has been widely used in both clinical practice and research for a range of adult and child problems. With any naturalistic observation the focus of the observation is inevitably restricted to a particular target behaviour or limited range of target behaviours. The target behaviour must also be clearly defined so that observers can code the behaviour accurately. Unlike self-report methods which rely on the client to provide the data, observational data is provided by other people such as the therapist, staff, spouse, or family. In a clinic or hospital setting the client's behaviour can be quantified as it occurs or audio- or video-recorded for subsequent coding. There are a number of alternative ways in which observed behaviour can be quantified.

If a few discrete behaviours (i.e. those with an evident onset and offset and with relatively invariant duration) are to be observed, then it may be appropriate simply to record the frequency with which that behaviour occurs during a given time period. Rates per minute or hour can then be obtained in order to make comparisons across observation periods.

An example is provided by Turner, Hersen, Bellack, and Wells (1979) who report behavioural observations conducted by trained nursing staff of the frequency of rituals for three obsessive-compulsive patients.

A measure of duration, the length of time a particular response lasts, is likely to be especially useful for continuous behaviour. Alternative duration measures include latency, the time between a particular event or stimulus and the onset of a particular response, or the time between successive responses.

Time sampling is appropriate with continuous or high-frequency behaviours. For example, a 10-minute period might be divided into 40 15-second intervals, and then the occurrence of one or more preselected target behaviours within each short interval recorded. The record would then be the number of intervals in which the behaviour occurred divided by the total number of observation intervals. Another method for high-frequency behaviours is momentary time sampling. In this instance the observer records, at predetermined moments, whether or not the client displays a particular behaviour at that particular point in time. There are a number of existing time-sampling coding systems which provide useful templates for observation. For example, the Family Interaction Coding System (FICS), which has 29 behavioural codes, was developed by Patterson and his colleagues (Jones, Ried, & Patterson, 1975) to monitor behavioural interactions in families with conduct-disordered children and has been used in a range of studies.

Although naturalistic observation inevitably provides the most valid method of behavioural assessment it is not always practical to implement, and observations in simulated contexts or role-play methods are often used as alternatives. It is also inevitable that certain behaviours such as those associated with sexual dysfunctions and deviancies are not open to direct observation, although Masters and Johnson (1966) observed and described sexual responses of sexually functional male and female volunteers in the laboratory.

The most frequently used simulated task is the behavioural avoidance test (BAT) where anxious clients are asked to approach the fear-eliciting stimulus, stopping when they feel too anxious to approach further. A variation of this used in agoraphobia research is the standardised or behavioural walk. Since first reported by Agras, Leitenberg, and Barlow (1968) this has been used in a number of studies over the past two decades. This typically involves clients walking along a course of specific length until they either reach the end of the course or feel too anxious to proceed. The course is usually divided into roughly equal parts (e.g. Mavissakalian, 1986). Similar procedures have been used with dental phobics (the number of procedures in a routine dental examination that they could complete; Ost & Hugdahl, 1985) and acrophobics (the distance they could climb up a fire escape; Emmelkamp & Felton, 1985). Observations of behaviour in simulated contexts have also been conducted in relation to a range of other problems. For example, Sobell, Schaefer, and Mills (1972) systematically observed the behaviour of male alcoholics and normal drinkers in a simulated cocktail bar environment.

The advantage of standardised behavioural assessments is that it facilitates direct comparison across clients and across treatments; it also makes it possible to monitor concurrently both subjective reports and physiological responses in vivo. One obvious disadvantage is that only one behavioural parameter (e.g. walking) is assessed; thus it does not necessarily provide an adequate assessment of clients whose primary difficulty relates to varied or multiple parameters (e.g. shopping, driving etc). A further problem relates to demand characteristics which means that a standardised assessment of this kind may not reveal the true nature of the person's difficulties.

Role-play tests have been used to assess behaviour in a number of studies with social phobics. Curran and his colleagues (e.g. Curran, 1982) have developed the Simulated Social Interaction test for this purpose. This consists of eight brief social interactions each initiated by a series of two confederate prompts delivered in face-to-face interactions. The situations used are representative of a good range of social encounters, with judges' ratings from the role-plays relating to nurses' ratings of the patients' everyday interactions. Another role-play, the Social Interaction Test was developed by Trower, Bryant, and Argyle (1978). This consists of a 12-minute interaction with a confederate of the opposite or same sex, with a general instruction to the patient to maintain or initiate a conversation with the other person. The client is subsequently rated for 29 behaviours (e.g. voice tone, pitch, volume, and clarity; posture; gestures; gaze) on a 5-point scale (0–4) to indicate acceptability of behaviours.

Commentary on behavioural observation

There are many potential threats to the reliability and validity of observational procedures (Wildman & Erickson, 1977) and it is important to keep these in mind when assessing behaviour.

First, it seems reasonable to assume that more reliable data will be collected by trained observers than by untrained observers. A particular problem with the recording of observational data relates to observer drift, the tendency for observers to alter, in idiosyncratic ways, how they observe and/or record behaviour over time. It can therefore be useful to retrain observers at regular intervals. There is some evidence that observers produce higher interobserver agreement when they know that agreement is being assessed than if they are unaware of this (Kent & Foster, 1977). The accuracy of observational data can be ascertained by evaluating interobserver agreement, a process facilitated by video-recording the behaviour. Although, as will be noted later, this in turn may influence the behaviour observed. Regular accuracy checks can be used to gauge the necessity of retraining. It is also important to select clearly defined target behaviours and to limit the workload on observers. The more vaguely defined the behaviour, the less likely it is that two observers will agree on its occurrence; the more behaviours there are to record the less reliable the data.

Second, the introduction of observers and/or recording equipment may itself lead to a change in the behaviour being assessed. Johnson and Bolstad (1973) identified four factors associated with observation which might result in behaviour change or reactivity: (i) conspicuousness of the observer and/or recording equipment; (ii) interaction of physical characteristics, such as age and gender, of the observer and subject; (iii) personal attributes of the observer which may determine changes in the subject's behaviour; and (iv) the rationale provided for the observation. Clearly there are practical steps one can take to reduce reactive effects, such as minimising subject–observer interaction or covert observational procedures (Haynes & Horne, 1982). The use of completely unobtrusive measures is ethically unacceptable as it would mean that the observee would not give informed consent.

A particular question raised by the use of role-play or simulated assessments is whether they provide a valid measure of behaviour that is generalisable to everyday contexts. In the case of role-playing the fact that performance is sensitive to a range of situational variables makes this a difficult question to answer. For example, relatively small changes in role-played scenes or instructions, or whether the role-play is videotaped or live can cause relatively large changes in the person's performance. In spite of these issues, however, the general conclusion seems to be that role-plays do provide useful data (e.g. Nelson, Hayes, Felton, & Jarrett, 1985).

Additional problems relate to demand characteristics and the perceived payoffs for performing a particular behaviour. This is illustrated by problems inherent in the behavioural avoidance test (BAT). Clearly the client may feel pressurised to approach in spite of their anxiety, and may perceive positive consequences from doing so in the assessment environment. This would not, however, give a true indication of their "normal" pattern of avoidance.

PSYCHOPHYSIOLOGICAL MEASURES

The main physiological response systems that have been of interest to clinical psychologists are cardiovascular, musculoskeletal, central nervous system, respiratory, and electrodermal. Measurements in the cardiovascular response system include electrocardiogram (ECG) to trace the electrical impulse that passes through the heart during contraction; blood pressure (BP), both systolic (the force with which blood leaves the heart) and diastolic (the force with which the blood flows back to the heart); and vasomotor activity consisting of blood volume (the absolute amount of blood in the tissue) and pulse volume (the blood flow through the tissue with each cardiac contraction).

The most common measurement taken in the musculoskeletal response system is the electromyogram (EMG) which records electrical activity of stimulated muscle fibres. Such measures have been most frequently taken from the forehead (frontalis muscle) as this is assumed to be an indicator of tension and arousal. Central nervous system activity is measured by electroencephalogram which provides a measure of the electrical potential difference between any two electrodes placed on the scalp. Measurements of respiration include rate and volume. Electrodermal responses include skin resistance and skin conductance; decreases in the former and increases in the latter are associated with increased sweating.

Psychophysiologically related symptoms are recorded in a range of disorders although this frequently relies on self-report data derived from interviews or questionnaires. For example, the Body Sensations Questionnaire is frequently used with panic/agoraphobic clients. However, direct measures are often taken for a range of physical health concerns such as hypertension and headache, and are commonly evaluated in anxiety problems and for the measurement of sexual responses, although such assessments are more usual for research purposes than for clinical practice. This is partly because the methods require reasonable technical skill to achieve a minimal level of competence, and training courses do not necessarily provide the opportunity to acquire such skill, but also because reasonable equipment is expensive.

A variety of sexual problems can be assessed by direct psychophysiological measures. Male genital arousal can be assessed by monitoring changes in penile circumference or penile volume, and female genital arousal can be measured by a vaginal photoplethysmograph (Wincze & Carey, 1991).

Electromyographic measures as well as measures of skin temperature and vasomotor activity are frequently used in the assessment of pain conditions (Karoly & Jensen, 1987).

Electromyographic, cardiovascular, and electrodermal measures are most likely to be included in any comprehensive assessment of anxiety. Such assessments have been recorded during in vivo exposure, such as during behavioural avoidance tests, while the subject is imagining scenes, when the subject is exposed to a stimuli such as a slide of the feared object, or more recently in the subject's natural environment. For example, in an early study of agoraphobia Stern and Marks (1973) monitored heart rate during phobic and neutral imagery, and during imaginal and in vivo exposure. In a study of patients with generalised anxiety disorder Barlow et al. (1984) assessed frontalis EMG and heart rate during a six-minute baseline period and during relaxation and a stressor task. With regard to panic attacks, the availability of microcomputer technology has made it possible to conduct ambulatory monitoring. For example, Freeman, Lanni, Ettedgui, and Puthezhath (1985) recorded heart rate, finger temperature, and ambient temperature continuously over two 12-hour periods using a Medilog cassette recording system.

In addition to providing baseline assessments against which to monitor treatment outcome, psychophysiological measures have also been used to determine patient characteristics in order to target interventions (Jerremalm, Jansson, & Ost, 1986) and to predict likely treatment response (Michelson et al., 1990). Thus, Jerremalm et al. (1986) classified subjects as physiological or cognitive reactors on the basis of heart rate measures taken during a social interaction test and cognitive reactions assessed immediately after the test. Within each category subjects were randomly assigned to a physiologically focused treatment method (applied relaxation), a cognitively focused method (self instructional training), or a waiting list control group. The results suggested that there were significant improvements on most measures for both groups, leading Jerremalm et al. to conclude that dividing social phobics into cognitive and physiological reactors does not predict differential outcome of targeted interventions. The results may, however, have been partly due to both measurement issues (comparing a self-report measure to direct physiological assessment) and the method of allocating subjects to groups (high and low reactor groups were assigned on the basis of a median split which may understate the magnitude of the "low" reactors' responses).

A number of studies have also evaluated desynchrony of response evident in many treatment outcome studies such that improvements are often evident in behavioural and cognitive measures but only weak or inconsistent for physiological indices such as heart rate. Some studies suggest that such desynchrony is associated with either poorer outcome and/or the likelihood of greater relapse (Michelson et al., 1990).

However, the results of such studies are mixed, making it difficult to evaluate the usefulness of predicting outcome on the basis of synchronous/desynchronous treatment responses. Such contradictory results are no doubt due in part to the measurement issues referred to previously.

Commentary on physiological assessment

It is widely recognised that assessing physiological parameters is not without its difficulties. For example, major problems arise in the selection of measures (i.e. which individual parameter or multiple set of parameters should be assessed), the reliability of equipment, intrusiveness of the techniques, and interpretation of the data (Ney & Gale, 1988). In general, the use of direct psychophysiological measures is expensive and necessitates a degree of expertise. More recently, however, the availability of user-friendly devices that can be linked to personal computers has broadened the opportunities for psychophysiological data recording and analysis. As noted, although it is possible for the client to monitor their reactions in real life situations, most psychophysiological assessments are taken during exposure of the client to a relevant stimulus in laboratories or clinics. It is assumed that reactions occurring in such circumstances will mimic those occurring in the natural environment, but this variable has rarely been investigated. It is well documented, however, that quite subtle changes in the stimulus can affect psychophysiological responses. In addition, psychophysiological measures are particularly sensitive to instrument errors and artifactual contamination. The latter involve any change in the psychophysiological response system not attributable to the relevant stimulus. Sources of artifacts include movement or electrical interference as well as more subtle environmental variables such as changes in noise, light, tactile stimulation, or ambient temperature which occur during recording.

Research has also questioned the reliability of physiological measures. Arena et al., (1983) found that although frontalis EMG was reliable across conditions when assessments were performed up to one month apart, hand temperatures and heart rate were only reliable when assessments were performed no more than one week apart, and measures of electrodermal activity, cephalic vasomotor response, and forearm flexor EMG were generally inconsistent. Holden and Barlow, (1986) found that during in vivo assessments, as well as during laboratory assessments, test–retest reliability of heart rate was quite low. Such findings point to the need for careful interpretation of physiological assessments as a measure of clinical change.

CONCLUDING COMMENTS

Being an effective clinician and researcher requires knowledge of a variety of assessment procedures. All methods have their advantages and disadvantages, and selecting the appropriate battery of measures requires careful consideration. Each method also has its limitations and it is important to bear these in mind when interpreting the data. Given the multifaceted nature of psychological problems, any comprehensive assessment should consist of several different measures tapping behavioural, physiological, cognitive, and affective domains. As the various measures may not agree and there is no prior basis on which to decide which is the one "true" measure, multiple assessment can provide a broader picture of the client's problem. Even if the measures are synchronous at one point in time this may not be the case as treatment progresses. In practice, however, as direct assessment of psycho-physiological parameters is expensive and necessitates a degree of expertise, and behavioural observation, especially in the client's natural environment, can be impractical and time consuming, extensive use is frequently made of just self-report measures. If this is the case then it is clearly important to select measures that are not only accurate but also sensitive and meaningful. The psychometric properties (i.e. reliability and validity) of questionnaires can help decide whether a measure should be used or avoided. Global measures of, say, depression or anxiety may be helpful in defining the presenting problem but may not be sensitive enough to chart therapeutic progress. Accurate assessment is important not only to define the presenting problem and hence to select the appropriate treatment, but also to monitor treatment progress. Effective assessment is thus a prerequisite for effective clinical practice.

REFERENCES

Abelson, J.L., & Curtis, G.C. (1989). Cardiac and neuroendocrine responses to exposure therapy in height phobics: Desynchrony within the 'physiological response system'. *Behaviour Research and Therapy, 271,* 561-567.

Abrahamson, L.Y., Seligman, M.E.P., & Teasdale, J. (1978). Learned helplessness in humans: Critique and reformulation. *Journal of Abnormal Psychology, 87,* 49-74.

Agras, W.S. (1987). *Eating disorders. Management of obesity, bulimia, and anorexia nervosa.* Oxford: Pergamon Press.

Agras,W.S., Leitenberg, H., & Barlow, D H. (1968). Social reinforcement in the modification of agoraphobia. *Archives of General Psychiatry, 19*, 243-427.

American Psychiatric Association (1980). *Diagnostic and Statistical Manual of Mental Disorders*, 3rd Edn. Washington DC: American Psychiatric Association.

American Psychiatric Association (1987). *Diagnostic and Statistical Manual of Mental Disorders*, 3rd Edn, rev. Washington DC: American Psychiatric Association.

Anthony, J.C., Folstein, M., Romanoski, A.J., Von Korff, M.R., Nestadt, G. R., Chahal, R., Merchant, A., Brown, C.H., Shapiro, S., Kramer, M., & Gruenberg, E.M. (1985). Comparison of the Lay Diagnostic Interview Schedule and a standardized psychiatric diagnosis. *Archives of General Psychiatry, 42*, 667-675.

Arena, J.G., Blanchard, E.B., Andrasik, F., Crotch, P.A., & Meyers, P.E. (1983). Reliability of psychophysiological assessment. *Behaviour Research and Therapy, 21*, 447–460.

Arrindell, W.A, Emmelkamp, P.M.G., & van der Ende, J. (1984). Phobic dimensions: I. Reliability and generalizability across samples, gender and nations. *Advances in Behaviour Research and Therapy, 6*, 207-254.

Barlow, D.H. (Ed.) (1981). *Behavioral assessment of adult disorders*. New York: Guilford Press.

Barlow, D.H. (1988). *Anxiety and its disorders*. New York: Guilford Press.

Barlow, D.H., Cohen, A.S., Waddell, M.T., Vermilyea, B.B., Kiosko, J.S., Blanchard, E.B., & DiNardo, P.A. (1984). Panic and generalized anxiety disorder: Nature and treatment. *Behavior Therapy, 15*, 431-449.

Barrios, B.A. (1988). On the changing nature of behavioral assessment. In A.S. Bellack & M. Hersen (Eds.), *Behavioral assessment. A practical handbook*. 3rd Edn. Oxford: Pergamon Press

Beck, A.T., Epstein, N., Brown, G., & Steer, R.A. (1988). An inventory for measuring clinical anxiety: Psychometric properties. *Journal of Consulting and Clinical Psychology, 56*, 893-897.

Beck, A.T., Steer, R.A., & Garbin, M.G. (1988). Psychometric properties of the Beck Depression Inventory: Twenty-five years of evaluation. *Clinical Psychology Review, 8*, 77-100.

Beck, A.T., Ward, C.H., Mendelsohn, M., Mock, J., & Erbaugh, J. (1961). An inventory for measuring depression. *Archives of General Psychiatry, 4*, 561-571.

Beidel, D.C., Turner, S. M, Stanley, M.A., & Dancu, A.V. (1989). The social phobia and anxiety inventory: Concurrent and external validity. *Behavior Therapy, 20*, 417-427.

Bellack, A.S., & Hersen, M. (1988). *Behavioral assessment. A practical handbook*. 3rd Edn. Oxford: Pergamon Press.

Benjamin, S., Decalmer, P., & Haran, D. (1982). Community screening for mental illness: A validity study of the General Health Questionnaire. *British Journal of Psychiatry, 140*, 174-180.

Blackwell, R.T., Galassi, J.P., Galassi, M.D., & Watson, T.E. (1985). Are all cognitive assessment methods created equal? A comparison of think aloud and thought listing. *Cognitive Therapy and Research, 9*, 399-414.

Borkovec, T.D., Weerts, T.C., & Bernstein, D.A. (1977). Assessment of anxiety. In A.R. Ciminero, K.S. Calhoun, & H.E. Adams (Eds.), *Handbook of Behavioral Assessment*. New York: Wiley.

Cacioppo, J.T., & Petty, R.E. (1981). The thought-listing technique. In T.V. Merluzzi, C.R. Glass, & M. Genest (Eds.), *Cognitive assessment*. New York: Guilford Press.

Carr, V., & Smith, J. (1985). Assessment of depression by questionnaire compared to DSM-III diagnosis. *Journal of Affective Disorders, 8*, 167-170.

Carroll, B.J., Fielding, J.M., & Blashki, T.G. (1973). Depression rating scales: A critical review. *Archives of General Psychiatry, 28*, 361-366.

Chambless, D.L., Caputo, C., Bright, P., & Gallagher, R. (1984). Assessment of fear of fear in agoraphobics: The Body Sensation Questionnaire and the Agoraphobic Cognitions Questionnaire. *Journal of Consulting and Clinical Psychology, 62*, 1090-1097.

Chambless, D.L., Caputo, C., Jasin, S., Gracely, E., & Williams, C. (1985). The mobility inventory for agoraphobia. *Behaviour Research and Therapy, 23*, 35-44.

Ciminero, A.R, Calhoun, K.S., & Adams, H.E. (1986). *Handbook of behavioral assessment* (2nd Edn). New York: Wiley.

Cone, J.D. (1979). Confounded comparisons in triple response mode assessment research. *Behavioral Assessment, 1*, 85-95.

Curran, J.P. (1982). A procedure for assessing social skills: The Simulated Social Interaction Test. In J.P. Curran & P.M. Monti (Eds.), *Social skills training: A practical handbook for assessment and treatment*. New York: Guilford Press.

Derogatis, L.R. (1977). *SCL-90 administration, scoring and procedures manual-l*. Johns Hopkin University Press.

DiNardo, P.A., Barlow, D.H., Cerny, J.A., Vermilyea, B.B., Himadi, W.G., & Waddell, M.T. (1985). *Anxiety Disorders Interview Schedule Revised (ADIS-R)*. Albany, NY: Center for Stress and Anxiety Disorders.

DiNardo, P.A, Moras, K., Barlow, D.H., Rapee, R.M., & Brown, T.A. (1993). Reliability of DSM-III-R anxiety disorder Categories using the Anxiety Disorders Interview Schedule-Revised (ADIS-R). *Archives of General Psychiatry, 50*, 251-256.

Edelmann, R.J. (1992). *Anxiety. Theory, research and intervention in clinical and health psychology*. Chichester: John Wiley & Sons.

Eifert, G.H., & Wilson, P.H. (1991). The triple response approach to assessment: A conceptual and methodological reappraisal. *Behaviour Research and Therapy, 29*, 283-292.

Emmelkamp, P.M.G., & Felton, M. (1985). The process of exposure in vivo: Cognitive and physiological changes during treatment of acrophobia. *Behaviour Research and Therapy, 23*, 219-224.

Endicot, J., & Spitzer, R.L. (1978). A diagnostic interview: The Schedule for Affective Disorders and Schizophrenia. *Archives of General Psychiatry, 3*, 837-844.

Foa, E.B., Steketee, G., Grayson, J.B., Turner, R.M., & Latimer, P.R. (1984). Deliberate exposure and blocking of obsessive-compulsive rituals: Immediate and long-term effects. *Behavior Therapy, 1*, 450-472.

Freeman, R.R., Lanni, P., Ettedgui, E., & Puthezhath, N. (1985). Ambulatory monitoring of panic disorder. *Archives of General Psychiatry, 42*, 244-248.

Glass, C.R., Merluzzi, T.V., Biever, J.L., & Larsen, K.H. (1982). Cognitive assessment of social anxiety: Development and validation of a selfstatement questionnaire. *Cognitive Therapy and Research, 6*, 37-55.

Goldberg, D. (1972). *The detection of psychiatric illness by questionnaire*. Maudsley Monograph, No 21, Oxford: Oxford University Press.

Goldfried, M.R., & Sprafkin, J.N. (1976). Behavioral personality assessment. In J.T. Spence, R.C. Carson, & J.W. Thibaut (Eds.). *Behavioral approaches to therapy*. Morristown, NJ: General Learning Press.

Gotlib, I.H., & Hamman, C.L. (1992). *Psychological aspects of depression. Towards a cognitive-interpersonal integration*. Chichester: John Wiley & Sons.

Haynes, S.N., & Horne, W.F. (1982). Reactivity in behavioral observation: A review. *Behavioral Assessment, 4*, 369-385.

Hersen, M., & Bellack, A.S. (1988), *Dictionary of behavioral assessment techniques*. New York: Pergamon Press.

Hodgson, R., & Rachman, S. (1977). Obsessional-compulsive complaints. *Behaviour Research and Therapy, 15*, 389-395.

Holden, A.E., & Barlow, D.H. (1986). Heart rate and heart rate variability recorded in vivo in agoraphobics and nonphobics. *Behaviour Therapy, 17*, 26-42.

Hulbert, R.T., Lech, B.C., & Saltman, S. (1984). Random sampling of thought and mood. *Cognitive Therapy and Research, 8*, 263-275.

Jerremalm, A., Jansson, L., & Ost, L-G. (1986). Cognitive and physiological reactivity and the effects of different behavioural methods in the treatment of social phobia. *Behaviour Research and Therapy, 24*, 587-596.

Johnson, S M., & Bolstad, O.D. (1973). Methodological issues in naturalistic observation: Some problems and solutions for field research. In L.A. Hamerlynck, L.C. Handy, & E.J. Marsh (Eds.), *Behaviour change: Methodology, concepts and practice*. Champaign IL: Research Press.

Jones, R.R., Ried, J.B., & Patterson, G.R. (1975). Naturalistic observation in clinical assessment. In P. McReynolds (Ed.), *Advances in psychological assessment* (Vol.3) San-Francisco: Jossey-Bass.

Karoly, P., & Jensen, M.P. (1987). *Multimethod assessment of chronic pain*. Oxford: Pergamon Press.

Kent, R. N., & Foster, S.L. (1977). Direct observation procedures: Methodological issues in naturalistic settings. In A.R. Ciminero, K.S. Calhoun, & H.E. Adams (Eds.), *Handbook of behavioral assessment*. New York: Wiley.

Kleinknecht, R.A, Klepac, R.K., & Alexander, L.D. (1973). Origin and characteristics of fear of dentistry. *Journal of American Dental Association, 86*, 842-848.

Lang, P. (1968). Fear reduction and fear behaviour: Problems in treating a construct. In J.M. Schlien (Ed.), *Research in psychotherapy*, Vol. 3. Washington DC: American Psychological Association.

Lindsay, W.R., Gamsu, C.V., Mcaughlin, E., Hood, E.M., & Espie, C.A. (1987). A controlled trial of treatments for generalized anxiety. *British Journal of Clinical Psychology, 26*, 3-15.

Marks, I.M., & Mathews, A.M. (1979). Brief standard self-rating for phobic patients. *Behaviour Research and Therapy, 17*, 263-267.

Marsh, E.J. (1985). Some comments on target selection in behaviour therapy. *Behavioral Assessment, 7*, 63-78.

Martzke, J.S., Anderson, B.L., & Cacioppo, J.T. (1987). Cognitive assessment for anxiety disorders. In L. Michelson & L.M. Ascher (Eds.), *Anxiety and stress disorders. Cognitive-behavioral assessment and treatment*. New York: Guilford Press.

Masters, W.H., & Johnson, V.E. (1966). *Human sexual response*. Boston, MA: Little, Brown.

Mavissakalian, M. (1986). The fear questionnaire: A validity study. *Behaviour Research and Therapy, 24,* 83-85.

Michelson, L., Mavissakalian, M., Marchione, K., Ulrich, R.F., Marchione, N., & Testa, S. (1990). Psychophysiological outcome of cognitive, behavioural and psychophysiologically based treatments of agoraphobia. *Behaviour Research and Therapy, 28,* 127-139.

Morganstern, K P. (1988). Behavioral interviewing. In A.S. Bellack & M. Hersen (Eds.), *Behavioral assessment. A practical handbook.* 3rd Edn. New York: Pergamon Press.

Morrison, R.L. (1988). Structured interviews and rating scales. In A.S. Bellack & M. Hersen (Eds.), *Behavioral assessment: A practical handbook.* 3rd Edn. New York: Pergamon Press.

Myers, J.K., & Weissman, M.M. (1980). Use of a self-report symptom scale to detect depression in a community sample. *American Journal of Psychiatry, 137,* 1081-1084.

Nelson, R. O., Hayes, S.C., Felton, J.L., & Jarrett, R.B. (1985). A comparison of data produced by different behavioral assessment techniques with implications for models of social skills inadequacy. *Behaviour Research and Therapy, 23,* 1-12.

Ney, T., & Gale, A. (1988). A critique of laboratory studies of emotion with particular reference to psychophysiological aspects. In H.L. Wagner (Ed.), *Social psychophysiology and emotion.* Chichester: Wiley.

Nietzel, M.T., Bernstein, D.A., & Russell, R.L. (1988). Evaluation of anxiety and fear. In A.S. Bellack & M. Hersen (Eds.), *Behavioral assessment: A practical handbook.* 3rd Edn. New York: Pergamon Press.

O'Leary, K.D., & Wilson, G.T. (1975). *Behaviour therapy: Applications and outcome.* Englewood Cliffs, NJ: Prentice Hall.

Ost, L., & Hugdahl, K. (1985). Acquisition of blood and dental phobia and anxiety response patterns in clinical patients. *Behaviour Research and Therapy, 23,* 27-34.

Parks, C.W., & Hollon, S.D. (1988) Cognitive assessment. In A.S. Bellack & M. Hersen (Eds.), *Behavioral assessment. A practical handbook.* 3rd Edn. New York: Pergamon Press.

Peck, D.F., & Shapiro, CM. (1990). *Measuring human problems. A practical guide.* Chichester: John Wiley & Sons.

Pilowsky, I., Levine, S., & Boulton, D.M. (1969). The classification of depression by numerical taxonomy. *British Journal of Psychiatry, 115,* 937-945.

Rachman, S., & Hodgson, R. (1974). Synchrony and desynchrony in fear and avoidance. *Behavior Research and Therapy, 12,* 311-318.

Radloff, L.S. (1977). The CES-D Scale: A self-report depression scale for research in the general population. *Applied Psychological Measurement, 1,* 385-401.

Rehm, L.P. (1984). Self-management therapy of depression. *Behaviour Therapy, 8,* 787-804.

Rehm,L.P. (1988). Assessment of depression. In A.S. Bellack & M. Hersen (Eds.), *Behavioral assessment. A practical handbook.* 3rd Edn. Oxford: Pergamon Press.

Robins, L.N., Heizer, J.E, Croughan, J., & Ratcliff, K.S. (1981). National Institute of Mental Health Diagnostic Interview Schedule: Its history, characteristics and validity. *Archives of General Psychiatry, 38,* 381-389.

Sanavio, E. (1988). Obsessions and compulsions: The Padua inventory. *Behaviour Research and Therapy, 26,* 169-177.

Seligman, M.E.P., Abramson, L.Y., Semmel, A., & von Baeyer, C. (1979). Depressive attributional style. *Journal of Abnormal Psychology, 88*, 242-247.

Sobell, M.B., Schaefer, H.H., & Mills, K.C. (1972). Differences in baseline drinking behaviour between alcoholics and normal drinkers. *Behaviour Research and Therapy, 10*, 257-267.

Speilberger, C.D., Gorsuch, R.L., & Lushene, R. (1970). *Manual for the State-Trait Anxiety Inventory.* Palo Alto, CA: Consulting Psychologists Press.

Spitzer, R.L., Williams, J.B.W., & Gibbon, M. (1987). *Instruction manual for the Structured Clinical Interview for DSM-III-R* (SCID; April 1987 Revision). New York: Biometrics Research Department, New York State Psychiatric Institute.

Stern, R.S., & Marks, I.M. (1973). Brief and prolonged flooding: A comparison of agoraphobic patients. *Archives of General Psychiatry, 28*, 270-276.

Trower, P., Bryant, B., & Argyle, M (1978). *Social skills and mental health.* London: Methuen.

Turkat. I.D. (1986). The behavioral interview. In A.R. Ciminero, K.S. Calhoun, & H.E. Adams (Eds.), *Handbook of behavioral assessment* 2nd Edn. New York: Wiley.

Turner, S.M., Hersen, M., Bellack, A.S., & Wells, K.C. (1979). Behavioral treatment of obsessive-compulsive neurosis. *Behaviour Research and Therapy, 17*, 95-106.

Turner, S.M., McCann, M., & Beidel, D.C. (1987). Validity of the social avoidance and distress and fear of negative evaluation scales. *Behaviour Research and Therapy, 25*, 113-115.

Tyrer, P. (1990). Personality disorder and social functioning. In D.F. Peck & C.M. Shapiro (Eds.), *Measuring human problems. A practical guide.* Chichester: John Wiley & Sons.

Watson, D., & Friend, R. (1969). Measurement of social-evaluative anxiety. *Journal of Consulting and Clinical Psychology, 33*, 448-451.

Watts, F., & Sharrock, R. (1984). Questionnaire dimensions of spider phobia. *Behaviour Research and Therapy, 22*, 575-580.

Wildman, B.G., & Erickson, M.T. (1977). Methodological problems in behavioral observation. In J. Cone & R.P. Hawkins (Eds.), *Behavioral assessment: New directions in clinical psychology.* New York: Brunner/Mazel.

Williams, M., Watts, F.N., MacLeod, C., & Mathews, A. (1988). *Cognitive psychology and emotional disorders.* Chichester: Wiley.

Wilson, P.H., Spence, S.H., & Kavanagh, D.J. (1989). *Cognitive behavioural interviewing for adult disorders.* London: Routledge.

Wincze, J.P., & Carey, M.P. (1991). *Sexual dysfunction: A guide for assessment and treatment.* New York: Guilford Press.

Wolpe, J., & Lang, P. (1964). A fear schedule for use in behaviour therapy. *Behaviour Research and Therapy, 2*, 27-30.

Zung, W.W.K. (1965). A self-rating depression scale. *Archives of General Psychiatry, 12*, 63-70.

CHAPTER FIVE

Analysing data

Paul R. Jackson *Department of Psychology, University of Sheffield*

Data analysis is impossible without presuppositions; it assumes world knowledge. The difference between statistics and arithmetic is that statistical analysis is about data and arithmetic is about numbers. Data are (usually) numbers with reference to some part of the real world. Consequently data analysis is not possible unless we ask questions of the data; about how they were gathered, what was measured, what measurement scale was used, and what choices were made in order to produce the data to hand.

The main purpose of statistical work is to derive summaries of some aspect of data, and in this way to reduce complexity in data without losing structure which is critical. Summary measures have to work hard and we cannot expect that a single index of structure will tell everything about a set of data. Summary measures are specialised tools; they capture one aspect of structure, so that it is generally necessary to produce several measures from the same data set, one for each aspect of structure. Simple examples are the arithmetic mean or median as a summary of location (or centredness) and the standard deviation or interquartile range as a summary of spread around a centre.

Most data analysis is concerned with either global or local structure in data. Global summaries describe the structure of the data set as a whole, and every observation contributes in some way to the summary measure. Consequently, they gloss over variations in structure from one part of the data to another; and such variations constitute the local structure of the data. In some circumstances the social scientist treats local structure as a nuisance (and is apt to call it 'error' variation); in other circumstances the scientist prefers to remove global structure in order to see changes in local structure more clearly.

A familiar example of the difference between the two kinds of structure comes from economic data such as the monthly unemployment statistics. Variations in average unemployment from year to year (or long-term trends upwards or downwards) are global structure; while seasonal trends are local structure and reflect the weather, school-leaving dates and so on. Here it is not sensible to take one aspect of structure as 'error'; rather we prefer to consider both kinds of structure but not at the same time. When unemployment figures are reported, they are accompanied by 'seasonally adjusted' figures to tell us about long-term trend. These adjusted figures use all of the data available but then discard seasonal factors using complicated and arcane formulae in order to make aspects of global structure clearer. If we wish to, we can look back at the local seasonal factors more clearly against the background of long-term trend.

In this chapter I want to draw together a number of approaches to the exploration of both global and local structure with illustrations of how they might profitably be used. The term 'exploration' is used quite deliberately for two reasons. Much of what I want to say is in the spirit of Tukey's Exploratory Data Analysis (1977) without the Tukeyesque obscurities. More important than this though is the fundamental point that analysing any set of data is a process of exploration; getting to know data can only be done step by step, without making unwarranted assumptions too soon.

The new procedures of Exploratory Data Analysis are of two general kinds. The first kind consists of procedures for looking at data in new ways: the development of more effective forms of display. Other procedures are for summarising data, but rely on summary measures that are cheap in assumptions. Taken together, these two classes of analytical tool can go a long way towards allowing the data to speak for themselves. The process of analysis is guided by two contradictory principles that are always in creative tension. On the one hand, data analysis is guided by what we already know of the world; and it is folly to pretend to do analysis without taking prior knowledge into account. On the other hand, the greatest payoff of intelligent data analysis comes when the analysis of the data we have reveal something we never expected to see.

UNIVARIATE SUMMARIES OF SHAPE

Summaries 'stand for' the data they replace. Univariate summaries describe the shape of a batch of data in terms of such features as location, spread, and symmetry. Other features of data distributions which are easy to see informally but hard to summarise are unimodality and connectedness. The commonest ways to summarise a data set are in terms of location and spread; and there are lots of different measures of each which could be used. For example, one researcher might choose to use the mean and the standard deviation; while another might prefer the median and the inter-quartile range (for further details of how to calculate these, see Howell, 1987). The word 'choose' here is quite deliberate, since using a particular summary measure is a choice. There are three criteria that matter in making this choice.

Ease of calculation is often the first criterion for the busy researcher, but it is really the least important. Doing things by hand might mean that we choose the measure that is easiest to work out; on a computer, we will probably pick what the program offers. These days, it is getting easier to calculate a wide variety of summary indices with the standard packages. The Examine procedure in SPSS for Windows is particularly comprehensive. Most of us are far too busy to spend a long time agonising over a location summary, but we really do have to learn to be fussy enough. Remember too that the choice depends on the data as much as on the mathematical properties of the summary measure itself. The summary 'stands for' the data.

The second criterion is efficiency in the extent to which the summary measure uses all the information in the data that is relevant to the feature being summarised. The most efficient measures milk the data dry of everything that each observation has to tell about what is being summarised. The arithmetic mean and the standard deviation are the most efficient summaries of location and spread respectively (statisticians define efficiency in terms of the standard error of an estimator—if you don't recognise the term, don't worry). While most of us would prefer to use statistical methods which are efficient (thus not wasting information that we worked hard to collect), the dilemma is that efficiency often contradicts with the final criterion for choosing a summary measure—robustness. In general, efficiency and robustness are opposite ends of a continuum: very robust measures are usually not efficient, and efficient measures are generally not robust.

The term robustness has several slightly different meanings (a lengthier account of these differences can be found in my chapter in Jackson, 1986). Statisticians argue over precise definitions of what the term robustness means, but for our purposes it can be taken simply as the sensitivity of a summary measure to departures from ideal assumptions. A summary index which changes dramatically when errors are introduced into a set of data is not robust; while a robust index is one whose value is not materially altered by the inclusion of error. Two kinds of departures have been the subject of technical analysis in the statistical literature, reflecting common occurrences with real data: large disturbances in a small number of observations, and small disturbances to a large number of observations.

Small numbers of large disturbances can come about by missing out the decimal point in recording a data value, or by lapses in concentration in transcribing data; and the result is likely to be a data distribution which contains outliers—extreme values either above or below the bulk of the scores. The presence of extreme scores within a data set may also indicate that the observations come, not from one distribution but from two distributions. For example, data for sickness absence are invariably positively skewed (with many low values and a few very large values); and it is quite likely that such data were obtained from a majority of healthy people with the occasional bout of sickness and also from a minority of people with chronic illness who are absent from work for lengthy periods.

In the presence of such outliers, whether arising from errors or mixtures of distributions, several strategies have been suggested. The least effective is to carry on regardless (maybe even without looking to see whether outliers are present!). Rather better, but still not a good idea, is to discard the outliers unconditionally, treating them as distracting contaminants. A much more effective strategy is to perform the same analyses with and without the outliers present and assess what difference it makes. If different results emerge according to whether outlying scores are included then the researcher has to decide which is appropriate. My own preference in these circumstances is to report the findings which come from the bulk of the data (excluding outliers) but also to report that outliers were present which materially altered the conclusions if they were included. Such an approach seems messy and unsatisfactory to many people, and perhaps the best solution is to use methods of analysis that are known to work well even in the presence of contamination introduced by gross errors to a few data points: robust statistical methods.

The second kind of problem occurs where values are rounded (either deliberately or because of limited accuracy in a measuring instrument) or where several values have been grouped together. Although the term 'errors' is often used for these, they are not necessarily mistakes; for they may not be accidental at all but simply by-products of the method used for recording the data. By way of example, consider pulse rate data measured in beats per minute. If the person recording the data followed normal practice and counted the number of beats in 15 seconds, then the count must be multiplied by four to get values in beats per minute. This procedure will lead to data values all of which are divisible by four, so that rounding errors or miscounts are also multiplied by the same amount. It would make no sense therefore to be overly concerned with numerical accuracy to several decimal places. One way of looking at this kind of data is to think of it as having been rounded quite coarsely, so that information is lost. The same thing happens when attitudes are measured on a Likert scale with a few categories used to record strength of opinion towards an issue.

The way in which summary indices are affected by these two kinds of data contamination has been studied in terms of *influence functions* which define the effect of each observation in a data set on a summary measure derived from it. Technical definitions vary slightly, but the commonest way of finding the influence of a data point is to calculate the summary measure from the whole data set, and then recalculate it dropping each data point in turn. The influence of a data point is the difference between the two summaries. Although the concept of influence can be applied to any summary measure (location, spread, correlation etc.), you are most likely to find computational analyses of the influence of each data point as part of regression analysis packages (see, for example, SPSS for Windows, Norusis, 1992).

In order to illustrate the idea of influence, we will take a very simple example and derive the influence curve for two familiar measures of location, the arithmetic mean and the median, as well as for a less familiar measure, the trimmed mean. The shape of the influence curve gives a precise way of assessing the properties of different kinds of summary and also some criteria for choosing between them. Consider a sample of 11 measurements in all, where 10 of them sum to zero and have fixed values. What will happen to the sample mean and median as the value of the remaining observation is allowed to change from very small to very large? Suppose that 10 of the observations have the values:

10, 7, 3, 3, 3, -2, -5, -5, -6, -8

which sum to zero (simply for convenience in the arithmetic). Because they sum to zero, the grand total including the 11th observation, x, must be x, and the sample mean is $x/11$. Thus the sample influence curve (shown in Fig. 5.1a) is a straight line with slope 1/11. The larger is our 11th observation, perhaps by a freak transcription error, the larger will be the mean. It is obvious, therefore, that the mean is not at all robust.

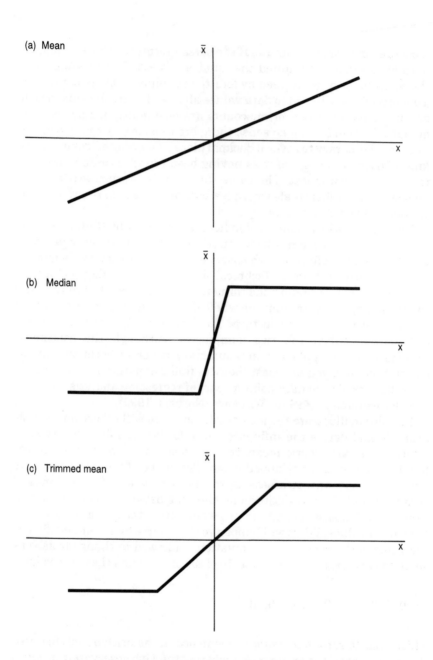

(a) Mean

(b) Median

(c) Trimmed mean

FIG. 5.1. Influence curves for three summaries of location.

Now consider the median. Because the sample has an odd number of observations, the middle observation is the median. If the extra observation, x, is bigger than or equal to 3, the median is 3; if x is smaller than or equal to -2, the median is -2; and if x is between the two the median is x. Try it for yourself and see. Thus the sample influence curve for the median (Fig. 5.1b) is composed of three straight lines segments— the central portion reflects the changing value of x, and the two horizontal lines on each side indicate that the median is unaffected by the size of x except within a narrow range. Apart from a small central range, therefore, the median is very robust.

Apart from the median, there are many different types of more robust summary measures (Jackson, 1986), but the most convenient family of summaries for everyday use is the family of trimmed means. Trimmed means can be calculated quite simply (at least for small to medium-sized batches of data). All that is required is to delete a proportion of extreme observations (called the 'trim proportion') from each end of the ordered batch, and then calculate the arithmetic mean of the remaining observations. It is easy to see that the zero-percent trimmed mean (i.e. no data trimmed from either end) is the familiar arithmetic mean; and trimming 50% of the observations (half from each end) gives the median.

The influence curve for the trimmed mean is shown in Fig. 5.1c, and trimming in this way gives a summary measure of location which is not unduly influenced by a small number of way-out values. Common trim percentages are 5% (one in twenty deleted from each end), and 25% trim. The 25% trimmed mean has a special name, the *mid-mean*: it's the mean of the middle half of the data. If we then label a dimension in terms of trim percentage, we have zero trim at one end (the mean) and 50% trim at the other (the median). Thus the trim dimension also indicates high efficiency/low robustness at the 0% end and low efficiency/high robustness at the 50% end. Statisticians have shown that 5 or 10% trim gives almost as high efficiency as the ordinary mean with a useful degree of robustness against outliers.

MAKING LOCAL STRUCTURE CLEAR—SMOOTHING

Scatterplots have been used for a long time as powerful tools for investigating the relationship between two variables. However, it can be difficult to see clearly the shape of a dependence relationship if either (a) there is a great deal of scatter around the basic relationship; or (b) the density of the scatter varies in different parts of the plot. The question of density changes is a difficult one as it is perceptually difficult to disentangle variations in level from variations in spread.

Moving averages have been used for a very long time to summarise slow changes in level in a series which is also subject to short-term fluctuations (remember seasonal and annual trends?). We can adapt this approach to the problem of analysing relationships by using robust summaries of location like those described earlier to give indications of level of one variable at each part of the other. (I should say that this process is harder to describe in words than to do.)

The basic idea can be grasped by using a simple three-point moving median for the data shown in Fig. 5.2, taken from an unpublished study described by Watson (1930). The study investigated adults throwing a dart at a target from a distance of 20ft (6m). Each of 10 people threw a dart every 2 minutes for 20 hours, with food (a cold meal with tea or coffee, taken between the throws) every 6 hours. After each throw, the distance from the target was measured and this is the index of accuracy used. The data points in the figure are averages for each hour over 30 throws from 10 people (300 throws in all, then). The purpose of the study was to examine the process of extended learning.

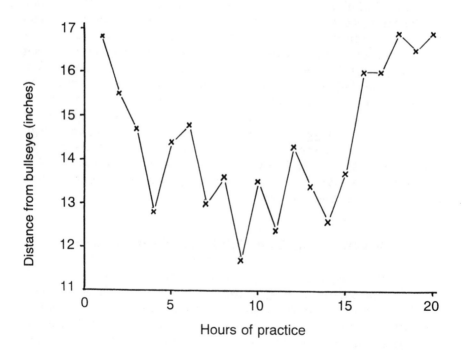

FIG. 5.2. Learning curve for dart throwing.

Take the three data points with the lowest scores on the horizontal axis (the ones farthest to the left of the plot), and replace the second point with the median accuracy value on the vertical axis. Now move on by one data point and do the same thing with the second, third and fourth points: replace the accuracy score of the third observation with the middle of the three values. And so on. The result is a smoothed sequence which is less spikey than the original. I call this an analysis of local structure because each of the summaries (the median values) applies only to values that are local to it. If you were to draw this smoothed sequence onto a plot of the original data, what you see is a picture of changes in local dependence of y on x through the levels of the x variable.

There are many variations on this theme. We could use running medians of 5 instead of 3, for instance. Can you see that a 20% trimmed mean of 5 is the average of the middle three observations? My trials with this data were done in less than half an hour using a spreadsheet program, Supercalc; but they could also be done by hand without too much problem. Velleman and Hoaglin (1981) described some sophisticated variations on the same principle they call compound smoothers, which involve applying several smoothing procedures one after the other; and the Minitab package implements them in an easy-to-use way (Minitab, 1989). The results can be most impressive: Fig. 5.3 shows the application of their 3RSSH smoothing to the data in Fig. 5.2. The method first involves repeated running medians of 3 (hence the 3R). This tends to flatten out peaks and troughs but leaves flat sequences with jagged 'cliffs' between them. These jumps in the sequence are smoothed by a procedure called 'splitting' (the S of the name). Finally, a procedure called 'Hanning' is used which is a weighted running average rather than a running median. Because the computer is doing the leg-work, we can afford to run the whole thing twice.

There are two main reasons for applying smoothing techniques like these. The first is to see changes in local structure clearly. The second reason is to remove this long-term change in order to see better another aspect of structure in the same data. Tukey (1977) gives the following simple but profound formula to describe the way in which a data set consists of systematic 'smooth' structure together with local variation:

Data = Smooth + Rough.

In our example, the smooth is a moving summary of level of the accuracy scores across time (Fig. 5.3); while the rough is what is left when the smooth is subtracted from the original data. Plotting the rough (often also called residuals) without the smooth as in Fig. 5.4 shows much more clearly any extra structure that may be present in the data.

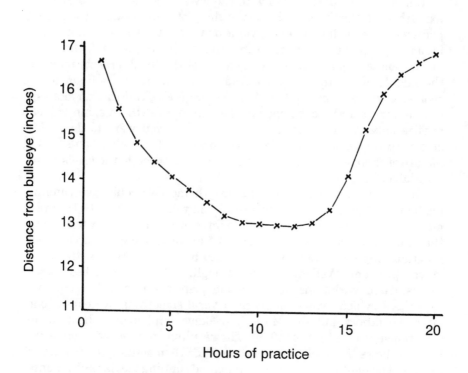

FIG. 5.3. Smooth learning curve for dart throwing.

In particular, it is possible to see whether the intake of food at the times marked on the plot has had any systematic effect on accuracy (it isn't very obvious that it does).

HYPOTHESIS TESTING

The logic of significance testing can be described quite simply, although the implications of each step are often subtle and non-trivial in their implications (good accounts are given by Leach, 1979; and Box, Hunter & Hunter, 1978). Suppose that you have been pursuing a testing programme for a number of months in a health centre as well as in an out-patients clinic of the local hospital. The same test is used in each site, and you also have a file of test results from your predecessor at the same clinic. You notice that the results from the health centre seem to be different from those obtained at the hospital clinic and you begin to wonder whether there really is a difference.

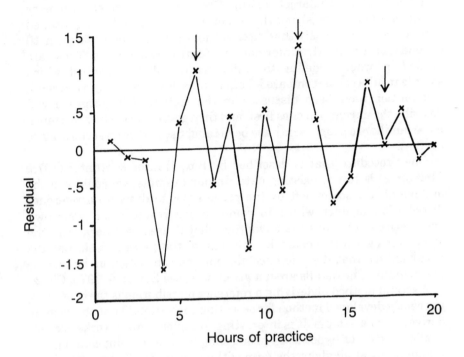

FIG. 5.4. Residuals from smooth learning curve.

First, define a null hypothesis, namely that the two sites generate the same results. If we can discredit this hypothesis then we can say that there is a statistically significant difference between the two sites. To do this we need more information, either in the form of extra data or in the form of assumptions about the data.

The second step is to calculate a summary measure for the test scores from each site (this might be a mean or a median). If the null hypothesis is true than we would expect the summaries to be similar, and the difference between them to be small. How small 'small' actually is can only be assessed from a reference distribution which shows what the distribution of differences would be if the null hypothesis were true. By using an appropriate reference distribution, we can calculate the probability that a difference at least as large as the one observed would occur by chance if the null hypothesis were true. If this probability is sufficiently small, then we can reject the null hypothesis in favour of an alternative that the two sites are different.

There are many different kinds of significance test developed specifically for particular jobs (Kanji, 1993, gives a convenient summary of commonly-used tests), but the essential logic of all tests is as outlined earlier. I said previously that discrediting the null hypothesis (or not!) depends either on extra information or extra assumptions. These are needed in order to define the reference distribution against which sample results can be compared. Four approaches to defining a reference distribution have been discussed in the statistical literature. I will describe the uncommon ones first, and then go on to two which are much more familiar to people who have been taught statistics on social science courses.

One procedure that is described by Box, Hunter & Hunter (1978, Chapter 2) is to use existing data. In our example, we could use the archive of test scores left by the predecessor to draw up a reference distribution against which to compare the results from your own observations. This has the advantage that it uses past data from the same setting which should be relevant to the present task; but the disadvantage that the reference distribution can sometime be tedious to calculate. (The details are not given here; see Box et al. 1978, Ch. 2.)

A second method of deriving a reference distribution is the bootstrap, a recently developed method for assessing the variability of an estimate derived from a sample. It is interesting to explore how it works because it allows tests of hypotheses about sample data without making any assumptions at all about the form of the parent distribution. The basic principle is that all the evidence we have about the parent distribution comes from the shape of the sample data itself. If we take this empirical distribution as an approximation to the unknown parent distribution then we can generate what is known as the bootstrap distribution of our estimate by taking repeated samples from the empirical distribution. The standard error of our estimate is then simply the standard deviation of all the estimates in the bootstrap distribution. Efron and Gong (1983) give a relatively non-technical exposition of the theoretical derivation of the bootstrap as well as some practical applications; I have used one of their examples in the chapter on robust methods (Jackson, 1986).

The third alternative for a reference distribution is to choose one of the standard theoretical distributions that statisticians have developed. In our example, the Gaussian distribution (sometime wrongly called the normal distribution, as if it were the normal thing to be distributed this way) or the t-distribution might be appropriate. These alternatives give relatively simple calculations, even by hand, although they sometimes make stringent and unwarranted assumptions about the process that generated the data. Most introductory statistics texts describe how to use these standard reference distributions to perform hypothesis tests.

A final approach to deriving a reference distribution is based upon ranks; so-called permutation tests. The principle behind permutation tests is the simple one that the observed outcome in a sample of data is only one of a number of possible orderings of the observations. Taking a null hypothesis that all possible ways of ordering the data are equally likely, then it is possible to draw up a reference distribution for a test statistic against which to compare that for the observed outcome (further details of the application of this principle are given in Leach, 1979; Neave & Worthington, 1988).

The data in Table 5.1 are taken from a study by Fryer and Payne (1984) of the relationship between aggregate unemployment levels in parts of South Yorkshire and the average number of books borrowed per day from local libraries. The data used here are just for the years 1975-1979 for Sheffield Central. The hypothesis of interest is whether book borrowing declines as unemployment levels rise; and we will use an index S which summarises the extent to which the two variables are ranked similarly (see Leach, 1979, for a readable account of the S-statistic generally).

If we order the pairs of values according to the unemployment level then we find that the book borrowing scores are ranked thus: 1, 3, 4, and 2. The question at issue is how likely this ranking is on the assumption that the two variables are independent of each other. If we reject the null hypothesis, then we can say that there is a significant correlation between the two variables. The S statistic for these data is 2, and Table 5.2 lists all 24 possible alternative rankings of 4 data points with their associated S values. Figure 5.5 shows the histogram of the permutation distribution for the S statistic. As you can see, 9 of the 24 possibilities generate an S value as high or higher than the value from the sample. The significance level associated with our S values is thus 9/24 = 0.375.

TABLE 5.1
Book borrowing and unemployment rates in Sheffield Central area
between 1975 and 1979

Registered unemployed		Daily book borrowing	
No.	Rank	No.	Rank
5,542	1	17,909	1
9,872	2	19,017	3
10,539	3	19,354	4
10,730	4	18,817	2

S statistic = 2

TABLE 5.2
All possible alternative rankings and their associated S statistics

Ordering				S	Ordering				S
1	2	3	4	6	2	3	4	1	0
1	3	2	4	4	3	1	4	2	0
2	1	3	4	4	4	1	2	3	0
1	2	4	3	4	2	4	3	1	-2
2	3	1	4	2	3	4	1	2	-2
3	1	2	4	2	3	2	4	1	-2
1	4	2	3	2	4	1	3	2	-2
1	3	4	2	2	4	2	1	3	-2
2	1	4	3	2	3	4	2	1	-4
3	2	1	4	0	4	2	3	1	-4
1	4	3	2	0	4	3	1	2	-4
2	4	1	3	0	4	3	2	1	-6

Taking a conventional significance level of 0.05 for rejecting the null hypothesis, we can say that there is no evidence for a correlation between unemployment level and book borrowing.

I have deliberately presented both commonly and uncommonly used methods in this section in order to draw out the way in which data analysis is much more than the unthinking application of statistical tests. Rather, it is the development of numeracy (Ehrenberg, 1975): thinking intelligently about data. While this may involve using conventional methods such as the t-test or the product-moment

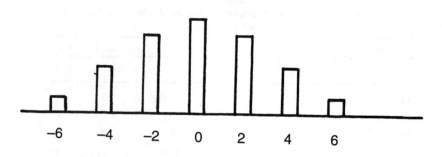

FIG. 5.5. Permutation distribution of the S statistic for sample size of four pairs of observations.

correlation, such choices should be to illuminate what the data have to say and not simply to conform to an ideal of what is 'proper'.

All integrated statistical packages offer tests based on standard reference distributions and the alternative permutation tests. Permutation tests such as the one illustrated earlier are deservedly popular because they are simple to perform and they make few assumptions about the measurement scales used. Because they work on the ranked data values rather than the original scores, they are much more robust than parametric procedures such as the t-test. The price paid for this robustness is a loss of efficiency: typically, more observations are needed to reject a false null hypothesis. For badly behaved data, quite different results may be obtained from tests of the same null hypothesis; and caution is obviously required. For well behaved data, however, there will often be little difference in the conclusions drawn.

REGRESSION—GLOBAL SUMMARIES OF DEPENDENCE

Correlation coefficients are often used as global summaries of the joint shape of a distribution, and their key feature is that they indicate a symmetric relationship—co-relationships. Often though, interest focuses on how to summarise asymmetric relationships—dependence of one variable on another. Dependence may reflect causal precedence, or simply be a matter of the convenience of using something that is easy to measure to stand for something else that is difficult or expensive to measure. Either way, regression relationships like this call for indices of global structure rather different from the indices of local structure; though they retain the essential features of summaries. (Remember that a summary stands for an aspect of the data, and an efficient summary is one that retains everything in the data that is related to the aspect being summarised.) At the same time, a good summary is simple, requiring fewer numbers than the original data.

This part of the chapter describes the general characteristics of a regression model as a summary of dependence and a number of techniques available to fit a regression model. The same steps apply, from the simplest model for two variables and a few observations to many variables and thousands of observations.

Characteristics of regression models
The purpose of a regression model is to summarise the dependence of one variable on at least one other: how the dependent variable behaves at different levels of the predictor variable. (Note in passing that we

cannot expect to make valid inferences about the effects on one variable of change in another without actually changing the predictor variable.) How can we seek a summary of such dependence? One way is shown in Fig. 5.6 where each point is joined to the next from left to right. We can see quite clearly in this plot that the dependent variable (shown on the vertical axis) tends to increase as the predictor variable scores (on the horizontal axis) increase.

Note some features of this figure:

1. The lines joining the points describe the relationship exactly—no information is lost—but at the same time we cannot say that we have a summary. It takes as much to present the lines as to present the points they join, so we have not reduced the information load at all.
2. Figure 5.6 does not really show a regression summary because we could reverse the two axes and draw exactly the same lines between points.
3. We can say exactly what is happening for two adjacent points but very little in a formal or precise way about the two variables as a whole. In fact we see local structure but not global structure.

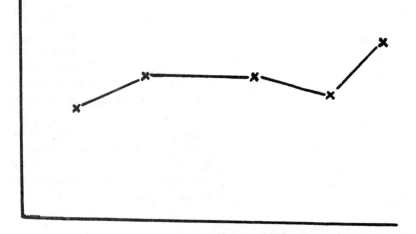

FIG. 5.6. Example of how to describe a dependence relationship exactly but not parsimoniously.

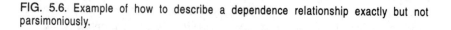

The most complex model describing two variables has almost as many lines as there are points available; the simplest model has just a single line which may or may not coincide with the recorded observations. Now defining a straight line requires very little information: to cross the Sahara Desert, start from here and go in that direction. All that is needed to draw a straight line on a page like this one is a starting point that fixes the level, top to bottom, and an angle that determines direction relative to the bottom of the page. Try it for yourself, by starting a line six inches from the bottom of the page at an angle of 45 degrees to the bottom of the sheet.

In algebraic language, statisticians often describe straight lines like this:

$$Y=a+bX.$$

Each symbol in this language stands for something (it's the Pitman shorthand of mathematics), Y stands for the dependent variable (lots of values), and X stands for the predictor variable (again, lots of values). The small letters, a and b, stand for the two pieces of information that are all we need in order to define where the line goes. The letter a tells about the level or height of the line from the bottom of the picture; and this is called either the constant or the intercept in textbooks or computer printouts. The letter b specifies the slope of the line, the angle relative to the horizontal axis or the bottom of the picture. For any particular line, the letters a and b have single values—different lines have different values. This means that the slope of the line is the same wherever we start to look at it—not like those slides at adventure parks which have bumps and hollows in them to increase the excitement! The two parameters which define a regression line are called regression weights; and the standardised versions are generally referred to as beta weights.

A straight line then has two characteristics that we value in a summary: it is simple (only two items of information needed to describe it) and it is global (the same two items describe the summary here and also there). We cannot say yet of course whether any particular straight line has the other two features of a good summary; does it summarise the proper pattern of dependence (maybe the line should be gently curving), and does it stand for the data adequately?

Fitting a regression line
There are many different procedures developed by statisticians for fitting a line. The differences between methods is nothing to do with the finished line—its properties as described earlier are intrinsic to its being

a line, not to how we calculate where to put it. Rather, the methods differ in terms of:

1.   Simplicity of calculation (often these days by computer).
2.   Efficiency in using the information in the data.
3.   Robustness, or invulnerability to the kinds of problems that data are heir to.

In this section, I will present three methods of calculating the parameters of a fitted regression line; the first is the standard conventional method, while the other two are more robust, but in different ways.

To illustrate the three methods, we will use data from 67 unemployed men (details of the study as a whole are given in Jackson, 1988). Among the variables measured in addition to the Zung Depression Scale was a shortened form of the Beck Hopelessness Scale, and here we will examine whether depression scores can be used to predict scores on the hopelessness scale. A scatterplot of the two variables is shown in Fig. 5.7.

Least squares.   The commonest, and often the worst because it is the least robust, method is the method of least squares; indeed many people think that least squares fitting is the only kind there is. This method is within the same mathematical tradition as means, standard deviations, and product-moment correlation coefficients as summaries of centre, spread, and co-spread respectively: mathematically elegant, highly efficient in idealised situations, and intuitively tough on the understanding. The value for the constant term is chosen so that the regression line goes through the point defined by the means of both variables. The value for the slope term is chosen such that the squared residuals from the line are as small as possible (the squaring is done because closeness of data points to the line is the criterion, and removing the minus sign from residuals by squaring is easier mathematically than taking the absolute value of the residuals).

The method of least squares makes maximum use of all the information within the data that is relevant to assessing dependence of one variable on the other (that's what the statistical term 'efficiency' means). However, in the process, it accepts every data point at face value, and gives greatest influence to those observations that are a long way from the regression line itself. In the language used earlier, the influence curve describing what happens by this method is similar to that shown in Fig. 5.1 for the mean. Thus the single data point at the bottom of Fig. 5.7 with scores of (11,26) has more influence on the positioning of the regression line than those in the centre of the plot.

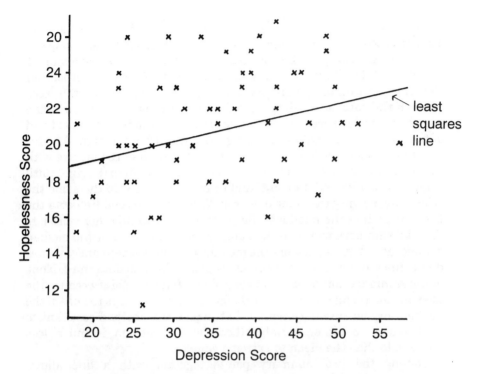

FIG. 5.7. Scatterplot of hopelessness and depression scores with least squares line.

The regression equation given by SPSS-X using the method of least squares gives the following results:

Hopelessness = 16.95 + 0.110 × Depression.

The regression line is superimposed upon the scatterplot in Fig. 5.7, and there is a modest difference in hopelessness scores for individuals who differ in depression scores. We can't tell from this plot alone how much the fitted line has been affected by the extreme observation at the bottom of the plot. When I played about with the data by changing this observation to (1,26) in order to see the result of moving it further away from the rest of the data, the least squares fit was affected considerably. The level of the line was pulled down closer to the outlying observation, while the slope value was larger, falsely overestimating the degree of relationship between the two variables. Alternative methods have been proposed by statisticians to get around this problem of the vulnerability of the least squares method. We will use two which have very different characteristics but share the feature that they are resistant to the influence of outlying values which may be rogue observations.

The three-point resistant line.   The first method gives what has come to be known as the three-point resistant line, and it has a long but little known history within statistics (see, for example, Velleman & Hoaglin, 1981). There are many refinements on the basic method but the principle is quite straightforward. The line required is one that goes through the data, so we divide the data into thirds using the ordering on the x variable; work out the middle of the points in the left-most third of the data and the middle of the right-most third of the data. 'Middle' is defined as follows. Using a ruler, start at the left of the picture with the ruler parallel to the vertical axis. Move the ruler in to the right until it meets the middle data point, and draw a line. Now do the same the other way, moving the ruler upwards. Where this second line cuts the first one defines the middle of that part of the data. In other words, to find the summary points in the outer thirds is to find first the median x-value, and then, separately, the median y-value. These x- and y-values define the coordinates of the summary points for each data third. None of the summary points needs to coincide with a data point because the medians for x- and y-values are calculated separately. It is the use of the median for the summary points that makes this method resistant to wild values in either variable (because the median is much less vulnerable than the mean to extreme values).

Joining the two summary points together with a line allows calculation of the slope, which is one of the two summary values needed. Finally, we need to look at all of the data points (those in the middle third as well). If we take 'throughness' to mean as many points above the line as below it, then we need to shift the line up or down using a ruler until we get the kind of symmetry required. This last step needs a little care to keep the line parallel to the one we started with. The end result is our regression line.

A useful quick test of whether a straight line is adequate to summarise dependence of Y on X is to calculate the summary point for the middle of the centre third of the data. If our fitted lines runs close to this summary point than a straight line will do.

That is the method in outline; now we need to consider some points in detail to see exactly how it works out. Forming three groups based on the X-values depends on whether the number of observations is divisible by three. If not, then aim to make the outer two groups equal in size: thus, for 9 points we get (3,3,3), for 10 points we get (3,4,3), and for 11 points we get (4,3,4). If there are ties in the X-values then additional complications arise (see Velleman & Hoaglin, 1981 for how to cope here).

The literature contains several variants on the basic method, including iterative procedures for 'polishing' the estimates of level and slope. The underlying principle is the same though. The computer program of Velleman and Hoaglin (1981) gives the following regression equation:

Hopelessness = 16.00 + 0.143 × depression.

Robust regression by M-estimation.   A more efficient as well as a more general method of fitting regression models is given by the group of procedures known as M-estimators. These methods combine the range of applicability of least squares regression fitting with the in-built protection against departures from ideal assumptions that the resistant line technique possesses.

The way in which M-estimation provides this protection is by applying to each observation a weight which depends on the distance of the observation from the fitted line. In least squares regression by contrast, every observation has the same weight. The effect of this equal weighting is that the observations farthest away from the fitted line have the greatest influence on where the line is located. This pays most attention to those observations least likely to be typical of the data set as a whole; and M-estimators down-weight such observations in order to reduce their influence. In extreme cases one or more observations may be given zero weight—they are ignored in defining the fitted line.

The simplest way to use robust regression is by repeated application of a weighted least squares algorithm (such as that offered by the Glim package), with the weights separately calculated at each step. Huynh (1982) describes how to do this using the SAS package. Taking the data shown in Fig. 5.7, robust M-estimates of level and slope were calculated using an M-estimator named after Huber, the statistician who developed it. The influence curve for this M-estimator is very similar to that for the trimmed mean shown in Fig. 5.1c.

The resulting regression equations is:

Hopelessness = 17.02 + 0.109 × depression

Comparing the results from the three methods of fitting a line shows close agreement between the non-robust least squares method and the two robust methods for these data. Interestingly, M-estimation has given the lowest observation in Fig. 5.7 a weight of 0.55 compared with a weight of 1.0 for most other observations, so that there is some suggestion that this observation, with scores of (11,26), should be given some special attention. The modified data set, with a gross error added to one observation, produced different values for both parameters in the model fitted by least squares. However, the robust regression model was identical with that reported earlier. The only difference was in the weight given to the offending observation: now given a weight of 0.25, rather than 0.55.

ANALYSIS OF INTERACTIONS

Many of the most interesting findings in applied work show up as interactions between predictor variables. For instance, Bolton and Oakley (1987) looked at the relationship between perceived social support and employment status in a study of the antecedents of depression. Unemployed men reporting low levels of social support had higher depression scores than unemployed men with high support scores; there was no corresponding difference for employed men. The authors concluded that there was an interaction between the two variables. This type of design is known as a between-groups design because each cell contains independent sub-groups of the total sample.

In many circumstances analysis of variance can be used to give appropriate tests of hypotheses of interest (see Keppel, 1973, for a lucid account of how to do this), though interpretation of the results it gives can sometimes be a problem. Consider for example what would happen in the Bolton and Oakley study if the sub-groups being compared also differ on some other variable which the researchers ignore or don't know about. Suppose that the low social support unemployed group were mostly single men, while the other groups were mostly married. In that case what looks like an interaction effect could equally be interpreted as a main effect of marital status showing lower depression scores for married men. This kind of confounding can make life very difficult in the interpretation of observational studies. You can see that the significance tests for interactions rely on the groups being equivalent on all other relevant variables.

It is this issue of the equivalence or non-equivalence of groups that has led many researchers to prefer designs where the same people appear in more than one cell of the design. These types of design are known as within-groups, or repeated measures designs, and they solve some of the problems inherent in between-groups designs (see Chapter 9). Looking at interactions in these designs involves the relationship between a group classification variable and time as a second explanatory variable: the dependent variable is measured on several occasions for two or more groups.

To illustrate some of the issues that arise with designs like these, let us look at a recent study by Milne (1984). He tested the efficacy of a course designed to train psychiatric nurses in elements of behaviour therapy. Two groups were selected from different hospitals; and individuals in the two groups were matched on a number of background variables. One group served as a control group and were simply tested on three occasions; while the experimental group received the training programme and measures were taken at the start of the course, after it finished, and again as a long-term follow-up. Two key tasks are required of the researcher in a study like this. First, he or she needs to assess whether the treatment and control groups were in fact equivalent on salient variables at the start of the study. The second task is to decide whether the treatment group has improved on relevant criteria by comparison with whatever changes may have occurred in the control group. The control group is needed to allow for the possibility of change brought about either by the process of measurement itself or as a result of external influences on both groups (such as organisational changes or a strike among workers). How should we make decisions on these questions?

There are a number of different types of analysis which can be used for this type of problem. Some of them are equivalent to each other, some are very complicated, and some are specifically tailored for tricky problems. One approach (in fact the one adopted by Milne himself) is to perform a series of comparisons using simple tests applied to data from different parts of the design. Table 5.3 shows part of the data from the original report, scores for the Knowledge of Behavioural Principles Questionnaire (KBPQ). He found no difference (using non-parametric tests throughout) between the two groups on the baseline test (column 1 of the Table), and a significant difference at post-test (column 2). Furthermore, the control group showed no change over time (row 2) while the treatment group changed significantly (row 1). This seems clear then, but there are some worrisome aspects of the Table. First, the control group started higher, and did improve over time. Second, we cannot infer from the tests reported that the change in the treatment group is significantly bigger than the change in the control group: all we are told is that change in one group was significant while change in the other group was not.

TABLE 5.3
Scores on Knowledge of Behavioural Principles Questionnaire
for control and behaviour groups, from Milne (1984)

	Baseline	*Post-test*
Treatment group (n = 41)	34%	56%
Control group (n = 18)	40%	45%

Milne's approach has the merit of keeping each bit of the analysis simple but has two damning drawbacks. It can be very hard to pull together lots of simple tests to give a clear overall picture; and the results so obtained can often be very misleading. My own strong preference is for procedures which, though more complicated, match the requirements of the design and deal effectively with the main threats to valid inference.

Two very common techniques are the two-way analysis of variance and the repeated measures t-test, and these will give identical results when applied to the same data. The interaction term in the analysis of variance indicates whether the time effect is the same for the two groups; and this is also what the t-test does using the difference score as the dependent variable. The technical term that statisticians use to describe these tests is that they focus on unconditional models: that is, we take the change score as it stands and ignore the individual's initial score. There are lots of settings where this gives sound results but also many occasions where it would be a foolhardy thing to do. For example, if our control and experimental groups were intact groups selected from very different organisations then aspects of the environments they work in could interact in important (but unknown) ways with the variables we focus on for study.

Interpreting comparisons of the absolute change in two groups depends a great deal therefore on the process whereby individuals were assigned to the groups in the first place. The unconditional approach makes sense if groups really are equivalent at the start of the study, and it is generally only safe to assume this if individuals are assigned randomly (and also if there is no differential loss of subjects from groups—for example, the healthier people in a control group refusing to continue, and the least healthy people in an experimental group being removed from the study for clinical treatment elsewhere). In quasi-experimental studies where random allocation is not possible or not desirable then unconditional models produce questionable and often misleading results.

Very often absolute change is much less meaningful than change which is relative to the individual's starting level—this might be recorded as percentage change or proportional change. When they want to look at relative rather than absolute change, statisticians turn to what they call conditional models. These are fundamentally different from the unconditional models already discussed in that they take measures on the first occasion as fixed, and then explore change over time conditional on the initial values of the dependent variable. In essence, the conditional model asks the question: if the groups had been alike on all relevant explanatory variables, then what difference would there have been between the groups at time 2? The simplest way to do this is to use analysis of covariance with the time-2 score as the dependent variable and the equivalent time-1 score as a covariate. Any initial differences between the groups are thus held constant statistically. An extended and very lucid account of the problems of analysing and interpreting change data is given in the book by Plewis (1985) which should be consulted by those who face such problems. An example taken from my own research on the consequences of change in employment status is reported in Jackson, Stafford, Banks and Warr (1983).

CONCLUSIONS

This chapter has covered a large number of issues in only a little detail. I have tried to give a flavour of how modern statistical procedures are being used on real data to address practical problems. Perhaps what has been included here, as well as what has been left out, is surprising. I have not tried to explain analytic procedures such as multivariate analysis or time series—these may be found in other specialist texts such as Everitt and Dunn (1983) and Plewis (1985). My purpose has been to focus on principles rather than on cookbook recipes, to increase statistical numeracy rather than number-crunching capacity. Behind it all is the conviction that data analysis is an enterprise involving the user and the computer jointly. The distribution of effort is that the user does the thinking while the computer does the easy bit—the calculation. Your job in analysing data is to ask intelligent questions of your data to understand part of the world better. If data analysis confuses rather than illuminates then something has gone wrong.

REFERENCES

Bolton, W., & Oakley, K. (1987). A longitudinal study of social support and depression in unemployed men. *Psychological Medicine, 17,* 453-460.

Box, G.E.P., Hunter, W.G., & Hunter, J.S. (1978). *Statistics for Experimenters.* Chichester: Wiley.

Efron, E,. & Gong, G. (1983). A leisurely look at the bootstrap. the jackknife and cross validation. *The American Statistician, 37,* 36-48.

Ehrenberg, A.S.C. (1975). *Data Reduction: Analysing and Interpreting Statistical Data.* London: Wiley.

Everitt, B.S., & Dunn, G. (1983). *Advanced Methods of Data Exploration and Modelling.* London: Heinemann Educational.

Fryer, D.M., & Payne, R.L. (1984). Book borrowing and unemployment. *Library Review, 32,* 196-206.

Howell, D.C. (1987). *Statistical Methods for Psychology* (second edition). Boston: PWS-Kent.

Huynh, H. (1982). A comparison of four approaches to robust regression. *Psychological Bulletin, 92*, 505-512.

Jackson, P.R. (1986). Robust statistics. In A.D. Lovie (ed.). *New Developments in Statistics for the Social Sciences*. London: Methuen and British Psychological Society.

Jackson, P.R. (1988). Personal networks, support mobilisation and unemployment. *Psychological Medicine, 18*, 397-404.

Jackson, P.R., Stafford, E.M., Banks, M.H., & Warr, P.B. (1983). Unemployment and psychological distress in young people: The moderating role of employment commitment. *Journal of Applied Psychology, 611*, 525-535.

Kanji, G.K. (1993). *100 Statistical Tests*. London: Sage.

Keppel, G. (1973). *Design and Analysis: A Researcher's Handbook*. Englewood Cliffs, NJ:Prentice Hall.

Leach, C. (1979). *Introduction to Statistics*. Chichester: Wiley.

Milne, D. (1984). The development and evaluation of a structured learning format introduction to behaviour therapy for psychiatric nurses. *British Journal of Clinical Psychology, 23*, 175-185.

Minitab (1989). *Minitab Reference Manual*. Pennsylvania: Minitab Inc.

Neave, H.R., & Worthington, P.L. (1988). *Distribution-free Tests*. London: Unwin Hyman.

Norusis, M.J. (1992). *SPSS for Windows: Base System User's Guide*. Chicago: SPSS Inc.

Plewis, I. (1985). *Analysing Change. Measurement and Explanation using Longitudinal Data*. Chichester: Wiley.

Tukey, J.W. (1977). *Exploratory Data Analysis*. Reading. MA: Addison-Wesley.

Velleman, P.F., & Hoaglin, D.C. (1981). *Applications, Basics and Computing of Exploratory Data Analysis*. Boston. MA: Duxbury Press.

Watson, J.B. (1930). *Behaviorism*. (revised edition). Chicago: University of Chicago Press.

CHAPTER SIX

Using computers

Christopher J. Colbourn *Department of Psychology, University of Southampton*

My aim is to provide busy clinicians and researchers with a relatively jargon-free introduction to using 'new technology'. You may think that wasted learning time outweighs potential benefits. Hopefully, this guide will clarify the issues, demonstrating potential uses and benefits. I start with an overview of the core uses of computers in research, framed by the central concept of the 'personal workstation'. Then each area will be considered to show how using a computer can assist you. Details of actual computer programs are not possible here, but selected references and information sources are provided for you to follow up. Finally, there is some practical advice on acquiring computing skills, and selecting suitable equipment. There is also a short glossary that attempts to explain basic computer jargon, which often baffles readers. Fuller descriptions of computing terms can be obtained from specialised dictionaries (e.g. British Computer Society, 1991; Gunton, 1992; Illingworth, 1990).

COMPUTERS IN THE RESEARCH PROCESS:
AN OVERVIEW

Range of applications

My comments are directed at clinical researchers as a specialist group, although there is considerable overlap in the ways professionals use computers. I shall concentrate on the equipment's functions and use, rather than specific products. First, let's specify the main type of 'office' functions where computer assistance is valuable:

1. Document and report production (including audio-visual presentations);
2. Quantitative and qualitative data manipulation;
3. Storing and retrieving textual and numerical information;
4. Mail and document communication;
5. Planning.

Second, some researchers require computers for extensive handling of numerical information, including complex statistical analyses. Third, many psychologists have developed computer techniques to control experimental procedures. These include 'automated clinical testing' which some clinicians use regularly in assessing patients. Finally, I refer to the computer tools called 'expert systems' which are intended to provide 'expert' advice and, possibly, instruction in fields like medical diagnosis, or psychological assessment.

Personal workstation

The 'personal workstation', a kind of electronically enhanced office desk, has built-in facilities for researchers to tackle most of their daily work independently of a large, and commonly inaccessible, office infrastructure. A 'business-type' desktop computer, the basis of such a workstation, offers considerable local processing power, and when connected to networks (via hardwiring or telephone), can access the greater facilities on more powerful remote computers. Figure 6.1 outlines the main current functions of such personal workstations as now found on many academic and business desks. The basic minimum hardware consists of a desktop computer with at least one floppy-disk and one hard-disk drive, and a printer. A computer network offering data storage and printing facilities could reduce these requirements. Note that while the acronym PC stands for 'personal computer' it is most commonly used to refer to IBM-type machines and their derivatives labelled IBM PC-compatibles. Therefore I prefer the term 'desktop computers' which I use to refer collectively to PCs, Apple Macintosh computers, and UNIX workstations.

A local area network (LAN) based within a department or office building/complex, enables colleagues to share expensive computing resources (secure disk storage of documents, etc; high-quality printers;

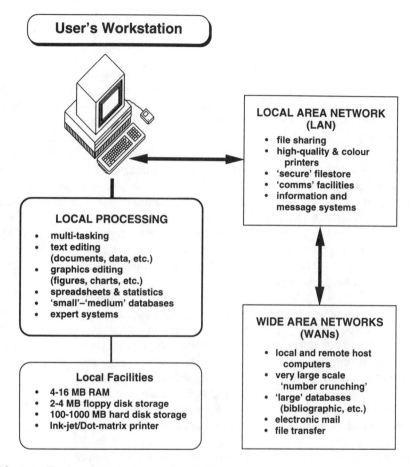

FIG. 6.1. The functions of a 'personal workstation'.

devices for telephone and direct-line communications to other computers and networks), and communicate with one another via 'electronic mail' (email) systems. A typical departmental LAN for personal computers was described by Colbourn (1991b) and a more general and accessible account of computer networking can be found in Apple Computer Inc (1989). Wide area networks enable use of distant computers when local software or databases are not available. They also facilitate access to national and global email systems (Fig. 6.1). Sproull and Kiesler (1991) give a readable account of the value and power of computer networking from the users' perspective.

MAIN FUNCTIONS: A MORE DETAILED LOOK

Electronic office

There is already heavy and beneficial computer use in many office tasks although, as yet, no 'paperless' office. A personal secretary's services (not widely available) cannot be replaced; but the workstation provides facilities impossible to command otherwise, and can pay handsome dividends in saved time and efficiency in everyday working lives.

You probably envisage users continually at their workstations, perhaps both suffering the posited health hazards of long exposure to the computer screen—although evidence for these, and the conditions of occurrence, are presently unclear (Bramwell & Davidson, 1989; Pearce, 1984); and missing essential social interaction (see Frude, 1991, and Oborne, 1985 for reviews of this aspect of 'computerisation'). The intention and purpose of office computer-use is reducing the time spent on many routine tasks, thus increasing the time for other, more central, aspects of one's profession.

The electronic office's major functions are document preparation and production using 'wordprocessing'/text-editing software and graphics editors/processors; manipulating sets of numerical data (e.g., departmental/project accounts, research data, etc.) using 'spreadsheet' software; storing and retrieving information (e.g., patients' records/ reports, research findings, bibliographical references, etc.) with 'database management' software (DBMS); email preparation and transmission involving text editors and 'communications' software; and time and resource management (appointments calendar, project planning, etc.). Johnson (1984) gives a general account of such facilities. An important principle is 'integrated' software allowing easy transferral of information between functions, e.g., references stored in a database can be retrieved and inserted into a paper you are writing on the wordprocessor.

Document preparation and production

Wordprocessing.   Many people's familiarity with computers is via document production. The idea of 'wordprocessing' (WP) has become very general. Much more than a clever form of typewriter, the WP function of a computer generally allows the user to design and control the format of documents simply and flexibly. The modification of text or formats is straightforward and advantageous whether a letter or a book is produced. The WP concept now extends to 'desktop publishing', where a combination of powerful desktop hardware (e.g. 'laser' printers using photocopier technology) and software enables production of documents almost indistinguishable from conventionally produced typeset material. Some WP software can produce computer files of your paper or book that will directly drive a printing press! However, these evolving products are still expensive. Conventional WP software abounds and most can produce a wide variety of documents. Differences mainly lie in: the relative ease of achieving different formats; how the user gives commands to the computer; the range of sophisticated features like merging a mailing list and other specific information with a standard letter to produce 'personalised' letters ('mail-merge' facility)—useful in research involving outpatient treatment where patients must be circulated with new information intermittently. There are built-in or add-on 'spelling checkers' (some use only American spelling), and 'grammar checkers'. Other facilities allow graphs and diagrams, produced using a graphics-editing program (rudimentary versions of which are commonly built into major WP packages), to be incorporated into the wordprocessed text. Seeing the exact printed form of the document on the computer screen is valued by many and labelled 'what you see is what you get' (WYSIWYG; pronounced 'wizzywig'!).

Useful general references here are Madron, Tate, and Brookshire (1985), and Schrodt (1987). Notable developments include 'outliners' (stand-alone or within WPs), containing facilities for developing papers, talks, etc. You can expand headings or 'ideas' with annotated sub-headings, text and graphics; and powerful versions allow you to zoom in or out, viewing any level of structure, etc. Making 'instant' overhead-projection slides from any part is another valuable feature. There are specific packages aimed at producing such visual aids also for full-colour 35mm slides, or for direct presentation to an audience via a computer-driven suitably-sized screen or video-projector often available in lecture theatres and conference centres. However, unless you need only to transport your floppy disk containing the 'slides', this is rarely worth the effort and overhead projection or 35mm slides produced from your computer graphics are preferable. This kind of software is commonly referred to as a 'desktop presentation' package, notable examples being Microsoft PowerPoint, and Harvard Graphics. Such developments are potentially valuable to researchers for speeding the production and enhancing the quality of conference presentations.

Text editing.   The compatibility between different types of hardware and software in terms of stored information is often queried. The transfer of information or data between computers (see later) may be necessary for processing that your own machine cannot carry out, or transferring your existing files to a new, more powerful computer. 'Pure text files', i.e. containing nothing but alphanumeric and punctuation characters, can be readily transferred between any two computers.

However, formatted material like manuscripts, databases etc. requires special 'translation' software, or their text re-formatted on the new machine. Such software is available for transfer between many of the standard software packages, but not always for the combinations that you require. Most WP packages can generate and read pure text files (ASCII files).

Graphics editing/processing.   Besides   text   for   reports   and publications, research can demand graphical representations of data, ideas, and theories. If you cannot draw well, the computer can assist you. Graphics-editing packages exist for everyone from mere doodlers to industrial designers. A good general-purpose 'drawing' program meets most researchers' needs. A range of on-screen tools facilitates the production of geometrical shapes, shading, and labelling. A package for creating various forms of graphs (i.e. histograms, line graphs, etc.) from an input of data and design specification (i.e. axes, labels, etc.) can also be helpful, though many spreadsheet and statistics packages now include such facilities which will be discussed later. Many of the major WP and desktop publishing packages now incorporate a basic graphics editor, and this may satisfy your needs.

Information handling
Computers are invaluable in other research activities, such as handling both numerical and textual information so that desired aspects are easily retrievable. Various software packages offer painless dealings with numbers and structured textual material, providing a powerful automated version of the pocket calculator (i.e. the spreadsheet-type program), and the filing cabinet or card index (i.e. the database-type). Truly portable battery-powered computers (i.e. those commonly labelled as 'notebook', 'sub-notebook', 'palmtop', and 'personal digital assistants, PDAs') can be used almost anywhere, so data gathering from fieldwork can be enhanced using conventional WP packages or purpose-designed data recording software (see Ager, 1985 for a review of this in mental handicap research; and Morley, 1991, reviews his use of such a machine in clinical psychology practice). Using 'communications' software (see later section), such a machine could 'telephone in' your collected data to a laboratory/office-based computer for processing. Portable computer use in fieldwork is specialised, but the information handling packages are potentially valuable to most researchers.

Spreadsheets.   Spreadsheet programs supposedly started the trend towards desktop computers in business. A spreadsheet is an electronic data sheet based on the squared paper used to set out research data at the first stage of analysis. Each row and column is labelled so individual squares can be cross-referenced, as on a graph or map. Each cell contains a data item (number or text). The advantage is that cells can alternatively contain a formula, which automatically calculates the cell's contents, usually from values held in other cells. Formulae can be defined once, then replicated across a specific row or column with automatic adjustment of the cell references. While the early programs were aimed at financial analysts, current programs offer extensive mathematical and statistical functions. Modern spreadsheets can calculate means, standard deviations, and be configured for exploratory data analysis, analysis of variance, etc. (see e.g. Bakeman, 1992), often required in mental health research. Once drawn up, such spreadsheets with their formulae can be saved for use with different data sets. Most packages can convert the sheet to a text file allowing transferral of data to other analysis software, or direct incorporation of financial planning into a grant proposal.

Researchers working on financial aspects of grant proposals will find these programs' facilities useful. Advantageous here is the ease of assessing 'what if' planning. Changing one or two cell entries representing salaries of research assistants, or project duration, provides an immediate outcome. Various options for project parameters could be entered and all the outcomes calculated together for you to choose the optimum.

Further details of spreadsheet use in research, including examples, are given by Madron et al. (1985), and Schrodt (1987).

Database management systems.   Mental health research, and the social and behavioural sciences deal with textual information almost as much as with numerical data. Software to organise and structure such information is called a 'database management system' (DBMS). Almost any set of structured textual information can be considered a database: Maintaining and searching a large file or conventional card index for literature sources, patient records, etc. is a daunting and time-consuming task where computer assistance can be invaluable.

DBMS packages come in two basic types:

1.   'File management systems': providing an electronic card index, with facilities for generating reports using database information; overall, a good text editor is almost as powerful.
2.   'Relational databases': contain flexible advanced features for information searches using both logical and mathematical operations on several database files at once. Facilities for creating new files from current ones exist, and a specialised programming

language for writing complete information management applications is embedded in the package. Mastery of the awesome facilities of the most popular DBMSs can be very time consuming.

Researchers commonly use a DBMS for computerised bibliographies (see Kornbrot, 1992, for a review of a purpose-designed DBMS for this task). Several reports emphasise the positive value of DBMSs in clinical work (notably Ericson, 1990; Kennedy, 1990; Robinson, 1990; and Romanczyk, 1991). Kapur (1984) noted the value of DBMSs in clinical decision-making, by cross-referencing patient and 'reference files' built up of particular diagnostic category information. Patient data records are an obvious choice, and useful for later adding an 'expert system' front-end (see later section) to aid diagnosis. Many complain of the time-consuming nature of database work, and suggest as a prerequisite a secretary or research assistant to set up and maintain the DBMS. It is worth noting though that simple databases can be established in most spreadsheet programs, or by using text files to contain the information and the search facilities of small utility programs or even the computer operating system to find items.

Inter-computer communications

While there are now relatively few tasks for which current desktop computers are unsuitable, some models may lack the processor power, and/or storage capacity to carry out certain tasks efficiently, e.g. analysing very large sets of data involving complex numerical procedures, and maintaining large bibliographic or other databases. However, most desktop computers communicate marvellously with computers capable of such tasks. Additionally, there is a wealth of relevant information available electronically via the global Internet and accessible by such inter-computer communications.

Necessities for computer communications. Inter-computer communication ('comms') requires your machine to be either 'networked' or connected via its serial interface to a 'modem' (see earlier section 'Personal workstation'). Access is needed to the target computer system, possibly via a modem, which links your computer to the telephone (assuming the target computer is either 'on' the telephone or connected to a network that is accessible by phone). The necessary communications software will emulate standard forms of inter-computer communications protocols ('terminal emulation'), and provide facilities for transferring files to and from other computers. For further details, see Engst (1995), Engst and Dickson (1994), Engst, Low and Simon (1995), Gilster (1994), or LaQuey (1994).

Why communicate with other computers?   The main reasons have already been mentioned: statistical analysis (see later section); literature searches; file and mail transfers (discussed shortly). Of value in the mental health context, possibly forming part of a research project, are on-line information systems ('bulletin board systems', 'computer conferencing systems', 'newsgroups', and 'mailing lists').

Bibliographic searches.   Literature searches by computer used to be made indirectly via library services. The trend now is to provide systems for end users, with many on-line bibliographic databases designed for use by individual researchers. In the UK, the Institute for Scientific Information's (ISI) well-known databases, the Science and Social Sciences Citation Indices are available for on-line searches by members of most higher education institutions (the so-called BIDS facility). Similarly, the British Library's Inside Information service which includes document delivery is now available. Equivalent services are available in North America.

Many such databases are not fully archival i.e. containing information on sources more than 12 years old. Examples of such searches are demonstrated by Gosling, Knight and McKenney (1989), Madron et al. (1985), and Reed and Baxter (1992). The first and last of these references also cover the use of CD-ROM databases that are now commonly provided in many academic libraries, and often made accessible over campus networks.

Online library catalogue systems (called 'online public access catalogues', OPACs; see Miter, 1986) promise a useful facility for busy researchers: from your workstation, you can check whether a particular book or periodical is in your institution's library, where it is located, if it is on loan, etc. You can search other libraries across the world just as easily.

On-line information.   Currently, the major focus of information exchange among professionals and academics is the Internet, the network of computer networks that spans the globe. While this has existed for some time it is only recently that easy access to all its facilities has become available to users of desktop computers. There is a rapidly expanding number of electronic documents (text, graphics, digital video and software) available on these networks, and these 'global network' resources can be searched using new desktop computer software tools that have become freely available. For example, electronic documents either titled with or containing particular user-specified keywords can be located and subsequently downloaded to your own machine using applications called 'gopher' and 'Mosaic'. Essentially these programs on your desktop machine, known as the 'client' version, interact transparently with 'server' versions of the program on remote computers holding electronic archives. There are various forms of these network navigation programs, some with strange names like 'archie', 'ftp', 'world wide web' (WWW or W3) browsers, etc. Developments in this area are rapid with much of the documentation being maintained electronically rather than in hardcopy, but LaQuey (1994), Engst (1995), and Engst, Low and Simon (1995) provide excellent overviews.

Electronic communication via email, computer conferencing, news groups, mailing lists and bulletin boards is now widely used by academics and professionals for scholarly discussion and information exchange. There are a number of electronic mailing lists, electronic newsletters and even electronic journals relevant to psychologists, some examples of which were reported by Colbourn (1993b). The 'server' software is now available for desktop computers and so it is easy for an individual to provide an on-line information system for say local mental health services, using a suitably connected desktop computer.

File transfer and electronic mail (email).   I have already mentioned most important uses of file transfer between computers, but the following may be less apparent. In the co-operative writing of books or papers between physically remote individuals, speedy electronic exchange of text documents can greatly facilitate the process (although conventionally mailed disks containing the text can have advantages if colleagues use the same WP). Cotton (1984) pointed out that 70% of the life cycle of a document transmitted by letter post is spent in the actual mail. Email and the file transfer is now easy so that from your personal workstation you can send and receive mail, chapter, and paper drafts and submit final copy to some publishers all over the world.

Work management
As the personal workstation provides a focus for one's work, much work management software has been produced; some, in the form of small applications that can run simultaneously or over the top of major applications like WPs, etc., in even quite modestly powered computers. Thus one can switch from entering data or writing a research paper to an electronic diary, calendar, notebook, or phonebook (which can even dial a voice call), etc., and then switch back to the main task. Some people feel these tasks are better done conventionally, but it is surprising how habits can change especially when working in an networked group where such software can even synchronise diaries. Complex time and project management could benefit from specialised packages especially

where there are deadlines. For example, when planning a one-year project, you break down the separate stages and estimate both time and the resources required. These packages work like spreadsheets although using critical path analysis as their underlying technique, and grid or network displays show how the project stages and resources dovetail. Similarly, sophisticated time management software when configured with your current appointments and other commitments, can quickly inform you of free time for extra appointments, etc. I have discussed such techniques more extensively elsewhere (Colbourn, 1991c).

However, the amount of usage and the time taken to learn the use of such software must be balanced. Researchers are not always planning projects, but should consider this form of software support as the need arises.

Data analysis

Given the familiar ground and substantial literature on statistical computing I attempt only an overview and address the question of what is feasible in this area on desktop computers at present.

The large integrated statistical packages, like SPSS, BMDP, GENSTAT, Minitab, SAS, etc., and specialised packages for particular forms of analysis like GLIM (General Linear Modeller), CLUSTAN (CLUSTer ANalysis), ECTA (Extended Contingency Table Analysis), MULTIVARIANCE (MULTIvariate analysis of VARIANCE), etc., have long been the researchers' first choice. These packages offer considerable flexibility in manipulating, organising, and recoding research data, and an extensive range of statistical analyses. Being very large and usually expensive, they mostly appeared on powerful multi-user mainframe computers. However, full versions of some of these (e.g., SPSS, BMDP, Minitab, and GLIM) have been implemented for most desktop computers. These 'micro' versions are still expensive, and generally require powerful (and therefore more expensive) desktop computers to run efficiently (or even at all). In some cases relatively cheap 'student' editions of these programs are available, although they usually contain only a relatively small subset of the facilities of the original package.

A key advantage is that such software is well tried and tested, and continually maintained and improved by a team of statistical programmers. Thus you can depend on the results, provided you input your data and specify the analyses correctly and accurately. They can almost certainly handle any size of data set. But they are complicated, so familiarising yourself with them requires time, although comprehensive manuals are readily available. The SPSS package is particularly good, with substantial user guides (e.g., Norusis & SPSS Inc., 1993a, 1993b, 1993c, 1993d), and statistical handbooks (e.g., Norusis, 1988) providing examples of different types of data analysis. Other authors have also provided useful guides to using this software (e.g., Foster, 1993; West, 1991). Additionally, the computing services at university and research establishments often run courses in their use.

For mainframe use, create the data and command files (which instruct the statistical software how to handle your data) using your computer's WP/text editor. Using your desktop computer as a terminal to a mainframe, you can transfer these files and initiate the analysis (see section on 'Inter-computer communications'). Results are presented as printed output, or a text file which can be downloaded into your machine for perusal and/or printing.

Clinical researchers may rely upon what can be achieved by a personal workstation. Many current desktop computers can run sophisticated statistical software with good graphical facilities (often lacking in mainframe packages) and can cope with substantial data sets. Schrodt (1987) discussed the problems of statistical software on a microcomputer, and highlighted speed, accuracy, and memory in particular. Microcomputers can represent numbers as accurately as mainframes, but need more storage resources to do so and hence longer processing times. However, statistical software must be carefully written for microcomputers to avoid rounding errors causing an erroneous result especially when test statistics are near to a critical value. One should always carefully check results from microcomputer-based statistics or numerical packages. Versions of the large well-established packages specially designed for micros (e.g., SPSS for Windows) can generally be considered free of such problems. Running micro versions of the well-established packages may not be cost effective, relative to using a mainframe service or purchasing other statistical software, for many small research groups. Smaller-scale and other more modestly priced statistical packages are available for desktop machines and I have discussed some major contenders in more detail elsewhere (Colbourn, 1993a).

Some micro-based packages can be relatively fragile, i.e., the novice can easily 'crash' them (a program or system failure) so data are lost and have to be re-entered. Also, menu-driven packages, where the computer constantly prompts you for the required inputs, can be irritating. The facility to bypass the menus or prompts and input direct commands is an advantage. Similarly, the possibility of inputting data via a text file (earlier, this section) is another advantage. Then if errors occur, there is no need to type all the data in again—having to re-type even 20 data points in a menu-driven system can drive researchers to distraction!!

Before buying try to find another user of the package to get both their opinion and some 'hands on' experience with some of your own data.

These smaller-scale packages are rarely entirely satisfactory and data exploration is often best achieved with a spreadsheet or purpose-designed software (see e.g., Lovie & Lovie, 1991). In fact a substantial amount of descriptive and graphical analysis can be done with standard spreadsheets, and data can be exported from these directly into most statistical software. Data entry rarely has to be carried out more than once. However, the attention of users of data graphics facilities should be drawn to Tufte's (1983) guidelines for excellent, unambiguous and economical graphical representation of data. These are clearly unknown to most producers of the software judged from some of the options offered to end users. The SYGRAPH manual, that accompanies the SYSTAT statistical package, is a notable exception to this, providing a discussion of not only Tufte's work, but also some of the psychology relevant to the perception of data graphics.

Mention must also be made of an important non-statistical area of data analysis: qualitative methods. In recent years considerable effort has been made to develop qualitative analysis techniques for handling interview, personal diaries, discourse and other text-based data, and to provide software tools to support them. Tesch (1990) provides one of the better sources on qualitative research with special emphasis on appropriate software tools, while Fielding and Lee (1993) have collected together a wider-ranging set of views and information on the use of computers in this area. The computer can also be a valuable tool in gathering interview data as Saris (1991) describes. Finally, it should be remembered, as Lovie (1986, p.17) aptly indicates, that data analysis packages should not and cannot be used instead of a knowledge of the actual analysis techniques and their interpretation. In Lovie's words, "The computer is an aid to thought not a substitute for it".

Automated testing and experimental control

For some 25 years psychologists have used computers to control experimental apparatus and procedures and record behavioural and physiological data. Widespread availability of cheap microcomputers pushed these techniques beyond the research laboratory into both undergraduate education and clinical practice. Automating various psychological test and assessment procedures essentially developed from computer control of psychological experiments.

The key advantages of transferring standard psychological tests to a computer are improved standardisation in presentation, and time saving for busy clinicians, enabling them to focus on understanding patient's problems and planning suitable treatments. It has been suggested that computer-driven initial screening interviews could help the clinician pinpoint problems and are generally accepted by patients, who sometimes find it easier to disclose sensitive details to the impersonal computer (Morris, 1985; Saris, 1991). The main rationale for computer use here is to utilise the clinician's time more efficiently.

Many traditional pencil-and-paper tests have now been converted, and are listed in the DRAT (1988). The DRAT gives the origins and specifications of a large number of automated psychological tests including those which have been developed in-house by individuals who are, in some cases, prepared to share or sell them. Tests mentioned include the Mill Hill Vocabulary Scale, Digit Span, Raven's Progressive Matrices, Eysenck Personality Inventory, Bexley-Maudsley Automated Personality Screening, Cattell's 16 PF, Myers Briggs Type Indicator, and tests of verbal reasoning and verbal fluency. The directory lists the addresses of software writers, the machines on which the software will run, the aim of the software, and research publications relating to its use.

O'Carroll, Brooks, Harrop and Shelton (1993) describe an innovative computer-assisted tutorial package they have developed for teaching psychometrics. The package takes its users through the whole process of developing a psychometric test and would appear to be valuable for those wishing to develop such skills.

Other popular software used in psychological testing is that designed to analyse repertory grids. For example, the freely available 'Circumgrids' (Chambers and Grice, 1986) allows the analysis and comparison of grids, together with a number of subsidiary analyses. It is usable only by those with a sound knowledge of repertory grid techniques and has a couple of irritating features: input and output are direct, and cannot be made through a file, and secondly it imposes a strict size limitation (Martin, 1993). Information on other repertory grid software can be found in Colbourn (1992) and Jankowicz (1990).

Both The British Psychological Society and the American Psychological Association have issued cautionary statements on test computerisation (see Standing Committee on Test Standards, 1984). Concern mainly relates to possible effects on the construct validity (although Morris, 1985, disagrees), and the possible use of untrained personnel.

Discussions of the advantages of computer-based testing can be found in Lockshin and Harrison (1991), Wilson and McMillan (1991), and Wexler (1990). Other, wider aspects of computer-based control of psychological research are reviewed by Colbourn (1993a).

Expert systems and artificial intelligence

The construction and application of 'expert systems' (ES) is a potentially important clinical research use of computers. ESs are computer programs which offer the advice and reasoning of a human expert. Popular domains are medicine, geology, financial investment, etc. Originally used experimentally, this software has now been commercially produced (e.g., Jackson, 1990), but assessing how widely it is routinely used is difficult. The techniques for building ESs were developed from 'artificial intelligence' (AI) research, aimed at building computer models of cognitive behaviour (e.g. see Boden, 1987 for an overview).

AI techniques are valuable in psychological theorising (Garnham, 1988); and Colby's research provides an example applied to mental health (see Boden, 1987, Chapters 2 & 3).

Earlier I cited Kapur's (1984) work, using a reference database, gradually constructed from patient data, to help assess new patients. ESs can be 'bolted-on' to certain DBMSs and the system itself will develop the rules for determining particular diagnoses from an established database of patient information, or allowing a clinician to input such rules directly. These are usually expressed in IF ... THEN form. A simple example might be:

IF memory-impairment mild
AND pattern-of-memory-performance atypical
THEN diagnosis depression/anxiety-state

These ESs are called 'knowledge-based systems' because they depend on encapsulating the expert's knowledge in the program (called an ES shell) in the form of rules and 'facts', e.g. a simplified 'fact' might be:

CEREBRAL TUMOUR-SYMPTOM-HEADACHE

representing that a symptom of a cerebral tumour is headache. Alternative approaches use Bayesian statistical inference on a substantial database of symptom-diagnosis probability relations.

The necessary software has been implemented on desktop computers, either as ES shell programs, or within flexible high-level programming languages like LISP and PROLOG. The latter is often favoured, and interested researchers can familiarise themselves using Bratko's (1990) thorough treatment.

More extensive yet concise discussions of this topic directly relevant to behavioural and mental health researchers can be found in Beaumont (1991), and Benfer, Brent and Furbee (1991).

PRACTICAL ADVICE ON ACQUIRING COMPUTING SKILLS AND CHOOSING APPROPRIATE HARDWARE AND SOFTWARE

Acquiring computing skills

Learning computing skills can seem unattainable to those whose education finished before the computer's widespread introduction. But this is not true.

Various strategies exist for the computer-naive. My emphasis here is on use because learning programming can take a considerable time, especially for producing useful software (although software tools like 'HyperCard' on the Macintosh, and 'Toolbook' on PCs do make this easy). The following requirements arise in learning to use computers:

1. A conviction that time spent learning computer use is well spent because it may not be especially productive in terms of your research and/or clinical work.
2. For a busy researcher or clinician, concentration on learning to use the computer only for those tasks of clear benefit to you is the best strategy. Having appreciated that, you may later feel confident enough to explore other potentially beneficial uses.
3. The realisation that you need know nothing about how the hardware works. A functional knowledge of the various components is sufficient (e.g., floppy and hard disks are for filing your data, text, programs, etc.). Some computer systems get this message across clearly (e.g., O'Malley, 1986; Williams, 1993).

The two main strategies for acquiring skills are:

1. Attend some intensive courses run by many university computing centres, often in an inexpensive adult education programme. These courses (2-5 full days) are generally better than a weekly hour or two for getting you using a machine; avoid expensive commercial courses inapplicable to the experience required in research or clinical applications. Any course must include actual use of a computer.
2. Obtain or borrow a desktop computer system fitting your requirements (see later); sit down with its tutorial and reference manuals and work through them alone; with a colleague also wishing to learn; or one knowledgeable about the hardware and software (preferably not a 'computer buff'). Many people prefer to master a machine alone, and consult others only when really stuck. That way you work at your own pace, with your own data,

documents, etc. Mistakes will happen, but remember that the computer only does what you ask, and you cannot damage it just by typing. Mistakes can be frustrating, especially if you erase a whole day's work. If you unfortunately encounter a software 'bug' (possible even in commercial software) which corrupts the data on your disk making it unreadable, the ensuing frustration encourages learning to make backup copies of important disks or files.

The second strategy is usually followed by academics and clinicians, owing to time constraints, and despite notoriously poor computer documentation (although standards are improving). There is a publishing boom in guides to particular computers and standard software packages. The level and helpfulness of these varies (see Colbourn, 1993c). As when choosing hardware and software, advice and comments from experienced colleagues, reviews in computer magazines, newspapers, etc., are still the main information sources. Dealers can be very helpful, but they are salesmen of specific products which they will be biased towards!

Finally, many potential users worry about unfamiliarity with the QWERTY keyboard used on most computers. Touch-typing is not a prerequisite for effective computer use but it may be more efficient in the long term. Many systems use a 'mouse' for some input. This device, attached to the computer by a lead, is moved around the desk to control an on-screen pointer. Using this to point to command words or small pictures, called 'icons', displayed on the screen, the computer can be made to execute various tasks. This type of 'graphical user interface' (GUI), as it is called, is simpler than recalling and typing command words.

Choosing appropriate hardware and software

Owing to continuous developments in the personal computer industry it is difficult to give firm advice on choosing particular products. Demonstrations of hardware and software can be misleading. You must be allowed to 'test drive' any product and see demonstrations of it solving the kind of problems you intend it to handle.

However, these additional points are important:

1. Hardware and software must be chosen together, since not all machines may have the applications you require. Perhaps you need a wordprocessor and a statistics package now; and later a communications package which is not a feature of your initial system. Do ensure that a system will cater for possible future needs as well.

2. Standardisation has always been a weak point; however, the three dominant desktop hardware platforms (IBM PC compatibles, Apple Macintosh, and UNIX workstations) are now closer than ever in terms of inter-working, and major software packages are produced in almost identical form for all three. This is partly because they all have GUI system software available. Nevertheless, choice should be also determined by existing personal computing equipment in your institution, which could determine the level of assistance obtainable when you need it.
3. Purchasing hardware and software from a local dealer often pays dividends despite a higher initial cost. Personal computers are very reliable, but if things go wrong then a good relationship with a local dealer should get them rectified quickly. You will find that the machine rapidly becomes integrated into your work and is therefore difficult to be without.

I trust that these brief comments will be useful to readers now wishing to become computer users. However, I have discussed these matters in more detail elsewhere (Colbourn, 1991a).

CONCLUSIONS

I hope this chapter has shown the computer to be a valuable tool, assisting researchers and clinicians, and that time spent acquiring the few necessary skills is well worth it. If you are not already a computer user, I hope you will be encouraged to become one. You won't regret it, but take care that the machine doesn't become an end in itself. If you are already a computer user, I trust that I may have helped you realise more potential applications to your work and provided some guide to further information.

ACKNOWLEDGEMENTS

During the writing of both editions of this chapter, I have had much valuable advice and comment from many colleagues, students, and friends with whom I have discussed, questioned, researched and taught the use of computers in psychology over a number of years. I particularly wish to mention Isobel Colbourn, Tony Gale, Martin Hall, Nick Hammond, Tony Hasemer, Narinder Kapur, Paul Light, Cliff McKnight, and Tony Roberts.

GLOSSARY OF SOME COMMONLY USED
COMPUTING TERMS

Terms given in italics are also defined in this glossary.

ASCII: 'American Standard Code for Information Interchange'; standard code using a *byte* to represent all alphanumeric and special control characters. A standard that allows just about all computers to intercommunicate.

BASIC: 'Beginners' All-purpose Symbolic Instruction Code'; easy to learn *high-level programming language* available on most computers.

BYTE: Commonly accepted measurement of computer storage. Used as a parameter for describing *RAM, ROM, Floppy disks, Hard disks*, etc. Equivalent to eight bits (binary digits) of information, the minimum required to represent alphanumeric characters, etc. using a standard code (e.g. *ASCII*).

CD-ROM: 'Compact Disk Read-Only Memory'; The same disk that has become the standard for audio recordings, can hold 550 to 630MB of permanently recorded electronic information. Recording and retrieval are via laser optics making the disks hard wearing in normal use. CD-ROMs are commonly used to distribute large *software* packages, and documents involving multimedia (i.e. text, graphics, photographs, audio and video) like electronic encyclopaedias, and other educational and entertainment materials.

CPU: 'Central Processing Unit'; nerve centre of a digital computer. The CPU coordinates and controls the activities of all other parts of the complete machine; carries out all the arithmetic and logical processes applied to data by following a program. CPUs are commonly implemented using *microprocessors.*

DOT MATRIX PRINTER: 'Hardcopy' peripheral device producing printed output via a printing head made up of a matrix of wires. Each character is formed by pre-programmed combinations of these wires striking a typewriter-like ribbon onto paper. Contrast with an *ink jet printer* and *laser printer.*

FLOPPY DISK: Commonest form of 'backing' storage, consisting of a lightweight flexible magnetic disk inside a protective square-shape sleeve. When rotated rapidly inside a computer disk drive it behaves as if rigid, allowing information to be written and read from it, providing a fairly permanent record. An older type of floppy disk, the 5.25in size protected by a cardboard sleeve and relatively easily damaged, is still occasionally found. The 3.5in type housed in a more robust hard plastic shell is now almost ubiquitous. Storage capacity depends on the computer system; generally ranges from 800K to 4MB. Disks are rarely directly interchangeable across machines using different *operating systems*, though software can enable this. Due to flimsiness, backup copies should always be kept.

GIGABYTE (G); One thousand *megabytes* (actually 1K times 1K times 1K or 1,073,741,824 bytes).

HARD DISK: Another form of backing storage, consisting of a rigid magnetic disk usually permanently housed with the associated drive components. Advantages are considerably faster read and write access to a greater quantity of stored information (typically between 160 and 1000MB). More reliable than floppies but important to make backup copies of stored information. Devices called 'tape streamers' offer a relatively high-speed economical form of backup. Hard disk storage devices also come in the form of removable cartridges (like very large capacity floppy disks), based on magnetic, optical, or magneto-optical (MO) recording technology.

HARDWARE: Computer system's electronic and mechanical components, i.e. the physical parts like the system units, monitor, keyboard, disk drives,etc.

HIGH-LEVEL PROGRAMMING LANGUAGE: Means of instructing a computer to carry out specific functions using a 'natural' or 'scientific' type of specialised language. There are many high-level programming languages like *BASIC*, C, C++, FORTRAN (FORmula TRANslation), LISP (LISt Processing), PROLOG (PROgramming in LOGic), etc., making the task of programming easier than using 'low-level' or 'assembler' languages, a mnemonic form of instruction codes used by the *CPU*.

ICON: Pictorial or ideographic representation of a computer function or feature shown on the *VDU*. A *mouse* device is used to point to an icon to initiate the function. Seen as a way of making computers easier and more 'friendly' to use.

INK JET PRINTER: Output device producing printed output by squirting ink drops selectively from a number of nozzles on to standard-sized sheets of paper. The ink drops are precisely directed by passing through an electrical field to quietly create high-quality monochrome or colour text and graphic images. The quality of output is close to that of laser printers but ink jets work more slowly and are not as suitable for serving a group of networked users.

INTERFACE: Usually a hardware device, internally fitted to pieces of computer equipment, enabling a computer to 'talk' to its printer, modem, disk drive, etc. Also used for important software interface between the computer and the human user, known as the 'human-computer interface' (HCI).

KILOBYTE (K): Considered to be a thousand bytes but actually 1024 bytes because of the base two arithmetic. Kilobyte has become a standard unit for specifying computer storage.

LASER PRINTER: The highest quality and fastest desktop hardcopy device producing printed pages via a xerographic process (as in plain paper photocopiers). The page image is built up pixel by pixel on a light-sensitive drum using a laser beam, or light emitting diodes. The drum then picks up toner and deposits it on the paper to rapidly and quietly create very high-quality monochrome or colour text and graphic images. The quality of output appears close to that of a printing press. These printers are now cheap enough to be used as personal printers but are more commonly found serving a group of networked users.

MAINFRAME: Large fast computers with substantial memory, and backing store capacity, offering multi-user fully managed services. Contrast with *microcomputers* and *minicomputers*.

MEGABYTE (MB); One million bytes (actually 1K times 1K or 1,048,576 bytes).

MICROCOMPUTER: Generally small desktop computers often housed within a single case containing electronic circuit boards and a keyboard. Now commonly called desktop or personal computers.

MICROPROCESSOR: Heart of most computers these days. Consists of a *CPU* encapsulated in a single microelectronic device or 'silicon chip'. Microprocessors are usually referred to in terms of size of 'word' or basic unit of processing that they use, e.g. 16-bit, 32-bit, and 64-bit being the current range, their type, e.g. *RISC* or *CISC*, and the name usually given to them by their manufacturer (e.g. 68040, 80486, Alpha, PowerPC 601, Pentium, etc.). 'Word' size indicates the largest number that the microprocessor can represent without resort to sophisticated processing routines.

MINICOMPUTER: Somewhat inexact term referring to machines somewhere in size and facilities between a microcomputer and a mainframe. Often have extensive *interface* facilities for use in laboratories, but computing power similar to high-specification desktop computers.

MODEM: 'MOdulator/DEModulator'; device to connect a computer to telephone lines for communication with another computer.

MOUSE: Device whose movements around a desktop are reflected by a pointer on a VDU. Used in a software environment with icons and menus to give commands to the computer.

MS-DOS: 'MicroSoft (major American software company) Disk Operating System'. Almost a de facto standard operating system for personal computers. There are variants produced by other companies including a superset of facilities. Often referred to simply as DOS.

OPERATING SYSTEM (OS): Program supervising the running of other programs, commonly incorporating facilities for managing disk files and other resources. First program run when a computer is started up. When an application program finishes, control usually passed back to the OS (e.g. MS-DOS, UNIX, OS/2, etc.).

RAM: 'Random Access Memory'; memory available for storing programs and data while they are being processed by the machine. Rapidly accessed for either read or write operations by *CPU*, but contents are lost when the power supply is turned off. Computers often described in terms of RAM capacity, e.g. 16MB RAM, giving an indication of size, and therefore sophistication, of programs and data files that can be handled.

RISC: 'Reduced Instruction Set Computer'; CPUs are generally of type RISC or CISC (Complex Instruction Set Computer). CISC processors use a vast number of instructions to specify all conceivable operations carried out by a computer. In contrast, RISC processors use a much smaller number of the most frequently required instructions, which are combined to carry out less frequently required operations. This enables the RISC processor to run much faster for most tasks.

ROM: 'Read Only Memory'; contrasts with *RAM* in that information can only be read and not altered. ROMs are usually chips installed inside computers, containing application programs termed firmware. Most personal computers have some ROM-based software, particularly associated with the *OS*.

SCSI: 'Small Computer System Interface'; A standard hardware interface used to connect desktop computers to fast peripheral devices like hard disks, scanners (for inputting printed materials to a computer), *CD-ROM* drives, etc. Equipment using the SCSI (usually pronounced 'skuzzy') interface can be simply connected together using the appropriate cables.

SOFTWARE: General term for computer programs, contrasted with hardware. Distinction between 'applications software', i.e. task-specific programs for wordprocessing, statistical analysis, etc., and 'system software', i.e. the operating system, high-level programming languages, etc.

VDU: 'Visual Display Unit'; screen where computer presents information that is input to and output from it.

WINDOW: A rectangular area of the *VDU* through which to view a wordprocessed document, a graphic, information about files on the hard disk, etc. The key principle involved is that many of these windows can be on screen at any one time, some of them overlapping, and they can be opened, closed, moved around, changed in size, and their contents edited, usually using a *mouse* device. These windows are a central part of *graphical user interfaces* (GUIs), also called 'point-and-click interfaces'. 'Windows' is also the name given by *Microsoft* to its widely used OS-like GUI application that fronts *MS-DOS*.

REFERENCES

Ager, A. (1985). Recent developments in the use of microcomputers in the field of mental handicap: Implications for psychological practice. *Bulletin of The British Psychological Society, 38*, 142-145.

Apple Computer Inc. (1989). *Understanding computer networks*. Reading, Mass.: Addison-Wesley.

Bakeman, R. (1992). *Understanding social science statistics: A spreadsheet approach*. Hillsdale, NJ: Lawrence Erlbaum Associates Inc.

Beaumont, J.G. (1991). Expert systems and the clinical psychologist. In A. Ager (Ed.), *Microcomputers and clinical psychology: Issues, applications, and future developments*. Chichester: Wiley.

Benfer, R.A., Brent, E.E.Jr., & Furbee, L. (1991). *Expert systems* (Sage University Paper series on Quantitative Applications in the Social Sciences, series no. 07-077). Beverly Hills & London: Sage.

Boden, M.A. (1987). *Artificial intelligence and natural man* (2nd edition). London: MIT Press.

Bramwell, R.S., & Davidson, M.J. (1989). Visual display units (VDUs) and reproductive health - The unresolved controversy. *The Psychologist, 8*, 345-346.

Bratko, I. (1990). *Prolog programming for artificial intelligence* (2nd edition). Wokingham, England: Addison-Wesley.

British Computer Society. (1991). *A glossary of computing terms* (7th edition). London: Pitman/British Computer Society.

Chambers, W.V., & Grice, J.W. (1986). Circumgrids: A repertory grid package for personal computers. *Behavior Research methods, Instruments, and Computers, 18*, 468.

Colbourn, C.J. (1991a). Issues in the selection and support of a microcomputer system. In A. Ager (Ed.), *Microcomputers and clinical psychology: Issues, applications, and future developments*. Chichester: Wiley.

Colbourn, C.J. (1991b, March). Local area networks (LANs): Southampton's choice. *The CTISS File, No. 11*, pp.19-20.

Colbourn, C.J. (1991c). Organization and management of research. In G. Allan & C. Skinner (Eds.), *Handbook for research students in the social sciences*. London: The Falmer Press.

Colbourn, C.J. (1992). Repertory grids revisited. *The Psychologist, 5*, 465.

Colbourn, C.J. (1993a). Desktop computers: Courseware and software. In *The British Psychological Society, Teaching Psychology: Information and resources* (3rd edition). Leicester: The British Psychological Society.

Colbourn, C.J. (1993b). Electronically speaking, and listening. *The Psychologist, 6*, 461.

Colbourn, C.J. (1993c). Broaden your bandwidth with books on computing? *Teaching Psychology Review, 2*, 151-154.

Cotton, K. (1984). Electronic mail. In A. Burns (Ed.), *New information technology*. Chichester: Ellis Horwood.

DRAT (*Directory of Research into Automated Testing*) (1988) S.L Wilson (compiler). London: The Royal Hospital and Home.

Engst, A.C. (1995). *Internet starter kit for Macintosh* (3rd end.). Indianapolis: Hayden Books.

Engst, A.C., & Dickson, W. (1994). *Internet explorer kit for Macintosh*. Indianapolis: Hayden Books.

Engst, A.C., Low, C.S., & Simon, M.A. (1995). *Internet starter kit for Windows* (2nd edn.). Indianapolis: Hayden Books.

Ericson, P. (1990). Clinical applications of computerized management information systems. In D. Baskin (Ed.), *Computer applications in psychiatry and psychology*. New York: Brunner/Mazel.

Fielding, N.G. & Lee, R.M. (1993). *Using computers in qualitative research*. London: Sage.

Foster, J.J. (1993). *Starting SPSS/PC+ and SPSS for Windows: A beginner's guide to data analysis* (2nd edition). Wilmslow: Sigma.

Frude, N. (1991). Psychological aspects of the new technological age. In A. Ager (Ed.), *Microcomputers and clinical psychology: Issues, applications, and future developments*. Chichester: Wiley.

Garnham, A. (1988). *Artificial intelligence: An introduction*. London: Routledge & Kegan Paul.

Gilster, P. (1994). *The Internet navigator* (2nd edn.). New York: Wiley.

Gosling, C., Knight, N., & McKenney, L.S. (Eds.) (1989). *Search PsycINFO: student workbook*. Washington, D.C.: American Psychological Association. [covers most psychological databases, both on-line and CD-ROM]

Gunton, T. (1992). *The Penguin dictionary of information technology and computer science*. Harmondsworth: Penguin.

Illingworth, V. (Ed.) (1990). *Dictionary of computing* (3rd edition). Oxford: Oxford University Press.

Jackson, P. (1990). *Introduction to expert systems* (2nd edition). Wokingham. Addison-Wesley.

Jankowicz, A.D. (1990). Review of Repgrid. *The Psychologist, 3*, 307.

Kapur, N. (1984). Using a microcomputer-based data management system for neuropsychological record filing, report generation, and as a clinical decision aid. *Bulletin of The British Psychological Society, 37*, 413-415.

Kennedy, R.S. (1990). Rudiments for establishing databases in mental health systems. In D. Baskin (Ed.), *Computer applications in psychiatry and psychology*. New York: Brunner/Mazel.

Kornbrot, D. (1991). EndNote Plus for the Macintosh. *The Psychologist, 4*, 551.

LaQuey, T. (1994). *The Internet companion: A beginner's guide to global networking* (2nd edn.). Reading, Mass.: Addison-Wesley.

Lockshin, S.B., & Harrison, K. (1991). Computer-assisted assessment of psychological problems. In A. Ager (Ed.), *Microcomputers and clinical psychology: Issues, applications, and future developments*. Chichester: Wiley.

Lovie, A.D. (1986). Getting new statistics into today's crowded curriculum. In A.D. Lovie (Ed.), *New developments in statistics for psychology and the social sciences*. London: The British Psychological Society/Methuen.

Lovie, A.D., & Lovie, P. (1991). Graphical methods for exploring data. In P. Lovie & A.D. Lovie (Eds.), *New developments in statistics for psychology and the social sciences*. Volume Two. London: The British Psychological Society/Routledge.

Madron, T.W.M., Tate, L.N., & Brookshire, R.G. (1985). *Using microcomputers in research* (Sage University Paper Series on Quantitative Applications in the Social Sciences. Series no. 07-052). Beverly Hills & London: Sage.

Martin, S. (1993). Circumgrids III package for personal computers. *The Psychologist, 6,* 511.

Miter, N.N. (1986). Users and ease of use: Online catalogues' raisons d'etre. *Program, 202,* 111-119.

Morley, S. (1991). Cambridge Z88: The original laptop. *The Psychologist, 4,* 496.

Morris, R.G. (1985). Automated clinical assessment. In F.N. Watts (Ed.), *New developments in clinical psychology*. Chichester: The British Psychological Society/Wiley.

Norusis, M.J. (1988). *The SPSS guide to data analysis for SPSS-X*. Chicago: SPSS Inc.

Norusis, M.J. & SPSS Inc. (1993a). *SPSS for Windows base system user's guide release 6.0*. Chicago: SPSS Inc.

Norusis, M.J., & SPSS Inc. (1993b) *SPSS for Windows base system syntax reference guide release 6.0*. Chicago: SPSS Inc.

Norusis, M.J., & SPSS Inc. (1993c) *SPSS for Windows advanced statistics release 6.0*. Chicago: SPSS Inc.

Norusis, M.J., & SPSS Inc. (1993d) *SPSS for Windows professional statistics release 6.0*. Chicago: SPSS Inc.

Oborne, D.J. (1985). *Computers at work: A behavioural approach*. Chichester: Wiley.

O'Carroll, P., Brooks, P., Harrop, A., & Shelton, A. (1993). Testing times: A demonstration of a computer-assisted tutorial for the undergraduate teaching of psychometrics. *Psychology Software News, 3,* 86-87.

O'Malley, C.E. (1986). Helping users help themselves. In D.A. Norman & S.W. Draper (Eds.), *User centred system design: New perspectives in human-computer interaction*. Hillsdale. NJ: Lawrence Erlbaum Associates Inc.

Pearce, B. (Ed.) (1984). *Health hazards of VDTs?* Chichester: Wiley. [To get to the most relevant aspects of this topic for researchers the following chapters are recommended: 2: Health hazards in perspective; 10: Issues in vision and lighting for users of VDUs; 13: Postural loads at VDT work-stations; 16: Optimal presentation mode and colours of symbols on VDUs.]

Quarterman, J.S. (1990). *The matrix: Computer networks and conferencing systems worldwide*. Bedford, Mass.: Digital Press.

Reed, J.G. & Baxter, P.M. (1992). *Library use: A handbook for psychology* (2nd edition). Washington, D.C.: American Psychological Association. [covers bibliographic searches via computer and CD-ROM].

Robinson, J. (1990). Use of computers in mental health management of information. In D. Baskin (Ed.), *Computer applications in psychiatry and psychology*. New York: Brunner/Mazel.

Romanczyk, R.G. (1991). Monitoring and evaluating clinical service delivery: Issues and effectiveness of computer database management. In A. Ager (Ed.), *Microcomputers and clinical psychology: Issues, applications, and future developments*. Chichester: Wiley.

Saris, W.E. (1991). *Computer-assisted interviewing* (Sage University Paper series on Quantitative Applications in the Social Sciences, series no. 07-080). Beverly Hills & London: Sage.

Schrodt, P.A. (1987). *Microcomputer methods for social scientists* (2nd edition) (Sage University Paper series on Quantitative Applications in the Social Sciences, series no. 07-040). Beverly Hills & London: Sage.

Sproull, L., & Kiesler, S. (1991). *Connections: New ways of working in the networked organization*. Cambridge, Mass.: MIT Press.

Standing Committee on Test Standards (1984). Note on the computerization of printed psychological tests and questionnaires. *Bulletin of The British Psychological Society, 37*, 416-417.

Tesch, R. (1990). *Qualitative research: Analysis types and software tools*. London and Philadelphia: The Falmer Press.

Tufte, E.R. (1983). *The Visual Display of Quantitative Information*. Cheshire, Connecticut: Graphics Press.

West, R. (1991). *Computing for Psychologists: Statistical Analysis using SPSS and MINITAB*. Chur, Switzerland: Harwood Academic.

Wexler, S. (1990). Computerized psychological assessment. In D. Baskin (Ed.), *Computer Applications in Psychiatry and Psychology*. New York: Brunner/Mazel.

Williams, R. (1993). *The little Mac book* (3rd edition). Berkeley, California: Peachpit Press.

Wilson, S.L., & McMillan, T.M. (1991). Microcomputers in psychometric and neuropsychological assessment. In A. Ager (Ed.), *Microcomputers and clinical psychology: Issues, applications, and future developments*. Chichester: Wiley.

CHAPTER SEVEN

Writing a research report

Glenys Parry   Sheffield Consulting and Clinical
Psychologists, Community Health Sheffield

It is surprising how many people undertake a piece of research and carry it almost to completion, but fail to take the final steps of writing about it in a formal paper and seeing it through to publication. Many of us have some results lying in a drawer which we intend to write up—one day—or an idea for a paper which has not been written—yet. There are a number of reasons for this. Sometimes, having embarked on a project, one can become disillusioned with it, believing it not to be worth publishing. This may be true, but until you have written at least a draft of a possible paper, it is difficult to be sure. A much more common reason is that people lack confidence in writing and find it difficult. We sometimes forget that to write successfully needs practice, as with any skilled behaviour. Unfortunately it is a skill often neglected during clinical and research training, and many people do not have anyone to help them acquire it. This chapter aims to help the relatively inexperienced researcher at every stage of writing a research report. I shall focus on writing an empirical paper for publication in a journal, but many of the points apply equally to other forms of writing, such as a case report, a review article or a dissertation for examination.

HOW TO START

Getting ready

Before you sit down to write, there is some important work to do in preparation. This time is well spent and will save a lot of problems later. The first question to mull over is 'What do I want to say?'. Writing is much easier if you have something you want to say. It is quite likely that there is no one clear idea in your mind. Perhaps your study addressed a range of questions which, in hindsight, are not closely related, or there may be some meaningless or negative results. These may be due to design flaws or measurement problems and cannot be interpreted. Despite this, I shall assume that you have some results which you find interesting and which are worth communicating. This is the purpose of the paper, to communicate your findings.

The same principle applies to writing a dissertation or a thesis. Here you have more room and more excuse to list your negative findings, but be careful. It has been remarked that there are many reasons for negative findings, but most of them are trivial. Do not spend pages over-interpreting the reasons why you did not find what you expected to; it is better to focus on what you did find. The quality of the dissertation will be enhanced by thinking carefully about what you found and presenting it as clearly as possible.

When writing up a case study or a piece of qualitative research, there are no numerical 'results' to present. The general importance of thinking through the purpose and the message of the paper is, if anything, even more important in language based research. In a case study, for example, it is easy for the reader to become lost in a mass of clinical detail. The case study is at its best when making a theoretical point. The clinical material, having previously been analysed by the author, can be used selectively to illustrate the argument, and, above all, presented in a logical sequence. There is some discussion of presenting findings from qualitative research in Chapter 12.

Having decided what it is you want to say, the next question, just as important, is 'Who wants to know about it?'. Even at this preliminary stage you should be thinking about the readers. The research paper is a communication from you to someone else. Imagine you were asked to give a talk about your work. You would find it disconcerting if the person who invited you refused to tell you who the audience was. American psychiatrists? Health visitors? Behaviour therapists? The same thing applies to writing a formal research report. You are not writing in a social vacuum, although it can feel like it sometimes. Think about which journal you are writing for, and what kind of readership it has. Study other articles published by the journal to get an idea of the style.

If you are writing with co-authors. you will need to allocate tasks and, just as important, decide in which order your names will appear. This can be a source of much bitterness to junior researchers who discover, when the paper reporting their research is nearly ready for submission, that a senior colleague expects to have his or her name first. Alphabetical ordering does not solve this problem, especially for people called Zug. There are, unfortunately, no hard and fast rules about author precedence. It seems fair that the person who did most work should be the senior author, but of course this is often not clear cut. Sometimes the person who planned the research or who wrote it up is not the one who carried it out or analysed the data. In any case, get the rules straight at the beginning, before starting to write—it will prevent acrimony later.

The next stage is to gather together all the ingredients for the paper. In empirical research, the results are the heart of the paper. Sort out all the findings you want to present and get them into a form you can work with. This means creating rough tables, graphs and figures rather than leaving it all on computer printout or scribbled on the backs of envelopes.

You will also need your notes on relevant articles. Ideally, you would have made notes on other papers at the time you first read them; a succinct but informative summary of each paper complete with a full reference. Alas, it is more likely that you have a few photocopies, a few references and several memories of interesting articles you read six months ago but cannot now remember—was it Bruddle and Dakey or Brobble and Daly? Was it 1985 or 1984? You can remember the journal had a green cover! Now is the time to spend some hours in the library searching out relevant articles. But beware! It is very easy to fall into the hands of the arch-enemy of academic writers—procrastination. This devious opponent can take many forms, and if you catch yourself, three weeks later, saying 'I can't possibly start to write my paper until I've managed to get hold of so-and-so's article', you must take this as an urgent signal to start writing, immediately.

The right conditions

By now you have some idea of what you want to say and to whom you wish to say it. You have gathered all your materials, or at least enough to be going on with. Now you must find the right conditions in which to work. This is a very individual thing. Different people have different strategies, from the well-known psychologist who is reputed to tackle the first draft walking along a towpath with a Dictaphone, to a colleague who can only write at the kitchen table surrounded by the tea things with the radio on. You must find your own style, and this is one area where you can be entirely self-indulgent. If you like to write in B pencil on yellow paper and only in your garden shed—so be it. There are some groundrules, though, which you ignore at your peril. The two most important are solitude and uninterrupted time. It's amazing how we expect to be able to dash off a quick paper between telephone calls, meetings and seeing patients, and then seem puzzled and disheartened when nothing happens. The single most common reason for failure to write is the lack of adequate clear time in which to do it. The longer you have the better, the more frequent and regular your sessions the better. You also need a refreshed, clear mind. Writing demands your highest cognitive functions, so it's a good idea to find your own best time of the day, when you have most energy. For many people that is first thing in the morning, so it seems a shame to waste this prime time opening the post or chatting to colleagues. Others like an evening session. Very few people can give their best at four-thirty in the afternoon at the end of a day in the clinic, or during the lunch hour. You also need support and encouragement.

Many would-be researchers working in health service jobs find their writing is not valued and can even be seen as an indulgence. You need to find someone, somewhere, who believes in you and will support you. This support can take many forms, for example shielding you from phone calls when you're writing, or reading and commenting on drafts. You are in the best position to know what kind of support you need and you should take yourself seriously enough to get it.

The final prerequisite for successful writing is having the right tools. A good dictionary is just as essential as pen and paper. Many people find word-processors invaluable as you can draft and re-draft, cut text or move it around on screen so easily. They are particularly liberating for those who are blocked by a perfectionist need to draft the perfect sentence on that blank sheet of paper.

So here you are, sitting in your locked room with the morning ahead of you, notes and results easily to hand and writing tools at the ready. It's time to start writing!

THE OUTLINE

The first thing to write is definitely not the introductory paragraph, but an outline, a plan of your paper. There are many excellent reasons for this. It is absolutely essential that the material you are presenting is organised so that there is a logical flow of ideas from beginning to end. There is nothing more frustrating for the reader than a muddled, formless paper which gets off to a few false starts, fails to explain why the study was undertaken, presents results in the method section and then describes previously unmentioned measures in the results. Taking the time to think through the content and structure is part of a genuine desire to communicate, since you are trying to help the reader. The outline is also a very good way of getting ideas down—you learn to tolerate partly formed ideas by sketching them in at an early stage under the appropriate heading. Gradually the structure of the paper takes shape without your getting bogged down in the minutiae of the method or results. A good outline also helps you to write the first draft.

There are a number of tools which can help with the outline. Many wordprocessors have an outlining facility where headings and subheadings are automatically numbered and indented. An even more effective method for organising ideas, when you have become familiar with it, is Buzan's (1974) approach to mapping concepts. He uses a sketch which allows different ideas to be related to the central theme and to each other. This type of map uses spatial positioning as well as a headings and subheadings structure and is invaluable as a creative tool.

The main headings

In an empirical paper, the standard headings are Introduction, Method, Results and Discussion. This format allows a logical and economic exposition of why you conducted the study, what you did, what you found and what it means. It is not meant to be a realistic account in chronological order of what you thought before you started, the whole story of the fieldwork, every piece of data you collected or how you changed the design twice in the middle. It is a formal, public account. It is scrupulously honest, but it is constructed. There may, for some purposes, be a better set of main headings, but convince someone else as well as yourself.

Under each main heading, sketch out subheadings. Don't worry if they are not all at the same level of detail. You may have quite a good idea of how your method and results will be written but be more hazy on the introduction and discussion. The aim is to have a working model of the paper, an overview of the whole thing. Under each subheading you can then sketch in rough notes of material you wish to include. There is no need to write in detail. An example might help—there is an initial outline of a paper in Example 1. This is as far as you need to take it before starting to write. The final paper will be rather different from the outline, but that is to be expected, since the paper develops in the process of being drafted and redrafted. The outline is your starting point. It is useful at this stage to make a list of all the tables and figures you want to present.

Example I

What the chapter is about
People undertake a piece of research but do not report it in a formal paper.
People lack confidence in writing and find it difficult.
Chapter aims to help the inexperienced.
Focus is on writing an empirical paper for publication in a journal. Mention case reports, review articles and dissertations for examination.

How to start
Getting ready
   What do you want to say? To whom do you want to say it?
   Gathering your results. Background reading and notes on other articles.
The right conditions
   Quiet solitude and uninterrupted time.
   A refreshed clear mind—support—the right tools.
What to do if you can't get started
   Why it is difficult.
   How to recognise procrastination.
   Getting into the habit.
   Some techniques to overcome a block.

The outline
Why bother?
   The supreme importance of a clear structure.
   If you can't write an outline the paper will be muddled.
   Good ways of getting ideas down—learning to tolerate partly formed ideas.
The main headings
Rough notes

The first draft
Using the outline.
What to write first—how much at a time.
The method—results—the introduction—the discussion.
Getting feedback.

Subsequent drafts
Redrafting and revising for major changes.
Re-analysing results.
Correcting for style.
Reading more articles—knowing when to stop.

Preparing the manuscript for submission
Tables and figures.
References.
The title and abstract.
Authors and addresses.
Acknowledgements.

The editorial process
The covering letter—packaging it.
Reviewers—how long to wait for the decision.
The decision and what to do about it.

THE FIRST DRAFT

Now you are ready to write the first draft of the paper. It is best to do this quickly. Some authorities advise us to complete the first draft at one sitting, but I have always found this impossible. Getting started is the most difficult part, as a law of inertia seems to apply. The basic principle is to work intensively on the paper over a short period, so that you can be completely immersed in it. One or two hours a week are useless for this, since you have to begin painfully each time; much better to clear a day or two completely. This enables you to build up a momentum where you can become preoccupied with what you are writing. If you do this, you will be surprised and pleased by how much you achieve. When you do stop work, leave your draft at a point in the middle of a section or paragraph where you know exactly what you want to write next. It will be much easier to start writing at the next session than if you had to start thinking afresh about a new section. The first draft can be written as an expansion of the outline, taking a section at a time. People sometimes wonder which section to write first. The books in the bibliography give a variety of opinion on this matter. Most authors are agreed, though, that it is unwise to start at the beginning and write through to the end. The introduction is often best left in outline form until the results and method sections are drafted. The method is often the easiest section to write, and on the principle that getting started is the most difficult thing, many people make life a little easier by beginning there. On the other hand, the whole reason for the paper is the findings, so it also makes sense to begin by examining these carefully and writing the results section first. Do not imagine that this will necessarily be the final set of results. In the course of writing a paper, gaps in the analysis are often revealed and extra analyses may be needed. The process is reiterative!

As you write the first draft, do not worry too much about niceties of style and grammar, just concentrate on getting it down. There will be ample time for revision later.

Method
In the method section you should aim to explain fully, but concisely, the procedures you used that yielded the data. There should be enough detail for a conscientious specialist to repeat your investigation. This would include the nature of the sample, how it was obtained, the context of the data collection, the procedures used, the measures used and the form of statistical analysis. Where measures are fully described elsewhere, a brief summary description should be given together with the reference. Never mention a measure without the reference, however

familiar it may be. If you have included measures of your own devising, give fuller details, including some indication of the measure's psychometric properties (for example, internal consistency, test-retest or inter-rater reliability, validity estimates) and one or two sample items.

Results

The results section should also have a logical order. Methodological checks need to be reported first, for example you may expect certain measures to correlate highly with each other, whereas others should be unassociated. Other checks might include an analysis to determine whether one group within the sample differs systematically from another group (such as where the sample consists of patients from different sites), or you may wish to check that two equivalent groups are well matched on crucial variables.

As a general rule, descriptive statistics precede exploratory data analysis which precedes confirmatory data analysis. If you are discussing the results in a separate section, simply report them here. On the other hand, do not refrain from comment if it helps to organise and structure the section. When reporting significance levels, use two-tailed tests. Don't use a one-tailed test simply because you had a hypothesis which predicted a particular direction. It is really only safe to do so if a result in the other direction would have no meaning. Do not report a p value without the statistic from which it was derived. Give enough information for someone else to check it (for example, an F ratio needs both degrees of freedom). A golden rule is not to report any statistical procedures which you don't understand. This sounds obvious, but the rule is often violated. Ideally you will have analysed your own data. If someone else carried out the analyses, you must know exactly what was done and why. It is much better to report simple procedures clearly and appropriately than complex ones which are muddled or, worse still, nonsensical.

Do not repeat in the text what is already clear from the tables or figures. These should be thought through very carefully. Do not include too much material in any one table or clarity suffers. Often it is better to have two smaller tables than one massive one, unless there is a good reason why the results must be presented together. Always make sure that each table and figure makes sense on its own without the reader having to refer to the text. This means it should have an explanatory title. Make sure you don't call a table a figure or vice versa. Avoid abbreviations if you can, but if you must use them, make sure they are explained on the table (and if used in more than one, on each table) rather than in the text. In graphs, all axes must be clearly labelled. In general, editors prefer tables to figures because they convey more information in a smaller space. Reserve figures for results that need them. In Example 2a, the information in Fig. 7.1 does not need a graphical presentation. It would be better presented as in Table 7.1. Figure 7.2 (in Example 2b) is useful, however, because the crucial point is communicated better visually. Having said all this, don't worry about perfection at this stage, so long as you have a 'working version' of all your tables and figures.

Example 2a

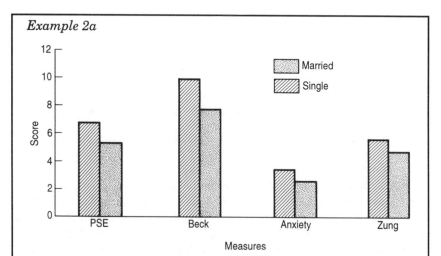

FIG. 7.1.   Comparison between single and married mothers on measures of psychiatric symptoms and psychological distress.

TABLE 7.1
Single (n = 21) and married (n = 172) mothers: Comparison between groups on measures of psychiatric symptomatology and psychological distress

		PSE	Beck	Anxiety	Zung
Single n = 21	mean (SD)	6.76 (7.06)	9.95 (9.72)	3.50 (2.39)	5.67 (4.10)
Married	mean (SD)	5.32 (6.27)	7.81 (7.12)	2.63 (2.48)	4.84 (3.78)
t-value (191 df) Significance		<1 ns	1.25 ns	1.48 ns	<1 ns

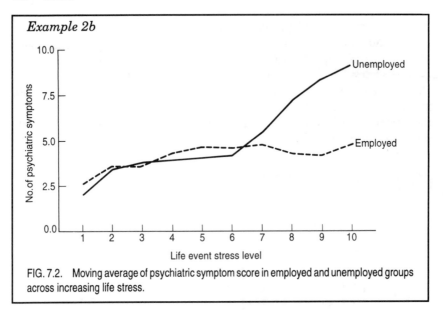

FIG. 7.2. Moving average of psychiatric symptom score in employed and unemployed groups across increasing life stress.

Introduction

The introduction should 'set up' the paper. You are trying to explain as economically as possible why you undertook the investigation, and why you approached it in the way you did. There is no point in writing a 2000- word literature review simply to demonstrate that you have read a lot! One hallmark of a badly written paper is a verbose and muddled introduction. The literature reviewed should be apposite, enabling you to make a series of points. If you find this difficult, imagine you are having a conversation with an interested and intelligent colleague (this may be quite a feat of imagination but try it anyway). You are asked a series of questions, such as 'Why was it important to do this investigation? Have other people examined this in the past? How might your study add to existing knowledge? Why did you choose this design? Did you have any special reasons for using these particular measures?'. Answer the questions in normal conversational English and you have the basis for your first draft. When you do describe someone else's study, be specific about the major details without being verbose. For example, compare the two descriptions of the same study in Example 3. The second is only a few words longer than the first, but it is much more informative. It is essential to be accurate when describing other people's results. Misreported findings have a habit of slipping into future papers by authors who don't bother to check them. Remember the reviewers of your paper may be the authors of the papers you cite, or are likely to be familiar with them. Your notes will be helpful here; but if you are in any doubt, check.

Example 3

First Version In a large scale survey, Kessler and McRae (1982) found a significant relationship between employment status and self-esteem in married women.

Second Version In a questionnaire survey of 532 married women whose husbands were employed, Kessler and McRae (1982) found paid employment was correlated ($p < 0.05$) with self-esteem measured by a short form of Rosenberg's scale.

Discussion

The discussion should not reiterate the results but should do what it says, discuss them. You are trying to explain what your results mean and to relate them to other people's work. Often you are pointing out the implications of the results. You can refer to material from the introduction in the light of your findings, but do not simply repeat it. You are taking it further now you have reported your results. It is appropriate in the discussion to take a sceptical view of your findings. If there are any design flaws (and there will be), this is the place to discuss how they might have affected your results. It is also the place to consider alternative explanations of your findings. If you are not able to think of these, wait until someone else has read and commented on the paper. Try to end the paper on a positive, interesting point. Do not finish it with any variant of the tedious cliché 'more research is needed to investigate this further'. We can take that for granted!

SUBSEQUENT DRAFTS

Your first draft is a major achievement. The good news is that everything gets easier from now on. The bad news is that you are only half-way there. Many inexperienced researchers assume that the first draft only needs tinkering with before it is submitted. Not at all. Many authors go through two or three major revisions before they are satisfied with the paper. Some do more. The first draft is the basis of your paper, not the paper itself. You can do the first revision yourself by reading through carefully, putting yourself in the reader's shoes. Is it clear? Are there any parts which are particularly muddled or clumsy? Do you stay in the same tense or oscillate between past and present? Have you overused a particular word or phrase? Iron out the worst faults and get it typed—now, as always, double-spaced with wide margins. This is the point at which the word-processor comes into its own, since it is so easy to print out new drafts—as many as you want. Typists (including yourself) are neither so tireless nor uncomplaining. Next, give the paper to at least one other person to read and comment on. Encourage them to write all over the draft. Tell them if there is something you particularly want them to do; for example, check that the results make sense, think of alternative explanations for the findings, spot unbuttressed assertions. One of these people could be a specialist who understands the field, but it is also useful for a non-specialist, even a layperson, to read the paper. They will be less tolerant of obscurities and the use of jargon. Remember that although your paper must be useful to the specialists, most of the journal's readers will not be; be considerate of them.

Your 'reader' may come up with a major problem, finding an error in your results or showing your argument is based on a fundamental misunderstanding. Don't be discouraged, however negative the feedback seems, since the value of writing the paper is to sort out these problems and to get it right. Having written the first draft you can more easily spot gaps in the argument or the analysis, and new ideas will occur to you. Again, this is one of the ways your work is improved, so don't shy away from new analyses at this stage, or a major redraft. Your adviser may also mention other research that you have missed but which bears on your paper. Again, it is worth checking this out and including new material, but don't fall prey to procrastination. At this stage you will probably find that the paper is too long and diffuse. You may have to rethink the central point of the paper and omit results that are not essential in order to provide a clear focus.

When you have redrafted the article to a point where you are happy with what it says, turn your attention to how you have said it; go through the paper carefully and correct the style. There are many useful guides to writing style, some are mentioned in the reference section at the end of this chapter. but the golden rule is to write as simply and clearly as you can. Ruthlessly cut out all the waffle, the redundant and circumlocutory phrases; fearlessly replace the passive verb forms with active ones, the clichés with fresh images, the 70-word, eight-clause sentences with two or more smaller ones (see Example 4). As well as trying your best to write in plain English, you must also observe the house-style of the journal. For example, the American Psychological Association publishes a guidebook on style (*The Publication Manual of the American Psychological Association*) which includes everything from whether to use single or double inverted commas to how to avoid sexist use of language.

Example 4: Correcting for style

First draft It is of interest to note that the approach employed by the present author is somewhat similar to that of Jones (1985) in terms of the assessment of individuals' conceptual structure, with the exception of the number of items included, where, in the present paper, ten is considered to be a sufficient number, as will be seen by examination of Table 3.

Second draft I used a ten-item version of Jones' (1985) method to measure conceptual structure (see Table 3).

PREPARING THE MANUSCRIPT FOR SUBMISSION

References, acknowledgements, abstract

You will find the reference list a time-consuming and frustrating job, but so does everyone else and there's no way round it. Write the references on cards or a word-processor so that the odd one can be popped in the right place without having to re-write the lot. The references must be complete and accurate. This sounds easy but isn't and you will have to take trouble over it, Follow the style of the chosen journal obsessionally, down to the last full-stop. Check that every reference you cite is in the reference list and that every reference in the list is cited in the paper.

The acknowledgements should include those who gave substantial help in supporting you, collecting data, advising on statistics, reading and revising the manuscript. On the other hand, do not mention absolutely everyone with whom you had a coffee-time conversation about the research. Always tell someone if you intend to acknowledge their help. The abstract should be a very brief summary of the paper, written with the non-specialist in mind. Try to include the main findings rather than the uninformative 'Results are reported of a comparison of two matched groups of outpatients'. It is better, for example, to say 'A group of depressed outpatients were found to have significantly smaller social networks than a matched group of anxious patients'. The journal will give a word limit for the abstract in the instructions to authors. Keep to it. You will have to draft and re-draft the abstract to whittle away every unnecessary word.

Tables and figures

When preparing the final version of the tables and figures, always double check that every number is correct. An error that creeps in at this stage has every chance of remaining undetected until after publication—an embarrassment so intense it is not worth risking. Eventually, you should have the figures professionally produced by a graphic illustrator, who will produce high-quality glossy prints suitable for reproduction. It is safer to wait until the paper is accepted, and the definitive version of the figures is known, before committing yourself to the expense.

The title page

Now you have to worry about the title of the paper. You have probably been using a working title, but think about it again now. The title should be as concise as possible, but should accurately describe the paper's concerns. Your own and any co-authors' names and affiliations should also appear on the title page, but nowhere else. This enables the editor to send your manuscript for blind review.

The final manuscript

Take loving care over the final manuscript, so that it looks really professional. This means, if you do use a word-processor, learn to use it properly. The life of an editor or an examiner is made miserable by poorly formatted manuscripts littered with misspelt words, produced by misguided authors who have prematurely dispensed with the services of a professional typist. If you cannot find the time or take the trouble to get a really good result yourself, you could use the word-processor up to the penultimate draft, then get a professional to produce the final one. The typing should be perfect, double-spaced (that means everything, including the references), with wide margins. Show in the text where each table and figure belongs (Fig. 7.3). Make a final check that all the references in the text are in the reference list (and vice versa) and that the names and dates are identical in both places. Similarly, make sure that all the tables are referred to in the text and that any table you mention does indeed exist. Read the manuscript for typing errors, checking every word. Use the spell-checking facility on the word processor, but don't rely on it entirely; these don't read for meaning and can pass a word which is quite wrong as long as it does exist (e.g. if you wrote 'experiential' when you meant 'experimental'.) Preferably, persuade someone else to proof-read it too, to pick up the mistakes you missed. The order in which the paper should be compiled is as follows:

1. Title page; includes title and authors' names and addresses. Some journals need index keywords here and a short title which will be used as a heading for subsequent pages (running head).
2. Abstract.
3. Text.
4. Acknowledgements.
5. References.

```
When the sample was split into 'cases' and non-cases',

all the measures showed a significant difference between

the two groups (see Table 1).

                    TABLE ONE ABOUT HERE

The two self-esteem measures most clearly reflected

differences between respondents. It is likely that even

for these measures, there is considerable overlap

between the distributions of scores of cases and

non-cases. The breakdown of means of the two self-esteem

measures across the eight ID levels is presented

graphically in Figure 1.

                    FIGURE ONE ABOUT HERE

There does seem to be a discontinuity in the linear

relationship between ID level and self-esteem, occurring

at ID5.
```

FIG. 7.3. An example of typed manuscript. (Originally on A4 paper; reduced to 60% on reproduction.)

6. Tables (each on a fresh page).
7. Figure legends.
8. Figures.

Before sending the manuscript off, check that all the pages are there, numbered and in the correct order. Send the top copy and two good photocopies, accompanied by a short, formal letter to the editor.

THE EDITORIAL PROCESS

The process of sending papers out for independent review does not only benefit the journal's editor, but gives you useful feedback on your paper and the research itself. The most frustrating thing is when you have no reply, save a postcard acknowledgement, for months on end. How long should you leave it before writing again to enquire about the decision? I think that three months is long enough, because if you have heard nothing by then your paper is probably sitting in the in-tray of one of the reviewers who needs to be reminded about it.

The decision you receive will be one of four—accept, accept subject to amendment, revise and re-submit, or reject. It is unusual to have a paper accepted outright, so please don't expect this. If it is accepted subject to amendment, you have done very well. After a celebratory night out, start the new version, so that the paper can be off your desk and back to the editor as soon as possible.

If you have been advised to revise and resubmit the paper, it will probably be sent to the reviewers again and there is no guarantee that it will be accepted. On the other hand, most revisions that are conscientiously undertaken do get accepted in the end. Don't think you can get away with a superficial readjustment of a few words; you must address the points raised by the reviewers and do everything you can to meet them. Read what they say carefully before deciding whether to attempt the revision or submit the paper as it stands to another journal. If you do revise the paper, an important part of the resubmission is the letter to the editor. Here you should list the points raised by reviewers, explaining how you have altered the paper, or what new analyses are included, corresponding to each point. A reviewer may suggest something with which you honestly disagree. If so, after the list of amendments you have made, explain why you have not made that particular change. Such a letter, if carefully written, can be very helpful to the editor and hence to your paper's chances of acceptance.

Rejection

The 'rejection' is a narcissistic blow and you will almost certainly feel bad about it. Read the reviewers' comments as objectively as possible and ask someone else to read them too.

If the editor advises you that the paper's subject matter is outside the scope of the journal, start to think where else you can resubmit it which would be more appropriate. Also submit it to another journal if the reviewers make a number of points which can be incorporated into the text, thus improving the paper and making it more likely to be accepted the second time. If the editor advises you that the results are unsound, do not submit it to another journal until you have thought how to improve the evidence in the paper.

If you are convinced that the editor's letter and the reviews are of poor quality, superficial, have missed the point or are just plain wrong, put the whole thing aside for a few days before reading them again. If you still feel unfairly treated, you are quite entitled to write to the editor explaining why and asking for the decision to be reconsidered. If you do this, take care that your letter is based on sound argument; avoid a shrill and acrimonious tone. Never telephone, and only write after thinking it over very carefully.

If you have taken care over the research and the earlier drafts of the paper, you should not be disheartened in the face of one rejection. Remember that there are very few academic writers, however distinguished, who have not had a paper rejected. Many good papers were rejected by the first journal to which they were submitted. Some journals are much more difficult to be published in than others, so you can patiently work your way down the hierarchy until you succeed. One important point though—always get the paper reprinted in the style of the journal to which you are submitting. A dog-eared manuscript clearly intended for a different journal will be at a big disadvantage from the start.

COMMON PROBLEMS

You can't get started

I have already said that the most difficult thing is beginning. For some people this is so difficult that they never do, putting off the fateful day for months on end. Procrastination is probably a response to anxiety about whether one is good enough; a fear of falling short of one's ideal, of failing, of being exposed, criticised, judged, vulnerable or lonely. It can sometimes feel as if something in you is actively blocking the work, rebelling against getting on with it. Successful avoidance (which includes a range of displacement behaviours like taking on too much work, getting drunk, suddenly deciding the house needs redecorating) does have a pay-off because one's anxiety level goes down. Alas, this only serves to reinforce the procrastination, which has you ever more firmly in its grip. Eventually, if you have someone else policing a deadline, there is an anguished and undignified last-minute scuffle in which, amazingly, the paper gets written. Unfortunately, for most research papers intended for publication there is no deadline at all; it is entirely your own affair. Procrastination is so deadly to productivity and so painful for the sufferer (and I speak from personal experience) that one wonders why it is so hard to relinquish. Perhaps it is because, as well as reducing anxiety in the short term, it also provides a ready-made attribution, an insurance policy against failure or criticism: 'Well, I know it isn't much good, but I only had two days to write it in'. Thus one can keep unsullied the fantasy of the perfect paper one might have written, given enough time.

The first step is to recognise these processes in oneself. The way out is to get into the habit of writing, doing it regularly. It is often helpful to set up a plan of the week's work, setting realistic goals and building in rewards for when they are achieved. What seems like an enormous task can be tackled by slicing it into small pieces and doing one at a time. Simply to put an end to the avoidance is useful. Set the time aside, find the right conditions and sit there. If you really can't get on with the paper itself, write something else—rough notes, ideas, notes on other people's papers—anything. The important thing is to be in the habit of setting pen to paper (or fingers to keyboard), to get practice at forming sentences, working with words. Even if you sit for the whole of your designated session staring at the wall, you are breaking the pattern of avoidance, starting to face the anxiety that freezes you. Since procrastination depends on self-deception, the next session will not be so difficult.

Isolation

The other major problem you are likely to face is being a lone researcher, trying single-handed to carry your project to completion. Do not struggle on alone if you are getting nowhere. Find someone else with whom you can share your work, on the basis that you give them the same kind of research support. This kind of reciprocal help can include a regular meeting to talk about research issues, how the writing progresses, to set deadlines. You can read and criticise each other's papers and help with boring jobs like checking the accuracy of references and proof-reading. You then also have someone with whom you can discuss the editor's letter, someone who will congratulate or commiserate as needed.

You will find more detailed guidance about the technical issues in writing a paper by reading the books in the reference section. I hope this chapter is a springboard to them and to achieving what is, in the end, a profoundly satisfying experience; seeing your own research paper published.

REFERENCES

Barzun, J. & Graff, H.F. (1977). *The Modern Researcher*. New York: Harcourt Brace Jovanovich. [Chapters 11, 12 and 13].

Bausell, R.B. (1986). Evaluating and communicating the results. In *A Practical Guide to Conducting Empirical Research*. New York: Harper and Row. [Chapter 17].

Buzan, J. (1974). *Use Your Head*. London: BBC Books

Day, R.A. (1979). *How to Write and Publish a Scientific Paper*. Philadelphia: ISI Press.

Fowler, H.W. (1978). *A Dictionary of Modern English Usage*, 2nd edn. Oxford University Press.

Gowers, E. (1986). *The Complete Plain Words*. 3rd edn. London: HMSO. [Also (1987) Harmondsworth: Penguin.]

O'Connor, M. & Woodford, F.P. (1978). *Writing Scientific Papers in English*. Tunbridge Wells: Pitman Medical Publishing.

CHAPTER EIGHT

Writing a grant application

Neil Brooks *Director, Case Management
Services, Northampton*

BACKGROUND

Obtaining research grants has never been easy. With the continuing heavy decline in Government funding for biomedical research, the situation concerning Government monies (the British Medical Research Council, Economic and Social Research Council, Science and Engineering Research Council, DOH, etc.) has become ever more difficult. Nevertheless, although the picture is gloomy for Government funded research, it is important to realise that research *is* being funded. For example, Haggard (1993) points out that in 1991-92, the Medical Research Council (MRC) invested £20.42m in research on the nervous system, £16.67m in mental health research, £8.5m in cognitive science, and £3.8m in health services research. Of course, some of this money went to fund units rather than single grants, but it is still a substantial investment. The charitable scene is particularly active in funding research, and a compilation of British Charities Funding Neuroscience Research (1986), identified 24 charities disbursing amounts from £300 to £20,000, and some charities (e.g. the Wellcome Trust) are major rivals to Government sources of research funding.

Whatever the amount and range of sources of research money available, the fundamental exercise is one of competition. Inevitably, any researcher seeking limited funds is competing with others equally keen to obtain those same funds. While it is rare that one can identify a direct competitor ('direct' in the sense that they are seeking similar money for an identical project), there are often a number of projects in a similar area, and one of the major deciding factors will then be the quality of the research application. The better the application the more likely it is to get funded. In defining what is meant by 'better' here, Haggard (1993) gives the following five determinants of whether or not a grant will be funded by any agency:-

- The importance of the question to the particular agency
- The amenability of the problem to progress
- The scientific quality of the case presented
- The clarity of the application
- The resources available

Although the 'bottom line' is one of quality of research application, any experienced obtainer of research monies will admit that the process of research application is at least partly a gamble, with an element of luck. The prudent applicant is the one who reduces the odds in his/her favour, and this can be achieved by a variety of means. This chapter is essentially about ways of reducing those odds. There are some very simple strategies that are worth describing at the outset, and then the chapter will discuss a series of more detailed procedures to assist in an application.

Whatever the source of the research money, an application involves a series of discrete processes. Firstly, the Officers of the funding body will check that the grant application matches the formal requirements and funding policies of that body (length of application, total amount of money requested, duration of grant, etc.). Secondly, the application will usually go to external referees who will concern themselves with the quality of the science, the adequacy of the case made for the amount of money requested, and the practicalities of the application (is it possible to complete the research in the time proposed, etc.). The referees will then report back to the awarding body with a recommendation for funding or not, and their recommendation will then often be considered in the light of the views of internal committee-based referees. For bodies such as the MRC, the names of committee members (the internal referees) are readily available, and it may be wise, at least in part, to tailor the application to the specific internal referees who may read it. Some bodies add an extra stage at which requests for clarification made by referees can be fed back to applicants for their comments prior to a final decision about funding. Finally, some bodies, in the event of an unsuccessful application, will give feedback of varying degrees of length and detail. An applicant should *never* ask referees personally for feedback, and should never lobby potential referees (see Bruce, 1991 for a further discussion here).

Any research application must address a range of issues. For the major grant-awarding bodies (in the UK, the Medical Research Council, Department of Health, Scottish Home & Health Department, Mental Health Foundation, Wellcome Trust, etc.) these may be addressed by means of the detailed application form with clear guidelines for submitting the proposal. The guidelines are crucial, and the applicant who fails to conform to them will quite simply not get past the first round. The exact information sought by the different fund-awarding bodies varies, but a number of headings appear so consistently on the application forms that they are worth using to structure much of the rest of the chapter. Even if the applicant is applying to a body that does not have clearly specified application procedures, the headings about to be described are worth using in order to impose maximum structure and clarity on the application.

THE RESEARCH APPLICATION—HOW TO FILL IT IN

Introduction

Obviously the purpose of an application is to obtain research funding, but bearing in mind that the applicant is competing with others for limited resources, it is worth considering the different justifications which need to be made. Any applicant must justify tackling a particular problem, in a particular department, using a particular method, with a particular group of patients/subjects in a particular amount of time. Applicants will have to indicate why they themselves and those whom they hire are so crucial to the project, and must justify why the research will cost the amount of money which is being requested.

Before even beginning to submit an application, applicants must ensure that the appropriate preliminary work has been carried out. A literature review should have been done, and the applicant should show that he/she knows enough about the population to be studied to avoid elementary blunders. This point is a particularly important one where experimentalists are attempting to study a clinical population. Lack of experience with that population can result in the submission of an inappropriate project simply because of failure to appreciate the constraints imposed by the condition (e.g. examining higher visual processing in Alzheimer's disease without appreciating the difficulty of finding well diagnosed cases). At this early stage it is well worth discussing ideas and tentative proposals with as many colleagues as possible, particularly those who have had successes in obtaining grants.

It can be particularly helpful to have a look at previously successful grants (Haggard, 1993). This is also the stage at which the clinician seeks the views of the theoretician and vice versa, and detailed and honest discussion here can prevent future disasters.

As a result of these discussions it may become obvious that the first stage of the research is to carry out a small pilot study to identify problems and propose solutions. Pilot studies are seldom wasted, and many research referees expect to see evidence that methods and procedures have indeed been piloted (Bruce, 1991).

Often during this early stage the researcher is not sure whether the research topic fits within the ambit of a particular grant-awarding body. In addition, there may be problems in understanding exactly what is required in the application, and this is the stage at which to seek advice from the officers of the body awarding funds. A telephone call here may save hours of needless work in the future. The call may identify that the resources of the grant-awarding body are too small for the project. It may indicate that the research area being proposed is one that the body does not wish to support, or alternatively, that it is one that has a high priority. It may result in helpful advice about 'marketing' a particular application. If in doubt, telephone.

Before considering detailed headings for the application, there are a number of other points to bear in mind in attempting to make the strongest application. Referees will need to know details about the applicants themselves, the Institution from which they are working, and the justification for the timing of the application.

It goes without saying that applicants must state who they are and what their relevant qualifications are. However, applicants should go beyond this. They should be able to communicate to the referees a sense of why it is that the applicants and only those applicants are so uniquely well qualified to obtain the research award. Applicants should not hesitate to spell out details of particular qualifications or particular past or current experience that bear on the current application. In addition, they should identify any research collaborators. Many referees and many sources of research funding are keen to develop collaborative interdisciplinary research. Indeed, research that marries the skills of a theoretician and clinician can be particularly valuable, and conversely, failure of a theoretician to secure guaranteed access to a well characterised and diagnosed clinical population can simply prevent research being carried out. Similarly, failure to secure access to appropriate computer hardware and software, or to data processing expertise can prevent research succeeding. Access to high-quality enthusiastic help in statistics and data processing can tip the balance in favour of funding an application. The wise applicant chooses his/her collaborators with care. Furthermore, as advised by Haggard (1993), the young applicant who has only recently completed a PhD may find it very beneficial to submit an application with a more senior colleague who has an established research track record. This not only strengthens the case as far as the awarding body is concerned, but also gives the young researcher a model of good practice in budgeting and managing a project.

Not only must applicants state who they are and with whom they are co-operating, but they will also need to spell out the nature of their institution. The referees will want to know where the research is to be based (university, clinical service department, etc.), and will need to be assured that the base is an ideal one for the proposed research. Relevant links with other institutions can with benefit be spelt out here, and letters of support from other institutions can always be included in an appendix. As a practical point, the awarding body will need to be assured that the host institution will administer financial aspects of the research (salaries, purchasing, etc.), and it is increasingly the case that institutions are charging for such a service. Does the host institution charge, and if so, will the grant-awarding body meet such a charge?

There is a further point to bear in mind here. With performance indicators assuming ever greater importance in the public sector, central funding to universities is based at least in part on the value of Research Council and similar peer-review funded awards obtained by the researchers within the university. Quite obviously some institutions and departments have suffered as a result of this, but others have benefited considerably. The scope for negotiation within universities is obvious. The research worker who brings in a substantial grant is directly benefiting his/her university, and may reasonably expect the university to benefit the researcher in turn. It is no longer enough for university finance officers to tell enthusiastic researchers that equipment purchase or laboratory refurbishing or hiring of extra staff is simply not possible. The researcher who has obtained a major grant, would be wise to delay formal acceptance of that grant until mutually beneficial bargains have been struck with the finance officer to purchase additional resources to allow the efficient running of a grant in addition to all the other duties facing the successful grant applicant. Precisely the same argument holds for clinician researchers in Health Service facilities, although here the situation is made very difficult to predict with the advent of Hospital Trusts. Trusts may or may not see research as a central part of their mission. However, if the Trust does want research to happen (remembering that the marketing advantages of good, relevant clinical audit and research are considerable), then the successful Trust-based applicant for research monies should expect to benefit in terms of time being freed up, access to travel monies etc.

Time is an important element of research, and two aspects of timing are particularly important. The first is the total amount of time for which the grant will be held, and the second is the amount of time that the applicant him/herself will be able to devote specifically to the project. Obviously the longer the project, the more expensive, so referees are particularly careful to scrutinise the justification for the length of time involved. If applicants are requesting funding for 3 years, but have not made a good case for this period, then referees are likely to advise that the research simply not be funded, or that funding be awarded for a 2- rather than 3-year period. As Bruce (1991) noted, don't over or under budget either in terms of time or resources.

Referees will want to be assured about the time that an applicant will be able to devote specifically to the actual research, or to supervision of researchers employed on the award. Experienced referees are well aware that active researchers manage to find 25 hours in every 24, but if it is obvious that the nature of the applicant's other duties mean that he/she simply cannot spend the proposed amount of time on the grant, then this will count against them in deciding on an award.

A thorny problem in deciding on the length of the award is the amount of time that should be devoted specifically and exclusively to data analysis and writing up the results. Grant awarding bodies differ in the extent to which they see these activities as crucial parts of the research, or as addenda which can be dealt with after funding has stopped. A careful reading of the guidelines for submission, and if necessary a telephone call to Officers of the body awarding the money can be invaluable here.

Headings for the application

Abstract.   Many bodies demand a simple abstract of the research, and this is usually the first thing that referees read. It gives the applicant an early opportunity to communicate clear thinking and excitement at pursuing an interesting project. The abstract should be brief, it should not over-run the number of words allowed in the guidelines for submission. It should be clear and informative, and should give a flavour of what is intended and why. It should communicate clearly and accurately to non-psychologists and non specialist psychologists who may well be part of the refereeing process. An example of an appropriate abstract might be:

> Although anecdotal evidence that ... exists, there is little empirical support for this. Our research proposes to

investigate ... by means of ...in ... patients. Our results should provide evidence that ...

Background and purpose of research.   This substantial section is where the applicant addresses the main conceptual and clinical issues, and communicates the sense of excitement and commitment which will excite referees. It incorporates the relevant literature review, and allows applicants to make the case that there is a crucial gap in knowledge that is important enough to be filled, and that only the applicant with his/her techniques and ideas can fill it. The background should be written with the knowledge that the application may be read by a variety of referees. Some will be at least as knowledgeable as the applicant, and will be able to detect major omissions, padding, incorrect citing of references, and inappropriate conclusions. Others may not be specialists in the applicant's area, but will expect to read a clear and understandable proposal. Bearing this in mind, the background should be as brief as possible, consistent with the guidelines for applicants, and with the need to communicate effectively. There is often a temptation to stray into areas that are not relevant, but which signal some aspects of the applicant's knowledge. This can only detract from the main central case.

This section of the application is one which referees often find very difficult to read. Applicants in their enthusiasm may present a closely argued and densely written case which is difficult for referees to follow, particularly if they are not specialists in the specific area of research. Applicants should try to help referees as much as possible by using a clear and logical structure to this section, with headings and subheadings, and a clear flow of ideas. At the end of the section, the applicant should be able to state a series of simple aims or questions or hypotheses, and ideally the background should have been so well structured that the knowledgeable referee should almost be able to complete the end of this section him/ herself.

Plan of investigation.   In this section, the applicant can spell out in detail the precise methods and procedures to be used, and the population of subjects or cases under investigation. Referees will expect the applicant to specify exactly the procedures that are to be used, and to justify why these rather than other related and apparently equally appropriate procedures are to be used. Applicants should try to be honest in identifying procedures that are up and running, and those that are being developed or have yet to be developed. If development work is required, then estimates of the likely timescale of this development should be included. Inevitably and quite appropriately, the methods will often incorporate novel procedures which have not been used before, or not with the specific population to be studied. The fact that procedures are novel may be very positive, but it also means that problems such as reliability and validity of procedures become important. A procedure that is appropriate for a 4-year-old child may not be appropriate for a mentally handicapped adult, etc. If very novel procedures are to be used, applicants must consider how reliable they are likely to be in the new population, and how accurately they are likely to measure the underlying processes being addressed in the application. When such novel procedures are being used, it is always worth including some conventional laboratory or clinical procedures which are known to work, and which would then act as 'marker variables' for the new procedures.

Precise details of the population under study should be given. Referees need to know how many subjects are to be studied, and will often expect a justification for the number chosen. Applicants, before writing this section, should ask themselves exactly how they arrived at the number of cases they proposed to study. Was it simply a convenient figure; a figure based on the size of the population; a figure based on statistical theory, etc? Not only should numbers be given, but the defining features of the population must be described. Ages, volunteer status, diagnostic categories and criteria, chronicity, etc., are all important. Applicants should also spell out how often and over what duration the subjects will be seen, and by whom. For example, is the researcher him/herself going to carry out the studies, or will it be wholly or partly in the hands of a research assistant? If the latter, is the assistant already competent, or will specific training be given? Following such training, what kind of ongoing supervision will be given, at what schedule, and for how long?

Finally, in clinical studies, the researcher often identifies clinical problems that have been missed in the routine clinical follow-up of patients. This faces the applicants with ethical and practical questions, and the wise applicant will have a policy for dealing with hitherto undetected clinical problems. If a decision is made to try to deal with the problems by the applicants themselves, then they must consider the extent to which this is ethically appropriate (is the applicant qualified, etc?); practically appropriate (are there others able and willing and competent to undertake clinical management?); and conceptually appropriate (will intervention by the researchers compromise the research design?). As a general rule, it is unwise for the researchers themselves to take on the management of clinical problems, and at the outset they should open lines of communication with clinical colleagues to enable patients to receive appropriate management wherever necessary.

Data analysis.   Whenever a research design involves very straight-forward data analysis, this section can be dealt with very briefly. If, however, the researcher is going to generate a substantial data base involving more than simple univariate analyses, applicants may have to spell out in detail how they propose to set up and manage the data base. If statistical help is going to be needed, applicants have to show that this is available, and that it is either free of charge, or can be paid for out of the research grant. If the results are to be analysed by means of a mainframe computer (increasingly rare now), applicants should demonstrate that they have ready access to the machine, and will have to budget appropriately for the cost of computing time. Some grant-giving bodies are reluctant to pay for computing costs, and applicants should ascertain the policy of the body before preparing the computing budget. As a matter of policy it is wise to plan a data analytic strategy that rests on micro computers rather than large centrally located machines. Such machines are likely to become the province of particular groups of scientists (physicists etc.) and will become increasingly unavailable to the average researcher. Data analysis should routinely be done via a micro-based statistics and data management package of which many are available. Loss of data held on hard disks is always a possibility, and it is sensible to budget for a backup system, perhaps a tape drive or removable hard disk. Neither are expensive, and their request shows that the researcher is thinking seriously about the practicalities of running a research project.

Frequently, research applicants make a common error in this section of the application. The error is to deal very sweepingly with data analysis, saying rather grandly that 'data will analysed by multivariate means'. Such a reference to multivariate analysis is unrevealing, and may raise suspicions in the minds of the referee that applicants have not in fact thought at all clearly about how they propose to handle the mass of data collected. It is rarely the case that multivariate analysis is the initial approach of choice, although with large data bases it will inevitably be one of the appropriate approaches to be employed.

Ethical and legal considerations.   Before submitting any grant application, the applicant should be aware of the basic ethical principles involved in conducting any research,whether with humans or other animals. A particularly useful statement of these principles vis a vis humans has been prepared by the British Psychological Society (BPS), and is published in the BPS journal *The Psychologist* (BPS, 1993). Any study carried out from a university or clinical base and involving patients will need to go through some form of ethical vetting. Clinically based submissions will need to have been cleared by the relevant hospital or unit Ethical Committee, and university and similar applications by the relevant departmental ethical committee. Such processes can take time, and ideally, ethical permission should be obtained in the very preliminary stages of the research application.

Although experiments involving volunteer adults do not usually pose serious ethical problems, such problems do arise as soon as the researcher studies groups who cannot readily give informed consent (children, handicapped, confused elderly, etc.). In fact, the BPS clearly advises that even with children 'real consent' (i.e. based on a clear understanding of what is involved) should be obtained. In addition, the consent of those *in loco parentis* should be obtained. If it is not possible for consent to be obtained from parents or teachers, it is particularly important for the researcher to have the approval of an Ethical Committee before proceeding with the research. Failure to do this would certainly be considered as serious professional misconduct. More subtle but no less real ethical problems arise when the researcher uses his/her students, clients or employees in research. Such people are at a real power disadvantage in dealing with the researcher, and may find it difficult to say 'No'. The BPS advise that the researcher must not allow the relationship he/she has with potential research subjects to pressurise them to participate in the research. In addition, research subjects (particularly children) must know that they can withdraw from the research at any time, and they should be confident that any data collected will be treated with complete confidentiality. They should be assured that any published reports of the research will not allow any individual subject to be identified. A further ethical problem is involved in withholding information from subjects. There may be very good conceptual reasons for doing this but if the participants are likely to show unease once debriefed then such withholding is probably ethically unjustifiable (BPS, 1993).

As soon as a computer data base is set up, the researcher comes within the ambit of data protection legislation, designed to protect personal data held in information repositories. Clinical data collected for research purposes may come within the restrictions imposed by the Act, and may demand two separate registrations (one from within the University, and one from within the Health Service). Institutions such as hospitals and universities will almost certainly have a Data Protection Officer from whom advice can be sought, and if applicants have any doubts about the restrictions and obligations placed upon them by the Act, they should seek advice early in the research application. A formal statement of how applicants will deal with their obligations under the Act can only enhance an application.

Financial aspects.   The application is designed to obtain money, and the money will be used mainly for hiring staff and purchasing equipment. Some bodies will only fund salaries; others only equipment. Some may have special schemes for purchasing a specific piece of equipment for a specific research project. Applicants should ascertain the policy of the body on funding. Both staff and equipment need to be justified in detail to show that without the exact staff and exact equipment proposed, the research could not be carried out. Applicants have to make a case for the type of staff they wish to employ (postgraduate or postdoctoral researchers, etc.), and also the level within the particular salary scale. Applicants frequently try to save money by quoting a starting salary for research staff which is at the bottom of a scale. As soon as they interview staff they find that the ones they want to hire will have to be paid some increments up the scale, but the money is not available. A case for extra funding has to be made, and this takes time and may not always be successful. A realistic appraisal of the needs of the research (in terms of level of staff, etc.) at the outset can prevent problems of this type later.

Obviously, applicants should aim to pare costs down as much as possible, but to do so without making the research impossible to carry out. For example, if medically qualified staff are to be hired, this will need an extra justification, as such staff are more expensive than nonclinical. In situations in which two or three staff are to be hired, it may be worth phasing their hiring over a period rather than hiring all at once. Often there is not enough work for all staff members at the beginning, and the volume of work increases steadily as the research gets underway. In this situation, phased hiring of staff may be advantageous scientifically as well as financially prudent. Wherever it is possible to save money, applicants should do so, but without jeopardising the scientific quality of the research.

Similarly with equipment, the aim is to cut costs as much as possible, while still allowing the research to take place. Equipment must be described and justified, and the case made to say why a specific piece of equipment is necessary rather than a cheaper alternative. In the UK there is a continuing decline in government funding for buildings and equipment. This results in a temptation for applicants to use a research grant as an opportunity to re-equip a laboratory, or to buy top quality equipment when a simpler and cheaper version would do perfectly well. Referees invariably scrutinise equipment requests very carefully, and often suggest pruning in this area to allow applicants to buy equipment that is sufficient for the research, but no more than that.

WHEN AN APPLICATION FAILS

Inevitably, many applicants will fail to obtain research funding, and often there is a very simple reason for this. The first reason is that the research was not good enough. The second is that although the research is fully up to standard, there was not enough money available. The third is that the research topic did not fall within the ambit of the grant-awarding body, and the fourth is that the research, while good enough, cheap enough, and appropriate to the awarding body, was presented in such a way that it failed to communicate adequately.

While these may be concrete reasons for failure to receive a grant, rejected applicants may consider themselves hard done by, and console themselves with a variety of common defences. Two are particularly frequent. The first is that the referees simply did not take the trouble to read the research carefully enough. Obviously there are occasions when the referees have been incompetent; but usually referees take their job seriously, and referee applications with care. The second common defence is to say that referees had a personal bias against the applicant or his/her particular area of research. Only the foolish would deny that this never happens, but the system regarding the larger grant-awarding bodies builds in a range of checks and balances. For example, in the UK the Medical Research Council uses both internal and external referees. The external referees are drawn from a very large panel, while the internal referees comprise members of the relevant Grants Committee, and membership of such Committees is public information which applicants should obtain. In this situation of internal and external refereeing, personal or professional bias soon becomes obvious, and the biased referee is unlikely to be asked for an opinion in the future.

If an application has been submitted and rejected, it is obviously disappointing for the applicant, but the situation can be helped by means of feedback. Differing grant-awarding bodies have very different policies about feedback, ranging from absolutely no information at all other than a statement of failure, to detailed summaries of referee's comments, or indeed copies of the comments themselves. There is a natural tendency for rejected applicants to argue against such comments, or to use them as a basis for a dialogue of the 'he said I did—I say I did not' variety, but this is likely to be counterproductive. If at all possible, applicants should read and listen to critical comments dispassionately and positively, and try to use such comments as a basis for a strategy for submission of a considerably strengthened application elsewhere.

SOURCES OF FUNDING

Major grant-awarding bodies are well known. These include the British Research Councils (MRC, ESRC), the American Institutes (e.g. Health. Mental Health, etc.) various Government Departments or Government sponsored organisations (DoH, SHHD), and charities and the like. The first two sources of money have clearly specified procedures, detailed application forms, Officers who are informed and helpful, and an understanding of the problems in setting up and running a research study. The charities range enormously from medical charities, such as the Wellcome Trust, which functions in a manner very similar to the Medical Research Council, to those that may be disbursing small amounts of money on an irregular basis. It is impossible to give a detailed list of grant-awarding bodies in a chapter like this (see Appendix 1 for a range of possible sources of funding) but a very useful directory has been compiled by Villemur (1983), and a more recent up-to-date list of UK charities funding specifically neuroscience research has been published (British Charities Funding Neuroscience Research, 1986). These are two particularly valuable sources of information. A further very helpful publication is by Burcham and Rutherfurd (1985) which discusses successful grant-obtaining strategies, and gives examples of successful applications. This is highly recommended.

Despite problems with shrinking funds for research, it is important to be aware that psychological research is still being carried out, and successful applicants are being awarded substantial sums of money. A brief letter in the *Bulletin of the British Psychological Society* asking researchers to supply details of research monies held resulted in replies from six researchers giving details about projects attracting support ranging from £2000 to £75,000. The sources of funding included the conventional Research Councils, the Wellcome Trust, the Mental Health Foundation, the Leverhume Trust, DHSS, SHHD, the Parkinson's Disease Society, NATO, and Sainsburys. For the right projects directed to the right body, money is still available.

REFERENCES

British Charities Funding Neuroscience Research (1986). *Trends in The Neurosciences, 9*, viii-ix.
British Psychological Society. Ethical principles for conducting research with human participants. *The Psychologist, January 1993*, 33-35.
Bruce, V. Applying for research grants. *The Psychologist, October 1991*, 439-441.

Burcham, W.E. & Rutherford, R.J.D. (1985). *Writing Applications for Research Grants*. Educational Development Advisory Committee Occasional Publication. No. 3. University of Birmingham. [For further information contact Dr Rutherford at Advisory Service on Teaching Methods. University of Birmingham, Birmingham B15 2TR.]

Haggard, M.P. Multidisciplinary research. *The Psychologist, May 1993*, 221-223.

Viilemur, A. (ed.) (1983). *Directory of Grant-Making Trusts*. Tonbridge. Kent: Charities Aid Foundation.

APPENDIX:
SOME SOURCES OF RESEARCH FUNDING

Alzheimer's Disease Society,
Third Floor, Bank Buildings,
Fulham Broadway,
London SW6 1EP, Tel: 0181 381 3177

Association for Spina Bifida and Hydrocephalus,
22 Woburn Place,
London WC1 0EP, Tel: 0171 388 1382

Association to Combat Huntington's Chorea,
34a Station Road,
Hinckley,
Leicestershire LE10 1AP, Tel: 01455 615558

Back Pain Association,
31-33 Park Road,
Teddington,
Middlesex TW11 0AB, Tel: 0181 977 5474/5

British Diabetic Association,
10 Queen Anne Street,
London W1M 0BD, Tel: 0171 323 1531

British Foundation for Age Research,
49 Queen Victoria Street,
London EC4N 4SA, Tel: 0181 236 4365
British Heart Foundation,
14 Fitzhardinge St.,
London WC1H 4DH, Tel 0171 935 0185

British Migraine Association.
178A High Street,
Byfleet,
Weybridge,
Surrey KT14 7ED, Tel: 01932 352468

Cancer Research Campaign,
2 Carlton House Terrace,
London SW1 5AR, Tel: 0171 930 8972

Carnegie Trust (For the Universities of Scotland),
Merchant's Hall,
22, Hanover St.,
Edinburgh EH2

The Chest Heart and Stroke Association,
Tavistock House North,
Tavistock Square,
London WC1E 9JE, Tel: 0171 387 3012

Children Nationwide Medical Research Fund,
Nicholas House, 181 Union Street,
London SE1 0LN, Tel: 0181 928 2425

Department of Health and Social Security,
Alexander Fleming House,
Elephant & Castle,
London, Tel: 0171 407 5522

Education and Social Research Council,
1 Temple Avenue,
London EC4 0BD, Tel: 0181 353 5252

The Epilepsy Association of Scotland.
48 Govan Road,
Glasgow G51 1JL, Tel: 0141 427 4911

Foundation for the Study of Infant Deaths
5th Floor, 4 Grosvenor Place,
London SW1X 7HD, Tel: 0171 235 1721

Iris Fund for the Prevention of Blindness,
York House (ground floor),
199 Westminster Bridge Road,
London SE1 7UT. Tel: 0171 928 7743

Leverhulme Trust,
15-19, New Fetter Lane,
London EC4B 1NR, Tel: 0171 822 6938

Medical Research Council,
20 Park Crescent,
London WIN 4AL, Tel: 0171 636 5422

The Mental Health Foundation,
8 Hallam Street,
London W1N 6DH, Tel: 0171 580 0145

The Migraine Trust,
45 Great Ormond Street,
London WC1N 3HD, Tel: 0171 278 2676

Multiple Sclerosis Society of Great Britain and Northern Ireland,
25 Effie Road,
Fulham, London SW6 lEE, Tel: 0171 381 4022

The Muscular Dystrophy Group of Great Britain and Northern
Ireland,
Nattrass House,
35 Macaulay Road,
London SW4 0QP, Tel: 0181 720 8055

National Fund for Research into Crippling Diseases,
Vincent House, North Parade,
Horsham,
West Sussex RH12 2DA, Tel: 01403 64101

National Schizophrenia Fellowship,
78 Victoria Road,
Surbiton,
Surrey KT6 4NS, Tel: 0181 390 3651

Parkinson's Disease Society of the United Kingdom,
36 Portland Place,
London WIN 3DG, Tel: 0171 323 1174

Royal National Institute of the Blind,
224 Great Portland Street,
London W1N 6AA, Tel: 0171 388 1266

Schizophrenia Association of Great Britain,
International Schizophrenia Centre,
Bryn Hyfryd,
The Crescent, Bangor,
Gwynedd, Wales, Tel: 01248 354048

Science and Engineering Research Council,
Polaris House,
North Star Avenue,
Swindon, SN2 1ET, Tel 01793 411000

Scottish Home and Health Department,
Chief Scientist Office,
St. Andrew's House,
Edinburgh EH1 3DE, Tel: 0131 556 8501

Spastics Society,
12 Park Crescent,
London W1N 4EQ, Tel: 0171 636 5020

The Wellcome Trust,
1 Park Square West,
London NW1 4LJ, Tel: 0171 486 4902

PART TWO
Methods

CHAPTER NINE

Experimental abnormal psychology

Fraser N. Watts *Faculty of Divinity,*
University of Cambridge

Experimental abnormal psychology is concerned with the investigation of the psychological dysfunctions of patients with mental health problems. Many such patients show impairment of a wide range of psychological functions, so it is relatively easy to select a psychological task and to demonstrate that a clinical group performs less well at it than a control group. This is especially true of people suffering from schizophrenia (Neale & Oltmanns, 1980) or depression (Watts, 1988) as these have a broad impact on psychological functioning. At this level, experimental psychology is easy, indeed too easy, to do.

The challenge is to carry out an experiment that does more than add to the catalogue of psychological dysfunctions shown in a particular group of patients. To meet this challenge, you need a good reason for choosing to study a particular dysfunction. The key difference between worthwhile and trivial studies in experimental abnormal psychology lies in the rationale for the experiment. No amount of technical competence in the execution of the experiment makes up for not having a good reason for doing it.

There can be various reasons for choosing to study a particular dysfunction. This chapter will be organised around three such reasons.

First, you may select a particular dysfunction for study because it is a prominent symptom of the condition that you wish to treat. The reason for investigating it lies in the hope that understanding it better will enable you to treat it. A variant of this strategy is to select for investigation a dysfunction that is a close analogue of the symptom of therapeutic interest, but this raises difficult issues about the choice of the right analogue.

A second possible reason for studying a particular dysfunction is more theoretical. To help in reaching a theoretical formulation of a particular condition, you may want to know what are the most striking impairments of the patients concerned. Identifying specific tasks which are affected particularly severely may guide you towards a theory of the disorder concerned. A key technical issue here as we shall see, is demonstrating clearly that patients are significantly more impaired on the task of interest than on a related control task.

Thirdly, a researcher may focus on a particular dysfunction because he or she has a hypothesis that it plays an important part in the aetiology of the clinical condition in which it is found, or that it influences the risk of relapse after symptomatic improvement. Such 'vulnerability' factors are important both theoretically and practically. They make an important contribution to understanding the nature of the disorder; they also indicate where preventive clinical work should be targeted.

These three rationales for studying particular dysfunctions will be considered in turn. Space does not permit a more general discussion of the design of psychological experiments, though these are obviously relevant to abnormal psychology. Kerlinger (1973) may be useful on general experimental design and Barber (1979) on common pitfalls. Kihlstrom and McGlynn (1991) have provided a comparable discussion of the application of experimental methods to the investigation of clinical disorders.

RESEARCH ON CLINICALLY IMPORTANT DYSFUNCTIONS

If a dysfunction is selected for study because of its clinical importance, in the hope that better understanding will have implications for treatment, two alternative strategies are available. One is to do experimental research on the target dysfunction itself; the other is to select for initial investigation a close analogue of the target dysfunction. For example, if learned helplessness (Garber & Seligman, 1980) is a close analogue of depression, studying learned helplessness in detail may have important implications for clinical work with depressed people.

Analogues can be classified on various dimensions. Firstly there is the range of subjects in whom the analogue is found. Some analogues are laboratory phenomena found only in the group of patients concerned, not in the normal population. An intermediate situation is where the analogue phenomenon is found in a sub-group of non-patients with personality characteristics somewhat similar to those of the patients concerned. For example, people with obsessional personalities may provide phenomena which are a useful analogue of symptoms found in obsessional patients. Secondly, there is the dimension of the closeness of the analogue phenomenon to the clinical phenomenon. For example, intrusive, repetitive, adhesive, upsetting thoughts in non-patients may be considered a close analogue of obsessional ruminations, and have 'face validity' as such. Lack of confidence in performance on a reality monitoring task (in which subjects have to distinguish events that have been externally supplied from those that have been internally generated) is a less obvious but nevertheless interesting, analogue of the checking problems of obsessionals (Sher, Frost & Otto, 1983). A third distinction between analogues concerns whether they occur naturally, or whether, like learned helplessness, they are experimentally created.

The reasons for choosing to study experimental research on analogues of clinical phenomena rather than on the phenomena themselves are not difficult to discern. Firstly, laboratory analogues are more tractable. More reliable measures can be obtained, background conditions can be manipulated more readily, and so on, Secondly, by choosing the kind of measure that has been studied in general experimental psychology, a large body of knowledge and theory relating to those measures becomes immediately applicable. The application of experimental psychology to the study of the psychological functioning of clinical groups is thus facilitated.

However, there are also reasons to be cautious about this strategy of studying 'analogue' tasks (i.e. tasks that are interesting because they appear to be an analogue of clinical phenomena). In experimental research, minor changes to a task can make a decisive difference to whether or not a particular phenomenon is demonstrable. If the phenomenon does not generalise from one laboratory paradigm to another slightly different one, the chances of it generalising from the laboratory to the outside world are not good. Further, there are many clinical phenomena that are known to be powerfully affected by the social context. For example, compulsive checking is generally much worse when patients are on their own. For similar reasons, the artificial context of the laboratory will often be unlikely to produce a good analogue of some clinical phenomena. Similarly, some clinical phenomena, such as responses to threat, may only be manifest in the context of really significant threats that cannot be manufactured in the laboratory.

These concerns certainly do not provide grounds for the condemnation of all analogue research in experimental abnormal psychology. The situation is parallel to that which obtains for evaluations of treatments with 'analogue' populations. Borkovec and Rachman (1979) have argued that the generalisation of results from treatment research with 'analogue' subjects depends less on whether they have the administrative status of patients than on the nature and intensity of the problems they present. Similarly, a particular analogue dysfunction can be considered as a candidate for research on its merits. Some will repay study, others will not.

The issues can be illustrated in connections with Hemsley's (1977) instructive review of the possible relationships between the symptomatology of schizophrenics and types of responses to information overload (Table 9.1). The question is how close are the analogies between the two columns of this table? How similar, for example, are the phenomena found in schizophrenics' performance in a laboratory card-sorting task to clinical symptoms of over-inclusive thinking? Such questions require more careful empirical investigation than has generally occurred. It would be relevant to know the magnitude of the correlation between the occurrence of the clinical symptoms and the laboratory phenomena; also how similar are the situational conditions that influence the occurrence of the two sets of phenomena.

TABLE 9.1
Possible relationships between clinical phenomena and adaptations to information overload (from Hemsley, 1977; reproduced by permission of the British Journal of Psychiatry)

Methods of adaptation	Clinical phenomena
Errors intrusion of associated responses	Inappropriate responding Incoherence of speech
Omission lowered responsiveness Raised threshold for response	Under responsiveness* Poverty of speech* Flatness of affect*
Approximation simplified categorising system. Several stimuli elicit the same response rather than there being a differentiated response to each	Undifferentiated responding Delusions
Escape reduction of exploratory responses. Avoidance of situations of high information load	Social withdrawal* Catatonic symptoms
Queueing delayed responding	Retardation
Filtering increased attention of certain classes of sensory input	Narrowed attention*

*More prominent in chronic patients.

Recent years have seen a vigorous discussion of the similarity of depression in college students to clinical depression. Doubts about the clinical relevance of studies of depression in students were forcefully raised by Gotlib (1984), who argued that student depression was not only milder, but represented a broader and less specific form of pathology than clinical depression. He supported this conclusion with several lines of empirical evidence about the structure and correlates of depression in students. However, in a recent review, Vredenburg, Flett and Krames (1993) have argued that the empirical evidence supports the similarity of student and clinical depression, and that studies of the two populations have yielded similar results. Though this remains a matter of controversy, there is agreement that more sophisticated methods are needed to identify depression in student populations. High scores on a single depression questionnaire are not enough, and a diagnostic interview schedule is to be preferred.

One of the analogue phenomena that has been studied most fruitfully in recent years is the relative accessibility of positive and negative memories in depression. It is a common clinical observation that depressed people are likely to dwell on negative things about themselves and neglect positive ones. This probably applies to various kinds of thought content, but it is often best to choose one example that you hope will prove paradigmatic and to study it in detail. Recent research has focused on the relative accessibility of positive and negative memories, and has provided abundant evidence that memories are biased towards those that are congruent with mood (e.g. Ellis and Ashbrook, 1989). Such research assumes that the experimental task parallels a clinical phenomenon in the processes involved; for example, that memory latency when people try to recall negative material in the laboratory is an index of the likelihood of their recalling such material spontaneously in real life. Unfortunately, such assumptions are often made only tacitly and it is simply assumed, without discussion or evidence, that the analogy between an experimental result and a phenomenon of direct clinical interest is close.

Analogue research should exploit its potential to clarify issues that are not clear from clinical studies. For example, if people are clinically depressed, both when negative events occur and when they remember them, it is not clear whether it is mood at encoding or mood at retrieval which is responsible for the biasing effect of mood on memory. By using mood induction procedures to create depressed mood at encoding but not at retrieval (or vice-versa) it is possible to disentangle which is responsible for the mood congruency effect. Another issue concerns the size of the pool of memories on which people draw when remembering particular events. It might be argued that depressed people remember negative events relatively frequently simply because more of such things have happened to them. To rule out this explanation, it is necessary to work with a pool of memories of known size. For this purpose, memory for a specially constructed list of hedonically biased words can be studied.

If the investigation of an analogue of a clinically important target variable is to be really worthwhile, it should be carried to the point where it does more than simply demonstrate in the laboratory what most clinicians thought they knew already from direct observation. Rather, research should seek to advance our understanding of how and why the phenomenon arises, in a way that has treatment implications. Research on the effects of mood on the accessibility of personal memories is reaching this point. It is now clear that the difficulty that depressed patients have in recalling positive events arises at the stage of accessing a specific positive event (Williams, 1992) Depressed people are able to recall general classes of positive events, but these probably have less impact on mood than accessing specific events. Understanding where problems arise for depressives in recall of positive events may suggest retrieval strategies they could use to recall more easily the positive things that have happened to them.

One class of clinical phenomena for which it is particularly difficult to find a good analogue are those that are qualitatively different from anything that occurs in the normal population, rather than being a quantitative extension of a problem that is continuously distributed through the normal population. Psychotic symptoms are most obvious example of the former, and present a particular problem for the application of experimental psychology derived from the normal population. However, even where it appears that a clinical symptom is just an extension of a phenomenon that occurs in the normal population, the processes underlying it may be quite different. The avoidance of social situations by a paranoid patient might look like an extension of the social avoidance of a 'normal' shy introvert, but this would probably be a misleading assumption. Superficial analogies between clinical symptoms and phenomena found in the normal population often break down on close examination. However, it is sometimes possible to find unusual conditions under which qualitatively distinct clinical symptoms begin to be demonstrable in normal subjects.

Shapiro (1960) has provided an instructive discussion, illustrating this latter point, of the effects on visual perception of parietal-occipital lobe damage demonstrated by Bender and Teuber (1949). There were four principal phenomena: (a) a decrease in the intensity of percepts, (b) systematic changes in space values, (c) a tendency to see objects as smaller than they really were, and (d) increased fluctuation in visual thresholds. Because these phenomena were produced in normals by prolonged stimulation, Bender and Teuber hypothesised that very brief stimulation might reduce or eliminate the perceptual abnormalities of their parietal-occipital patients. Their results confirmed this prediction, with the exception of the size distortion phenomenon. It thus seems that a quantitative change in exposure durations regulates the appearance of a qualitatively distinct perceptual phenomena. All that is needed is the assumption of a different threshold in the brain-damaged patients.

A similar approach has been taken to formulating a psychological model of hallucinations, another phenomenon that is apparently qualitatively distinct from anything that occurs in normals (Slade, 1976). In fact, there is evidence that hallucinations can be induced, at least in people with a history of hallucinations, by physiological manipulations such as hyperventilation. This argues for the role of physiological arousal in inducing hallucinations. Though such interventions are apparently not sufficient to induce hallucinations in all people, those who are prone to hallucinations may not be qualitatively distinct from the rest of the population. Mintz and Alpert (1972) have proposed that high scores on two dimensions with continuous distributions in the normal population—vivid mental imagery and poor reality testing—constitute this predisposition to hallucinations.

Another component in Slade's model comes from subsuming hallucinations under the more generally occurring category of task-irrelevant thoughts. These are increased in the normal population by psychological distress, and by situations where tasks being undertaken require relatively little processing resources, and this has been shown to be true of hallucinations too. Desensitisation to sources of psychological stress, and increasing the demands made by a concurrent task, both reduce the frequency of hallucinations. This multi-component theory of hallucinations provides a good example of how the study of psychological parameters in normal people can be applied to the explanation of a qualitatively distinct phenomenon. (See Birchwood, Hallett and Preston, 1988, pp.213-221 for a review of recent research relevant to this model of hallucinations.) Both here and in the work of Bender and Teuber discussed earlier, theorising based on general psychology has led to direct experimental work on the psychological symptom concerned.

If the objective of experimental research on clinical symptoms (or their analogues) is to suggest treatment strategies, the central objective must be to bring the symptom under experimental control. Because general experimental psychology is largely devoted to investigating the conditions under which psychological phenomena occur, it is highly relevant to this enterprise. Understanding how to control a phenomenon in the laboratory can suggest how to 'treat' it in the clinic.

DIFFERENTIAL DEFICIT HYPOTHESES

Next, I shall consider investigation of dysfunctions which are interesting because they are particularly severe, and can be shown to be significantly greater than deficits among similar tasks. Demonstrations of differences between a clinical and a control group on a task are much more interesting theoretically if it is also shown that the groups do not differ (or differ less) on a control task. Thus the relevance of judgements of body size to anorexia are much clearer if it is known that it is just body judgements that are distorted. If all size judgements were equally distorted it would be much less clear how this was related to a clinical condition characterised specifically by reduced body weight. Similarly, an attentional disorder has been postulated as being fundamental to schizophrenia and it has been predicted that schizophrenics will be especially impaired on tasks where they are subject to distraction. However, for the relevance of this to be clear, a control condition is needed so that it can be demonstrated that the deficit in performance is greater under conditions of distraction than without it.

Without such controls, the demonstration of psychological deficit in a patient group is too poorly specified to be theoretically interesting. For example, it seems that some of the supposedly specific deficits that researchers claim to have demonstrated in schizophrenia might be due to nothing more than the fact that it takes schizophrenics longer than controls to learn to perform optimally on almost all psychological tasks. Familiarity with materials has quite a powerful effect on task performance (Baron & Treiman, 1980) and many of the chronic schizophrenics studied have probably under-performed on particular tasks solely for this reason. Interpretations of results that assume that a specific deficit has been demonstrated may thus miss the point.

We will now consider some of the technical problems of design and interpretation that arise in seeking to demonstrate specific (or 'differential') deficits.

First, if you wish to demonstrate that a deficit is specific to a particular clinical group, the choice of control groups is crucial. If a 'normal' control group is used, care must be taken to ensure that it does not differ in unintended ways from the clinical groups. For example, no good can come from comparing a depressed and a normal group on memory if the groups also differ on intelligence. However, an appropriate 'normal' control group is insufficient if you wish to claim that a specific deficit is unique to a particular clinical group. For example, if you want to claim that a particular deficit is unique to schizo- phrenia and may explain schizophrenic symptoms, it is necessary to show that it is not also found in depression (Chapman & Chapman, 1973a).

Suppose that we wish to test the hypothesis that depressed patients are specially impaired, relative to controls, in memory for positive materials, compared to neutral materials. The experiment might be arranged so that each subject was tested on both kinds of material. This has two advantages over the alternative arrangement in which two different groups of depressed subjects (and two different control groups) are tested on the two memory measures. One is the practical advantage that fewer subjects need to be recruited; the other is that it eliminates at a stroke the problems of ensuring that the two depressed groups are comparable (e.g. equally depressed, etc.). The snag is that testing subjects on one measure may influence their performance on the next. There may be either practice effects or fatigue effects. Usually these can be dealt with by 'counterbalancing' the order of the tests, i.e. some subjects have one test first and some the other. However, this solution breaks down in the case where the practice effect is asymmetrical i.e. where test (a) leads to an improvement on test (b) when it is given subsequently, but test (b) has less effect on test (a). Such asymmetrical transfer effects certainly occur (Poulton, 1982) and they can only be dealt with by having a design in which each subject is given only one test. However, it is generally reasonable, at least in a preliminary experiment, to give both tests to the same subjects and to evaluate statistically whether transfer has occurred.

An experiment of this kind is likely to lead to statistical tests employing a two-way analysis of variance (see Chapter 5), Such an analysis yields three main statistical tests. First, there will be the 'main effect' of subjects. In the present example, this would indicate that depressed subjects performed worse *overall*. This may well be the case, but will be of little theoretical interest as depressed patients tend to be at least slightly impaired on so many functions. Next, there will be the 'main effect' of tests which, unlike the previous one, will probably be a 'within-subjects' main effect that is computed differently from a 'between-subjects' one. In the present example, this would refer to whether all subjects taken together tend to do better on one memory test than the other. This would probably not be the case, but, even if it were, it would not be of direct relevance to abnormal psychology. The interesting test in the analysis would be the *interaction* between groups and tests. It is here then that the prediction that depressed patients are especially impaired, relative to normals, in remembering positive rather than neutral material would be tested.

A great deal of contemporary experimental psychology is built on predictions relating to such interaction effects. In abnormal psychology, one of the terms in the interaction almost always concerns different groups of subjects (a clinical and a control group), though in general psychology other kinds of interaction are tested too. Hypotheses concerning interaction effects in abnormal psychology are sometimes termed 'differential deficit' hypotheses, i.e. that a clinical group is relatively more impaired on one task than on another. A closely related statistical approach to testing a differential deficit hypothesis is to examine the *difference* between each subject's scores on the two measures using a one-way analysis of variance (or a 't' test) to compare groups on this difference score. This is mathematically equivalent to the interaction term in a two-way analysis of variance but, because it provides fewer cell means, provides a less useful description of the results of the experiment. Because a significant interaction term can mean so many things, it is essential to report the means for the various conditions. Post-hoc tests to compare two means should also be used if it is to be claimed that they differ significantly. It is also often helpful for the researcher to plot out the interaction effect as a graph. The analysis of variance alone is not enough.

The research literature on differential deficits, as Chapman and Chapman (1978) concluded at the end of a review, is 'rather a mess'. Though studies testing such hypotheses have been extremely common, the majority have been methodologically unsound and have probably drawn incorrect conclusions. Too few research workers have yet grasped the problems and what needs to be done to remedy them. The issues are complex and technical, and it will not be possible here to provide more than a general introduction. Unfortunately, there is not yet complete agreement on the most appropriate solution. More detailed discussions of this issue have been published in relation to schizophrenia (Chapman & Chapman, 1973b, Chapter 4; Chapman & Chapman, 1978), mental handicap (Chapman & Chapman, 1974 & 1985) children (Bogartz, 1976), the elderly (Kausler, 1982, Chapter 5), and neurological patients (Strauss and Allred, 1987). More general discussions have been published by Chapman and Chapman (1973c), Loftus (1978), Baron and Treiman (1980), and—in relation to clinical disorders—Kihlstrom and McGlynn (1991).

With all hypotheses relating to interaction effects, the success of the experiment depends on how well the two measures are matched. The basic principle here is the familiar one that in a controlled experiment two measures (just like two groups) should differ only on the variable of interest, but be alike in all other ways. There is one particular problem that arises so commonly here that it deserves special comment, which is where the two tasks differ in their general level of difficulty as well as on the dimension of theoretical interest. Suppose we hypothesise that what an amnesic group finds difficult is the active retrieval of material, but that their ability to recognise material is unimpaired. If we could demonstrate this, it would appear to be an important step in identifying the exact locus of the memory deficit in the amnesic group. However, the two tasks could easily differ, not only in whether or not they required active retrieval, but also in their overall level of difficulty. If the tasks differed in both respects the interpretation of an interaction involving them would be ambiguous. In experiments testing the differential deficit hypotheses, the most common situation has been to have one task of moderate difficulty (e.g. free recall) and one easy task (e.g. recognition). The finding is usually that groups differ on the former more than on the latter. The researcher then reaches for an explanation of this fact that ignores the implications of these differences in difficulty.

The difficulty of a task has important implications for how well it differentiates groups. In general a task on which 50% of people succeed on each of the component items will differentiate groups better than a very easy or very difficult task. Constructors of intelligence tests have long understood the value, for this reason, of including items that around 50% of the population will pass. Difficulty also has implications for the variance of the scores. With easy or difficult tasks, the variance tends to be restricted and the distribution skewed. Equating difficulty is valuable in part because it tends to equate the variance of the two measures. It is not essential that the difficulty level should be 50%, though this will maximise the variance and hence the capacity of the tests to differentiate groups.

To press home the seriousness of this issue, it may be helpful to summarise some of the points made by Chapman and Chapman (1978) in applying it to the literature on differential deficit in schizophrenia. Two thirds of the relevant studies have found that schizophrenics show more thought-disordered responses to affective than to neutral materials, but this may well be a product of greater discriminability of measures based on the former. In two studies where the tests were matched on psychometric properties, differences between schizophrenics and controls disappeared. Similarly, two-thirds of the relevant studies found that schizophrenics showed greater deficits in learning passages with high contextual constraint, but again this may have been an artefact of the different psychometric properties of measures based on the two kinds of passage. When a study was done in which these were matched, the difference between schizophrenics and normals disappeared.

Matching tasks on psychometric properties (difficulty of items, variance of scores, internal homogeneity of the scale) avoids generating interaction effects that are in reality just an artefact of differences in those properties. However, it may have costs. It is often necessary to introduce some other difference between the tasks to avoid differences in psychometric properties such as difficulty. For example, Raulin and Chapman (1976) equated the difficulty of high and low contextual constraint by making the low constraint word lists shorter. An interaction effect of these matched tasks is thus still ambiguous, but in a new way. Is it due to differences in list length or contextual constraint? In principle the implications of varying both textual constraint and list length could have been explored by introducing additional versions of the tasks. Most problems of design and interpretation can in principle be resolved by an escalation of the number of groups or tasks, but this is not always sensible. A judgement needs to be made about the scientific pay-off of this method of choosing between alternative interpretations. A course needs to be steered between designs that are watertight at the cost of being prohibitively cumbersome and designs that are so leaky they are effectively useless. It is often prudent to take a calculated risk, whilst keeping a clear head about how the problems might affect the interpretation of results.

Having discussed the value of matching pairs of tasks in their level of difficulty, we should note that there are often good theoretical reasons to compare tasks of *different* levels of difficulty. Suppose for example, that the gap between the performance of schizophrenic patients and controls is greater on digits backwards than on digits forwards. A common theoretical approach to such a situation is in terms of 'component processes' (Sternberg, 1977)—that there is a common process that underlies performance on both tasks, and an additional process that is required for the more difficult one. The assumption is then made that this additional component is more sensitive to the effects of schizophrenia than the component common to both tasks. Another common theoretical approach is in terms of limited resources. The basic assumption is that the clinical group has less capacity to allocate processing resources to a task than the control group, as Ellis and Ashbrook (1988) have argued for depression. This will result in their being at a relatively severe disadvantage in performing a demanding task that requires resources greater than they generally have available, but which are within the scope of the control group.

Matching of tasks on psychometric properties such as difficulty is not the only approach to the problems of differences in discriminability, and three others involving supplementary analyses will now be discussed briefly. None is foolproof, but they each make at least a limited contribution to guarding against claiming spurious support for a differential deficit hypothesis.

1. Tests designed to be sensitive to the properties of a clinical group often produce not only a different mean for the clinical group but also a different variance. The variance in the clinical group is often higher and the distribution skewed. Transforming the scales (e.g. applying a log transformation to the skewed scale) to eliminate such differences in variance does not deal with underlying differences in the discriminative power of tests, but it does deal with some statistical artifacts produced by having tests with different kinds of variances (Winer, 1971, pp. 449-452). If a particular interaction survives this treatment, the amount of confidence the experimenter can have in it is increased.

2. If one test differentiates between a clinical and a control better than another simply because of its psychometric properties, this pattern of results should also be found when two normal groups with different levels of performance are compared. To check on this, you might divide the control subjects into high-IQ and low-IQ subgroups, and examine whether they also differed on one test more than the other. If an interaction is found only when one of the groups is clinical, and not with two normal groups, you can be more confident that the interaction is due to the characteristics of the clinical group, rather than just to the different psychometric properties of the test.

3. There are some interaction effects involving a 'cross-over' that are not subject to the problems of interpretation that have bedevilled so much abnormal psychology. For example, if a depressed group performs better than a control group in memory for negative materials, but worse in memory for positive materials. this cannot be an artefact of psychometric differences between tests. This suggests another post-hoc method of dealing with the problems of interpreting an interaction effect where the tasks are not matched on difficulty. Take, for example, an experiment in which the clinical group has performed worse than the control group on both tasks. You can select for a post-hoc analysis just the better clinical subjects and the poorer control subjects. This may change the relative positions on the graph of the lines representing the clinical group and the control group so that they now cross over (Fig. 9.1). If this happens, it is relatively unlikely that the interaction effect is an artefact of differences in the discriminating power of the tests.

However, obtaining convergent data from different kinds of experiment probably provides the most powerful support for the theory from which a particular interaction effect is predicted. Where there is a

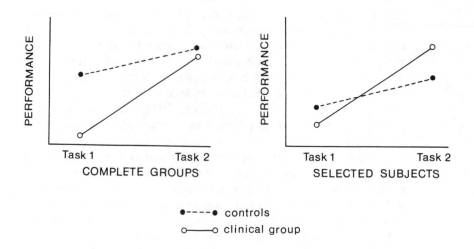

FIG. 9.1. How a cross-over interaction may emerge in a sub-groups clinical and control subjects matched on overall performance.

clear theory underlying the prediction of an interaction, there are often two or more interaction effects that can be predicted from the same underlying assumptions. For example, it might be hypothesised that imaginal processes in memory are relatively unimpaired in elderly subjects. Imagery can be introduced into a memory experiment either through direct instructions to use imagery, or through materials that lend themselves to imagery (e.g. concrete vs. abstract nouns). It would be predicted that in both cases the gap between the performance of elderly and young subjects would be narrowed. Clearly it is advantageous to have such converging experiments relating to the same basic hypothesis.

Another approach to the specification of differential deficits which has been less widely employed, but which has considerable promise, is based on task decomposition (i.e. breaking it down into its components). Decomposition research is well established as a way of identifying the effective components in a treatment package. For example, imaginal desensitisation can be decomposed into (a) relaxation alone and (b) imagery without relaxation. However, decomposition of tasks on which performance is impaired is attempted less often.

When a researcher is faced with the phenomenon of a clinical group which performs a task conspicuously badly, it is often possible to decompose it into its constituent parts to discover where the difficulty comes in. Levy (1973) has provided an excellent exposition of the decomposition approach to the construct validity of psychological tests. One of the unpublished studies he cites is a decomposition of the Digit-Symbol subtest of the WAIS. Several simplified versions of the tasks were devised including a test of writing speed in which the same symbol has to be written repeatedly for 90 seconds, a version in which there were just two possible symbols rather than the usual nine. This study has a single 'normal' group and the study focused on correlations between these simplified tests and the normal versions (and consequently the variance in the normal versions accounted for by the simplified version). With a clinical and an abnormal group to compare, an analysis could be undertaken of where the deficit in the abnormal group arose. For example, there might be no difference between groups in writing speed, but the abnormal group might become slower than the control group as soon as a choice of symbols was introduced. (Issues about the effect of the relative difficulty of components, parallel to those already discussed in this section, arise again here.) It might also be found that writing speed correlated with the normal version less highly in the clinical than the control group. The work of Luria (1966, part III) represents another example of the study of intra-individual discrepancies in performance.

DYSFUNCTIONS OF AETIOLOGICAL IMPORTANCE

A third reason for being interested in a particular psychological dysfunction rests on it being hypothesised to have an important role in aetiology. It should be noted here that 'dysfunction' is being used in an extended sense and can include any dimension along which people differ in the normal population and which has consequences for the development of clinical conditions. Vulnerability factors are obviously of enormous importance, though unfortunately they are very difficult to study. We will consider some of the problems that arise and the solutions that can be attempted. (For another discussion of the methodological issues concerning vulnerability factors, see Neuchterlein, 1990.)

The first step in vulnerability research is relatively simple. Clearly, people who manifest a particular abnormality would also be predicted to show high levels of the hypothesised vulnerability factors. Thus to return to an example used earlier in the chapter, hallucinators would be expected to have vivid imagery and poor reality testing. The main issue at this first stage (apart from constructing reliable measures of the hypothesised vulnerability factors) is the choice of the control group. As in studies of differential deficits, this should be similar to the target group in all respects except the presence of the particular abnormality in question. Thus Mintz and Alpert (1972) compared hallucinating schizophrenics, not with normal controls, but with non-hallucinating schizophrenics. When two such generally similar groups are shown to differ on the hypothesised vulnerability factors, the chances are much increased that they really are relevant to the target symptom. This is too often neglected, and when it is eventually done the results tend to be disappointing. For example, though conflict between the verbal and non-verbal components of communications may be characteristic of the families of schizophrenics, it is not specific to them. When Bugenthal, Love, Kaswan and April (1971) investigated the families of delinquents, they too proved to have a high level of double-bind communications.

A number of models of onset assume a 'diathesis-stress' process in which it is assumed that the vulnerability factor interacts with a triggering event to generate symptoms. Such models require a 2×2 factorial design including groups with/without the vulnerability factor and with/without the triggering event. A diathesis-stress model that has attracted considerable interest stems from the learned helplessness model of depression, and proposes that people with a negative attributional style are particularly likely to become depressed when they experience stressful events (Abramson, Metalsky & Alloy, 1989). So far, however, the evidence for this theory has not been strong, and Brewin (1985) has argued that it is consistent with symptom, recovery or coping models of the relationship between attributional style and the onset of depression, but not with vulnerability or onset models.

The first step in any vulnerability model is to show that the vulnerability factor is characteristic of people with a particular abnormality. However, at best, this only establishes an association between the two variables and you cannot infer a causal relationship from a correlation. The alternative causal hypotheses, that the abnormality has caused the hypothesised vulnerability factor, or that they have both been caused by a third variable, cannot yet be ruled out.

The ideal solution to this problem is a prospective study in which you identify which people have the vulnerability feature, and predict on this basis which ones will develop the abnormality concerned. However, prospective studies tend to be cumbersome. The problem is partly that the rate of inception of a disorder is often so low that you have to use extremely large groups. Sometimes, if the hypothesis relates to a delayed effect, like the effect of early upbringing in increasing the risk of schizophrenia in adulthood, a very long-term study is also needed.

The problem of low numbers can be alleviated somewhat by studying a high-risk group, like people in families with a history of schizophrenia (see Birchwood, Hallett & Preston, 1988, Chapter 10) Depression, being such a ubiquitous disorder, is probably the most feasible to study prospectively. For example, you might obtain a high-risk group by studying people about to undergo an event such as childbirth that is thought to increase the risk of depression.

It is important to notice that there can be considerable variation in how unusual each of the two factors are (Meehl, 1973, pp. 244-250). The extremes are (a) cases where the vulnerability factor is common, but the triggering stress is rare; and (b) cases where the vulnerability factor is rare, but the triggering stress is common. Which of these patterns is presumed to apply will affect exactly how you test a diathesis-stress model. There is a particular need for caution over hypothesising that a common variable is a vulnerability factor for a relatively rare disorder.

Even a prospective study has potential problems (see the sections on path analyses and cross-lagged correlations in Chapter 11). There is always a possibility, even if a strong correlation is found between the vulnerability factor at time one and symptomatology at time two, that what is taken to be a vulnerability factor is in fact an early prodromal symptom. This is most likely when only one premorbid occasion is sampled, and it is quite close in time to the full onset of symptomatology. Also, there is the possibility that in those subjects who have had symptoms on a previous occasion, the presence of the hypothesised vulnerability factor at time one is really a residual symptom of a previous episode of depression. This last problem can be handled to some extent by selecting for a supplementary analysis subjects who have never been depressed.

Prospective studies are sufficiently problematic that it is reasonable to look for alternatives to them. Let us now consider some of those available. The available designs are summarised in Table 9.2. A general caution about retrospective studies is that a clinic-based sample may be unrepresentative in their aetiological processes, and that a general population study is the best way of avoiding this potential problem (see the section on hypothesis testing epidemiology in Chapter 16).

There are also problems in assessing vulnerability factors retrospectively, though this problem melts away like snow in the sun if the vulnerability factor you are concerned with is known to be stable. Sex is an unusually stable characteristic. Therefore, when you find that most agoraphobics are women, it is entirely reasonable to infer that being a woman increases vulnerability to agoraphobia, though of course it says nothing about how this vulnerability is mediated. Irritability, in contrast, is not stable. So, if you find that patients with angina tend to

TABLE 9.2
Methods of investigating vulnerability factors and their problems

1. Prospective studies:
   Often needs a very large sample (or a 'high-risk' sample).
   The supposed vulnerability factor may be just an 'early' symptom.

2. Concurrent assessment of stable vulnerability factors (e.g. sex):
   Few sufficiently stable vulnerability factors.

3. Retrospective assessment of vulnerability factors:
   Need to use objective measures so as to minimise retrospective distortion.

4. Use of 'recovered' groups as a guide to what pre-morbid groups would be like:
   Need to check that supposed vulnerability factors are not just residual symptoms.

5. Prediction of response to induction procedures:
   Susceptibility to the induction procedure may not accurately reflect vulnerability to the clinical condition.

be irritable, you can make no causal inferences. (Much of the older research on personality factors that are assumed to increase vulnerability to psychosomatic illness is flawed in this way.) There are in-between cases of hypothesised vulnerability factors that are not necessarily stable (like sex) but are presumed to be so. Conditionability is an interesting example. If patients with neurotic problems show higher-than-average conditionability, this might be interpreted as a vulnerability factor. The assumption here is that conditionability is a stable characteristic, but the alternative hypothesis that the clinical condition has affected conditionability cannot be ruled out.

A variant of this strategy is to get self-report measures of stable (i.e. 'trait') aspects of personality. The state/trait measures of anxiety (Spielberger et al., 1983) are the most widely used example of this approach. Though the subject completes both scales at the same time, it has often been shown that they have different patterns of correlates that are consistent with their different intentions.

Another approach is to try to get retrospective measures of vulnerability characteristics. The problem with these is that they are likely to be unreliable. However, there are important exceptions. Sometimes a pre-morbid feature can be found that is a sufficiently good marker of the hypothesised vulnerability factor to be of interest and also sufficiently objective that there is no reliability problem. For example, school records have been used as a source of objective information about the pre-morbid sociability of people who subsequently became schizophrenic. Obviously the availability of such indices is severely limited, but researchers have so far been less ingenious than they might have been in generating them. Rawls' (1971) report on the capacity of objective measures drawn from pre-morbid life (such as school reports) to predict readmission to mental hospital is a good model of ingenuity.

Thirdly, there are 'recovered' groups. The current spate of studies of whether recovered depressives show the cognitive vulnerability factors hypothesised by Beck and others is a good example of this approach. But how far are you justified in assuming that 'recovered' people have reverted to their pre-morbid state? One problem is that recovery is often only partial. If you take an administrative criterion of recovery (e.g. discharged from treatment) you will probably have many people who still have mild symptoms. On the other hand, if all people with mild symptoms are excluded, it will be difficult to find an adequate sample and they may be so highly selected as to be unrepresentative in other ways. Statistical techniques are sometimes helpful in disentangling the effects of (a) current mood state from (b) whether or not people have had a depressive illness. Monitoring the relapse process carefully may also provide rich time-course data that are helpful in disentangling alternative hypotheses. However, even people whose symptoms have fully remitted may show residual effects of a depressive episode that render them different from people who are vulnerable to depression but who have not yet actually become depressed.

There is no statistical solution to this problem. When recovered depressives are shown to have particular characteristics, we can never be sure whether these are pre-morbid vulnerability features or the permanent residue of a depressive episode. Finally, there is the problem of finding a comparable 'never-ill' group with whom to compare the recovered group. The group may differ in various incidental ways from the clinical group, producing differences on the measure of the hypothesised vulnerability factor that will be misinterpreted. Researchers can and should match groups on some of the more obviously relevant variables, but other unnoticed differences between groups may remain.

Related to hypotheses about pre-morbid vulnerability factors are hypotheses that a particular symptom of a clinical condition is 'primary'. Many psychological disorders have features that span multiple domains. Depression, for example, affects physiological, cognitive and behavioural systems. In such cases there is a tendency to claim primacy for one or other domain of dysfunction; for example, that negative cognitions are the primary symptoms of depression. In fact, primacy seems to be rather rare in abnormal psychology. It is probably much more common for there to be mutual interactions between the different systems of a complex condition such as depression. Thus cognitive and physiological aspects often affect each other. A strong 'primacy' theory would be refuted by such a state of affairs; the thesis that negative cognitions are the primary aspect of depression predicts not only that cognitions generate other features of depression including dysphoria, but also that dysphoria does not similarly generate negative cognitions. The latter claim is clearly incorrect, as evidence for the effects of mood on negative memories indicates (Ellis & Ashbrook, 1989). In its strongest form, a primacy theory would also claim that all cases of the primary symptom should lead to the other symptoms of the condition, and would be refuted by cases in which the primary symptom occurs alone, except as a temporary phase of the aetiological processes. Primacy theories also make predictions about the course of onset. The primary symptoms should always develop first and the secondary symptoms later. The converse pattern of development would refute a strong primacy theory.

Strong primacy theories are perhaps something of a 'will o' the wisp', and perhaps scarcely worth chasing. However, within the framework of the more plausible assumption of mutual interaction between symptoms, it can be important to know whether one aspect of disorder can induce other aspects. This requires an experimental manipulation, such as psychological or physiological induction procedures. Studies of the effects of mood induction procedures (currently the best known example of a psychological induction procedure) have made a substantial contribution to research on depression (Goodwin & Williams, 1982). Studies of the effects of alcohol (see Huesmann, 1982, p. 238) are an example of a physiological induction procedure that has contributed to the understanding of alcoholism.

Two cautions are required in such studies. One is that care should be taken not to over-extrapolate from rather loose similarities between clinical symptoms and the state induced by the experimental procedure. The other is to ensure that the effects of the procedure do not merely reflect the effects of demand characteristics. This is more problematic with psychological than with physiological procedures because they are less easily disguised. However, it is possible to include a condition in which counter-demands are given, in which for example an elation induction procedure is used but subjects are told it will make them feel unhappy (e.g. Polivy & Doyle, 1980).

One of the uses of induction studies is to allow theories about vulnerability factors to be tested directly. Hypotheses about the antecedent events that lead to particular conditions can be tested by the use of procedures designed to induce the disorder concerned. The use of insoluble problems in the 'learned helplessness' paradigm is a widely used example. The application of conditioning procedures to produce a sexual fetish (Rachman, 1966) is another. Clearly, there can be ethical problems with such procedures. There is a research dilemma here that applies to all induction procedures in abnormal psychology. If the state induced is too close to a clinical disorder there will probably be ethical problems in inducing it. Alternatively, if it produces only a weak simulation of the disorder, its relevance to the explanation of the clinical disorder is doubtful. But even if the simulation of the clinical disorder is perfect, all that is established is that the clinical disorder can be induced in this way, not that this is the normal genesis. There may be different paths to the same disorder, and the route represented by the experimental procedure may be an atypical one.

An alternative approach to studying the genesis of a clinical condition is to look at the course it follows after inception. Knowing how to predict, or even control, changes in the severity of a condition is clearly of practical value. Of course, nothing can be inferred about the original genesis of the disorder, but it is always a plausible hypothesis that factors known to affect the course of a disorder might also contribute to its genesis. Ideas about possible vulnerability factors can be translated into hypotheses about factors which will predict the course of the disorder, and in this new form are much more tractable. Thus research on the prediction of the course of schizophrenia from patterns of communication involving high levels of expressed emotion in the family (e.g. Leff & Vaughn, 1985) has been more fruitful than research on the role of family processes in the genesis of schizophrenia. Research on prognostic factors is always difficult to interpret causally, though sometimes careful analysis can at least be suggestive. For example, current marital status predicts outcome in schizophrenia but it seems that both are predictable from pre-morbid sociability (see Watts, 1983, pp. 300-301), suggesting that current marital status does not have a direct casual impact.

Sometimes social variables known to be associated with the course or severity of a disorder can be manipulated experimentally, such as in the work of Purcell and Weiss (1970) showing the beneficial effects of separating a small group of asthmatic children (those who were less steroid-dependent) from their parents. Of course, when children leave home too many aspects of the environment are changed simultaneously for unambiguous conclusions to be drawn. The key manipulation was one in which children were cared for in their own homes by a substitute mother while the rest of the family were away. It was shown that this led to improvements in the children's asthmatic symptoms. Where manipulations are used to test hypotheses about causal factors the key requirement is for a 'clean' intervention whose effects are known. Because a substantial component of the effectiveness of so many interventions can be attributed to non-specific factors, the fact of their effectiveness doesn't necessarily confirm the principles on which they are based. For example the clinical success of an intervention designed to reduce the level of expressed emotion in the family of a schizophrenic doesn't necessarily confirm the specific relevance of expressed emotion. The intervention may have achieved its clinical results in other more non-specific ways.

CONCLUSIONS

Inevitably, this chapter has focused on some of the difficulties of doing research in abnormal psychology. The intention has not been to discourage the reader, but to lay bare the scientific process. Researchers are naturally always ambitious in the sense of wanting to draw bold conclusions from their work, but it is an essential characteristic of the scientific process that this must be balanced by caution. Because it is so easy to draw incorrect conclusions from research, scientists need to be constantly on their guard. The methodological cautions of experimental research should not be seen as off-puttting, arcane or elitist. They are just the distillations, from much research experience, of how scientists can avoid fooling themselves into thinking they have proved something when they haven't. Only in this way can we decide whether our bold conjectures about clinical conditions are actually true.

REFERENCES

Abramson, L.Y., Metalsky, G.I. & Alloy, L.B. (1989) Hopelessness depression : A theory-based sub-type of depression. *Psychological Review, 96*, 358-372.

Barber, T.X. (1979). *Pitfalls in Human Research ... Ten Pivotal Points*. Oxford: Pergamon Press

Baron, J. & Treiman, R. (1980). Some problems in the study of differences in cognitive processes. *Memory and Cognition, 8*, 313-321.

Bender, M.B. & Teuber, H.L. (1949). Disturbances in visual perception following cerebral lesion. *Journal of Psychology, 28*, 233-234.

Birchwood, M., Hallett, S. & Preston, M. (1988) *Schizophrenia : An Integrated Approach to Research and Treatment*. London : Longman.

Bogartz, R.S. (1976). On the meaning of statistical interactions. *Journal of Experimental Child Psychology, 22*, 178-183.

Borkovec, T. & Rachman, S. (1979). The utility of analogue research. *Behaviour Research and Therapy, 17*, 253-261.

Brewin, C.R.(1985) Depression and causal attributions : What is their relation? *Psychological Bulletin, 98*, 297-309.

Bugenthal, D.E., Love, L.R., Kaswan, J.W. & April, C. (1971). Verbal-non-verbal conflict in parental messages to normal and disturbed children. *Journal of Abnormal Psychology, 77*, 6-10.

Chapman, L.J. (1985) Methodological problems in the study of differential deficits in retarded groups. *Current Topics in Human Intelligence, 1*, 141-153.

Chapman, L.J. & Chapman, J.P. (1973a). Selection of subjects in studies of schizophrenic cognition. *Journal of Abnormal Psychology, 86,* 10-15.

Chapman, L.J. & Chapman, J.P. (1973b). *Disordered Thought in Schizophrenia.* New York: Appleton-Century-Crofts.

Chapman, L.J. & Chapman, J.P. (1973c). Problems in the measurement of cognitive deficit. *Psychological Bulletin, 79,* 380-385.

Chapman, L.J. & Chapman, J.P. (1974). Alternative to the design of manipulating a variable to compare retarded and normal subjects. *American Journal of Mental Deficiency, 79,* 404-411.

Chapman, L.J. & Chapman, J.P. (1978). The measurement of differential deficit. *Journal of Psychiatric Research, 14,* 303-311.

Ellis, H. & Ashbrook, P.W. (1988). Resource allocation model of the effects of depressed mood states on memory. In K. Fiedler and J. Forgas (Eds) *Affect, Cognition and Social Behaviour.* Toronto: Hogrefe.

Ellis, H. & Ashbrook, P.W. (1989) The "state" of mood and memory research: A selective review. *Journal of Social Behavior and Personality, 4,* 1-21.

Garber, J. & Seligman, M.E.P. (1980.) *Human Helplessness: Therapy and Applications.* London: Academic Press.

Goodwin, A. & Williams, J.M.G. (1982). Mood induction research: its implications for clinical depression. *Behaviour Research and Therapy, 20,* 373-382.

Gotlib, I.H. (1984) Depression and general psychopathology in university students. *Journal of Abnormal Psychology, 93,* 19-30.

Hemsley, D.R. (1977). What have cognitive deficits to do with schizophrenic symptoms? *British Journal of Psychiatry, 130,* 167-173.

Huesmann, L.R. (1982). Experimental methods in research in psychopathology. In P.C. Kendall and J.N. Butcher (Eds) *Handbook of Research Methods in Clinical Psychology.* New York: John Wiley.

Kausler, D.H. (1982). *Experimental Psychology of Human Aging.* New York: John Wiley.

Kerlinger, F.N. (1973). *Foundations of Behavioural Research: Educational, Psychological and Sociological Enquiry.* New York: Holt, Rinehart & Winston.

Kihlstrom, J.F. & McGlynn, S.M. (1991) Experimental research in clinical psychology. In M. Hersen, A.E. Kazdin, & A.S. Bellack (Eds) *The Clinical Psychology Handbook.* New York: Pergamon Press.

Leff, J. & Vaughn, C. (1985). *Experienced Emotion in Families: Its Significance for Mental Illness.* New York: Guilford Press.

Levy, P. (1973). On the relation between test theory and psychology. In P. Kline (Ed.) *New Approaches in Psychological Measurement.* London: John Wiley.

Loftus, G.R. (1978). On the interpretation of interactions. *Memory and Cognition, 6,* 312-319.

Luria, A.R. (1966). *Higher Cortical Functions in Man.* New York: Plenum.

Meehl, P.E. (1973). Why I do not attend case conferences. In P.E. Meehl (Ed.) *Psychodiagnosis: Selected Papers.* Minnesota: University of Minnesota Press.

Mintz, S. & Alpert, M. (1972). Imagery vividness, reality testing and schizophrenic hallucinations. *Journal of Abnormal Psychology, 79,* 310-316.

Neale, J.M. & Oltmanns, T.F. (1980). *Schizophrenia.* Chichester: Wiley.

Neuchterlein, K.H. (1990) Methodological considerations in the search for indicators of vulnerability to severe pathology. In J.W. Rohrbaugh, R. Parasaraman, & R. Johnson. (Eds) *Event-Related Brain Potentials.* New York: Oxford University Press.

Polivy, J. & Doyle, C. (1980). Laboratory induction of mood states through the reading self-referent mood statements: affective changes or demand characteristics. *Journal of Abnormal Psychology, 89,* 286-290.

Poulton, E.C. (1982). Influential comparisons: effects of one strategy on another in within-subjects designs of cognitive psychology. *Psychological Bulletin, 91,* 673-690.

Purcell, K. & Weiss, J.H.(1970). Asthma. In C.G. Costello (Ed.) *Symptoms of Psycho-pathology: A Handbook.* New York: John Wiley.

Rachman, S. (1966). Sexual fetishism: an experiment analogue. *Psychological Record, 16,* 293-296.

Raulin, M.L. & Chapman, L.J. (1976). Schizophrenic recall and contextual constraint. *Journal of Abnormal Psychology, 85,* 151-155.

Rawls, J.R. (1971). Toward the identification of readmissions and non-admissions to mental hospitals. *Social Psychiatry, 6,* 58-61.

Shapiro, M.B. (1960). *Introductory notes to the work of Bender and Teuber on disorders of perception.* Unpublished observations. Institute of Psychiatry. University of London.

Sher, K., Frost, R.O. & Otto, R. (1983). Cognitive deficits in compulsive checkers: an exploratory study. *Behaviour Research and Therapy, 21,* 357-363.

Slade, P.D. (1976). Towards a theory of auditory hallucinations: outline of an hypothetical poor-factor model. *British Journal of Clinical Psychology, 15,* 415-423.

Spielberger, C.D., Gorsuch, R.I., Lushene, R., Vagg, P.R. & Jacobs, G.A. (1983). *Manual for the State-Trait Anxiety Inventory (Form Y).* Palo Alto : Consulting Psychologists Press.

Sternberg, R.J. (1977). *Intelligence, Information Processing and Analogical Reasoning.* Hillsdale, NJ: Lawrence Erlbaum Associates Inc.

Strauss, M.E. & Allred, L.J. (1987) Measurement of differential cognitive deficits after head injury. In Levin, H.S., Grafman, J. & Eisenberg, H.M. (Eds) *Neurobehavioral Recovery from Head Injury.* New York : Oxford University Press.

Vredenburg, K., Flett, G.L. & Krames, L. (1993) Analogue versus clinical depression. *Journal of Abnormal Psychology, 113,* 327-344.

Watts, F.N. (1983). Socialization and social integration. In F.N. Watts & D.H. Bennett (Eds) *Theory and Practice of Psychiatric Rehabilitation.* Chichester: John Wiley.

Watts, F.N. (1988). Cognitive impairments. In J.M.G. Williams, F.N. Watts, C. M MacLeod & A. Mathews (Eds). *Cognitive Psychology and Emotional Disorders.* Hove: Lawrence Erlbaum Associates Ltd.

Williams, J.M.G. (1992). Autobiographical memory and emotional disorders. In S.-A. Christianson (Ed) *The Handbook of Emotion and Memory: Theory and Research.* Hillsdale, NJ: Lawrence Erlbaum Associates Inc.

Winer, B.J. (1971). *Statistical Principles in Experimental Design.* 2nd edn. New York: McGraw Hill.

CHAPTER TEN

Outcome research

David A Shapiro *Department of Psychology,*
University of Leeds

Mental health practice is composed of a large variety of interventions. These range from admission to a psychiatric ward to participation in a self-help group or taking a course of psychotropic medication. In relation to any of these, it seems reasonable and indeed socially important to ask, 'Does it work?', or 'Does intervention X work better than intervention Y?'. This chapter sets forth the basic principles of outcome research, which lies at the heart of efforts by clinical psychologists and others to build a scientific foundation for mental health practice. The aim is to provide a guide both to the design of outcome studies and to the critical reading of published outcome research, Examples will be taken from research on psychological treatments, because this is the field I know best. However, most of the principles discussed are common to all mental health interventions. Indeed, the basic research approach or paradigm of outcome research was originally developed for the evaluation of drug treatments.

CHOICE, COMPROMISE AND INFORMATIVENESS

The investigator seeking to establish the effectiveness of one or more interventions is faced with a large number of decisions about how to proceed. Research design is the discipline governing such decisions. It incorporates a number of key principles which must be attended to in framing an outcome study. Given the practical and resource constraints limiting any one study, however, the demands of these principles have an unfortunate tendency to conflict with one another; beginners should take heart from the fact that it is therefore impossible to design the 'perfect' study. The art of outcome research design thus becomes one of creative compromise based upon explicit understanding of the implications of the choices made (Aveline, Shapiro, Parry, & Freeman, 1995).

A good way to go about research design is to imagine that we have already completed the study we envisage, and that the results are available (Horowitz, 1982). This imaginative exercise should be repeated assuming all the patterns of results that we can envisage. Such an exercise will enable us to fulfil the central purpose of research design, which is to maximise the informativeness of the results by minimising the number of plausible explanations for them.

CHOOSING A DESIGN

The simplest approach to evaluating a treatment is to measure the symptoms or well-being of a series of patients before they undertake the treatment, and to repeat this measurement when treatment is complete. However, many competing explanations will reduce the informativeness of data obtained using this 'pre-post' design. In the technical terminology of outcome research, this method lacks 'controls' to exclude these alternative explanations (Table 10.1). Thus if patients are found to be, on average, no better off at the end of treatment than before, then this

TABLE 10.1
Outcome designs

Design	Features	Controls for:
Pre-post	One group, compare post-treatment with pre-treatment scores	
No-treatment control	Patients assigned to treatment or to no-treatment control group	(1) 'Spontaneous remission' or passage of time
Placebo control	Patients assigned to treatment or placebo-treatment control group	(1) as above (2) Expectations of benefit
Comparative outcome study	Patients assigned to one of several active treatments	(1) As above (2) As above but more convincing and ethical

appears to suggest that the treatment, as practised, is ineffective. However, one of several plausible alternative explanations is that the patients were on a deteriorating course which was effectively stemmed, albeit not reversed, by the treatment.

If, on the other hand, patients are on average much better off at the end than at the beginning of treatment, different explanations suggest themselves. There is of course the optimistic interpretation that the treatment is effective. However, alternatives include the possibility that the patients would have got better anyway. In psychotherapy research, this is known as 'spontaneous remission' (Lambert, 1976). Even if patients do not invariably improve without treatment, their mental health will undoubtedly vary over time and with changing circumstances, and they tend to seek help when they are at their worst.

Considerations such as these have led to the use of no-treatment control groups in the basic design for outcome research (Table 10.1). Rather than simply following a single group of treated patients, changes in those undertaking a treatment are compared with changes in others, the control group, not receiving that treatment. The logic of this comparison is that any changes in the control group give us an estimate of what would have happened to the treated group if they had not undertaken the treatment. This logic requires, of course, the assumption that the groups are composed of individuals whose personal characteristics and circumstances are comparable or interchangeable. Formally speaking, this assumption is expressed as follows: the treatment and control groups are comprised of individuals drawn and assigned to one or other treatment at random from the same parent population, every member of which enjoyed an equal probability of being assigned to either of the two groups.

So far, we have considered alternative explanations arising from changes in the treated individuals not attributable to treatment. Other alternative explanations arise from the possibility that the mere fact of receiving a treatment that participants believe to be effective may predispose them to experience or report benefits, irrespective of the efficacy or otherwise of the treatment procedures themselves. In the evaluation of drugs, this consideration gave rise to the use of placebo controls—the administration of inert tablets. In drug research, this preferably takes the form of a double-blind placebo trial, in which patients receiving an active drug are compared with others receiving an apparently identical but pharmacologically inert placebo, with both the patient and the administering personnel ignorant of (i.e. 'blind' to) the nature of the tablets taken by any one person. This contrasts with the simpler, single blind, method in which only the patient is unaware of the nature of the treatment.

Unfortunately, however, this method has limitations. First, there may be side-effects or other features that distinguish the active and placebo treatments and thus enable participants to 'break the blind'. In psychological treatments, participants (patient and therapist alike) cannot be ignorant of the procedures they are following, and cannot be prevented from formulating their own hypotheses and expectations as to the effectiveness or otherwise of the activities in which they are engaged. Personnel employed to interview patients to assess their progress are seldom able to avoid exposure to information (especially within patients' accounts of their experiences) that gives away the nature of the treatment they have undergone.

In addition, the conceptual distinction between 'active' and 'placebo' treatments that is so clear with pharmacological treatments is blurred when we consider psychological treatments (Wilkins, 1984). With physical treatments, the efforts of physicians to encourage the belief that the treatment is helpful are clearly separable, in terms of both operations and impact, from the biochemical pathways differentiating active from placebo treatments. In contrast, the encouragement of positive expectations is a psychological process much closer to those mediating the effectiveness of psychological treatments. Indeed the engendering of such positive expectations is probably a part of every psychological treatment, although different psychological treatments achieve this via differing means.

These considerations have led many outcome researchers to elaborate their designs one step further. Instead of—or sometimes as well as—comparing an active treatment with a placebo, they very often compare two or more active treatments in the same study (Basham, 1986). To the extent that all active treatments share the non-specific benefits arising from participants' belief in their value, this design reduces the need for a placebo condition. Dispensing with the placebo condition has the ethical advantage that no one is denied treatment, and that all patients are receiving something that has at least a good chance of being helpful. This design has the practical advantage of mirroring the actual choices available in clinical practice, which are more often between alternate courses of action than between 'doing something' and 'doing nothing'. Such comparative studies provide a concurrent opportunity to compare the contents or processes of the two treatments, which may help us identify the active ingredients within each treatment, and to find out just how different or similar these may be in the methods under comparison (Stiles, Shapiro & Elliot, 1986; Shapiro, Barkham, Hardy, Morrison, Reynolds, Startup, & Harper, 1991).

Important practical and ethical problems arise for any study in which the decision about which treatment a patient receives is influenced by research considerations as well as by the likely benefit to that patient. Practically, the researcher must consider the likely impact on the patient of becoming aware that alternatives to the treatment actually received are available within the same facility. Thus, for example, in-patients, or out-patients living or working in the same setting as one another can encounter other patients receiving different treatments. If one treatment is apparently superior (e.g. involves more patient-therapist contact), knowledge of this may well influence the reactions of patients assigned to the different treatments. Ethically, most would consider that the principle of informed consent requires that the patient be told that there are alternative treatments under comparison.

The investigator designing an outcome study should begin with a careful specification of the research question or questions to be answered in the study. This should define the nature of the two or more conditions to be compared. Next, the possible outcomes and their implications should be evaluated to ascertain to what extent each would provide unambiguous answers (i.e. answers not susceptible to alternative explanations) to the research questions. Several attempts at this may be necessary to yield a worthwhile design. The next step is to consider the details of its implementation. The methodological problems that must be overcome in carrying out an outcome study are considered next.

FOUR TYPES OF INVALIDITY

Many of the methodological problems faced in outcome research (Aveline & Shapiro, in press; Kazdin, 1978, 1986; Mahoney, 1978) may be subsumed within Cook and Campbell's (1979; Cook, Campbell, & Peracchio, 1990) discussion of validity and invalidity (Shapiro & Shapiro, 1983).

Cook and Campbell (1979; Cook, Campbell, & Peracchio, 1990) distinguish four types of validity, shown in Table10.2. Statistical conclusion validity refers to the validity with which a study permits conclusions about covariation between the assumed independent and dependent variables. Threats to statistical conclusion validity typically arise from unsystematic error rather than systematic bias. Internal validity refers to the validity with which statements can be made about whether there is a causal relationship from independent to dependent variables, in the form in which they were manipulated or measured. Threats to internal validity typically involve systematic bias. Construct validity of putative causes and effects refers to the validity with which we can make generalisations about higher order constructs from

TABLE 10.2
Aspects of validity

Validity type	Focus	Major issues	
Statistical conclusion	Covariation between independent and dependent variables	1. 2. 3	Statistical power Treatment delivery Heterogeneity of patients
Internal	Causal relationship between independent and dependent variables	1. 2.	Bias from pre-treatment differences Bias from attrition
Construct	Theoretical constructs	1. 2. 3. 4. 5. 6.	Representativeness of treatments Concomitant variation in non-specifics Investigator bias Reactivity of measures Specificity and relevance of measures Timing of assessment
External	Generalisability over persons, settings and times	Representativeness of: 1. Patients 2. Therapists 3. Settings	

research operations. Finally, external validity refers to the validity with which conclusions can be drawn about the generalisability of a causal relationship to and across populations of persons, settings, and times. Frequently encountered threats to each of the four types of validity will now be considered in detail.

Statistical conclusion validity

A central issue in statistical conclusion validity concerns statistical power; the probability of rejecting the null hypothesis when it is false. This depends upon the size of the difference between groups in relation to the variation within groups that an experimenter is seeking to detect, the level of statistical significance adopted in the test, and the numbers of subjects in the groups (Cohen, 1962, 1977).

Comparing a psychological treatment with no treatment, it is reasonable to expect a large effect of around one standard deviation unit (i.e. mean of treated group one standard deviation better than mean of untreated group). To detect such an effect, sample sizes around 20 are sufficient (Kraemer, 1981).

In marked contrast, the average effect obtained in studies comparing two different treatments is only one-half of a standard deviation (Kazdin, & Bass, 1989). To detect an effect of this magnitude, requires considerably larger groups—around 64 people completing each treatment. Power problems are exacerbated by attrition (missing data), which reduces the available sample size (in addition to introducing possible bias).

If a study has insufficient statistical power, the most likely outcome is no significant difference between the conditions. This does not prove that they are equally effective, but merely that the research has failed to detect a difference in their effects.

Uncontrolled variation in the way a treatment is delivered or implemented presents a second major threat to statistical conclusion validity. Shapiro and Shapiro (1983) found that the majority of the outcome studies they reviewed were deficient in this respect. However, this problem is increasingly being overcome by the preparation of manuals defining the treatment procedures to be followed (Beck, Rush, Shaw & Emery, 1979; Klerman et al., 1984; Luborsky, 1984). Project therapists are then trained to implement the techniques as specified in the manual, and their adherence to the manual is empirically assessed via process analysis of recorded sessions (Hill, O'Grady, & Elkin, 1992; Moncher & Prinz, 1991; Startup & Shapiro, 1993). The importance of this methodological advance is heightened by sustained concern with variations in the skilfulness with which therapists are found to deliver a treatment procedure (Schaffer, 1982). Just how far it is feasible or appropriate to go in the direction of specifying an intervention in writing will, of course, vary with the nature of that intervention. In principle, however, this should be done as much as possible (Luborsky & DeRubeis, 1984).

A third threat to statistical conclusion validity arises from excessive heterogeneity amongst the patients treated in an outcome study. It is often argued that patients differing in presenting problems, personality or life circumstances must be expected to differ in their response to a given treatment. On this argument, investigators admitting varied individuals to their treatment groups are subscribing to a 'uniformity myth' that invalidates their research. The increasingly common solution to this problem is to select patients on the basis of specified inclusion criteria, such as minimum scores on questionnaires such as the Beck Depression Inventory (Beck et al., 1961) or psychiatric diagnoses based on such systems as DSM-IV (American Psychiatric Association, 1994) or the PSE-ID-CATEGO system (Wing, Cooper, & Sartorius, 1974). Despite the obvious logical attractions of this approach, it has drawbacks. At a purely practical level, the more restrictive the inclusion criteria the longer it will take to locate suitable patients and the less willingly will other professionals refer to the research programme. Notoriously, patients meeting given criteria suddenly become much rarer when a researcher launches a trial requiring such patients! Furthermore, the more restricted the population from which the patients are drawn, the narrower is the range of patients to whom the results may be generalised. In addition, making the patient population homogeneous may prevent the investigator from finding out which patient characteristics are prognostic of good versus poor outcome in the treatments being studied.

Another problem is that the measures used to select patients may not tap the most important and treatment-relevant similarities and differences between individuals—for example, similarities in terms of symptoms could conceal large differences in terms of underlying personality or be overshadowed by differences in social integration. Finally, it must be acknowledged that the available selection criteria often fail to meet the rigourous scientific standards of precision that inspired their introduction into an outcome design. For example, DSM-IV criteria for affective disorders are based upon an interviewer's judgement as to the presence of a certain number of symptoms drawn from a menu-like list. Thus although homogeneous patient groups are in principle desirable in outcome research, the gains may sometimes be more apparent than real, and, like most design advances, carry some drawbacks too.

A different perspective on statistical conclusion validity derives from the growing concern with clinical as opposed to statistical significance of results. From a practitioner's perspective, statistical power may be counterproductive if it enables researchers to report statistically reliable results based upon trivially small differences between groups assigned to alternative treatments. Procedures to ascertain the clinical significance of change have been developed (Hugdahl & Ost, 1981; Jacobson, Follette, & Revenstorf, 1984; Kazdin & Wilson, 1978; Yeaton & Sechrest, 1981). For example, an individual may be deemed improved to a clinically significant extent if their score on a clinically relevant measure improves more than could be expected on the basis of measurement error alone, and reaches a level after treatment that would be more characteristic of the general population than of people requiring treatment.

Internal validity

Threats to internal validity chiefly concern sources of possible bias in the comparison between experimental conditions. A primary requirement is to ensure that the groups of individuals assigned to different experimental conditions are comparable at the outset.

The most common solution to this problem is random assignment (Shapiro & Shapiro, 1983). However, randomisation can often result in nonequivalent groups, especially if the samples are small, with consequent opportunities for the groups to differ by chance. When this happens, investigators must attempt to 'correct' for the initial differences in some way. One solution is the use of 'residual gain scores' from which the effects of initial differences are statistically partialled out. The principles underlying this are illustrated in Figs 10.1 and 10.2.

In Fig. 10.1, every individual is represented by either a circle or by a cross, depending on which of two treatments they received. The individual's position in the figure is determined by that person's scores before treatment (along the horizontal axis) and after treatment (along the vertical axis). The relationship between pre- and post-treatment scores for the sample as a whole is represented by the regression line shown. This line provides the 'best fit' to the complete set of data. This fit is determined by the criterion that the sum of the squares of all the vertical distances from individual points to the line be as small as possible. Note that, in the example shown, the circles tend to be above the regression line, and the crosses below it. These vertical distances

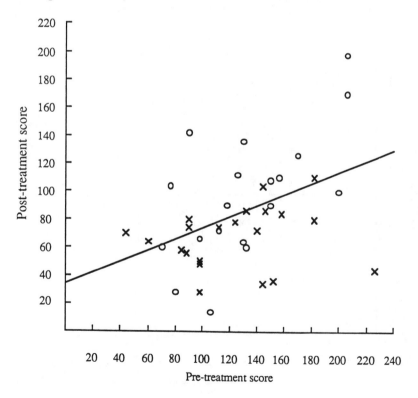

FIG. 10.1. Regression of post-treatment on pre-treatment scores.

are known as residuals. Figure 10.2 shows these rescaled, as residual gain scores. Here, the regression line is now the horizontal axis, so that points on the line have a score of zero.

Thus this method substitutes for each raw post-treatment score the difference between that score and the score that would have been expected, given the pre-treatment score obtained for that individual and the relationship for the sample as a whole between pre- and post-treatment scores. This method is only useful if the correlation between pre- and post-treatment scores is large enough for sufficient correction to be obtained (Mintz, Luborsky, & Christolph, 1979).

Another solution is to analyse arithmetic differences between post- and pre-treatment scores. However, these difference scores compound the error components in the two scores from which they are derived, with a consequent loss in statistical power. A third solution is known as 'blocking'. This comprises post-hoc division of the participants into two or more groups, according to the level of their pretreatment scores, and then using two-way analysis of variance to establish whether the post-

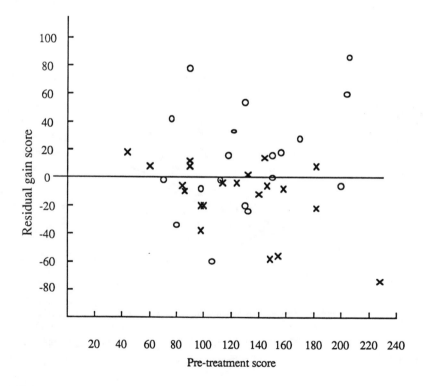

FIG. 10.2. Residual gain scores.

treatment difference between treatments is similar or different for people at different levels on the pretreatment variable.

A variant on blocking is to stratify the sample in advance into two or more levels of severity of disorder before randomising to treatment conditions (Shapiro, Barkham, Rees, Hardy, Reynolds, & Startup, 1994). This does not guarantee equivalent pretreatment groups at each level of severity however; Shapiro et al. (1994) obtained pre-assignment differences between their high-severity groups randomised to two durations of treatment.

Whenever two samples differ before treatment, no merely statistical manipulation can guarantee that the initial difference between the groups under comparison was not responsible for the post-treatment differences observed; such corrections do not address the question of whether the two samples were drawn from the same population and would have changed similarly if given similar treatments. In order to avoid these problems, it has sometimes been suggested that randomisation be abandoned altogether in favour of prematching individual pairs or sets of individuals to each of the two or more treatment conditions, but this raises tricky statistical issues.

A second, related source of bias derives from attrition or loss of subjects from the study (Howard, Krause, & Orlinsky, 1986). Howard et al. point out that this begins before inclusion in the study, as there is a natural filtering process whereby some members of the population deemed to be appropriate for inclusion in the study become unavailable, either through choice or through intervening circumstance; whereas other members have a disproportionately better chance of inclusion.

After inclusion in a study, subjects may be lost for a variety of reasons, most of which threaten to bias the study because they cannot be dissociated from the treatment and the subject's reactions to it. People may discontinue treatment, opting to seek alternative treatment or believing that they no longer need help. They may continue treatment, but fail or refuse to supply post-treatment data. When the rates of post-inclusion attrition differ across groups being compared, the causes of that attrition are likely to differ also, so that the groups are no longer comparable. It is difficult to place an upper bound on acceptable attrition rates, as these will vary with the treatment and assessment demands of the study and with the population under investigation. In the light of data presented by Shapiro and Shapiro (1983) on typical post-inclusion attrition rates, however, it is reasonable to expect of investigators the loss of no more than the reported mean 10% of participants from any treatment group.

Howard et al. (1986) review several methods that have been developed to compensate for the effects of attrition, but note that these all rest on the untenable assumption that 'attritors' and 'completers' are equivalent samples of the same population. These authors recommend the elimination from data analyses of all cases missing any independent variable data and the use of only those cases that are not missing data on a dependent variable in any analysis involving that particular dependent variable.

More radically, however, Howard et al. (1986) propose a reorientation of research strategy away from the pretence of control for what cannot be controlled, towards a new perspective in which the basic unit of study is the individual case, described with as much dependent and independent variable information as is required at the present state of development of psychotherapy research. In this new strategy, it is the knowledge of which points in the independent variable space are associated with the best average outcomes that is ultimately of clinical importance. Thus if dependent variable data are missing from a point in the independent variable space represented by the combination of two independent variable values, each of which is associated with better than average outcomes, it becomes important to design a study that will capture data at this point.

Construct validity

Representativeness of treatments.   Cook and Campbell (1979) consider the adequacy with which the independent variable is represented within a study as an important aspect of construct validity. It is important that the treatments incorporated within a study be designed to represent the techniques of interest, both with respect to such obvious structural features as the number and duration of sessions, and more subtle aspects such as the specific interventions or general interpersonal style of the therapist. Kazdin (1986) presents a careful discussion of 'treatment integrity', noting that in some comparative studies it may be appropriate to allow some features of the treatments to vary to represent the treatments more faithfully, even though the variations may also be looked upon as confounds. This arises, for example, when different treatments are expected to require differing numbers of sessions to attain their optimal effectiveness.

Control for non-specific effects.   A major issue in psychotherapy research has been the extent to which treatment effects are attributable to the specific techniques under investigation, rather than to so-called 'non-specific' factors such as the arousal of expectations on the part of clients that the treatment will be beneficial. If such factors are present to different degrees in different treatments, this concomitant variation threatens the construct validity of the research by suggesting that the mechanism whereby one treatment is more effective than another may be quite different from the more specific one envisaged by the theory underlying that treatment. In the 1960s and 1970s, increasingly sophisticated controls for such effects were incorporated into research designs, on the basis of an explicit analogy with the use of pharmacologically inert placebos in drug research (Shapiro & Morris, 1978). An early example of this was Paul's (1966) incorporation into his comparative outcome study of an 'attention placebo' condition.

Subsequently, however, the adequacy of such controls was questioned (Borkovec & Nau, 1972; Kazdin & Wilcoxon, 1976; Shapiro, 1981). Specifically, it was suggested that optimal control for non-specific effects required empirical demonstration that the control condition was as credible as the active treatments with which it was to be compared. Failing that, Kazdin and Wilcoxon (1976) advocated a treatment-element control strategy, in which the control procedure resembles the active treatment as closely as possible. For example, Holroyd et al. (1984) found that tension headache sufferers improved as much with electromyographic (EMG) feedback increasing muscle activity as with feedback reducing it. Shapiro and Shapiro (1983) report that only a small minority of comparative outcome studies incorporated such controls.

Subsequently, however, it has been argued that the predominant conceptualisation of non-specific effects in psychotherapy as analogous with the placebo effect in drug therapy (Shapiro & Morris, 1978) is misguided (Wilkins, 1984; Parloff, 1986).

For example, Parloff (1986) argues that under the necessarily nonblind experimental conditions of psychotherapy research, it is well-nigh impossible to ensure that therapists and their patients will view the experimental and placebo treatments as equally credible. The neat medical distinction between core somatic pathology and symptoms cannot be sustained with respect to psychological disorder. The effectiveness of all psychological treatments is likely to be based in part upon common factors arousing hope and expectation of benefit. Thus it is misguided to seek a true placebo, controlling for the actual active ingredients of a treatment, whether such ingredients are characteristic or incidental, unique or common. These considerations lead Parloff (1986) to recommend research designs comparing known alternate treatment forms and modalities, which can serve as natural placebo controls for each other (Rosenthal & Frank, 1956).

Investigator bias.   Closely linked with the question of non-specific effects is the likely impact of experimenter bias upon psychotherapy studies. Reasons for suspecting the influence of subtle, unwitting demands by investigators upon the responses made by subjects include the substantial evidence for experimenter effects in psychological research (Rosenthal & Rubin, 1978). These effects are the social influences at work in a situation defined as one in which one person is professionally engaged in the task of helping another, the strong and enthusiastic allegiances of psychotherapists to their preferred orientations and treatment methods, and the previously noted impossibility of double-blind conditions in psychotherapy research.

Smith, Glass and Miller (1980) found a substantial correlation between the allegiance of investigators (inferred from analysis of their published reports) and the results they obtained for a given treatment. There is a tendency for new psychotherapeutic methods to show outstandingly good results in early studies published by their originators, followed by more modest findings characteristic of the field as a whole when studied by less committed workers. For example, Berman, Miller and Massman (1985) attribute the failure of more recent studies to confirm earlier reports of the superiority of cognitive therapy over other methods (Shapiro & Shapiro, 1982a) to the greater allegiance of earlier investigators to cognitive therapy. Independent replication in several institutions is required for the true importance of any mental health treatment to be established.

Reactivity of outcome measures. A further, related construct validity issue concerns the vulnerability of outcome measures to the biasing effects discussed earlier. For example, measures administered 'blind' by individuals unaware of the treatment condition to which subjects have been assigned tend to yield smaller treatment effects (Shapiro & Shapiro, 1983). This is despite the fact that the impact of the blind is in reality reduced by unavoidable disclosures to experimenters of the subject's treatment assignment. For example, during interviews subjects often refer, directly or indirectly, to their treatment experiences; if the interviewer knows which treatments are under comparison, it is often impossible to avoid matching these incidental remarks to the treatment conditions.

Different outcome measures vary in the extent to which they are vulnerable to bias. Thus therapist ratings or self-report measures of the severity of the problem for which the person is seeking help are highly reactive to demand characteristics, whereas a physiological index is much less so. There is evidence that more reactive measures yield more favourable results (Shapiro & Shapiro, 1983; Smith et al., 1980). Whilst therapist ratings and self-reports have their place, this implies that every study should include at least one non-reactive measure of change.

Specificity and relevance of measures.   The construct validity of a study is threatened if the outcome measures used are not sufficiently specific to the problem under treatment, or not relevant to the goals of treatment. Some investigators (e.g. Rachman & Wilson, 1980) attribute the equivocal findings of much outcome research to excessively general, crude outcome measures based upon simplistic models of such constructs as anxiety. Shapiro and Shapiro (1983) found more powerful effects with measures that were more specific to the goals of treatment.

It is a commonplace observation in psychotherapy research that different outcome measures applied to the same clients in the same treatments may yield quite different results. For this and other reasons, there is general agreement (Lambert, Christensen, & DeJulio, 1983; Kazdin, 1986; Lambert et al., 1986) that outcome assessment needs to be multifaceted, involving different perspectives (the treated individual, significant others, professional observers), different aspects of the individual (e.g. behaviour, affect, and cognition) and different modalities of assessment (e.g. selfreport, direct observation, and clinician ratings). However, Shapiro and Shapiro (1983) found that most investigators confined themselves to only one or two out of five assessment modalities.

Another measurement issue is that it may be important to distinguish the effects of a mental health treatment from the value attached to such effects. Some investigators have argued that different psychotherapies may have different and potent effects that are valued differently by different people (Stiles, 1983; Strupp & Hadley, 1977). Projecting multiple dimensions onto a single dimension of 'improvement' or 'change' by using averaged scales makes therapies comparable but at a cost of masking their diversity and potency of effect (Stiles et al., 1986).

A final aspect of measurement that bears on construct validity relates to the timing of outcome assessment. In principle, outcome research should demonstrate the maintenance of treatment effects over time. Although Nicholson and Berman (1983) have provided persuasive evidence that follow-up data are typically very similar to data obtained immediately after the completion of treatment, there are striking exceptions to this generalisation for particular problems and treatments (Kazdin, 1986). For example, Kingsley and Wilson (1977) found that individual behaviour therapy was more effective in achieving weight reduction at post-treatment when compared with a group treatment based on social pressure; 1 year later, however, weight loss data favoured the social pressure treatment. In the review by Shapiro and Shapiro (1983), 77% of outcome data were obtained immediately after treatment, and only 6% were obtained 4 or more months after the end of treatment. Investigators' reluctance to present long-term follow-up data is readily explicable: such data are costly to obtain, and are often compromised by attrition or by participation in additional treatment.

External validity

External validity is defined by Cook and Campbell (1979) in relation to problems of generalising to particular target persons, settings, and times; and of generalising across types of persons, settings, and times. For psychotherapy research, the central problem is the extent to which the persons and settings studied in the literature represent those of clinical practice.

Much psychotherapy research has taken the form of 'analogue' studies in which undergraduate students are solicited to participate in brief treatments designed to help them overcome circumscribed and relatively minor problems such as public speaking anxiety or specific phobias (Kazdin, 1978; Mathews, 1978; Borkovec & Rachman, 1979), conducted in laboratory or academic rather than in clinical settings. There is some evidence that such studies may show larger gains in treatment than are found in settings and with populations more representative of clinical practice (Smith et al., 1980; Shapiro & Shapiro, 1983). On the other hand, therapists in such research tend to be trainees, unrepresentative of qualified and experienced therapists, and likely, if anything, to yield less favourable outcomes. Krupnick, Shea and Elkin (1986) reviewed 14 studies presenting direct comparisons between solicited and non-solicited patients receiving treatment in clinically representative settings. These authors concluded that results of studies using solicited patients alone must be interpreted with caution. Not only may such studies over- or under-estimate response to treatment, but they may also yield conclusions concerning the relative efficacy of different treatments that do not hold up when tested with non-solicited patients.

Of course, there are often good reasons to choose solicited populations. Within the resource limitations and practical constraints under which mental health researchers operate, the demands of external validity are often in conflict with those of internal or construct validity. For example, random allocation to different treatments may not be feasible in an established clinical service, with referral patterns based on the reputations and preferred treatment methods of individual practitioners. A comparative design that allowed individuals to be assigned to treatments in such a biased way would confound the treatment variable under test with features of the therapists, the patients, and their circumstances which influenced the referral decisions. These same features would also probably contribute substantially to the outcome obtained in each case. This would present a fatal threat to the internal validity of the study as a comparison between treatments. In these circumstances, the preferred compromise would almost certainly be to sacrifice external to internal validity and solicit patients via new channels outside the established referral system, to enable random assignment to treatments.

In the long run, it is probably best to divide research efforts on a given type of intervention into distinct phases during each of which the conflict between internal and external validity is resolved differently. For example, initial development of a new method may be best carried out in practice settings. When the method appears promising, controlled experiments high on internal validity are the next step in establishing its effectiveness. Finally, however, conclusions from such controlled trials need to be tested in the 'real world' of uncontrolled clinical practice. Salkovskis (1995) describes these three phases as forming an 'hourglass', the breadth of whose shape at top and bottom represents generalisibility to the highly variable conditions obtaining in clinical practice.

MAKING SENSE OF EXISTING
OUTCOME RESEARCH

A vast number of controlled and comparative outcome studies of mental health treatments have been published over the past 40 years. This large amount of information is difficult to integrate in such a way as to provide clear guidelines for future practice, training and research. Indeed, reviewers attempting such integrations of outcome research on mental health treatments, particularly psychotherapy, have reached disparate conclusions. In relation to 'verbal', non-behavioural therapies, for example, the negative conclusions drawn by Eysenck (1952) and by Rachman and Wilson (1980) conflict sharply with the more optimistic evaluations of Bergin (1971; Bergin & Lambert, 1978), Meltzoff and Kornreich (1970), and Luborsky, Singer, and Luborsky (1975).

Such debates may in part reflect subjective and unsystematic elements of the traditional approach to reviewing scientific literature. The terms *meta-analysis* and *research synthesis* denote a family of approaches and techniques based upon the application to the literature review process of the methodological principles of empirical social science (Cooper & Hedges, 1994; Glass, McGaw, & Smith, 1981; Shapiro & Shapiro, 1982a; Shapiro, 1985). Meta-analysis entered clinical psychology with the appearance of Smith and Glass's (1977; Smith, Glass, & Miller, 1980) review of psychotherapy outcome studies. This work has been widely praised (Fiske, 1983; Rosenthal, 1978), criticised

(Eysenck, 1978; Wilson & Rachman, 1983) and built upon (Andrews & Harvey, 1981; Landman & Dawes, 1982; Prioleau, Murdock, & Brody, 1983; Robinson, Berman, & Neimeyer, 1990; Shapiro & Shapiro, 1982b) by other reviewers.

Table 10.3 summarises some differences between traditional and meta-analytic reviews. A traditional, narrative review was qualitative in orientation, with rational and interpretive considerations governing its scope, procedures and conclusions. It commonly excluded studies from consideration which the reviewer considered severely deficient from a methodological point of view. Studies were grouped according to characteristics shared in common, and results of such grouped studies were presented in tabular form.

In contrast, a meta-analysis is primarily quantitative in orientation. Selection of studies is governed by sampling principles; a sample of studies is drawn, following replicable procedures, from the population of studies addressing the issue at hand. Exclusion of individual studies on the basis of evaluative judgements of their quality, made in full knowledge of the findings of the study, is typically avoided. Rather, studies are scored for their methodological attributes, using defined coding schemes of proven reliability, and these methodological attributes are subsequently correlated with the findings of each study, to determine empirically the impact of study quality on the results obtained. Meta-analysis thus takes account of study quality, but in a quantitative fashion rather than by selection of 'good' studies. This process does not eliminate the need for human judgement in evaluating research, but, rather, attempts to systematise the exercise of such judgement in accordance with the canons of social science.

TABLE 10.3
Traditional versus meta-analytic reviews

	Traditional	Meta-analytic
Orientation	Qualitative	Quantitative
Coverage	Selective	Representative or exhaustive
Quality control	By exclusion	Expirical evaluation
Organisation	Study by study	By features
Representation of findings	Narrative statements	Quantitative and/or probabilistic
Description of study features	Qualitative	Systematic coding schemes
Linking study features to outcomes	Narrative statements	Disaggregation and statistical analysis

Other attributes of each study are similarly coded, so that the study-by-study narrative of the traditional review can be replaced by generalisations across studies, organised according to features common to or differing between groups of studies. In mental health treatment research, for example, the literature can be described in terms of such parameters as the types of patients treated, the treatment methods used, the length and format of treatment, and the instruments used to assess client change.

Meta-analysis differs from traditional reviews in how the findings of each study are represented. The outcome of each study, or of each treatment comparison contained within each study, is expressed quantitatively. Most commonly, a difference between group means is expressed in standard deviation units. Such a standardised difference score is known as an effect size. The meaning of this statistic can be illustrated with reference to a hypothetical example shown in Fig. 10.3. This diagram represents a study in which the difference between treated and untreated control subjects is equal to an effect size of 1.0.

If we assume that the scores on the outcome measure follow the familiar, bell-shaped normal distribution, an effect size of 1.0 implies that 84.1% of the members of the treated group are better off in terms of the outcome measure than the average member of the control group. Another way to think of an effect size is in terms of the percentage of variance it accounts for. Considering the variation in outcome between all the individuals in both groups, for an effect size of 1.0 it turns out that 20% of this variation amongst individuals can be attributed to their membership of one or other of the two groups, with the remaining 80% of the variation being due to other factors probably unrelated to

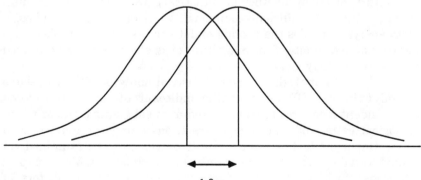

1.0σ

FIG. 10.3. Effect size of one standard deviation.

treatment. Yet a third way of understanding an effect size is based upon the idea of dividing the combined sample into 'successes' and 'failures' according to a dichotomous criterion appropriate to the particular sample and circumstances. In the case of an effect size of 1.0 as between treated and untreated groups, we find that treatment enhances subjects' success rate by 45% (Rosenthal, 1983).

Another approach involves cumulative testing of the null hypothesis of no treatment differences across studies by combining the probabilities obtained in each study (Rosenthal, 1978). Yet another method is to divide mean pre-post difference scores by mean pre-treatment scores in each group (Blanchard, Andrasik, Ahler, Teders, & O'Keefe, 1980). This method takes no account of within-group variation.

Reviewers summarising data from a series of studies traditionally tallied the number of positive (i.e. statistically significant) and null (i.e. not statistically significant) findings in a 'box score' total (e.g. Luborsky et al., 1975). All the meta-analytic methods described here preserve more information about the magnitude of effects obtained in each study than this simple, binary, box score. The box score procedure compounds the statistical conclusion validity problems which ensue if each study has inadequate statistical power when considered alone. The box score method misrepresented every study whose results were in the predicted direction, but did not attain significance on account of inadequate statistical power, as evidence against the hypothesised relationship between treatment and outcome. This difficulty is overcome in meta-analysis, because each finding is represented as an effect size, expressing in standard deviation units the magnitude of the difference between treatment groups, irrespective of the statistical significance of each result considered alone.

As will be readily apparent, meta-analysis can overcome some of the difficulties created by insufficient statistical power of individual studies. Provided there is sufficient commonality across a set of studies, a meta-analysis enables the pooling of data across several studies, for a more reliable estimate of the magnitude of an effect than can be derived from any one study alone.

Finally, meta-analysis involves statistical analysis of the correlates of study outcomes. Effect sizes or other indices of outcome are considered as dependent measures to be predicted from substantive and/or methodological features of each study. The relations of single parameters such as treatment method or sample size to outcome can be examined via simple statistics such at t tests or zero-order correlations. More complex questions (such as the identification of independent predictors of outcome from amongst sets of predictors, or the search for interactions between client and treatment parameters in the determination of outcome) can be addressed with correspondingly complex statistical procedures such as multiple regression. Large and varied data sets (such as are found in mental health treatment outcome research) are particularly suited to this type of analysis. which offers the potential for a much richer account of the relationships between study parameters and outcome than the traditional narrative review.

Perusal of any recent issue of the review journal *Psychological Bulletin* will demonstrate that meta-analysic methods have become the norm in the integration of research data throughout the behavioural and social sciences. Meta-analytic findings were drawn upon to illuminate several of the methodological issues discussed earlier in this chapter. The contrast between meta-analytic and traditional reviews, presented in Table 10.3, is becoming obsolete as most reviewers use meta-analytic techniques, which are themselves subject to continuing development and refinement by their own methodologists (e.g. Hedges & Olkin, 1985; Cooper & Hedges, 1994).

However, it remains the case that no technique is free of problems; specifically, careful attention is required to the impact of the assumptions made in carrying out the meta-analysis upon the conclusions drawn. Furthermore, there may be insufficient studies looking at new or unusual treatments to permit a meaningful meta-analysis. The advent of meta-analysis has thrown into new relief some recurrent weaknesses of outcome studies, together with avoidable limitations in the precision with which their methods and data are reported. Investigators planning outcome research should anticipate the inclusion of their published work within future meta-analytic reviews. This has implications both for the conduct of the research itself and for how it is reported. For example, the informativeness of meta-analyses is enhanced if investigators use closely comparable outcome measures and patient inclusion criteria in different studies, and if they ensure that all necessary information is included in their reports (Shapiro & Shapiro, 1983).

COSTS, BENEFITS AND EFFECTIVENESS

In health service practice, it is painfully obvious that the availability of mental health treatments is limited by resource constraints. Treatment decisions for individual patients are influenced by the availability of therapists, office space and other resources. For example, the waiting list for the best available treatment may be so long that immediate access to a less oversubscribed intervention may be preferable for the patient. Underlying such individual dilemmas are the strategic choices made by health districts in deciding how much of which kinds of service to make available, which would in an ideally rational world be governed by evidence showing how to gain the maximum benefit to the patient population from available resources. If outcome research is to facilitate such rational policy formulation, therefore, it must measure the costs as well as the effects of interventions (Yates & Newman, 1980; Newman & Howard, 1986). Drummond, Stoddart and Torrance (1987) discuss the economic evaluation of healthcare in general.

Following Newman and Howard (1986), we may define the costs of an episode of treatment in terms of the cost of each 'unit of service activity' (such as an individual psychotherapy session). Each unit cost consists of the salary and fringe benefit cost for the professional(s) involved for that proportion of their working time, plus the costs of material resources used and of allocated overheads (such as accommodation, support staff, heating, etc., also expressed as a proportion of annual figures). The total cost of an episode of treatment is obtained by summing the costs of the units of service it comprises. As noted by Newman and Howard (1986), however, such cost measures are no more than an estimation procedure for describing the human efforts and material ingredients invested in an intervention. In addition, these authors have extended the cost concept to that of 'therapeutic effort', also encompassing the degree to which an intervention imposes restrictions upon the freedom of the patient.

Costs can be related to effects in two ways. First, cost-effectiveness analysis expresses the yield of an intervention in terms of units of effectiveness per unit of cost, without attempting to scale effectiveness in monetary terms. Thus we might compare treatments in terms of the costs in £s per symptom point reduction on a standard measure such as the Present State Examination. In a study by Piper, Debbane, Bienvenu, and Garant (1984) comparing four forms of psychotherapy (long-term versus short-term variants of both individual and group therapy), cost considerations altered the relative merits of the four conditions as compared with their ordering with respect to effectiveness alone. In contrast, cost-benefit analysis takes the further step of assigning financial value to the effects of treatment. For example, the financial benefits to the state of a successful psychotherapy might include the reduced benefits liabilities and increased taxation income consequent upon the patient's return to employment. Cost-benefit analysis entails several complex and debatable economic assumptions and value judgments, and is thus too ambitious and fraught an enterprise for many outcome researchers. Cost-effectiveness analysis, on the other hand, can be recommended as a helpful addition to most comparative outcome studies. In summary:

1. Treatment decisions depend on costs as well as effectiveness of treatment.
2. Therapeutic effort reflects costs of treatment episode plus restrictions on patient's freedom.
3. Cost-effectiveness analysis expresses yield in terms of units of effectiveness per unit of cost.
4. Cost-benefit analysis expresses yield in terms of financial benefit per financial unit of cost.

CONCLUSION

This chapter has reviewed the most common designs for outcome research studies, discussed methodological issues bearing upon the validity of such studies, outlined the meta-analytic approach to summarising existing research findings, and introduced the appraisal of costs as an important element in the evaluation of mental health treatments. As noted at the outset, the art of outcome research design is one of creative compromise, since practical constraints and the countervailing demands of different methodological criteria preclude the 'perfect' study. In practice, the definitive evaluation of a given method requires complementary and convergent evidence from a body of methodologically diverse studies ranging from laboratory analogues with good internal and statistical conclusion validity to field trials with good external validity.

Under-resourced and possibly inexperienced investigators working in service settings should take heart from this state of affairs. Careful attention to the principles discussed here will enable them to make worthwhile contributions to outcome research. The goal in planning such studies, of course, is to maximise the yield from the design strengths available whilst minimising the weaknesses stemming from unavoidable deficiencies. Given the benefits of methodological diversity in outcome research, there is a continuing need for soundly designed, albeit modestly resourced, studies in service settings.

REFERENCES

American Psychiatric Association (1994). *Diagnostic and Statistical Manual of Mental Disorders*, 4th edn. Washington. DC: American Psychiatric Association.

Andrews, G. & Harvey, R. (1981). Does psychotherapy benefit neurotic patients? A reanalysis of the Smith, Glass and Miller data. *Archives of General Psychiatry, 38*, 1203-1208.

Aveline, M., & Shapiro, D.A. (eds.) (in press). *Research foundations for psychotherapy practice*. Chichester: John Wiley.

Aveline, M., Shapiro, D.A., Parry, G., & Freeman, C. (1995). Building research foundations for psychotherapy practice. In M. Aveline & D.A. Shapiro (eds.) *Research foundations for psychotherapy practice*, pp.301–322. Chichester: John Wiley.

Basham. R.B. (1986). Scientific and practical advantages of comparative design in psychotherapy research. *Journal of Consulting and Clinical Psychology, 54*,88-94.

Beck, A.T., Rush, A.J., Shaw, B.F., & Emery, G. (1979). *Cognitive Therapy of Depression*. New York: Guilford Press.

Beck, A.T,. Ward, C.H., Mendelson, M., Mock, J., & Earbaugh, J. (1961). An inventory for measuring depression. *Archives of General Psychiatry, 4*, 561-571.

Bergin, A.E. (1971). The evaluation of therapeutic outcomes. In A.E. Bergin & S.L. Garfield (eds.), *Handbook of Psychotherapy and Behaviour Change: An Empirical Analysis*. New York: John Wiley.

Bergin, A.E. & Lambert, M.J. (1978). The evaluation of therapeutic outcomes. In S.L. Garfield & A.E. Bergin (eds.), *Handbook of Psychotherapy and Behavior Change: An Empirical Analysis*, 2nd edn. New York: John Wiley.

Berman, J.S., Miller, R.C., & Massman, P.J. (1985). Cognitive therapy versus systematic desensitization: Is one treatment superior? *Psychological Bulletin, 97*, 451- 461.

Blanchard, E.B., Andrasik, F., Ahler, T.A., Teders, S.J., & O'Keefe, D.O. (1980). Migraine and tension headache: A meta-analytic review. *Behavior Therapy, 11*, 613-631.

Borkovec, T.D. & Nau, S.D. (1972). Credibility of analogue therapy rationales. *Journal of Behavior Therapy and Experimental Psychiatry, 3*, 257-260.

Borkovec, T.D. & Rachman, S. (1979). The utility of analogue research. *Behaviour Research and Therapy, 17*, 253-261.

Cohen, J. (1962). The statistical power of abnormal-social psychological research: A review. *Journal of Abnormal and Social Psychology, 65*, 145-153.

Cohen, J. (1977). *Statistical Power Analysis for the Behavioral Sciences*, 2nd edn. New York: Academic Press.

Cook, T.D. & Campbell, D.T. (1979). *Quasi-experimentation: Design and Analysis for Field Settings*. Chicago: Rand McNally.

Cook, T.D., Campbell, D.T., & Peracchio, L. (1990). Quasi-experimentation. In M.D. Dunnette & L.M. Hough (eds.), *Handbook of Industrial and Organizational Psychology*, Second Edition, Volume 1, pp 491-576. Palo Alto, CA: Consulting Psychologists Press.

Cooper, H., & Hedges, L.V. (1994). *Handbook of Research Synthesis*. New York: Sage.

Drummond, M.F., Stoddart, G.L., & Torrance, G.W. (1987). *Methods of economic evaluation of health care programmes*. Oxford: Oxford University Press.

Eysenck, H.J. (1952). The effects of psychotherapy: An evaluation. *Journal of Consulting Psychology, 16*, 319-324.

Eysenck, H.J. (1978). An exercise in mega-silliness. *American Psychologist, 33*, 517.

Fiske, D.W. (1983). The meta-analytic revolution in outcome research. *Journal of Consulting and Clinical Psychology, 51*, 65-70.

Garfield, S.L. (1983). Introduction to special section. *Journal of Consulting and Clinical Psychology, 51*, 3.

Glass, G.V., McGaw, B., & Smith, M.L. (1981). *Meta-analysis in Social Research*. Beverly Hills, CA: Sage.

Gottman, J.M., & Rushe, R.H. (eds.). (1993). Special section: The analysis of change. *Journal of Consulting and Clinical Psychology, 61*, 907-983.

Hedges, L.V., & Olkin, I. (1985). *Statistical methods for meta-analysis*. London: Academic Press.

Hill, C.E., O'Grady, K.E., & Elkin, I. (1992). Applying the Collaborative Study Psychotherapy Rating Scale to rate therapist adherence in Cognitive-behaviour Therapy, Interpersonal Therapy, and Clinical Management. *Journal of Consulting and Clinical Psychology, 60*, 73-79.

Holroyd, K.A., Penzien, D.B., Hursey, K.G., Tobin, D. L., Rogers, L., Holm, J.E., Marcille, P.J., Hail, J.R., & Chila, A.G. (1984). Change mechanisms in EMG biofeedback training: Cognitive changes underlying improvements in tension headache. *Journal of Consulting and Clinical Psychology, 52*, 1039-1053.

Horowitz, M.J. (1982). Strategic dilemmas and the socialization of psychotherapy researchers. *British Journal of Clinical Psychology, 21*, 119-127.

Howard, K.I., Krause, M.S., & Orlinsky, D.E. (1986). The attrition dilemma: Toward a new strategy for psychotherapy research. *Journal of Consulting and Clinical Psychology, 54*, 106-110.

Hugdahl, K. & Ost, L. (1981). On the difference between statistical and clinical significance. *Behavioral Assessment, 3*, 289-295.

Jacobson, N.S., Follette, W.C., & Revenstorf, D. (1984). Psychotherapy outcome research: Methods for reporting variability and evaluating clinical significance. *Behavior Therapy, 15*, 336-352.

Jacobson, N.S. & Truax, P. (1991). Clinical significance: A statistical approach to defining meaningful change in psychotherapy research. *Journal of Consulting and Clinical Psychology, 59*, 12-19.

Kazdin, A.E. (1978). Evaluating the generality of findings in analogue therapy research. *Journal of Consulting and Clinical Psychology, 46*, 673-586.

Kazdin, A.E. (1986). Comparative outcome studies of psychotherapy: Methodological issues and strategies. *Journal of Consulting and Clinical Psychology, 54*, 95-105.

Kazdin, A.E., & Bass, D. (1989). Power to detect differences between alternative treatments in comparative psychotherapy outcome research. *Journal of Consulting and Clinical Psychology, 57*, 138-147.

Kazdin, A.E. & Wilcoxon, L.A. (1976). Systematic Desensitization and non-specific treatment effects: A methodological evaluation. *Psychological Bulletin, 83*, 729-758.

Kazdin, A.E. & Wilson, G.T. (1978). *Evaluation of Behavior Therapy: Issues, Evidence, and Research Strategies*. Cambridge Mass.: Ballinger.

Kingsley, R.G. & Wilson, G.T. (1977). Behavior therapy for obesity: A comparative investigation of long-term efficacy. *Journal of Consulting and Clinical Psychology, 45*, 288-298.

Klerman, G., Rounsaville, B., Chevron, E., Neu, C., & Weissman, M. (1984). *Manual for Short-term Interpersonal Therapy for Depression*. New York: Basic Books.

Kraemer, H.C. (1981). Coping strategies in psychiatric clinical research. *Journal of Consulting and Clinical Psychology, 49*, 309-319.

Krupnick, J., Shea, T., & Elkin, I. (1986). Generalizability of treatment studies using solicited patients. *Journal of Consulting and Clinical Psychology, 54*, 68-78.

Krupnick, J.L. & Pincus, H.A. (1992). The cost-effectiveness of psychotherapy: A plan for research. *American Journal of Psychiatry, 149*, 1295-1305.

Lambert, M.J. (1976). Spontaneous remission in adult neurotic disorders. A revision and summary. *Psychological Bulletin, 83*, 107-119.

Lambert, M.J., Christensen, E.R., & DeJulio, S.S. (Eds) (1983). *The Assessment of Psychotherapy Outcome*. New York: Wiley.

Lambert, M.J., Shapiro, D.A., & Bergin, A.E. (1986). The effectiveness of psychotherapy. In S.L. Garfield & A.E. Bergin (eds), *Handbook of Psychotherapy and Behavior Change*, 3rd edn. New York: Wiley.

Landman, J.T. & Dawes, R.M. (1982). Psychotherapy outcome: Smith and Glass's conclusions stand up under scrutiny. *American Psychologist, 37*, 505-516.

Luborsky, L. (1984). *Principles of psychoanalytic psychotherapy: A manual for supportive-expressive treatment*. New York: Basic Books.

Luborsky, L. & DeRubeis, R.J. (1984). The use of psychotherapy treatment manuals: A small revolution in psychotherapy research style. *Clinical Psychology Review, 4*, 5-14.

Luborsky, K., Singer, B., & Luborsky, L. (1975). Comparative studies of psychotherapies: Is it true that 'Everyone has won and all must have prizes'? *Archives of General Psychiatry, 32*, 995-1008.

Mahoney, M.J. (1978). Experimental methods and outcome evaluation. *Journal of Consulting and Clinical Psychology, 46*, 660-672.

Mathews, A.M. (1978). Fear reduction research and clinical phobias. *Psychological Bulletin, 85*, 390-404.

Meltzoff, J. & Kornreich, M. (1970). *Research in Psychotherapy*. New York: Atherton Press.

Michelson, L. (1985). Editorial: Meta-analysis and clinical psychology *Clinical Psychology Review, 5*, 1-2.

Mintz, J., Luborsky, L., & Christolph, P. (1979). Measuring the outcomes of psychotherapy: Findings of the Penn Psychotherapy Project. *Journal of Consulting and Clinical Psychology, 47*, 319-334.

Moncher, F.J. & Prinz, R.J. (1991). Treatment fidelity in outcome studies. *Clinical Psychology Review, 11*, 247-266.

Newman, F.L. & Howard, K.I. (1986). Therapeutic effort, treatment outcome. and national health policy. *American Psychologist, 41*, 181-187.

Nicholson, R.A. & Berman, J.S. (1983). Is follow-up necessary in evaluating psychotherapy? *Psychological Bulletin, 93*, 261-278.

Parloff, M.B. (1986). Placebo controls in psychotherapy research: a sine qua non or a placebo for research problems? *Journal of Consulting and Clinical Psychology, 54*, 79-87.

Paul, G.L. (1966). *Insight vs. Desensitization in Psychotherapy*. Palo Alto: Stanford University Press.

Piper, W.E., Debbane, E.G., Bienvenu, J.P., & Garant, J. (1984). A comparative study of four forms of psychotherapy. *Journal of Consulting and Clinical Psychology, 52*, 268-279.

Prioleau, L., Murdock, M., & Brody, N. (1983). An analysis of psychotherapy versus placebo studies. *Behavioral and Brain Sciences, 6*, 275-310.

Rachman, S. & Wilson, G.T. (1980). *The effects of psychological therapy*, 2nd edn. New York: Pergamon Press.

Robinson, L.A., Berman, J.S., & Neimeyer, R.A. (1990). Psychotherapy for the treatment of depression: A comprehensive review of controlled outcome research. *Psychological Bulletin, 108*, 30-49.

Rosenthal, R. (1978). Combining results of independent studies. *Psychological Bulletin, 85*, 185-193.

Rosenthal, R. (1983). Assessing the statistical and social importance of the effects of psychotherapy. *Journal of Consulting and Clinical Psychology, 51*, 4-13.

Rosenthal, R. & Frank, J.D. (1956). Psychotherapy and the placebo effect. *Psychological Bulletin, 53*, 294-302.

Rosenthal, R. & Rubin, D.B. (1978). Interpersonal expectancy effects: The first 345 studies. *Behavioural and Brain Sciences, 3*, 377-415.

Salkovskis, P.M. (1995). Demonstrating specific effects in cognitive and behavioural therapy. In M. Aveline & D.A. Shapiro (eds.), *Research foundations for psychotherapy practice*, pp.191–228. Chichester: John Wiley.

Schaffer, N.D. (1982). Multidimensional measures of therapist behavior as predictors of outcome. *Psychological Bulletin, 92*, 670-681.

Shadish, W.R., Montgomery, L.M., Wilson, P., Wilson, M.R., Bright, I., & Okwumabua, T. (1993). Effects of family and marital psychotherapies: A meta-analysis. *Journal of Consulting and Clinical Psychology, 61*, 992-1002.

Shapiro, A.K. & Morris, L.A. (1978). Placebo effects in medical and psychological therapies. In S.L. Garfield & A.E. Bergin (eds.) *Handbook of Psychotherapy and Behavior Change,*. 2nd edn. New York: Wiley.

Shapiro, D.A. (1981). Comparative credibility of treatment rationales: Three tests of expectancy theory. *British Journal of Clinical Psychology, 20*, 111-122.

Shapiro, D.A. (1985). Recent applications of meta-analysis in clinical research. *Clinical Psychology Review, 5*, 13-34.

Shapiro, D.A., Barkham, M., Hardy, G.E., Morrison, L.A., Reynolds, S., Startup, M., & Harper, H. (1991). Psychotherapy research program, University of Sheffield. In L.E. Beutler (ed.) *Psychotherapy Research Programs*. Washington, DC: American Psychological Association.

Shapiro, D.A., Barkham, M., Rees, A., Hardy, G.E., Reynolds, S., & Startup, M. (1994). Effects of treatment duration and severity of depression on the effectiveness of cognitive–behavioural and psychodynamic–interpersonal psychotherapy. *Journal of Consulting and Clinical Psychology*.

Shapiro, D.A. & Shapiro, D. (1982a). Meta-analysis of comparative therapy outcome studies: A replication and refinement. *Psychological Bulletin, 92*, 581-604.

Shapiro, D.A. & Shapiro, D. (1982b). Meta-analysis of comparative therapy outcome research: A critical appraisal. *Behavioural Psychotherapy, 10*, 4-25.

Shapiro, D.A. & Shapiro, D. (1983). Comparative therapy outcome research: Methodological implications of meta-analysis. *Journal of Consulting and Clinical Psychology, 51*, 42-53.

Smith, M.L. & Glass, G.V. (1977). Meta-analysis of psychotherapy outcome studies. *American Psychologist, 32*, 752-760.

Smith, M.L., Glass, G.V., & Miller, T.I. (1980). *The Benefits of Psychotherapy*. Baltimore: Johns Hopkins University Press.

Startup, M., & Shapiro, D.A. (1993). Therapist treatment fidelity in prescriptive vs. exploratory psychotherapy. *British Journal of Clinical Psychology, 32*, 443-456.

Stiles, W.B. (1983). Normality, diversity and psychotherapy. *Psychotherapy: Theory, Research and Practice, 20*, 183-189.

Stiles, W.B., Shapiro, D.A., & Elliot, R.K. (1986). "Are all psychotherapies equivalent?" *American Psychologist, 41*, 165-180.

Strupp, H.H. & Hadley, S.W. (1977). A tripartite model of mental health and therapeutic outcomes: With special reference to negative effects in psychotherapy. *American Psychologist, 32*, 196-197.

Waltz, J., Addis, M.E., Koerner, K., & Jacobson, N.S. (1993). Testing the integrity of a psychotherapy protocol: Assessment of adherence and competence. *Journal of Consulting and Clinical Psychology, 61*, 620-630.

Wilkins, W. (1984). Psychotherapy: The powerful placebo. *Journal of Consulting and Clinical Psychology, 52*, 570-573.

Wilson, G.T. & Rachman, S. (1983). Meta-analysis and evaluation of psychotherapy outcome: Limitations and liabilities. *Journal of Consulting and Clinical Psychology, 51*, 54-64.

Wing, J.K., Cooper, J.E., & Sartorius, N. (1974). *The Measurement and Classification of Psychiatric Symptoms*. Cambridge University Press.

Yates, B.T. & Newman, F.L. (1980). Approaches to cost-effectiveness analysis and cost-benefit analysis of psychotherapy. In G.R. VandenBos (ed.) *Psychotherapy: Practice, Research, Policy*. Beverly Hills, CA: Sage.

Yeaton, W.H. & Sechrest, L. (1981). Critical dimensions in the choice and maintenance of successful treatments: Strength, integrity, and effectiveness. *Journal of Consulting and Clinical Psychology, 49*, 156-167.

CHAPTER ELEVEN

Patient series and quasi-experimental designs

R. Glynn Owens *University of Auckland,*
New Zealand

Peter D. Slade *Department of Clinical Psychology,*
University of Liverpool

Dorothy M. Fielding *St James University Hospital, Leeds*

Experimental procedures have become widely accepted as an appropriate means of conducting research in the mental health field. Such experimentation may range from the small-N ABAB and similar designs beloved of applied behaviour analysts to large-scale statistical studies of experimental and control groups. Common to all such procedures, however, is the general principle of holding constant all factors except the independent variable under study; where these cannot be controlled directly, some form of statistical control, involving the 'balancing' of these factors between conditions, is adopted. Most frequently such balancing of factors is achieved by some form of randomisation; either baseline and experimental conditions are randomly varied, or subjects in large-N designs are randomly allocated to one or other group.

Such an approach has a clear strength in permitting any differences between conditions to be attributed to the only factor which has been permitted to vary systematically, and designs following such principles are now commonplace in mental health research. Often, however, there are reasons that render a tight experimental design undesirable or impractical. As a result researchers have developed a number of alternative approaches to the study of various types of problem, permitting topics to be studied that lie outside the scope of traditional experimental methods. Two methods that have had particular impact in psychological settings are the patient series and quasi-experimental designs, approaches which, whilst not without their own problems, side-step certain difficulties encountered by straightforward experimentation.

PATIENT SERIES DESIGNS

Even the slightest acquaintance with clinical problems brings an awareness that patients are very much individuals (Kiesler, 1966). A corollary of this is that a researcher's behaviour is likely to vary considerably from patient to patient. Such variation may present problems to a traditional experimental design, producing considerable heterogeneity within comparison groups and also considerable overlap between them. Thus a therapist who attempted to compare, say, directive and non-directive psychotherapy would probably find it difficult to be entirely directive to one group and entirely non-directive to another group (the difficulty of being nondirective has been demonstrated by Truax, 1966). In consequence, groups that were meant to be distinct may in fact turn out to be not at all dissimilar. Where a therapist would normally, in practice, use elements of both of the methods being compared, an attempt to use only one for the purposes of an experiment might result in a totally artificial experiment the results of which would have little or no relevance to actual clinical practice.

The problem is compounded when it is recognised that in many cases such groups as 'no treatment' control groups may be unacceptable on ethical grounds. In such cases it may be appropriate to provide treatment to all individuals involved, reporting the results of such interventions as they stand without direct comparison with similar untreated individuals. Finally, it is notable that the similarities between individuals often become apparent only at a relatively abstract level; that is, while similar processes may operate, the specific factors may none the less be quite disparate (Shapiro, 1966). For example, two people may show aggressive behaviour in response to some disturbing or irritating event, yet the specific events may be peculiar to each. In such cases it may be important to study in detail each individual, rather than to summarise the subjects in terms of means and variances. Indeed a number of writers have pointed out how similarities of process may be masked by such activities as averaging. Sidman (1960) for example illustrates how subjects showing basically similar (but parametrically different) performances may give rise to a totally different average performance.

Because of problems such as these a number of important works have presented their results not as experimental findings but rather as a description of a series of patients. Such a 'patient series' design may be traced back to the case history reports of workers like Freud. Modern patient series designs, however, show considerably more sophistication than these early reports. Two well-known and much-quoted examples are Masters and Johnson's studies of psychological methods of treatment for sexual dysfunction patients (Masters & Johnson, 1970) and Beck's studies of cognitive processes and therapy in patients presenting with depressive and anxiety problems (Beck, 1976). The basic underpinning of patient series research designs was formulated by Cronbach (1975) in his principle of 'intensive local observation', as follows:

> An observer collecting data in one particular situation is in a position to appraise a practice or proposition in that setting, observing effects in context. In trying to describe and account for what happened, he will give attention to whatever variables were controlled. But he will give equally careful attention to uncontrolled conditions, to personal characteristics, and to events that occurred during treatment and measurement. As he goes from situation to situation, his first task is to describe and interpret the effect anew in each locale, perhaps taking into account factors unique to that locale ... As results accumulate, a person who seeks understanding will do his best to trace how the uncontrolled factors could have caused local departures from the modal effect. That is, generalization comes late and the exception is taken as seriously as the rule.

It can be seen from this that the basic principle underlying the 'patient series approach' involves a combination of systematic observation and manipulation of relevant variables, where possible, while maintaining a clear focus on the individual rather than the average group member. As such this research lends itself to many clinical problems and situations. We shall now consider some of the methods and possibilities associated with such an approach.

Prediction of outcome

When a more or less standard psychological treatment is given to a group of patients who apparently share a similar problem (for example, an exposure treatment for agoraphobic patients or a controlled drinking programme for problem drinkers) the outcome of treatment is likely to vary. Some patients are likely to show a good response, others a poor response, while the outcome for still others will be intermediate between the two extremes. This is a common clinical observation and one that lends itself to analysis by the clinician-researcher.

There are good reasons why the clinician may wish to investigate the issue of which patients respond well and which poorly to the treatment. If the patients who are likely to respond poorly can be predicted in advance from pretreatment variables, such patients can be offered a different type of treatment by the clinician or referred on to someone else who offers a different kind of treatment. Similarly, if the likelihood of a poor eventual outcome can be predicted from variables relating to initial treatment response, the clinician may change the treatment approach at an early stage. Thus the investigation of prediction of treatment response has much to commend it for practical reasons.

The common approach to this issue is to collect data on the nature and severity of the target problems in a sizeable and unselected sample of patients, both before and after exposure to a standard treatment regime. Such measures are likely to be quantitative in nature, such as how close a snake-phobic patient can approach to a live snake or an agoraphobic patient's rating of their anxiety at various distances from home. A quantitative index of improvement can be obtained by subtracting the post-treatment from the pre-treatment values, although the use of such improvement scores is not always straightforward. Indeed the use of such change scores can sometimes require careful thought. For example, two patients may be given a pre-treatment measure of anxiety; if one scores the maximum possible on the test, the only possible post-treatment results are no change or improvement. A second patient, however, whose pre-treatment score was only moderately raised, can either appear to improve, stay the same or deteriorate. Note that both patients might in reality deteriorate; since the first has already scored the maximum however, their deterioration will be recorded by the researcher as 'no change'. This will of course apply even where the only changes which occur are a result of random fluctuations: the observed results will be biased by the 'ceiling effect' of the first patient's maximum score. Such 'ceiling effects' (and the corresponding 'floor effects' associated with very low scores) can complicate the use of change scores. A discussion of the complex statistical issues in the measurement of change is given by Harris (1963.)

Change scores can be treated either as continuous treatment-outcome measures or used to establish discrete outcome categories such as 'good', 'intermediate' or 'poor response'. In either case, they can be used as dependent measures in the analysis of treatment prediction. As previously indicated, the predictors of interest will either be pretreatment variables or treatment variables. The former may well include demographic variables (e.g. age, sex, occupation, marital status, etc.), severity of problem variables (e.g. duration of drink problem, severity, etc.), assessments of personal, social and marital satisfaction, general measures of anxiety, depression and other problems, expectancies for treatment success, etc. Treatment variables may include number of attendances, number of homework assignments completed, rapport achieved by therapist, etc. Initial response to treatment is a particularly useful treatment variable, as research with a variety of different treatment approaches and clinical problems has shown that response to the first one of two sessions of treatment is a good predictor of eventual clinical improvement.

The type of statistical analysis which can be performed with the data will depend largely on the nature of the outcome criterion variable used (Table 11.1). If it is continuous, correlational measures will probably be the most appropriate: if discrete, then analyses of variance and discriminant function analysis will be required. However, whether the dependent variable is continuous or discrete the clinician will no doubt wish to know which of the predictor variables has the strongest influence on outcome. For this the clinician-researcher will need to carry out 'multiple regression analyses'.

One cautionary point needs to be raised when carrying out statistical analyses of outcome prediction data. Often the relationship between the 'dependent or criterion' variable and a 'predictor' variable is not linear (i.e. a straight line). For example, the relation between severity of agoraphobic symptoms and treatment response may be curvilinear one, with 'mild' and 'very severe' patients showing much less of a response than 'moderately severe' patients. Such relationships may be

TABLE 11.1
Summary of methods for investgating response to treatment

| Outcome criteria | Predictor variables | | Methods of statistical analysis |
	Pretreatment	Treatment	
Continuous, i.e. Degree of change	Age, sex, severity of problem, etc.	No. of attendances No. of homework assignments completed, etc.	Correlations, multiple regression analyses, etc.
Discrete, i.e. Good vs. intermediate vs. poor response	Same	Same	ANOVAS, discriminant function analyses, multiple regression analyses

investigated using correlational measures suitable for curvilinear relationships such as eta; a description of this can be found in Wiseman (1966). Alternatively it may be possible to transform the data either algebraically to produce a linear relationship or to approximate such a relationship by 'folding' around the peak.

There may also be an asymmetrical relationship between the predictor and the criterion, for example where patients with good motivation show varied responses to treatment though patients with poor motivation never respond well. Where such non-linear relationships obtain, the statistical methods outlined in Table 11.1 are probably inappropriate. Bivariate plots or scattergrams taking two variables (one dependent one predictor) at a time will usually serve to sort out this complication. Non-linear relationships should not be regarded merely as a statistical nuisance; they can be of theoretical interest and practical importance.

Model-building

As well as lending itself to investigations of prediction of treatment outcome, or indeed any kind of prognostic outcome such as for example recovery of function following post-traumatic amnesia, the 'patient series' approach is useful for model-building. In such an exercise the clinician-researcher is concerned with extracting general principles or processes from consideration of a sample of individual patients presenting with apparently similar problems. One method of model-building which is becoming increasingly popular is that of functional analysis. Descriptions of functional analysis can be found in Owens and Ashcroft (1982), and discussion of some of its characteristics and problems in subsequent papers (e.g. Samson & McDonnell 1992, Jones & Owens 1992, Owens & Jones 1992, Owens & MacKinnon 1993)

In its simplest form the functional analysis approach involves analysis of behaviour in terms of Antecedents, Behaviour and Consequences—the A-B-C paradigm. Examples of each of these may be seen in the functional model of aggressive behaviour of Owens and Bagshaw (1985). This model is summarised in the form of a flow diagram in Fig. 11.1. Basically antecedents include such factors as aversive stimulation (reactive aggression paradigm), personality factors, physiological factors, drugs (including alcohol), etc. whereas the consequences include the various pay-offs or reinforcers to the individual.

Clearly, whilst the model points to the types of factor that may be involved in aggressive behaviour, it does so only in a very general way, with reference to 'aversive stimuli', 'reinforcers', etc. In any given episode of violent behaviour the actual variables may be specific to the

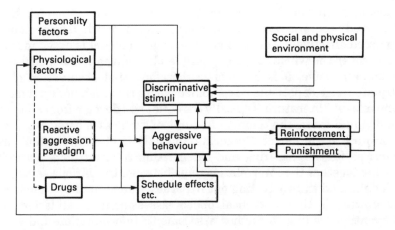

FIG. 11.1. Outline of a functional analysis of aggression. (Reproduced from Owens & Bagshaw, 1985, by permission of Plenum Publishing.)

individual concerned. Thus for one individual the aversive stimulus may take the form of being mocked by a friend; for another it may be a physical blow. Stimuli that are aversive to one individual may not be so to another, as has been demonstrated elegantly by Vernon and Ulrich (1966), who showed how particular learning experiences could result in previously neutral stimuli acquiring aversive properties and giving rise to reactive aggression. This individuality is a common aspect of models derived from a patient series design, particular features of each case being grouped according to their functional, rather than their physical similarities. Thus rather than listing each different type of aversive stimulus encountered in the patient series it is recognised that the various stimuli play similar roles and may therefore be grouped together. In the same way other functionally similar but physically different events (e.g. reinforcers) may be subsumed under a single heading.

The model presented in Fig. 11.1 illustrates several aspects of patient series designs. First, it should be recognised that different processes may operate in the development and the maintenance of a problem; in extreme cases these two aspects may reflect almost totally different formulations. Secondly, it is clear that not all of the variables potentially used in the problem may be present in any given episode or example. Thirdly, and perhaps most importantly, the variables involved are usefully classified in terms of their functional status within the system rather than in terms of their physical property.

Practical aspects

Developing a model of a clinical problem or phenomenon from a patient series study comprises several practical aspects if such development is to proceed effectively. The data on which such a model is based must of course cover the whole range of possible phenomena if the model is to be comprehensive; it is important, therefore, that observation of an adequate range of patients be combined with a thorough understanding of the relevant literature. Typically the series will develop from analyses of individual cases, the common features of such cases being extracted to form a general model. Producing an analysis of an individual case comprises firstly gathering and categorising relevant data, secondly drawing together the interrelationships between the various aspects of such data, and thirdly testing out hypotheses generated by the model. The process is thus a cyclical one of assessment, formulation and intervention leading to further assessment, reformulation and so on (Fig. 11.2). For example, the clinician may, on the basis of data gathered from interviews and other forms of assessment, produce a model according to which the behaviour or the problem 'makes sense'. Armed with this understanding of the problem it is possible to devise an intervention which, in principle, will alleviate the problem. By further assessing the results of such an intervention the adequacy of the original model may be tested and on the basis of such testing the model refined further as necessary.

Patient series studies thus provide a framework for the derivation of general models of specific psychological phenomena. Such designs have permitted the construction of functional analyses of a number of psychological problems including anorexia nervosa and bulimia nervosa

FIG. 11.2. The cyclical nature of functional analysis.

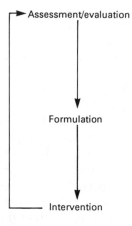

(Slade, 1982), childhood enuresis (Fielding, 1982), alcohol abuse (Sobell & Sobell, 1981), etc.

Strengths and weaknesses of patient series designs

As with any approach to research, patient series designs have both advantages and disadvantages. Perhaps the most obvious strength of a patient series design is its clear ecological validity. That is to say, since the use of such a design requires little if any alteration to a clinician's normal practice, results obtained are easy to link with the 'real world'; the artificiality of the experimental laboratory may be completely avoided. A second clear advantage is the avoidance of many of the ethical problems which constrain more traditional designs, particularly in the use of 'no-treatment' or placebo control groups. Failure to use any form of control procedure, however, may also constitute one of the major disadvantages of such a design, making it difficult to determine exactly how much of any result obtained is due to the procedures adopted. It may be argued, for example, that individuals treated in patient series designs may have improved irrespective of the treatment used. Whilst this may be evaluated to some extent by using a waiting list or similar control, the problem of interpretation will remain. Even if the rate of improvement by patients in treatment is greater than the rate in the waiting list, the possibility remains that the improvement is due to some non-specific aspect of the treatment. In most cases, therefore, investigation of a topic by means of a patient series design will need to be supplemented by consideration of experimental material. Such experimental material may reflect existing literature on the topic (as in the functional analysis of aggression) or may suggest its own experimental research (as in the functional analyses of anorexia and bulimia nervosa).

A second difficulty with the patient series design stems from its dependence on the specific individuals included. In most cases the individuals taking part in such studies will be, at least to some extent, unrepresentative. Rarely will their participation reflect random sampling from a suitable population. To some extent such a problem may be overcome by careful selection of participants in the series so as to permit a degree of systematic replication (as in single case research). That is to say, individuals are selected so as to produce a systematic variation of factors suspected to be of relevance. For example, a young male patient may be followed by an older female patient; if the results are similar, doubt is cast on the possible involvement of age and gender in the process. Whilst it will not usually be possible for patient series to adopt such systematic variation, careful monitoring of the status of individuals with respect to such variables may permit post-hoc consideration of their role.

For many researchers, however, there is little to compare with direct experimental manipulation of relevant variables. Such direct manipulation permits a degree of assessment of the role of such variables widely surpassing that provided by simple observation. The desirability of investigating problems of real clinical significance experimentally in a naturalistic setting has thus led to the development of procedures capable of direct application in a number of contexts; these include the procedures that have come to be known as quasi-experimental designs (Campbell & Stanley, 1963; Cook & Campbell, 1979).

QUASI-EXPERIMENTAL DESIGNS

Often a topic will be suitable in principle for experimental investigation but a truly experimental treatment will be inappropriate for practical, political, ethical or other reasons. In such cases it may be appropriate to approximate as far as possible an experimental procedure within the constraints that are operating. Thus, in a traditional experimental design, subjects may be randomly allocated to experimental or control groups. In some circumstances such random allocation may be impossible. Amongst the factors that may restrict the use of such random elements we may include the following.

Practical issues.   The investigation of such questions as the effects of natural disasters obviously rules out the production of a truly random design. Comparing psychological morbidity in survivors of the Hiroshima and Nagasaki atrocities with that in other similar cities provides some information as to the effects of such events, but a number of confounding variables inevitably remain. Each city is, for example, to some extent individual; the factors that led to the choice of Hiroshima and Nagasaki as targets may in principle also be the factors that produce any subsequent findings in research studies. Such practical issues are illustrated by Maes et al. (1993) who decided on the use of a quasi-experimental methodology in investigating two different health promotion programmes in nursing homes. Although their study involves 1200 subjects, these are drawn from only six nursing homes; it would be impractical to allocate individuals randomly to two conditions, since this would lead to individuals in the same nursing home receiving different information. Almost certainly there would be some comparison by these individuals of what they had been taught, and as a result each group would be to some extent 'contaminated' by the other. By allocating different programmes on the basis of the homes, rather than individuals, such risks of cross-contamination could be minimised.

Political issues.   Often it is desired to investigate the effects of some event whose occurrence depends largely on political circumstances. Perhaps one of the best known of such questions concerns the investigation of the effect of introduction or withdrawal of capital punishment on the incidence of violent crime. Experimentally, it is desirable that the introduction and withdrawal of the death penalty take place at random points in time. By observing the effect of such introduction and withdrawal on the incidence of violent crime a link to the penalty could be established, since the latter is the only factor varying systematically. However, such random introduction and withdrawal is usually politically (and arguably morally) unacceptable. Rather, changes in judicial policy tend to be associated with other political and social changes, and it can always be argued that these, rather than the change of punishment, are responsible for any changes observed.

Ethical issues.   Often the evidence that a measure will be of benefit is associated with such a high initial plausibility that to withold it from certain individuals would be questionable on ethical grounds. Thus evaluation of the compulsory wearing of seat belts in motor cars, or crash helmets on motor cycles, might ideally be done by imposing such a requirement on a randomly selected subgroup of such individuals. Yet not only would such a procedure be politically impractical, it would also be tantamount to deliberately increasing the risk of death or injury amongst those on whom no such obligation was placed. In the same way, the evaluation of the benefit of introducing pedestrian crossings or subways near schools would not normally be considered an appropriate subject for a truly randomised design.

Methodological issues.   In many cases the appropriate use of randomisation design may itself produce a degree of confounding in the experiment. A study by Dean et al. (1983), for example, looked at the psychological benefits of breast reconstruction in mastectomy patients by providing reconstruction to a randomly determined subgroup and comparing psychological morbidity in the two groups thus obtained. Unfortunately, such a design immediately encounters its own problems as a direct consequence of the randomisation. Firstly, since the experiment required informed consent on the part of the patients, it is perhaps unsurprising to find that a substantial proportion (almost half) of the patients refused to participate. Not surprisingly, many women were unwilling to have the decision of being given breast reconstruction determined by a toss of a coin in the operating theatre. Generalisation of the results is therefore limited as a result of the patients participating being an atypical subgroup. Secondly, there is the possibility that the randomisation may have its own psychological effects. In this example, some women who awake from the operation to find that they had been given reconstruction may have seen this as evidence that they were 'lucky', and a good omen for their future prognosis; others who were not given reconstruction may have interpreted this as evidence of being unlucky and an omen for poor prognosis. Comparison of the data obtained with other studies on the psychological outcome of mastectomy lend some support to such an argument (Owens, Ashcroft, Leinster & Slade, 1986).

As a result of problems such as these much research has adopted what have come to be known as 'quasi-experimental' designs, defined as those in which, for some reason, random allocation of subjects to groups is not possible (Campbell & Stanley, 1963). Quasi-experimental designs in which a cause is studied after it has exerted its effect (as in the Nagasaki/Hiroshima example) are sometimes decribed as 'ex post facto' or 'causal comparative' designs; for the purpose of the present chapter the term 'quasi-experimental' will be used throughout. In a quasi-expermental design, the basic structure is that of a traditional experiment, but it is acknowledged that certain factors in addition to the one under study will vary between experimental and control conditions. Thus in dealing with the problems described earlier, a study of the effects of nuclear bombing might include a comparison between the survivors of Hiroshima and Nagasaki and other inhabitants of similar, unbombed cities. Studies of the effects of road safety measures, or of capital punishment, have typically used either before and after measures (acknowledging that other changes in society may be concurrent with those under study) or comparison of settings which are broadly similar except with respect to the dimension of interest (e.g. the comparison of adjacent American states that differ in policy on capital punishment). Examples of such studies may be found in Campbell, 1969 (road safety) or Walker, 1968 (capital punishment). Ethical problems of withholding treatment may be circumvented by making comparisons between all current patients who are given a treatment and others seen before the treatment became available (e.g. Owens, Ashcroft, Leinster & Slade, 1986). A similar strategy may be employed to circumvent methodological problems associated with randomisation.

Example: The effect of choice of treatment on wellbeing of breast cancer patients

In a study reported in detail elsewhere (Ashcroft, Leinster & Slade, 1986) a quasi-experimental design was used to investigate the psychological consequences of allowing women with early breast cancer to make their own choice of treatment. The study arose from recognition by a number of surgeons that for certain patients there was no medical basis for selecting one of two different treatments, lumpectomy with radiotherapy or mastectomy. In effect the surgeon could provide no better way of choosing treatment than tossing a coin. Whilst such random selection of treatment would provide a classic experimental method for investigating the effects of various treatments, it is perhaps unsurprising to note that few women were willing to have their treatment selected in this way. In consequence, since there was no basis according to which the surgeon could determine the treatment for these women, it was decided to allow the women themselves to make the choice. Such a procedure immediately renders a true experimental design impossible. Consideration of the psychological outcome of the different treatments, for example, is confounded by the fact that other systematic differences would exist between those choosing mastectomy and those choosing the lumpectomy/radiotherapy combination (e.g. differences in degree of concern about body image). Whilst it could be argued that the effect of choice itself could be investigated by making choice available to only a random subgroup of women, ethical considerations argued against this; those women not given choice would be having their choice made (by no better method than the toss of a coin) by the surgeon, and as has already been noted few women were willing to allow this. Nevertheless, the issue was of obvious importance and investigation of the effects of choice desirable.

As a consequence of these considerations a decision was made to allow all suitable patients (i.e. all those for whom no medical grounds for preferring a particular treatment could be determined) to make, if they wished, their own choice of treatment. A battery of psychological tests was administered and scores along these dimensions compared with similar measures used in studies of breast cancer patients where choice had not been permitted. The results are too complex to go into detail here, but perhaps the most remarkable finding was that these patients, unlike similar patients in the literature, showed good psychosocial adaptation to their disease and treatment. Such good adaptation could not be attributed to the particular treatment chosen, with no differences being found between those opting for each of the two treatments. However, a significant difference was found between those patients who were allowed to chooose their own treatment and those who were not. The results were thus consistent with the notion that allowing patients to choose their own treatment, where this is feasible, is associated with improved psychological outcome. Such a conclusion is implied from the observations that (a) women in this study given a choice showed a better outcome than those who were not given such a choice, and (b) women in this study given a choice showed a better outcome than comparable patients in other studies who were not given a choice

Although the findings were consistent with the conclusion that choice is associated with improved psychological outcome, such a conclusion is not necessarily implied. Patients in the present study given a choice differed in ways additional to their choosing their own treatment, most notably in the staging of the disease (only those patients at a suitably early stage were permitted to choose). Similarly, the choice patients in the present study differed from patients of similar staging in the literature in a number of ways, most obviously in terms of the individuals concerned with their treatment (a surgeon sufficiently progressive to consider allowing patients their own choice of treatment and a clinical psychologist available to help women make their decision). In principle, these or other differences may have accounted for the results obtained. Nevertheless, the study provides support for the provision of choice of treatment where practical; the notion that choice is beneficial may thus be considered to have passed at least minimal testing. Although the study does not permit the definite conclusion that choice is of benefit, to have obtained the opposite results would have dealt a severe blow to such a notion.

To summarise, then, in this example the use of a quasi-experimental design permitted investigation in an area where practical and ethical constraints would have precluded a conventional experiment. The information gathered, whilst not permitting definite conclusions, provided a reasonable preliminary test of the hypothesis that choice is a significant variable and encourages further work in the area. According to the notion that a concept is scientific to the extent that it is falsifiable, the use of such a design permits at least one route to possible falsifiability, in that, for example, the patients concerned may have turned out to have shown no psychological benefit relative to others reported in the literature or to others in the same study not given a choice.

Practical aspects of quasi-experimental designs

Implicit in the definition of a quasi-experimental procedure is that any results obtained will be open to more than one possible interpretation. It is the responsibility of the researcher, therefore, to take whatever steps are possible to minimise the number of such alternative explanations. In general such steps involve enhancing as much as possible the comparability of comparison conditions, and then taking whatever steps are possible to assess the potential significance of any remaining differences.

Enhancing the comparability of the comparison conditions requires, first and foremost, a good understanding of the subject matter under investigation. The researcher should know what factors are likely to have an effect on the dependent variables and take whatever steps are possible to match these between the two groups. In the case of the breast cancer project, for example, it would obviously have been more difficult to interpret the results if the patients given a choice of treatment for breast cancer had been compared with women suffering from some totally different disease. The researcher establishing a quasi-experimental design needs to identify as many as possible of the factors that may affect the dependent variables and attempt to equalise these across the comparison conditions. Thus in examining the effects of the death penalty on rates of offending, it is more sensible to compare American states which are similar in terms of population density, urban/rural distribution etc., as well as in rates of other offences for which penalties differ only slightly or not at all (Sutherland & Cressey, 1970). The identification of a good comparison group requires considerable skill and knowledge on the part of the quasi-experimental researcher.

Another obvious method for minimising alternative interpretations of data obtained from quasi-experimental studies is to include relevant and robust pre-intervention/post-intervention measures. Even more powerful still is a design in which change during an experimental phase is compared with change during a control phase, with measures taken before and after each phase. The strongest form of this design is probably that in which a treatment is introduced, withdrawn, and then reintroduced, with measures being taken between each phase of the design. Even when the inclusion of a carefully matched no-treatment control group is impossible, the results obtained with satisfactory pre/post measures may still prove convincing and difficult to set aside.

Supplementary analyses

No matter how much effort the experimenter puts into increasing comparability of comparison groups and ensuring the inclusion and relevant pre/post measures, it is likely that some variables will still be confounded. Supplementary analyses may therefore be useful. The first stage is to test whether there were any unintended differences between the experimental condition and the comparison condition (or comparison phase). If it can be shown that there were not, the case for a causal interpretation of the data is enhanced. However, if unintended differences between conditions are discovered, further analyses may focus on either reducing the total amount of data variance or eliminating the confounding influence of uncontrolled variables. For example, if the experimental and comparison samples were found to differ in terms of average age, several methods might be used to rule out the hypothesis that the age factor was responsible for the important group differences in the dependent variable.

One method (the age-matched subgroup analysis) would involve selecting subsamples from the experimental and comparison groups who were comparable in age and then determining whether or not they differed in terms of the crucial dependent variables. An alternative method would to use an analysis of covariance; in this approach the relationship between age and the dependent variables is assessed from the data. The dependent variables are then 'adjusted' to take account of the initial differences (sometimes referred to as 'partialling out' the effect of age). If the differences on crucial dependent variables remain significant, it is clear that such differences cannot be explained away in terms of the original differences in age—the differences are too great to be simply an age effect. Such an approach can of course be used for other variables, besides age, in terms of which the groups showed initial differences.

In practice the calculation of analyses of covariance is complex, and is now almost always performed by computer. Most statistical packages, even those designed for desktop machines like IBM PC compatibles and Apple Macintosh, will have facilities for such analyses (see Chapter 6 of this volume).

Finally, when carrying out analyses of a clinical data set, it may be helpful to test out clinical formulations of the cause-effect relationships between hypothesised variables. A number of statistical methods are available for doing this, including 'path-analysis' and 'cross-lagged correlation analysis'.

Path analysis.   Path analysis can contribute to causal theory building in two different ways: first in terms of general theoretical clarification and secondly in the estimation of specific causal impacts. For a general introduction to the area the reader is referred to the book by Cook and Campbell (1979).

We will illustrate the theoretical contribution that path analysis can make to the understanding of one clinical problem, namely anorexia nervosa. Several years ago, Slade (1982) developed a functional-analytic account of this disorder involving two major setting conditions (general dissatisfaction and perfectionism) which, it was argued, could lead to anorexia nervosa if the individual went on a serious diet. It was suggested that general dissatisfaction in turn developed from three further factors (adolescent problems, interpersonal problems, and stress and failure experiences). The two major setting conditions were hypothesised to lead to a 'need for total control' which might then lead on to pathological dieting. The important point is that the theoretical model of anorexia nervosa was spelt out in a form suitable for path analysis.

We will consider the application of this statistical method by reference to a restricted part of this model. Namely, that adolescent problems (A) and interpersonal problems (B) contribute independently to general dissatisfaction (C) and that the latter contributes directly to dieting behaviour (D). The path diagram based on this model is outlined in the upper, left-hand quadrant of Fig. 11.3. The corresponding correlation coefficients are shown in the upper, right-hand quadrant.

The less specific model against which the latter could be tested is shown in the lower quadrants of Fig. 11.3. This model suggests that not only do (A) and (B) contribute to (C), which in turn affects (D) but that (A) and (B) have an independent effect on (D). Thus the models outlined in the upper and lower quadrants of Fig. 11.3 give rise to testable differences in terms of correlations. Sharrock and Gudjonsson (1993) give a similar illustration of the use of path analysis in the context of false confessions in criminal cases.

Cross-lagged correlations.   The cross-lagged correlation technique may be useful for investigating the cause-effect relation between two variables assessed concomitantly at two points in time (Fig. 11.4) (Cook

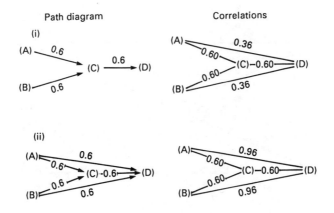

FIG. 11.3. Hypothetical path diagrams and the corresponding correlation coefficients.

& Campbell, 1979). As an example of where it might be used, we may be interested in the causal relationsbip between 'negative self-statements'(NSS) and 'depressed mood'(DM) where either direction of causality is possible. Another example is the investigation of Golin, Sweeney and Shaeffer (1981) of the role of attributions in the onset of depression. Although the statistical technique is subject to major deviations and problems (Rogosa, 1980), well-balanced and normally distributed data such as those presented in Fig. 11.4 are open to clear interpretation. Basically, a causal influence is suggested where the correlation between one variable at time one (NSS1) and the other variable at time two (DM2) exceeds the correlation observed between the second variable at time one (DM1) and the first variable at time two (NSS2).

As with many statistical procedures, the development of relatively simple but powerful statistical packages for small computers (e.g. the Windows version of SPSS—see Chapter 6) has made analyses of this kind straightforward and relieved the researcher of much of the burden of computation. Arguably such widespread availability can be seen as a danger as well as a benefit, and it is of critical importance that users ensure that they fully understand the principles of their analyses.

Strengths and weaknesses of quasi-experimental designs
Clearly quasi-experimental designs may share with the patient series designs the benefits of ecological validity and the circumvention of numerous ethical problems. Thus in the example of the breast cancer and choice of treatment study it was possible to investigate a variable

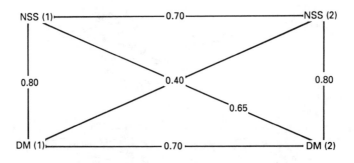

FIG. 11.4. Hypothetical cross-lagged correlation pattern between negative self-statements (NSS) and depressed mood.

of significance without the ethical problem of withholding choice from a subsample of patients. In such circumstances it may be the case that the use of a quasi-experimental design provides methodological as well as ethical advantages. Comparison of the studies of breast reconstruction reported by Dean et al. (1983) and Owens et al. (1986) reveals that the former, although a true randomised trial, is at least as difficult to interpret as the latter quasi-experimental procedure. Firstly, the percentage of patients willing to participate in the former is low, leaving open the question of generalisability to other patients similar to those who refused. Secondly it is apparent that those randomly allocated to the 'no-treatment' control group showed a poorer outcome than might have been expected, suggesting that the relatively good results of the experimental group may be confounded. It is thus possible then that the use of a traditional random trial may create at least as many problems as a quasi-experimental procedure.

Besides the advantages of ethical simplicity and ecological validity a quasi-experimental design has the advantage of permitting the direct assessment of the role of variables under investigation by their systematic manipulation. To the extent that an outcome variable fluctuates systematically with changes in an experimental variable, the hypothesis that the two are indeed related is supported. Whilst such a test of a relationship is obviously not as strong as in a true experimental design (because of the presence of confounding variables), it may nevertheless prove highly informative.

On the other hand, the use of a quasi-experimental design will always, by its very nature, permit alternative interpretations as a result of confounding variables. It is thus an inherent weakness of the quasi-experimental design that positive results do not unequivocally indicate the role of the variables under study. However, it will often be possible, in the light of data obtained from quasi-experimental procedures, to initiate further studies which clarify remaining doubts. Consider, for example, the investigation of the effects of introducing a speed limit on a road where the accident rate has been high. It can be argued that any reduction following the limit reflects nothing more than the effect of confounding factors; accidents may, for example, have been random, but the limit prompted by a particular peak. Since such a peak would (on a random model) occur only infrequently, research may indicate a spurious reduction. If, however, such a quasi-experimental study does indicate a reduction, it may then be possible to introduce further limits on other roads without requiring an accident 'peak' to prompt such introduction. Reduction of the accident rate on these additional roads following reduction in the speed limit would not be explicable in terms of the random model and would thereby strengthen the case for reduction. Thus although a quasi-experimental study may not in itself give strong evidence for a relationship, a series of such studies may permit greater and greater confidence in the results obtained. Often the use of a quasi-experimental procedure on an exploratory basis will lead to the removal of objections on political or ethical grounds and permit the introduction of a full-scale experimental design.

SUMMARY AND CONCLUSIONS

Whilst the experimental tradition is of considerable value in the conduct of psychological research, it is not without its problems. Statistical large group designs may have difficulty with participation rates, drop-out rates, and other sampling problems; even with single subject designs there may be problems in isolating the experimental variable of interest. Attempts at statistically balancing variability by averaging may give rise to results which can be generalised only to groups, not to individuals, or may require such distortion of procedure to prevent overlap between groups that the techniques under investigation bear only a slight resemblance to real clinical practice. Difficulties such as these are exacerbated when political, ethical or similar issues constrain the extent to which an experimental design can be initiated.

In the light of difficulties such as these it may often be appropriate to withhold traditional experimental procedures and look instead to patient series or quasi-experimental designs. Figure 11.5 indicates a possible basis for choosing between patient series, quasi-experimental or more traditional experimental designs. In the patient series design, careful investigation of individual patients, coupled with a thorough analysis of the features of each case, may permit considerable clarification of important issues to do with treatment (e.g. Masters & Johnston, 1970) or indeed the whole theoretical analysis of a topic (e.g. Slade, 1982). In the case of a quasi-experimental design, the presence of confounding variables may limit the confidence which may be placed in the results, but the information provided may none the less be of considerable value; indeed such a design may often turn out to be at least as useful as a traditional randomisation once consideration is given to issues such as participation rate, and the status of control groups. In many instances, the minimal interference with normal clinical procedures required by patient series and quasi-experimental designs may permit a study that is much less artificial than one following more traditional approaches. Reasons such as these suggest that they will continue to complement more conventional research designs.

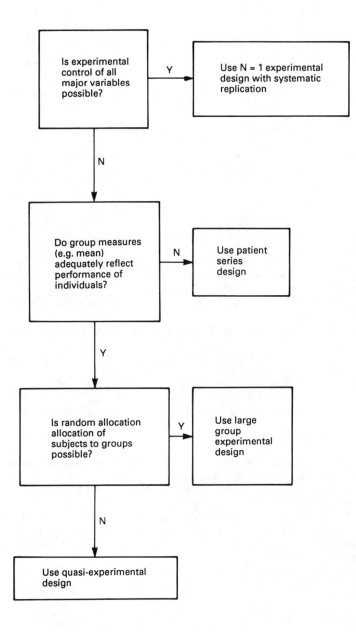

FIG. 11.5. A possible strategy for chasing research problems.

REFERENCES

Ashcroft, J.J., Leinster, S., & Slade, P.D. (1985). Breast cancer; patient choice of treatment. *Journal of the Royal Society of Medicine, 78*, 43-46.

Beck, A.T. (1976). *Cognitive Therapy and the Emotional Disorders*. New York: International Universities Press.

Campbell, D.T. (1969). Reforms as experiments. *American Psychologist, 24*, 409-429.

Campbell, D.T. & Stanley, J.C. (1963). Experimental and quasi-experimental designs for research. In N.L. Gage (ed.) *Handbook of Research on Teaching*. Chicago: Rand McNally.

Cook, T.D. & Campbell, D.T. (1979). *Quasi-experimentation; Design and Analysis for Field Settings*. Chicago: Rand McNally.

Cronbach, L.J. (1975). Beyond the two disciplines of scientific psychology. *American Psychologist, 30*, 116-12 7.

Dean, C., Chetty, U., & Forest, A.P.M. (1983). Effects of immediate breast reconstruction on psychosocial morbidity after mastectomy. *Lancet, i*, 459-462.

Fielding, D.M. (1982). An analysis of the behaviour of day and night wetting children; towards a model of micturition control. *Behaviour Research and Therapy, 20*, 49-60.

Golin, S., Sweeney, P.D., & Shaeffer, D.E. (1981). The causality of causal attributions in depression: a cross-lagged panel correlational analysis. *Journal of Abnormal Psychology, 90*, 14-22.

Harris, C.W. (ed.) (1963). *Problems in Measuring Change*. Madison: University of Wisconsin Press.

Jones, R.S.P. & Owens, R.G. (1992) Applying functional analysis. *Behavioural Psychotherapy, 20*, 37-40

Kiesler, D.J. (1966). Some myths of psychotherapy research and the search for a pradigm. *Psychological Bulletin, 65*, 110-136.

Maes, S., van der Gulden, J., van Elderen, T., Senden, T., Kittel, F., Hertog, C., Seegers, G., van der Doef, M., Engels, J., & Gebhardt, W. (1993). *Healthier work in nursing homes*. Presented to conference of European Health Psychology Society, Brussels.

Masters, W.H. & Johnson, V. (1970). *Human Sexual Inadequacy*. Boston: Little Brown.

Owens, R.G. & Ashcroft, J.B. (1982). Functional analysis in applied psychology. *British Journal of Clinical Psychology, 21*, 181-189.

Owens, R.G. & Ashcroft, J.B. (1985). *Violence; A Guide for the Caring Professions*. Beckenham: Croom Helm.

Owens, R.G., Ashcroft, J.J., Leinster, S., & Slade, P.D. (1986). Psychological effects of the offer of breast reconstruction in mastectomy patients. In M. Watson & S. Greer (eds.) *Psychosocial Issues in Malignant Disease*, Vol. 2. Oxford: Pergamon.

Owens, R.G. & Bagshaw, M. (1985). First steps in the functional analysis of aggression. In E. Karas (ed.) *Current Issues in Clinical Psychology*, Vol. 2. New York: Plenum.

Owens, R.G. & Jones, R.S.P. (1992) Extending the role of functional analysis in challenging behaviour. *Behavioural Psychotherapy, 20*, 45-46.

Owens, R.G. & MacKinnon, S.A. (1993). The functional analysis of challenging behaviours: some conceptual and theoretical problems. In R.B. Jones & C. Eayrs (eds.), *Functional Analysis and Challenging Behaviour*. British Institute of Learning Difficulties, Clevedon.

Rogosa, D. (1980). A critique of cross-lagged correlation. *Psychological Bulletin, 88*, 245-258.

Samson, D.M. & McDonnell, A.A. (1990). Functional analysis and challenging behaviours. *Behavioural Psychotherapy, 18*, 259-272.

Shapiro, M.B. (1966). Generality of psychological processes and specificity of outcomes. *Perceptual and Motor Skills, 23*, 16.

Sharrock, R. & Gudjonsson, G.H. (1993) Intelligence, previous convictions and interrogative suggestibility: a path analysis of alleged false-confession cases. *British Journal of Clinical Psychology, 32*, 169-175.

Sidman, M. (1964). *Tactics of Scientific Research*. New York: Basic Books.

Slade, P.D. (1982). Towards a functional analysis of anorexia nervosa and bulimia nervosa. *British Journal of Clinical Psychology, 21*, 167-179.

Sobell, M., & Sobell, L. (1981), Functional analysis of alcohol problems. In C.K. Prokop & L.A. Bradley (eds), *Medical Psychology; Contributions to Behavioural Medicine*. New York: Academic Press.

Sutherland, E.H. & Cressey, D.R. (1970). *Criminology*. Philadelphia: J.P. Lippincott.

Truax, C.B. (1966). Reinforcement and non-reinforcement in Rogerian psychotherapy. *Journal of Abnormal Social Psychology, 71*, 1-9.

Vernon, W. & Ulrich, R. (1966). Classical conditioning of pain-elicited aggression. *Science, 152*, 668-669.

Walker, N.D. (1968). *Crime and Punishment in Britain*. Edinburgh: Edinburgh University Press.

Wiseman, S. (1966). *Correlation Methods*. Manchester: Manchester University Press.

CHAPTER TWELVE

Qualitative research

David A. Good *Department of Social & Political Sciences, University of Cambridge*

Fraser N. Watts *Faculty of Divinity, University of Cambridge*

The expression 'qualitative research' is a loose description for a varied set of techniques. An examination of relevant books yields a long list of qualitative methods, ranging from the familiar to the exotic, and including participant observation (e.g. Festinger, Riecken & Schacter, 1956; King, 1978); case studies (e.g. Yin, 1984; Bromley, 1986); discourse analysis (e.g. Labov & Fanshel, 1977); protocol analysis (e.g. Ericsson & Simon, 1984); conversation analysis (e.g. Schegloff, Jefferson & Sacks, 1977); voice-centred techniques (e.g. Gilligan, 1993); photographic analysis (e.g. Becker, 1981); diary studies (e.g. Pollock, 1983); document analysis (e.g. Bogdan, 1974); computational modelling (e.g. Colby, Weber & Hill, 1971; Hand, 1985) and many others. All these methods are concerned with both data collection and analysis. Some are purely qualitative, though many can also generate quantitative data. Most are relatively new to psychology, and have their origins in the related disciplines of anthropology, linguistics, and sociology. This is not to say, though, that the assumptions at the heart of good qualitative work are alien to the psychologist. Clinical psychologists, in particular, are well acquainted with making judgments of a qualitative character and one of the attractions of qualitative research is the possibility it offers for developing such judgments into a formal research strategy capable of yielding substantive and reliable contributions to knowledge.

Though recent years have seen growing sophistication in qualitative research, its foundations within mental health research are still not as secure as the more traditional methods. We shall therefore give particular attention to the problems that any qualitative method needs to solve, and examine how they have been addressed in particular pieces of qualitative research of clinical relevance. First, however, we will consider some common misapprehensions about qualitative research.

In the minds of many researchers, any move towards non-numerical forms of analysis is associated with a retreat from clarity and rigour into a conceptual and methodological quagmire. Quantitative and qualitative approaches are seen as representing fundamentally different perspectives on how research should proceed. It is often assumed that there is little, if any, constraint on what is done in qualitative research, and that at best it can only be used at the exploratory, hypothesis-generation stage of research. While it is true that qualitative methods face difficulties that are avoided by quantification, there is a growing recognition that good qualitative research is both necessary and possible. As Miles and Huberman (1984) note, a number of leading methodological specialists have increasingly turned to the collection and analysis of qualitative data, and for good reason.

The first point to make is that quantification is by no means the only way to rigour. In fact, quantification is often necessary in psychology because of the imperfection of its theories and measurement procedures. With greater precision, the statistical analysis of quantitative data can become redundant. Conversation analysis, perhaps the most rigorous qualitative technique, depends on the search for counter-examples to fully specified claims (see Wootton, 1987, for a discussion of this point, and Schegloff, 1968, for a classic case). Such work also emphasises the point that qualitative research need not be associated only with exploratory and descriptive studies, even though it is likely that it will have its greatest attractions for many at those stages of empirical research. Qualitative research may be a relatively open-ended endeavour, but it is not the case that 'anything goes'. Different methods have different requirements. For example, an anthropologist attempting 'thick descriptions' of the type recommended by Geertz (Geertz, 1983), will admit quite different materials than will the conversation analyst examining 'adjacency pairs' (Schegloff & Sacks, 1973). Each qualitative method has its own rules and constraints.

A related point is that far from being an alternative to quantification, good qualitative analysis is necessary for good quantitative analysis. It is easy to lose sight of the fact that the process of quantification both forces and enables the researcher to solve a number of problems that are always present. but harder to identify and solve in qualitative research. Some procedure is always necessary to turn observed performances into a numerical index. That index can only be as good as the procedure on which it is based, and this in turn is derived from a piece of qualitative work.

In orthodox quantitative research, there necessarily exist procedures that can provide the appropriate numerical values which is the basis of the study. These procedures are effectively a function (F) which takes as input the information-rich set of raw observations, and gives as output a value or set of values (V) as a representation of that initial set. Both F and V may be more or less complex, and aspects of F may be built into the very design of the study. For example, reaction time data are the product of a contrived situation which usually require little or nothing of significance in F to produce V. The contrivance has pre-empted the task F might have accomplished. At the other extreme, the raw data might be a video of a group of children playing. F could then be a complex coding scheme for categorising the behaviours, and V might be a set of frequencies, co-occurrence relationships, or the like.

In producing V, F clearly provides a representation of the subject matter of the study which permits the making of comparisons, and the drawing of inferences. The provision of access to this inferential machinery is clearly the major benefit of quantification, but it produces two others that are of great value to the researcher. It reduces the complexity of the data to a small number of indices, and it provides a simple concise way of displaying the data. These are essential to any research, and they are harder to achieve in qualitative work. Researchers using qualitative methods can quickly find themselves overwhelmed by a mass of data which cannot be easily inspected in the search for patterns and relationships, or corralled into a useful format for reporting and presenting.

We will give relatively little attention to the purported philosophical bases of qualitative methods, partly because we want this chapter to have a practical focus, but also because we suspect that the link between qualitative methods and philosophical assumptions is much weaker than some advocates claim. Of course, some advocates of qualitative methods regard any attempt at quantification as misguided. However, as Stalin once remarked, bourgeois trains can easily accommodate socialist passengers pursuing socialist goals, and so too can qualitative methods be turned to other ends, no matter what their origin.

Because qualitative clinical research is relatively unfamiliar, we will present good illustrative examples. In doing so, we will consider three key questions: How were the data collected? How were they transformed into a manageable and meaningful representation for both analysis and report? What kinds of inferences were drawn, and how were they validated?

Despite the heterogeneity of qualitative methods, three key issues will recur. These will be discussed in detail in specific contexts later in the chapter, but we want to draw attention to them in relatively abstract form at this stage:

1. It is seldom sufficient to use a single source of data. Usually, conclusions will be much more secure if supported by both direct and indirect measures, both objective records and personal accounts, material with both participants and observers, etc. Exactly which combination of data sources is best will vary from one piece of research to another. Investigators should consider what will give them maximum assurance of validity within the constraints of time and feasibility. Campbell and Fiske (1959) coined the term 'triangulation' to refer to the use of multiple data sources to confirm an interpretation in a situation in which any single source would lack sufficient credibility. It is a common and important principle of qualitative research.

2. The researcher should be clear whether he or she is doing exploratory reconnaissance or hypothesis testing. There is a place for both, but their methodological requirements are very different, and attempts to switch into hypothesis-testing mode in mid-stream are not likely to be fruitful. In hypothesis testing it is always essential for the hypotheses to be sufficiently clear to ensure that they are actually testable. With qualitative research, it is especially important that the categories on which the research is based should be clearly specified. The question for the researcher to ask himself or herself before beginning is 'what would be a counter-example to this hypothesis?'.

3. Because the qualitative researcher is not using the 'short-cuts' to apparent objectivity provided by quantification, he or she must take special care to consider their personal connection to what he or she is studying. The ideal is to be sufficiently in tune with the culture under study to understand the nuances of psychological transactions, but for impartiality and commitment to scientific validity to remain unclouded. This is often a counsel of perfection, but then researchers must realise where they fail short, what risks this brings, and how they can compensate. Clinicians will have no difficulty in principle with grasping the importance of their personal involvement with what they are trying to understand.

THERAPEUTIC DISCOURSE—AN ECLECTIC
APPROACH TO CONVERSATION

Qualitative analyses of conversation are one of the best developed techniques currently available, and we will take as an example the study of a psychotherapeutic interview by Labov and Fanshel (1977). It is the most rigorous of a number of qualitative studies of psychotherapeutic discourse, though there are others (e.g. Havens, 1986; Russell, 1987). It is not representative of any particular school of thought on how conversation research should proceed, but draws on an eclectic background which includes the work of linguistic philosophers (e.g. Austin, 1962), ethnomethodologists (e.g. Schegloff & Sacks, 1973), and linguistic microanalyses (e.g. Pittenger, Hockett & Danehy, 1960), It is an interesting and informative example in that it attempts to move beyond simple exploration and description; it also illustrates the wealth of detail that is available in a single case. However, because of the great commitment of time and resources it required, it is not one that many would be able to imitate.

Labov and Fanshel sought to address not only the description and explanation of the particulars of psychotherapeutic exchange, but also the more general conversational rules and procedures upon which it was built. Clearly, most research has a less ambitious intent. The study was based on just 15 minutes of the twenty-fifth psychotherapy session between a 19-year-old anorexic woman and her therapist. The data collected were an audio recording of this exchange, and the observations of the therapist after listening to the tape and being interrogated by the authors. They offer two justifications for this empirical base. First, by this stage in the series, the therapist and client will have established a routine way of dealing with one another that will be repeatedly exemplified, so it would not matter exactly which session was sampled. Second, the detailed study of individual cases has often proved to be a powerful tactic in science (see Davidson & Costello, 1969; and Chapter 13); the conclusion they yield can be validated against further cases.

In their presentation of each part of the conversation, they detail the background knowledge relevant to the structure and character of the interchange, which they present in the form of an expansion of the observed utterances. This permits the representation of the conversation as a set of actions. An example of an analysis of a brief interchange is given in Table 12.1.

TABLE 12.1
Example of Labov and Fanshell's analysis of a brief episode

Text	*Cues*
[a] Rhoda: and *then-n*, with everything.	Tension: *with everything* (ellipsis)
[b] my sister wanted to go to *work* again.	exasperation
[c] So sh- stayed *Tuesday*.	

Expansion

[a] Rhoda: And then, in spite of everything that happened and all the trouble that had been caused at her house and ours,
[b] my sister wanted to go to work and call on my mother to help some more which was an unreasonable thing to do.
[c] so my mother stayed at my sister's house one more day, Tuesday, but my sister didn't go to work after all so she wasn't being unreasonable because she had no good reason to have asked my mother to stay..

Interaction

Rhoda: continues the narrative, giving information to show that her mother did not have any obligation to fulfil in Household 2, and asserts indirectly that the circumstances for her problem were caused by her sister's unreasonable behaviour.

From such analysis of individual utterances, Labov and Fanshel were able to build a picture of the various significant characters and issues in the patient's life. The major criterion for the evaluation of this process was the internal consistency of the resulting representation of the dialogue, which is assessed by three sorts of questions:

1. Do the rules for the designation of various speech actions group together utterances which are ostensibly similar in the eyes of the therapist and the authors?
2. Are the expansions of the utterances legitimised by the participants' subsequent reactions?
3. Did the final characterisation of the dialogue avoid implications which conflicted reconcilably with the therapist's knowledge of the client?

Two points are of specific interest. First, in looking for counter-intuitive characterisations that their procedures might produce, they are seeking disproof by single counter-example, which makes the claims more vulnerable and thus more interesting if they survive. Second, their use of different sources of information, such as therapists' intuitions, their own experience of other therapy sessions, the client's own subsequent behaviour, illustrates the use of 'triangulation' in qualitative research.

The way in which Labov and Fanshel achieve their extended description is similar to Kreckel's (1981) work on the Wilkins family, who were the subject of a 'fly-on-the-wall' television documentary series. This reflects an approach to the study of social life as quasi-linguistic and open to the same research methods as language (Harre, 1979). Kreckel's findings emphasise the importance of studying the relevant social microcosm if we are to interpret properly the significance of the personal actions observed. This in turn depends on understanding the meanings that the participants ascribe to their actions. Labov and Fanshel see the correct characterisation of such interpretations as the key problem to be solved, as writers in the hermeneutic tradition have also realised (Bauman, 1978).

A different tradition of conversation analysis has examined the structural regularities which may be found in conversation. It is a (less adventurous) style of work than that of Labov and Fanshel in that it relies less heavily on interpretation, but is capable of producing more solid, if more limited, findings. Researchers in this field move inductively from corpora of recorded conversations to a claim about how some facet of a conversational sequence is organised, and then test it by seeking counter-examples in a wider range of cases. If one is found, the claim is reformulated and tested in the same way. For example, using this method Schegloff et al. (1977) have studied how the 'repair' of a conversational error or infelicity may be initiated and accomplished by each participant.

This approach has not often been applied to clinical materials, but is potentially of clinical relevance. For example, the ability to initiate and accomplish a 'repair' depends upon the ability to monitor one's own and someone else's speech at various levels, and to produce a suitable reformulation. The selective losses found in the aftermath of head injury will be reflected in which kinds of error (for example, phonological lexical or syntactic) are noticed and redressed in spontaneous speech, and so an analysis of an aphasic's repair strategies could provide a guide to the precise nature of the impairment. See, for example, Schlenck, Huber and Willmes (1987).

Another example is that of Rochester and Martin (1979) on schizophrenic discourse. Using Halliday and Hasan's (1976) analysis of discourse coherence they constructed a coding scheme which was then applied to schizophrenic productions. This resulted in both further qualitative and quantitative analyses, which revealed important differences between thought-disordered and non thought-disordered schizophrenics and normals in the cohesiveness of the texts produced.

PARTICIPANT OBSERVATION

Participant observation (PO) is a research method that has seen greatest use in sociology and anthropology. In contrast to the micro-analytic approach to conversation, PO ostensibly requires much greater effort in the data collection process, but given that the researcher is basing the primary data on his or her own interpretation of the events being witnessed, the division between data collection and data analysis is not so clear. In essence, it refers to a method that places the researcher in the community of interest as the recording apparatus, and thus its success depends greatly on the researcher's personal skills. It can provide data of great authenticity and validity, although it is fraught with many problems, and is probably of greatest use in the descriptive and exploratory stages of research when the researcher needs to develop greater insight into those in whom he or she is interested.

The aspect of PO to which most attention has been given is data collection. The main issues that need to be considered here are (a) gaining access, (b) sampling, and (c) investigation effects.

The normal problems of gaining access to subjects are heightened in qualitative research by the level of involvement required. Considerable preliminary work may well be needed before satisfactory access is gained. In fact, the form of participation that researchers achieve is often beyond their control, and they may be forced by the circumstances to be more or less active and overt than they intended. Also, the personal characteristics of the researcher will dictate the role taken. For example, it would be impossible for a middle-aged white researcher to be accepted as a participant in a black juvenile gang in the South Bronx.

It might be thought that clinical researchers could never be covert in their own institution, but it should be remembered that the overt clinical status can provide a cover for research activity. Furthermore, the researcher's own background will radically affect their understanding of what they observe. As Alaszewski (1986) has pointed out, there is a sharp difference between operating in familiar and alien cultures. In the latter case the researchers can suffer from not knowing enough to make sense of what is observed. In the former, it can be difficult for the researcher to recognise the full significance of highly familiar actions.

The sampling problems in qualitative research are more familiar than might be imagined. If one is to make claims about some class of condition or person, it is necessary to ensure that the correct beast has been trapped. In qualitative research this sometimes results in a post-hoc appraisal of the class of entity which has been studied, rather than an attempt to identify the class precisely before the data collection is conducted.

In any research on humans, the investigator and the investigation can inevitably exert an influence. In experimental work, there is the problem of demand characteristics; in survey research, there is the concern with the exact wording of the question and the interviewer's style, and so on. Given the extent of the researcher's role in PO, these effects can be of such magnitude that they form the basis of the subsequent theorising. However, it is always the hope that the investigator will provoke more activities of the type that would have occurred anyway rather than changing the character of what is observed.

The PO researcher who is not completely covert always faces problems in concealing his or her purpose, and avoiding disingenuous presentations by the subjects. These take many forms, ranging from subtle evasions to blatant lies, and are conveniently summarised by Douglas (1976, Ch. 4). The separation of the investigator and observer roles, though unusual in PO work, can be highly beneficial, and was recommended long ago by Katz (1953). It forces the researcher to have a more explicit observational agenda, permits the use of a greater number of observers, and spreads the burden of responsibility for the conduct of the study, thus making it easier for competing views about the quality of the observations and their significance to surface.

Being covert, however, causes problems too. The report by Festinger et al. (1956) of their well-known study of the infiltration of an apocalyptic group is instructive here, because it gives more explicit attention than is usual to methods and observations. They noted that it was impossible for their observers to maintain a completely passive role because often they were directly requested to act; not to have done so may have led to their expulsion from the group. Thus, inevitably, some of the events that were recorded would have had a different character, and perhaps would not have occurred at all, if the observers had not been there. Secondly, they could not enlist native informants in the same way that overt observers would have done, but this did not inhibit all the lines of questioning with informants. As new and keen members of this type of group the observers had every reason to ask many questions. Finally, covert observers face peculiar difficulties in recording their observations. The observers needed to find time alone when they could jot down their observations where such time is hard to find; the quality of observations will vary as a function of the memory load that the observers faced at different times.

The strategy of having several observers was a good feature of Festinger's study because it offers the possibility of 'triangulation' from different data sets. As Friedrichs and Ludtke (1975, p. 20) and Pelto and Pelto (1978) point out, this increases the probability of eccentric observations being rooted out when there are conflicting reports, and also enhances the prospects of building a richer account of specific events of which individual observers might only be able to offer a partial report. Pelto and Pelto also point out the necessity of estimating the knowledge base on which reports are made. For some simple concrete matters (such as the number of people present at a small meeting) the observer is well placed to provide reliable data; for some other issues (such as the projected internal states of other participants) observations will obviously be on a less sound footing.

This point brings us to the most difficult part of the observations of Festinger et al. They were interested in how individuals' reactions to events varied as a function of their previous commitment to the belief system. They attempted to validate observations of individual commitment, first by seeking confirmation of the level of commitment from a variety of different actions, second by always considering alternatives. They considered this to be like detective work (see Festinger et al., 1956, p. 249). Bromley in another context has referred to it as the quasi-judicial method; we return to this later.

Festinger's work provides a good methodological model of PO, and is much more satisfactory from this point of view than the work of Goffman (e.g. Goffman, 1961) which, in terms of content, is of more direct relevance to the clinician. Goffman's work does not provide an instructive exemplar because so little of his method and direct observations are revealed in the final reports. This is regrettable as particular issues arise relating to PO in hospitals, which is where clinicians are most likely to carry out research. However, there is an instructive discussion of the problems in setting up clinical PO in Alaszewski's (1986) report of his study of a mental handicap hospital.

A particularly good and recent example of the psychological use of participation observation is *Ecological Studies of Family Life* by Vetere and Gale (1987). Though the families studied were not explicitly 'clinical', the relevance to clinical research of this approach to the study of family processes is clear. Vetere and Gale also provide a good discussion of the benefits and problems of participant observation.

ACCOUNT ANALYSIS

The observation of behaviour can be supplemented by analyses of people's accounts of their behaviour. Nisbett and Wilson (1977) argued that such protocols are of little use because people do not usually have access to the relevant cognitive processes, but their argument is flawed in several ways (Kraut & Lewis, 1982; Wright & Rip, 1981). Nevertheless, their general point that such reports must not be taken always at face value must be remembered.

The area where accounts have been studied most rigorously is in the analyses of people's accounts of performance on psychological tasks, such as how they solve problems. Ericsson and Simon (1984) have presented a full exposition of the case for studying protocols obtained from subjects as a supplement to the experimental study of task performance. Normally, 'think-aloud' reports are obtained during actual performance, and more likely to be accurate than those obtained subsequently. Ericsson and Simon make an important distinction between (a) verbalising covert encodings or articulating material that is in focal attention at least in a compressed internal format, and (b) explaining other task-related thoughts or hypotheses that are not in focal attention. They make out a good case that the former can normally be reported with a high degree of accuracy, and that doing so affects neither the speed nor quality of performance.

Think-aloud protocols have a potential, so far largely unrealised, to contribute to the analysis of performance deficits in clinical groups, and they can supplement the experimental methods described in Chapter 9. However, caution is needed about requiring subjects to verbalise material that would not normally be in awareness. For example, requiring subjects to articulate hypotheses in a problem-solving task is an example of a 'think-aloud' requirement that goes beyond what is already in focal attention, and is likely to change performance.

The first step in the analysis of a protocol is to transform it into segments, formed in a consistent vocabulary so that linkages can be identified, and to check the reliability of this transformation. Reliability can be maximised by fine segmentation of the protocol, though it may also be necessary to sacrifice a degree of detailed specification of each segment to achieve good reliability. There then follows an analysis of the implicit grammar represented by the protocol. The methods for doing this are similar to those already described in this chapter for analysing discourse. Ericsson and Simon (1984) also give many examples of the analysis of decision-making and problem-solving protocols. Another example of protocol analysis of clinical interest is Foulkes' (1978) analysis of the grammar implicit in protocols of dreams.

An extension of account analysis to a limited segment of social interaction is the technique of Interpersonal Process Recall, which is now well developed and researched (Kagan, 1984; Barker, 1985). As soon as possible after an interaction, a videotape of it is played to each of the participants separately. The researcher stops the tape frequently and asks for a detailed analysis of moment-to-moment thoughts and feelings. This technique yields a wealth of data, and has important professional uses, both in the training of novice therapists and in the 'unblocking' of cases which have become stuck. It has the potential to yield interesting research data (such as data showing that the perspectives of client and therapist on a single event can be very different; Caskey, Barker & Elliott, 1984), though as yet it has led to few well-substantiated general findings.

A different kind of account analysis, so far less rigorously developed but with wide potential application, is based on people's accounts of their social actions. This kind of account analysis makes the assumption that social behaviour is rule-based and that participants are capable of supplying the implicit rules. Such accounts can be an important constraint on social behaviour in two ways. First, knowledge of the alternative accounts which could be offered of an action will force consideration of possible consequences, and these will matter to the actor. Second, an account that has been publicly offered will crystallise the definition of an event, and this can either permit or prohibit other subsequent acts (see Semin & Manstead, 1983).

An interesting example is a study of the accounts of football violence given by fans who participated in it (Marsh, Rosser & Harré, 1978). However, this example also reveals a problem with account analysis. Marsh's protocols revealed two different kinds of account that were often closely intertwined. One emphasised the violent intentions of the behaviour of the fans, the other that it was constrained by conventions that limited the actual violence that occurred. Marsh accepted the latter as being the correct account, apparently on the grounds that it coincided with his observations of violent behaviour. However, it is not clear that the accounts alone revealed any basis for deciding which strand to accept as the correct one. The moral seems to be the value of seeking convergent data from different sources. This is, once again, the principle of 'triangulation'. Accounts of social action can provide valuable insights that can be checked against observations made in other ways. However, it cannot at present be regarded as a secure basis on its own for drawing conclusions.

There are, of course, incidents that are driven, stage by stage, by people's perceptions of what is happening. In such cases, accounts are of central explanatory relevance, regardless of whether the participant's accounts are veridical by some external criterion. An excellent example is Hans Toch's (1969) study of participants' accounts of how violent incidents arose. He obtained detailed participants' accounts of 344 incidents of assault on police officers. An interesting feature of the study was the use of 'peer' interviewers, albeit equipped with an interview schedule, to obtain these accounts. Thus a prison inmate would be interviewed by another prison inmate. As is normal in such qualitative research, the interviews were first transcribed. Each stage of the incident was then coded, so that the material was reduced to standard form (e.g. C2 = violence in an effort to prevent being transported or moved after being arrested). The analysis then focused on common sequences. Thus, the researcher would start with the 164 incidents that began with 'officers' orders or instructions'. A branching tree would then be constructed showing the possible routes from this starting point to violence against the police officer. The most frequent sequence that was discovered by this method of analysis is shown in Fig. 12.1. The presentation of results in this form is an elegant solution to something that is often a problem in qualitative research. Clearly, this is a form of research that is of potential relevance to a wide range of clinical behaviour disorders.

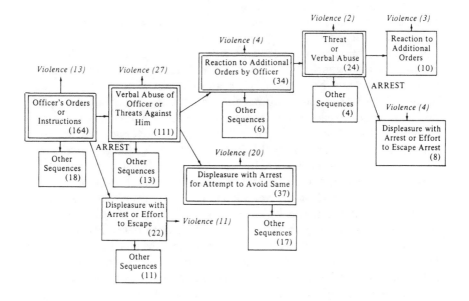

FIG. 12.1. Sequences leading to police arrests (N = 344).

CATEGORISATION STUDIES

Probably the form of qualitative research that has so far been most fruitful in the clinical field is that which seeks to establish a categorisation of a series of cases of 'instances'. The cases concerned are often individual patients (see the discussion of case series in Chapter 11), but there are of course other categorisations that are of potential clinical interest. At the other extreme, it would be possible to do a taxonomic study of recurrent events within a single case, such as a categorisation of meetings between a patient and a critical relative, of episodes of violent behaviour, or amnesic episodes. For such a categorisation study to be fruitful, it is of course necessary that there should be sufficient variety in the instances under study, and that this variety should be lawful in the sense that each of the categories of the taxonomy has a cluster of features spanning different domains that come together to define it. Again, categorisation studies normally draw on a variety of different data sources; both accounts and observations are often used.

A rigorous qualitative approach to clinical categorisation provides a clear example of the path between 'off-the-top-of-the-head' clinical methods on the one hand and quantitative approaches to taxonomy on the other. Both are in common use. Numerous clinicians have reflected on their clinical experience and derived an intuitive classification of the patients that they have seen, such as different types of depression. Equally, there have been numerous quantitative studies that have recorded numerical scores on features in a patient series, and subjected these to a statistical technique such as factor analysis that yields a categorisation. These approaches suffer from different problems. The purely clinical approach is wholly unconstrained, subject to no kind of empirical checking, and of unknown (and doubtful) reliability. The quantitative approach is in some ways too constrained, for example in the range of data that can be considered; only those features that can readily be captured in numerical scores contribute to the results of the analysis. Information from patient accounts, for example, is nearly always excluded. Also, though it is well known that techniques such as factor analysis can lead to a wide range of different solutions depending on the exact technique used, there is normally little place for the taxonomic process to be steered by the researcher's rich personal familiarity with the material. Qualitative approaches to categorisation seek to introduce greater rigour into the process than occurs with purely clinical approaches, but without the impoverishment both of data and the researcher's personal contribution, that often occurs with quantitative approaches.

There are three important methodological guidelines about qualitative approaches to categorisation.

1. The categories must be defined sufficiently explicitly for the allocation of instances to categories to be a reliable process, and the reliability should be checked empirically.
2. The set of categories used should be exhaustive, so that every instance can be allocated to one or other category.
3. Every category should be internally coherent; exhaustiveness should not be achieved by having a waste-basket category.

In practice it is often helpful to develop categories sequentially, beginning by grouping together instances that are very closely related. This produces an initial sorting into a large number of categories that have few instances each, but are at least coherent. These initial categories can then be combined as far as is compatible with the requirement that each resulting category should be internally coherent.

We shall illustrate qualitative approaches to categorisation with two main examples, one from cognitive performance, the other from social action research.

Our cognitive example is Baddeley and Wilson's (1986) study of autobiographical memory in amnesic patients. A standard technique of eliciting the data was used, in which subjects were presented with a series of cue words and asked to produce a memory suggested by each. The test was repeated after a week, and the interviews transcribed. Baddeley and Wilson then sought dimensions on which their amnesics' autobiographical memories varied, and on which a categorisation could be based. Some of the patients studied had normal autobiographical memory. Those in whom it was abnormal fell into three main groups:

1. 'Clouding' of autobiographical memory in which memories that were available on one occasion were largely unavailable on the next.
2. Those in whom fluency of memory was poor but there was little confabulation.
3. Those who were fluent but showed extensive confabulation.

The distinction between the latter two groups is of considerable theoretical interest in pointing to a distinction between the generation and checking of autobiographical memories. Indeed, the significance of this categorisation of pathologies of autobiographical memory comes largely from the integration of observation and theory that it represents. There is no need for qualitative research to be atheoretical.

Other important recent examples of qualitative categorisation studies in related fields are the studies of approaches to learning in higher education initiated by Ference Marton at Gothenburg (Marton, Hounsell & Entwistle, 1984). Analyses, both of students' accounts of how they approached the learning process, and of their performance when they recalled a passage they had studied, led to a distinction between deep and surface approaches to studying that had wide empirical ramifications. Recent work categorising slips of action (Reason & Mycielska, 1982) is also interesting both methodologically and substantively. In the field of social action, Toch's (1969) study of violent men is a good example of a categorisation study. He worked with detailed accounts of violent incidents from 69 people who had been engaged in them. Each case was then reduced to a summary pattern description or personality sketch. The cases were then subjected to a process of content analysis and grouping. The result was a list of 10 types of violence, six were classified as being self-preserving strategies, in which violence is used to bolster and enhance the person's ego in the eyes of himself and of others, the other four occurred in people who see themselves and their needs as being the only fact of social relevance.

One good methodological feature of this study is that it was subjected to a reliability check. It should be possible for any other investigator who spends the time to work through the protocols and correctly allocate each to one of the categories provided. A categorisation should ideally always be checked for reliability, and this should be included when the study is published. However, the presentation of results remains problematic, and it is usually necessary to fall back on the presentation of examples. It may be helpful to present delimiting as well as typical instances.

CASE STUDIES

Finally, we will consider qualitative case studies, which can be distinguished from both the experimental and intensive studies of individual cases discussed in Chapters 13 and 14 respectively. Qualitative case study research can also be distinguished from routine clinical case work both by its theoretical purpose, and its methodological rigour.

Case study research aims to make a general contribution to knowledge, which is not normally true of clinical case reports. The aims and objectives of the study should be clearly formulated, and determine both the selection of the case and the way in which it is studied. No case study can be fully comprehensive, but its limitations should flow from clearly specified objectives. A successful study from this point of view is Garfinkel's (1967) well-known study of 'Agnes', a patient who presented for a sex-change operation. This arose as part of Garfinkel's interest in how institutional realities are maintained; this unusual case permitted a rich study of the institution of gender. Similarly, Strauss and Glaser (1970) studied the dying trajectory of 'Mrs Abel' as part of a broader study of the dying process, examining how aware patients are of it and how they cope. Case studies are also frequently undertaken to illuminate the process of treatment; Dewald's (1972) study of a patient in psychoanalytic treatment is an exceptionally thorough study of this type.

Case studies can also draw explicitly on a particular theoretical background, such as the social-phenomenological position which influenced Garfinkel's study of Agnes. This is allied to the hermeneutic tradition of research, which Packer (1985) has distinguished both from rationalistic research that seeks to discover an abstract system of relations in which social context and individual differences are minimised, and from empiricist research that sees behaviour as resulting from the interaction of causal forces. Hermeneutic research, in contrast, is said to investigate 'the semantic or textual structure of everyday practical activity' (Packer, 1985, p.1086). In particular, hermeneutic analysis is concerned with how the significance of an action can be understood by reference to its setting, the personal and cultural practices within which it arises. However, as we have already observed, links between theoretical assumptions and practical methodology are often weak. Garfinkel's 'Agnes' is very different from the hermeneutic work on the laboratory game of 'Prisoner's Dilemma' that Packer presents; on the other hand 'Agnes' is very similar to other case studies that don't explicitly use Garfinkel's theoretical orientation.

Case study research aspires to a degree of methodological rigour beyond what is normally required in clinical reports. Like most other qualitative research it cannot afford to make do with a single source of data. Again, it is necessary to 'triangulate' from a variety of different vantage points. The principal sources are the subject's own account, the accounts of informants, relevant documentary evidence, and the researcher's direct observations. These can be checked against each other. As far as possible, any factual claims that are crucial to the case study should be corroborated from more than one source. Bromley (1977, 1986) has made the helpful suggestion that the evaluation of evidence in the case study is 'quasi-judicial'. Hearsay is not enough. Neither can researchers be content with simply stating how things appear to them. Evidence must be evaluated, and the conclusions reached must be ones that a reasonable and fairminded group of people would accept if the evidence for them was set out. Moreover, evidence should be distinguished from conclusions in the way the case study is presented; the arguments and evidence for preferring one conclusion to another should be explicitly laid out. Unfortunately, many published case studies are unsatisfactory from this point of view, and present evidence and interpretations indistinguishably in a homogeneous narrative format.

Spence (1982) has argued that the truth criteria appropriate to ideographic material are those of 'narrative truth' rather than 'historical truth'. Narrative truth depends essentially on 'coherence' rather than 'correspondence' truth criteria. There can be legitimate debate over this point; what is essential is that if a case study is to be presented as having historical truth it must have satisfied the appropriate criteria. Clearly, meeting criteria for narrative truth does not mean that historical truth has been achieved.

Bromley is not the first to have made recommendations about how study research should be presented. A series of other rather similar recommendations have been made over the last 50 years (see Runyan, 1982, Chapter 8). However, Bromley's are perhaps the clearest and most comprehensive guidelines to have been set out so far. His suggestions regarding the content and organisation of a case report are set out in Table 12.2.

Concurrently, de Waele has developed methods for producing assisted autobiographies, in which the subject effectively writes his or her own case study with the assistance of an expert team (de Waele & Harré,

TABLE 12.2
The contents and organisation of a case-report (adapted from Bromley, 1977)

1.	The problem under investigation and the authorship of the report, including a statement of its purpose and terms of reference.
2.	The identity of the individual, his or her physical appearance, location and other routine information.
3.	The life-history and present circumstances of the individual and related issues.
4.	The psychological attributes of the individual
5.	The social positions and social relationships of the individual.
6.	The relationship of the individual to the investigator (or informants).
7.	An evaluation of the individual in terms of accepted and explicit ethical standards.
8.	A review of the evidence and arguments in relation to the purposes and terms of reference of the investigation.
9.	A summary of the methods used in, and the conditions governing, the investigation, together with any associated reservations or implications.
10.	Conclusions: findings, recommendations and forecasts.

1979). Of course, this can also be seen as an application of account analysis, but we have included it here because of its similarity to case studies. The subject writes an initial autobiography in his or her own terms, but this is then subjected to negotiation with a team of experts. For this purpose, it is dismembered into a series of topics (e.g. living conditions; family and groups, etc.). An extensive inventory has been developed covering nine such topics, which is used in the process of 'negotiating' the autobiography. The Focused Account Eliciting Interview is itself recognised as a social episode in which the material produced will be determined by how the interview is perceived; each interview therefore begins and ends with reflexive questions about the interview process. Finally, key longitudinal themes are identified, and the autobiography is often organised around how the subject has coped with conflicts or crises. It is a statement of how the subject interprets his or her own life, but because of the procedure of negotiation and authentication, everything included in the final version has been considered and evaluated by an expert team. Initially, de Waele has concentrated his research using this method on developing assisted autobiographies of murderers, but substantive conclusions have apparently not yet been published.

A variety of ideographic methods are available which do not aspire to the comprehensiveness of a case study, but which analyse in detail part of the material on which a case study would be based (see Runyan, 1982, Chapter 9). One example is Horowitz's study of Janice, a college student in psychotherapy, by his technique of 'configurational analysis' (Horowitz, 1979). One aspect of this technique is concerned with identifying key recurrent states and the patterns of change between them.

Analysis of the material from Janice's sessions led to the identification of several recurrent states. These were described, partly using her own terms, as 'tra-la-la', 'hurt and not working', 'hurt but working', 'acute self-disgust', etc. The second stage of the investigation focused on the circumstances that effected a transition from one state to another. For example, difficult material in therapy such as a reminder of shortcomings. often produced a change from 'tra-la-la' to 'hurt but working'. However, if this was followed by further difficulty, such as a loss of support, 'hurt but working' could give way in turn to 'acute self-disgust'. Such analyses led to the model of transitions between states given in Fig. 12.2. A further stage of the analysis focused on the recurrent images of self and others associated with each state. For example, when in the 'hurt but working' state. she perceived herself as an impaired but learning student, and the other person as a teacher.

Though Horowitz's initial 'configurational analysis' of Janice was a qualitative exercise, this can (and has been) supplemented by using

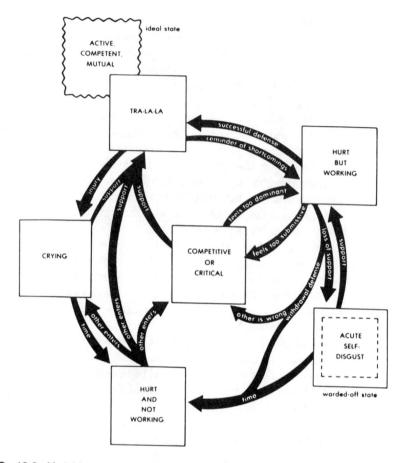

FIG. 12.2. Model for the cycle of the states.

intensive quantitative methods. Allport's analysis of over 100 letters written by the subject Jenny is another example of a partly qualitative, partly quantitative analysis of a corpus of material from a single subject (Allport, 1965).

CONCLUSIONS

Qualitative research techniques have enormous scope and adaptability. It can hardly be doubted that they are good at the research task of generating hypotheses. However, we have argued that some qualitative techniques are also sufficiently rigorous to yield conclusions in which researchers can have confidence. Recent years have seen growing enthusiasm for qualitative research, and as a result of this, it is now possible to be more precise than previously about how to do it. There remains a need for the refinement and specification of qualitative research methodologies, and this will happen as more researchers use these methods. At present, the greatest need is for good examples of projects that have produced significant findings. This is, in the end, the test by which qualitative research will properly be judged.

The number of books and articles on qualitative methodology that researchers may find useful to consult has grown substantially since the first edition of this volume was published. Amongst those which clinical researchers might find it useful to consult are the following: Ashworth, Giorgi and de Koning (1986), Bryman (1988), Henwood and Pidgeon (1992), Maanen (1983), Miles and Huberman (1984), Patton (1990), Reason and Rowan (1981), Silverman (1985), Stiles (1993), Strauss (1987), Strauss and Corbin (1990), Walker (1985), and Wolcott (1990). Though many of these are not explicitly concerned with clinical questions, it is often straightforward to see how the methods described could be applied in mental health research.

REFERENCES

Alaszewski, A. (1986). *Institutional Care and the Mentally Handicapped.* London: Croom Helm.

Allport, G.W. (1965). *Letters from Jenny.* New York: Harcourt, Brace and World.

Ashworth, P.D., Giorgi, A. & de Koning, A.J.J. (eds) (1986). *Qualitative Research in Psychology.* Pittsburgh: Duquesne University Press.

Austin, J.L. (1962). *How to Do Things with Words.* Oxford: Clarendon Press.

Baddeley, A.D. & Wilson, B. (1986). Amnesia, autobiographical memory and confabulation. In D.C. Rubin (ed.) *Autobiographical Memory.* Cambridge University Press.

Barker, C. (1985). Interpersonal process recall in clinical training and research. In F.N.Watts (ed.) *New Developments in Clinical Psychology.* Leicester: British Psychological Society.

Bauman, Z. (1978). *Hermeneutics and Social Science.* London: Hutchinson.

Becker, H.S. (ed.) (1981). *Exploring Society Photographically.* Evanston, Ill.: Mary & Leigh Block Gallery, Northwestern University.

Bogdan, R. (1974). *Being Different: The Autobiography of Jane Fry.* New York: Wiley.

Bromley, D.B. (1977). *Personality Description in Ordinary Language.* London: John Wiley.

Bromley, D.B. (1986). *The Case Study Method in Psychology and Related Disciplines.* Chichester: John Wiley.

Bryman, A. (1988) *Quantity and Quality in Social Research.* London: Unwin Hyman.

Campbell, D.T. & Fiske, D.W. (1959). Convergent and discriminant validation by the multitrait-multimethod matrix. *Psychological Bulletin, 56,* 81-105.

Caskey, N., Barker, C. & Elliott, R. (1984). Dual perspectives: clients' and therapists' perceptions of therapist responses. *British Journal of Clinical Psychology, 23*, 281-290.

Colby, K.M., Weber, S. & Hill, F.D. (1971). Artificial paranoia. *Artificial Intelligence, 2*, 1-25.

Davidson, P.O. & Costello, C.G. (eds) (1969). *N=I: Experimental Studies of Single Cases*. New York: Von Nostrand.

de Waele, J.-P. & Harre, R. (1979). Autobiography as a psychological method. In G.P. Ginsburg (ed.) *Emerging Strategies in Social Psychological Research*. Chichester: John Wiley.

Dewald, P.A. (1972). *The Psychoanalytic Process: A Case Illustration*. New York: Basic Books.

Douglas, J.D. (1976). *Investigative Social Research*. Beverly Hills: Sage.

Ericsson, K.A. & Simon, H.A. (1984). *Protocol Analysis*. Cambridge, MA: MIT Press.

Festinger, L., Riecken, H.W. & Schacter, S. (1956). *When Prophecy Fails*. New York: Harper Row.

Foulkes, D. (1978). *A Grammar of Dreams*. Hassocks, UK: Harvester Press.

Friedrichs, J. & Ludtke, H. (1975). *Participant Observation: Theory and Practice*. Farnborough, UK: Saxon House.

Garfinkel, H. (1967). *Studies in Ethnomethodology*. Englewood Cliffs, NJ: Prentice-Hall.

Gilligan, C. (1993). *In a Different Voice*. Cambridge, MA: Harvard University Press.

Goffman, E. (1961). *Asylums*. Harmondsworth, UK: Penguin.

Halliday, M.A.K. & Hasan, R. (1976). *Cohesion in English*. London: Longman.

Hand, D.J. (1985). *Artificial Intelligence and Psychiatry*. Cambridge University Press.

Harré, R. (1979). *Social Being: A Theory for Social Psychology*. Oxford: Blackwell.

Havens, L. (1986). *Making Contact: Uses of Language in Psychotherapy*. Cambridge, MA: Harvard University Press.

Henwood, K.L. & Pidgeon, N.F. (1992) Qualitative research and psychological theorizing. *British Journal of Psychology, 83*, 97-112.

Horowitz, M.J. (1979). *States of Mind: Analysis & Change in Psychotherapy*. New York: Plenum Press.

Kagan, N. (1984). Interpersonal process recall: basic methods and recent research. In D. Larsen (ed.) *Teaching Psychological Skills*. Monteney: Brooks/Cole.

Katz, D. (1953). Field Studies. In L. Festinger & D. Katz (eds) *Research Methods in the Behavioural Sciences*. New York: Holt, Rinehart & Winston.

King, R. (1978). *All Things Bright and Beautiful? A Sociological Study of Infants' Classrooms*. Chichester, UK: Wiley.

Kraut, R.E. & Lewis, S.H. (1982). Person perception and self-awareness: Knowledge of one's influences on one's own judgements. *Journal of Personality and Social Psychology, 42*, 448-460.

Kreckel, M. (1981). *Communicative Data and Shared Knowledge in Natural Discourse*. London: Academic Press.

Labov, W. & Fanshel, D. (1977). *Therapeutic Discourse*. New York: Academic Press.

Maanen, J. Van (ed.) (1983). *Qualitative Methodology*. Beverly Hills, Cal.: Sage.

Marsh, P., Rosser, E. & Harré, R. (1978). *The Rules of Disorder*. London: Routledge & Kegan Paul.

Marton, F., Hounsell, D. & Entwistle, N. (1984). *The Experience of Learning*. Edinburgh: Scottish Academic Press.

Miles, M.B. & Huberman, A.M. (1984). *Qualitative Data Analysis: A Sourcebook of New Methods*. Beverly Hills, Cal.: Sage.

Nisbett, P.E. & Wilson, T.D. (1977). Telling more than we can know: Verbal reports on mental processes. *Psychological Review, 84*, 231-259.

Packer, M.J. (1985). Hermeneutic inquiry in the study of human conduct. *American Psychologist, 40*. 1081-1093.

Patton, M.Q. (1990). *Qualitative Evaluation Methods*, 2nd edition. Beverly Hills, Cal.: Sage.

Pelto, P.C. & Pelto, G.H. (1978). *Anthropological Research: The Structure of Enquiry*. Cambridge University Press.

Pittenger, R.E., Hockett, C.F. & Danehy, J.J. (1960). *The First Five Minutes*. Ithaca, New York: Paul Martineau.

Pollock, L.A. (1983). *Forgotten Children: Parent-Child Relations from 1500 to 1900*. Cambridge University Press.

Reason, J. & Mycielska, K. (1982). *Absent-Minded: The Psychology of Mental Lapses and Everyday Errors*. London: Prentice-Hall.

Reason, P. & Rowan, J. (1981). *Human Inquiry*, Chichester, UK: John Wiley.

Rochester, S. & Martin, J.R. (1979). *Crazy Talk: A Study of the Discourse of Schizophrenic Speakers*. London: Plenum.

Runyan, W.K. (1982). *Life Histories and Psychobiography*. Oxford University Press.

Russell, R.L. (ed.) (1987). *Language in Psychotherapy: Strategies of Discovery*. London: Plenum.

Schegloff, E.A. (1968). Sequencing in conversational openings. *American Anthropologist, 70*, 1075-1095.

Schegloff, E.A. & Sacks, H. (1973). Opening up closings. *Semiotica, 8*, 289-327.

Schegloff, E.A., Jefferson, G. & Sacks, H. (1977). The preference for self correction in the organisation of repair in conversation. *Language, 53*, 361-382.

Schlenck, K-J., Huber, W. & Willmes, K. (1987). 'Prepairs' and repairs: Different monitoring functions in aphasic language production. *Brain and Language, 30*, 226-244.

Semin, G.R. & Manstead, A.S.R. (1983). *The Accountability of Conduct*. London: Academic Press.

Silverman, D. (1985). *Qualitative Methodology & Sociology*. Guildford, UK: Gower.

Spence, D.P. (1982). *Narrative Truth and Historical Truth: Meaning anti Interpretation in Psychoanalysis*. London: Norton.

Stiles, W.B. (1993) Quality-control in qualitative research. *Clinical Psychology Review, 13*, 593-618.

Strauss, A.L. (1987) *Qualitative Analysis for Social Scientists*. Cambridge: Cambridge University Press.

Strauss, A.L. & Corbin, J.M. (1990). *Basics of Qualitative Research*. Newbury Park: Sage.

Strauss, A.L. & Glaser, G.B. (1970). *Anguish: A Case Study of a Dying Trajectory*. London: Martin, Robertson.

Toch, H. (1969). *Violent Men*. Chicago: Aldine.

Vetere, A. & Gale, A. (1987). *Ecological Studies of Family Life*. Chichester, UK: John Wiley.

Walker, R. (1985). *Applied Qualitative Research*. Guildford, UK: Gower.

Wolcott, H.F. (1990). *Writing Up Qualitative Research*. Newbury Park: Sage

Wootton, A. (1987). Remarks on the methodology of conversation analysis. In D. Roger & P. Bull (eds) *Conversation: An Interdisciplinary Approach*. Bristol, UK: Multilingual Matters.

Wright, P. & Rip, P.D. (1981). Retrospective reports in the causes of decisions. *Journal of Personality and Social Psychology, 40*, 601-614.

Yin, R.K. (1984). *Case Study Research*. Beverly Hills, Cal.: Sage.

CHAPTER THIRTEEN

Single case research

Stephen Morley *Division of Psychiatry and Behavioural Sciences, School of Medicine, University of Leeds*

For the clinician single case research has one overwhelming advantage; the material for research is the same as their clinical work. There is no need to seek out special populations, control groups and large numbers of subjects. Research can be completed within a matter of months rather than years and there is every opportunity for the investigator to build up expertise and data rapidly and sequentially. Furthermore, some single case research can be carried out relatively cheaply without the taxing need to devote time and resources to applying for and administering research grants. But single case research should not be approached casually, there are many pitfalls and difficulties. Care must be taken over the articulation of the research question, development of measures and the implementation of the interventions.

A compelling reason for adopting single case methods is that they can be useful aids to satisfying a clinician's everyday curiosity about clients. Most clinicians are curious about their clients and ask questions about the aetiology and maintenance of problems, the effect of treatment, whether another treatment is more effective or why a treatment fails (Table 13.1).

For clinicians who approach case work as an applied scientist, single case methods provide a flexible and logical way of evaluating their clinical activity. Nevertheless, there is a tension between the approach one must take as a clinician and the ideal which is expressed in the literature. Much of the published work is derived from applied

TABLE 13.1
Questions for curious clinicians

Questions about formulation:
  What contributes to the development and maintenance of a problem?
  What are the controlling factors for the target variables?

Simple outcome question:
  Has the client improved?

Simple treatment question:
  Is the improvement a result of treatment?

Complex treatment question:
  Does the treatment have a specific effect or do the non-specific components of the treatment account for the change?

Comparative treatment question:
  Is one treatment more effective than another?

Questions about a theory:
  Does the therapy work for the reasons given in the theoretical rationale?

behaviour analysis (ABA) which espouses single case methodology as the methodology for investigating behaviour. ABA researchers have selected to investigate potent treatments which produce rapid changes in behaviour in carefully defined problems in research settings. This represents an ideal that many practising clinicians will not be able to attain. Many of the examples cited in this chapter come from the behavioural tradition and are used because they illustrate particular points clearly. There are, however, sufficient published accounts of single case work carried out in settings using treatments not derived from ABA (Barlow & Hersen, 1984; Fonagy & Moran, 1994; Hilliard, 1993) to encourage the use of single case methods in routine clinical work: especially if the clinician has access to a relatively homogeneous population which will enable the development of techniques and replication across individuals.

A PROTOTYPE CASE STUDY

Deriving a testable hypothesis is the key activity of any research enterprise. Arriving at a clinical formulation is the end product of a complex cognitive process whereby the clinician constructs a model of the patient's problem, but even simple problems can produce elaborate formulations (see Hallam, 1976) with several interrelated hypotheses. Developing a formulation is a creative enterprise involving several sources of information, as follows (the references in parenthesis provide a detailed example of the point in question):

1. Prototypicality judgements (induction): case is like a previous class of problems.
2. Hunches (intuition): gut feeling that certain ideas are right.
3. Historical correlation: there is evidence of a relationship between events and the target problem (Turkat & Carlson, 1984).
4. Passive observation: prospective record keeping reveals a correlation between events and the target problem (Snyder, 1987).
5. Accidental manipulation: the pattern of behaviour changes with a concurrent change in the person's environment (Morley, 1987).
6. Deliberate manipulation: investigator makes a deliberate attempt to manipulate events which are thought to be causally related to the target problem (Mace & Lalli, 1991).

Only the tactic of deliberate manipulation is a true experiment but it will be apparent that some or all of the preceding items are necessary prior steps to deliberate manipulation. The following case illustrates this and other features of single case research.

Case study 1: The case of Mrs S (Turkat & Carlson, 1984)

Mrs S reported a sudden onset of a cluster of anxiety and dysphoric symptoms (sleep and mood disturbance and some avoidance activity) following the diagnosis of her daughter as a diabetic. After several interviews the therapists were unable to arrive at a satisfactory explanation of why Mrs S should be so anxious. On the basis of past experience with anxiety cases (prototypicality, hunches) they decided to treat the patient by relaxation and hierarchically determined in vivo anxiety management. The initial success of this treatment was followed by rapid relapse for reasons which could not immediately be discerned. The therapists reasoned that her relapse might be connected with factors that had caused the onset of the problem. During treatment the therapists observed that Mrs S continually sought reassurance that she was performing anxiety management properly (passive observation). This reassurance had been withdrawn at the termination of treatment. They reformulated the problem postulating that the main functional determinant of the Mrs S's behaviour was a hypersensitivity to independent decision making. Re-examination of Mrs S's history (historical correlation) revealed that her decision making about trivial things such as buying food was accompanied by anxiety and reassurance seeking. She reported being made anxious when reassurance was denied or when her decision making was approved of by one person but criticised by another. Finally the therapists discovered that her early upbringing showed that the patient had been characterised by a lack of independent decision making and a surfeit of criticism and anxiety surrounded her attempts at independence. Some objective evidence (passive observation) for this formulation by obtaining measures of 'Autonomy' and 'Emotional reliance on others' from a standardised personality questionnaire. As a result of the formulation the therapists designed an intervention to reduce her anxiety about decision making. They constructed a hierarchy and obtained daily ratings of her anxiety on the items. These data were used as the main outcome measure. The results are shown in Fig. 13.1.

SOME BASIC ISSUES IN SINGLE CASE RESEARCH

Case study 1 illustrates three important features of single case experimentation.

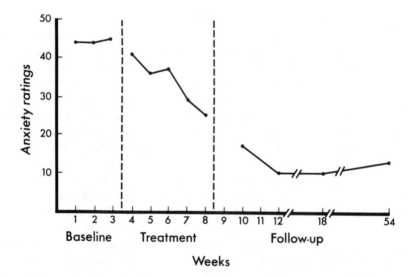

FIG. 13.1. The effects of formulation based treatment on the anxiety ratings of Mrs S. The graph illustrates an A-B 'design' with a short baseline (A) and a treatment phase (B). (Reprinted with permission from: Turkat, I.D. and Carlson, C.R. (1984). Data-based versus symptomatic formulation of treatment: the case of a dependent personality. *Journal of Behaviour Therapy and Experimental Psychiatry, 15*, 153–160. Copyright 1984, Pergamon Journals Ltd.)

1. Data driven experimentation

Single case experiments can be 'data driven'. The results of one phase of the experiment can provide information which will determine the course of action to be taken in the next phase, allowing scientific curiosity to be indulged (Sidman, 1960). This approach has ecological validity for the practising clinician as it encourages active monitoring of clinical problems and the investigation of serendipitous findings. The emphasis of data driven, or exploratory, experimentation, should not detract from the use of single case experiments as a method for confirmatory investigation (Elashoff & Thoresen, 1978).

2. Repeated measures and variability

The second feature of single case research is the emphasis on repeated measurement within one subject and the investigation of variability within a person. The Achilles' heel of group-based research is the problem of generalising from group data to an individual; a functional relationship shown in group data is not necessarily reflected in an individual. A similar issue arises with respect to time. Behaviour, whether it be overt responses or thoughts and feelings, fluctuates in time, and it is assumed that in some way it is caused by preceding events. Group research assumes that the dependent variable is the result of the same preceding processes in all individuals and aggregates data to control error processes. Little attempt is made to assess or control what may be important sources of variability within individuals. That variability between subjects is not the same as variability within subjects is a truism which is nevertheless worth emphasising. Sidman (1960) and Johnston and Pennypacker (1980) argue that the most appropriate way to study behaviour is to identify and isolate the determinants of an individual's behaviour. Generalisation proceeds by replicating functional relationships across individuals, i.e. the reverse order from group research.

Variability is a two-edged sword. On one hand minimum variability within each phase of the experiment is required so that inferences about the impact of an intervention can be made by comparing sets of data points obtained under different conditions. On the other hand a certain degree of variability is required to facilitate the development of a clinical formulation. Variability is the 'window through which to observe the workings of basic controlling relationships' (Johnston & Pennypacker, 1980, p. 70). A practical resolution of this conflict is shown in Turkat and Carlson's (1984) study. Variability in Mrs S's anxiety led them to a formulation concerning her difficulties in decision making. If we examine the baseline phase of Fig. 13.1 in which daily ratings were averaged there is very little variation in anxiety. This enables us to be reasonably confident that the change in anxiety occurring in the treatment phase is not just part of the random variation displayed by the patient. In this case the simple tactic of averaging data reduces the variability. On the other hand experimental analysis of this variability might have revealed potentially controlling variables.

Sidman (1960) pointed out that variability can be regarded as either an *intrinsic* feature of individuals, or due to *extrinsic* controlling factors. Uncritical acceptance of the intrinsic hypothesis precludes the investigation of variability. This affects measurement tactics and the type of variables which one seeks to investigate. (See Johnston & Pennypacker, 1980, pp. 207-8 for detailed discussion of these points.) The assumption that behavioural variability is extrinsically controlled leads one to search for and isolate the sources of control. This will ensure that accurate measurement is obtained and controlling influences on the behaviour determined where possible.

Good clinical and experimental practice demands that variability in a person's performance should be investigated whenever possible. There are three general categories of variation to be considered. Firstly variability might be due to changes in the individual's state. Common examples of this are diurnal rhythm, drug induced changes and variation in mood. In the latter two examples one would need to investigate the cause of change of state. The second source of variability is attributable to variations in the setting in which the person is observed. Experimental settings are normally very precisely controlled. This is not always the case in clinical work where a person may be seen in different settings across the period of contact. Variations in lighting, decor, ambient noise and dress of the investigator may all have subtle but important influences on some variables. Understanding the sources of variability in a person's everyday environment is also crucially important. For example, Wahler (Wahler, 1980; Wahler & Graves, 1983) demonstrated that mothers could successfully implement behavioural strategies to control their childrens' oppositional behaviour but gains were often not maintained. Further analysis revealed that the mothers' own social environment determined whether they would implement the therapeutic strategies. Discovery of this source of variability in the treatment environment has led to a better understanding of the problem and development of new methods for helping families.

Finally, variation in measurement is an important consideration, often overlooked in clinical practice and fieldwork. Variables may be poorly defined, e.g. use of ambiguous anchor statements on rating scales, and assessment of a measure's reliability is often neglected. Problems of instrumentation and observer drift need constant monitoring.

3. Levels of measurement

The third feature of single case research concerns the type of measure employed, Herbst (1970) argues that individuals live in their own 'behavioural worlds'; they have unique ways of interacting with the environment. This is reflected by the fact that they have unique sets of measurement scales which are only partly related to others. For example, a standardised 10-item hierarchy in a behavioural avoidance test will not capture the critical features for all subjects, Careful scaling of the subjective distances between the items would reveal considerable differences between subjects. While much effort in measurement technology has gone into devising ways of maximising the common variance contained in scales one must question whether many issues of interest to psychologists, especially clinicians, can be satisfactorily tackled using measurement techniques that regard individual variation as error (Shapiro, 1975, 1985).

What is required are measures of criterion variables scaled for individuals. Clinical researchers coming from a background of applied behaviour analysis achieve this objective by counting frequencies of specified target events. This measurement strategy ensures that the accuracy and reliability of measurements taken on particular occasions for a single individual may be assessed (Cone, 1988; Hartmann, 1984). There are procedures derived from psychophysics which enable similar levels of psychometric sophistication to be applied to the measurement of subjective states. Shapiro's (1961; Phillips, 1986) personal questionnaire technique uses simple pair comparison methodology to assess the internal consistency of a measure of subjective state on every occasion of administration. Developments of Stevens's magnitude estimation method can be used to quantify the subjective distances between items on a scale (Lodge, 1981; Morley & Hassard, 1989).

Set against the need to use sensitive individual measures is the requirement that useful experiments should be generalisable to other individuals. This issue is ultimately resolvable only by empirical replication. However, it is prudent to take other measures of variables which one suspects might be important determinants of generalisation across cases. Commonly these measures concern the classification of subjects into homogeneous groups representing some type of pathology or common psychological process. The measures have two characteristics:

1. They are standardised on specified populations so that several psychometric features are known, e.g. test-retest reliability, concurrent validity.

2. They measure 'global' variables, such as depression, which are made up of a series of imperfectly correlated items which may be functionally separate within individuals.

For these reasons they may not be the most sensitive measures of individual pathology but they contain enough information to use as reliable and valid general outcome measures (Beutler and Hamblin, 1986).

To meet the requirements of specificity and generality it is suggested that investigators should adopt an assessment strategy which uses the assessment funnel shown in Fig. 13.2. Examples of its use in an experimental clinical investigations are given by Chadwick and Lowe

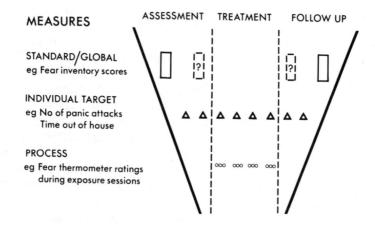

FIG. 13.2. The assessment–evaluation measurement funnel. The figure depicts a general strategy for selecting measures and determining when to take them. *Standard–global* measures are those that have been developed for known populations and problems. Ideally they have well-researched psychometric properties and can be used to index a person to known populations. By design these measures are often not suitable for rapidly repeated administration. They contain items selected for the population as a whole and they may not be sensitive to an individual's target problems. *Target* measures are measures developed for a particular individual and are the main outcome measures in single case research. The psychometric characteristics of target measures should be determined for each case. *Process* measures are taken more frequently than target measures and may not be taken during baseline phases or throughout treatment. They are deployed to monitor treatment sessions. They very often have a spurious validity, e.g. SUDs (subjective units of discomfort), so that the investigator is lulled into thinking that they have the properties of standard–global measures. Little attention is usually paid to their psychometric properties.

(1990), Parry, Shapiro and Firth (1986) and Salkovskis and Warwick (1985).

ELEMENTS OF EXPERIMENTAL DESIGN

The purpose of experimentation is to eliminate alternative explanations for a phenomenon. Common alternative explanations, or threats to the validity of experiments, are discussed by Campbell and Stanley (1966) and Cook and Campbell (1979). Kazdin (1982) discusses these issues with respect to single case experiments. The central feature of experimentation is the comparison of two or more conditions. In single case research these comparisons are made within an individual. Formal single case designs have been developed that specify sequences of baseline and treatment comparison, but within this framework investigators must make decisions about implementing and withdrawing treatments. These decisions should be governed by the data collected during the experiment and the lengths of different phases of the experiment are not necessarily pre-planned as in conventional group research.

When should the intervention be applied/withdrawn?
In laboratory experiments it is usual to wait until the baseline behaviour has stabilised within prescribed limits. While every effort should be made to obtain stable baselines there are many clinical situations where complete control is not possible. Other criteria for introducing treatments may be used.

1. Treatments may be introduced as quickly as possible to reassure the client. This is not good experimental practice and it has dubious clinical validity because there will be inadequate baseline data and no testable formulation.
2. Treatments may also be applied as soon as the therapist is convinced that an adequate formulation has been made but this may be before adequate baseline data has been collected.
3. Treatments can be introduced or withdrawn in a *reactive* manner (Glass, Willson & Gottman, 1974). In this case the therapist makes a decision to manipulate the treatment on the grounds that the target behaviour is 'out of control'. This is often a misguided decision. Extreme behaviour is rare and usually returns to a median value without intervention (Glass et al., 1974). Reactive interventions are likely to be confounded with naturally occurring changes in the behaviour and they also preclude the opportunity

of investigating and understanding the problem as illustrated in case study 2.

Case study 2: A reactive intervention

T was a young woman with a long history of schizophrenia. Her most distressing symptoms were hallucinations in which voices told her to harm herself. She had fractured both legs and her pelvis after jumping in front of a bus. At times she appeared very distressed and her behaviour made staff anxious and protective. T was an inpatient for five days a week, returning to her mother's home at weekends. Invariably on her return to the ward she showed signs of distress. The staff responded to this by increasing or changing her medication. T improved during the next few days, thereby reinforcing the staff's belief in the efficacy of the intervention and the implicit hypothesis that her behaviour was determined by neurochemical mechanisms. The data are plotted in phase A of Fig. 13.3.

Three alternative hypotheses were considered:

1. That T forgot to take her medication during the weekend. Analysis of blood serum levels and careful questioning of T and her mother invalidated this.

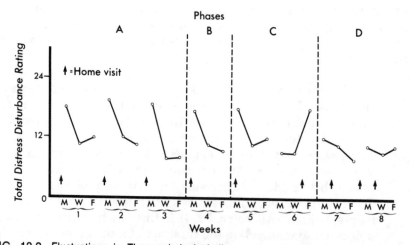

FIG. 13.3. Fluctuations in T's psychological distress (case study 2). Distress was measured as the sum of a checklist of symptoms derived from an analysis of T's problems and rated by nursing staff 3 days a week; Monday (M), Wednesday (W) and Friday (F). T's visits to her mother's home are shown by the arrows. Phases A, B, C, and D are described in the text.

2. That T's distress had a seven-day periodicity for unknown reasons (intrinsic variability).
3. That the social environment at the weekend was a causal factor. Clinical records and interviews suggested that T's mother might be considered over protective and provide a high expressed emotion environment (Leff & Vaughn, 1985).

Three tests of the hypotheses were made. Firstly no drug changes were made on her return to the ward. The data plotted in phase B show that T returned to her usual level of activity without the drug intervention. Secondly, weekend leave was deferred and T was sent home mid-week. This resulted in increased distress after her return from leave and not during the weekend (phase C); suggesting that hypothesis 2 was wrong. Finally hypothesis 3 was tested by asking T to return to her mother's home for shorter periods but more frequently (phase D). This procedure was satisfactory for T, her mother and the staff.

The final criterion for deciding when to implement treatment is based on statistical and design considerations. Randomisation tests (see later) require that the interventions should be implemented and withdrawn at randomly chosen points in the experiment. This approach to single case experiments is particularly powerful when the investigator wishes to test a treatment of known efficacy and where the likely time course of the treatment is known. Under these conditions the investigator can pre-plan the experiment in some detail. Clements and Hand (1985) investigated the impact of a programme to help parents manage sleeping problems in young handicapped children. The length of the baseline was set in advance and because the investigators anticipated that treatment would not take effect for several days, decisions about the form of data analysis could be specified in advance. In experiments where two or more conditions are repeatedly administered it is necessary to plan the order of presentation to ensure that there is no confounding with extra-experimental events.

For how long should the treatment be applied?
Three factors must be considered:

1. Stability in the baseline.
2. The magnitude of the treatment effect.
3. The speed of the treatment effect.

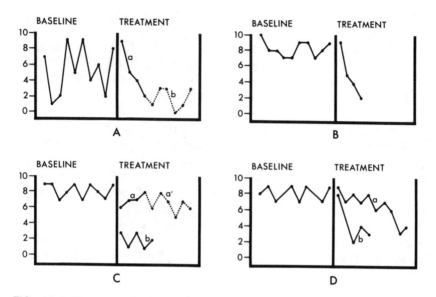

FIG. 13.4. The effects of baseline variability on the interpretation of changes in a target variable following the introduction of treatment. In (A) there is a highly variable baseline. The effect of a treatment for the period **a** is uninterpretable. If the treatment were extended for the period **b** greater confidence in its effects would be justified. In (B) there is a short treatment phase but because the baseline is stable and longer than the treatment phase it is easier to judge the impact of the treatment. (C) illustrates the effect of the magnitude of treatment. With a small effect is is necessary to obtain more measures, extending the period **a** to **a'**. (D) illustrates the role of the speed of change in interpreting the impact of treatment. Slow changes (**a**) will require longer periods of observation than fast-acting changes (**b**).

Figure 13.4 illustrates some of the effects of baseline variability, and treatment strength and magnitude on the interpretability of the data. For example, if the data displays considerable variability during the baseline, (Fig. 13.4A), treatment should be extended for at least the length of the baseline. With a variable baseline and a relatively weak treatment long baseline and treatment phases are essential. In contrast to this if the baseline is stable and the treatment is powerful (Fig. 13.4C) a short treatment phase will suffice. As a general rule baselines should always be longer than the time in which it is expected that the treatment will take effect: slow acting treatments require long baselines, fast acting treatments can be evaluated against shorter baselines.

Decisions about withdrawing or changing treatments will depend on the nature of the target behaviour, the treatment and the experimental design. Treatments can also be withdrawn for clinical reasons. A common one is when the treatment is counter-therapeutic. It is advisable to analyse why this effect has taken place. It may be apparent that the change is transient and that treatment should not be withdrawn, e.g. an increased response rate during extinction. Treatments may also be withdrawn because they appear not to be working; there may be a lag between the start of the treatment and its effect. For example some antidepressives and psychological interventions, such as relaxation for headaches, may take several weeks before their effects are felt. Investigators should guard against reactive withdrawal of treatments.

Specifying the treatment

In experimental work treatments are specified in advance. While this is usually true in clinical work there will be occasions when changes in treatment are made as a function of client feedback. In all cases investigators should take great care to document exactly what treatment strategies and tactics are employed. A conceptual analysis of the differences obtaining in each of the different phases should be conducted as part of the analysis of the experiment. This should include an analysis of events occurring during baseline phases. An excellent example of this process is given by Youell and McCollough (1975).

Is the treatment being applied? (Manipulation validity)

It is necessary to obtain evidence that the treatment is actually being applied as stipulated. Where overt environmental manipulations are part of the treatment there is no apparent difficulty in ensuring that the treatment is intact. The monitoring of covert treatments (psychotherapy and cognitive therapy) is more problematic. One strategy is to use brief within-session manipulations of the treatment to determine functional relationships between the treatment and a target variable (Teasdale & Fennell, 1982). For example, in exposure sessions for phobic anxiety, changes in subjective anxiety measured by the fear thermometer can be tracked as the intensity of the exposure is varied. This strategy of course depends on the presence of a functional relationship. If the expected changes do not occur it should not be assumed that the treatment is not in effect; it may be that there are moderating variables that mitigate its impact. With obsessional patients it is not uncommon to find that exposure to the anxiety-provoking stimulus is managed by a form of covert avoidance. Careful interrogation of the patient usually reveal this and counter-measures can be taken. In general manipulation validity must be inferred from a number of sources of evidence which will vary from experiment to experiment.

BASIC EXPERIMENTAL DESIGNS

Simple time series; A-B design

Measurement before and after an intervention does not enable causal inferences about an intervention to be made. Changes in the measures might reflect changes in variability, the conditions of measurement, or the sensitivity of the measure, or be due to a coincidental extra-treatment event. Increasing the number of measurements taken during baseline (A) and treatment (B) phases can partly override these alternative explanations. The extent to which alternative explanations can be eliminated depends largely upon the length and stability of the baseline and the rapidity with which treatment takes effect. Long stable baselines followed by a rapid change on the introduction of the treatment are more believable than other patterns of data. If the baseline phase has remained stable despite the presence of other documented changes in the client's life then the likelihood that the change occurring with the introduction of treatment is due to anything but treatment is reduced.

Several experimental designs have been developed to overcome the problems of eliminating alternative explanations. These designs all have the same underlying logic. The logic is that if the introduction of the intervention is uniquely associated with changes in the target variable, i.e. there are no changes in the target variable at other times, then the likelihood that other explanations for the change in behaviour are true is reduced. Several basic designs are illustrated here but the reader should be aware that these represent prototypes from which countless variations can be developed in order to suit particular circumstances.

The A-B-A-B design

The causal effect of an intervention is more believable if the effect can be replicated. The obvious way to achieve this is repeatedly to withdraw and re-introduce the intervention. If the target behaviour changes consistently in association with changes in treatment alternative explanations become less plausible.

Case study 3: An A-B-A-B experiment

P was a 6-year-old boy with mild asthma. He had a persistent dry cough which was especially prominent just before bedtime. An attempt was made to bring the cough under control. During the experiment all sessions were scheduled during the reading of a bedtime story and were

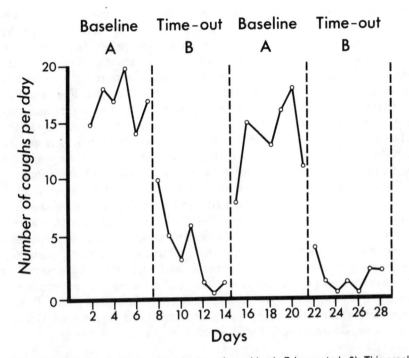

FIG. 13.5. The effect of time-out on the rate of coughing in P (case study 3). This graph shows the results of an A-B-A-B experiment. In this case the treatment was powerful and took effect rapidly. These factors coupled with its reversibility produced results which are easily interpreted.

carried out by his father. During the baseline P and his father recorded the frequency of coughing. Treatment was a time-out procedure contingent on coughing. After a cough the father turned the book over and he and P counted slowly to 10. If there was no cough during this period reading was resumed. Treatment was subsequently reversed and reinstituted. Figure 13.5 shows that the cough was suppressed by time out. At follow-up, nine years later, the father reported that several booster sessions had been necessary following recovery from asthma attacks.

The A-B-A-B experiment has a simple elegance about it but in clinical research there are many occasions when it cannot be used. An intervention may not be reversible, either because the person has learned new behaviour which is now under self-control, or when it is ethically inappropriate to withdraw treatment.

Changing criterion design

This can be used if there is one target variable and when treatment is considered irreversible. Experimental control is demonstrated by manipulating some aspect of the treatment other than its total withdrawal. After a baseline phase several treatment phases are introduced sequentially. Each treatment phase differs with respect to the amount of change in the target behaviour expected. For example, the investigator may ask the subject to meet a specified target and only to reward behaviour which meets this criterion target. Once the behaviour has met this target and is stable a new criterion can be introduced. Experimental control is demonstrated if the changes in the target behaviour closely follow the changes in treatment conditions.

This design was originally applied to overt behaviour under the control of external reinforcement contingencies where systematic changes in parameters of reinforcement schedules could be studied (e.g. Handen, Apolito & Seltzer, 1984). Setting target criteria is a common example of the changing criterion design but any systematic change in the therapy, provided that it is variable along the same dimension, can be used to manipulate the behaviour and demonstrate experimental control. For example, it would be possible to demonstrate the effect of increasing accurate empathy on the amount of self-exploration. Certain guidelines should be considered for changing criterion designs.

1. The minimum number of changes is two although increasing this number is advisable.
2. It is important to vary the length of each treatment phase. This will ensure that the changes are not coincidental with cyclic extra-treatment events.
3. Wherever possible the magnitude of the criterion should be varied, although for some problems large changes may be impossible, at least in the early stages of treatment, e.g. addictive behaviour.
4. It is advisable to consider whether the direction of criterion changes can be reversed. This may be possible in the later stages of the experiment and adds to the power of the design. If a full reversal cannot be considered brief probe withdrawals should be attempted. There are many published examples of the changing criterion design reviewed by Barlow and Hersen (1984). This design may be especially useful in studies of patients undergoing psychiatric, physical and neuropsychological rehabilitation, when the functional control of irreversible changes needs to be demonstrated (e.g. Hegal, Ayllon, VanderPlate & Spiro-Hawkins, 1986).

Case study 4: A changing criterion experiment

(Bernard, Dennehy & Keefauver, 1981.) Mary was concerned about her excessive drinking of coffee and tea. She reported a number of unsuccessful attempts to reduce her intake. During baseline the average number of cups drunk per day was 11.54. She agreed to a response-cost programme whereby she would be fined $5.00 if she exceeded the criterion by one cup. Additional cups were fined at $2.00. The final target was 6 cups per day and the first criterion was set at 11 cups. Figure 13.6 shows the course of treatment. Each criterion was set at one cup less than the previous one. The data reveal that Mary was able to meet each criterion without incurring a penalty. The step-wise nature of the data is apparent as is the variable duration of each criterion. Follow-up data collected some three months after the end of treatment showed that Mary had successfully reduced her consumption to less than four cups per day.

Hayes (1981) has suggested a variant of the changing criterion design, the periodic treatment design, where the treatment is applied only at the start of each phase. In this case changes in behaviour should be observed only at the onset of treatment. Hayes has suggested that this design could be used in outpatient work where sessions are

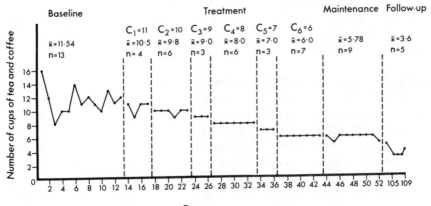

FIG. 13.6. The results of a Changing Criterion experiment (case study 4). This graph illustrates the step-like nature of a Changing Criterion experiment. Notice the irregular spacing of the criterion changes which contributes to good experimental design. The power of the experiment would be improved by varying the magnitude of the criterion changes and by reversing the direction of the criterion changes on one or more occasions. (Reproduced from Bernard, M.E., Dennehy, S., & Keefauver, L.W. (1981). Behavioral treatment of excessive coffee and tea drinking: a case study and partial replication. *Behavior Therapy, 12*, 543–548. Copyright 1981, the Association for the Advancement of Behavior Therapy. Reproduced with permission of the publisher and author.)

irregularly spaced. To date there appears to be only one extant example of this design given in Hayes's original paper.

Multiple baseline design

This design uses control variables to demonstrate the effect of an intervention. The variables can either be other measures taken on the subject, the same target variable observed in other settings or the same measure observed in other persons in under the same conditions (Harris & Jenson, 1985; Hayes, 1985). Experimental control is demonstrated if the target variable changes with the introduction of treatment but there are no corresponding changes in the control variables. Further demonstration of experimental control is obtained by sequentially applying the treatment to the control variables. The logic of this design is that if treatment is responsible for change then change will be observed in the target variable only. If, however, the introduction of treatment corresponds with an influential extra-treatment event then concurrent changes will be seen in the control variables. The logic of this design is clearly inconsistent as it is assumed that treatment will produce specific changes in behaviour while non-treatment events will produce general changes. In practice, results from multiple baseline designs can only be unambiguously interpreted when there is only change in target variables when treatment is introduced. When other patterns of data are observed it is impossible to know whether the results are due to a generalised treatment effect or to the coincidental effect of an extra-treatment event (Kazdin & Kopel, 1975).

Case studies 5 and 6: Multiple baseline experiments

(Barmann & Murray, 1981; Barmann & Vitali, 1982.) These studies by Barmann report the use of facial screening to suppress undesirable behaviour in children with a learning difficulty. During treatment the subject wore a terry cloth bib which was pulled over the face for five seconds following the production of the target response. Barmann and Murray (1981) treated one subject in three different settings; home, the school bus and the classroom. Jimmy was a mentally handicapped boy with a record of sexually inappropriate behaviour. He rubbed his crotch and displayed his penis. Treatment was sequentially introduced into the three settings. Figure 13.7 shows that the introduction of treatment corresponded with a reduction in self-stimulation in the situation where it had been implemented but not in other situations.

In the second study Barmann and Vitali (1982) treated three children who displayed trichotillomania (compulsive hair pulling). The data shown in Fig. 13.8 come from 90-minute sessions collected at home and show the frequency of hair pulling.

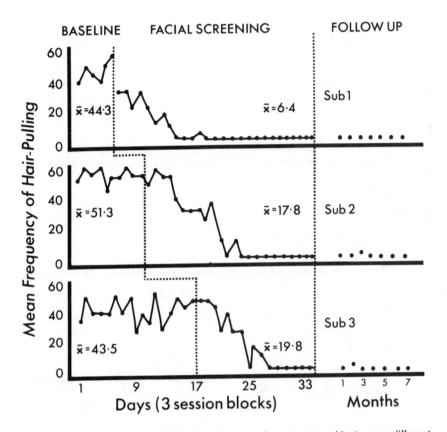

FIG. 13.7. An example of a multiple baseline experiment on one subject across different experimental settings. The graph shows the delayed sequential introduction of the treatment in the three settings. In this case the treatment produced a large and rapid change in the subject's behaviour. (Reproduced from Barmann, B.C., & Murray, W.J. (1981) Suppression of inappropriate sexual behavior by facial screening. *Behavior Therapy, 12*, 730–735. Copyright 1981, the Association for the Advancement of Behavior Therapy. Reproduced with permission of the publisher and author.)

Although Fig. 13.8 shows that the treatments were successful in reducing the frequency of hair pulling there is one feature about the graph which is notable. Unlike the previous case (Barmann & Murray, 1981) the facial screening technique did not produce an immediate improvement in the target response. Generally the treatment took several days before an effect was observed. In all cases treatment was introduced to the other subjects before the effect on the previous subject had stabilised. Under some conditions (i.e. where different subjects are being treated in the same setting at the same time) it would be possible to argue that the effects of treatment are not specific to a single subject

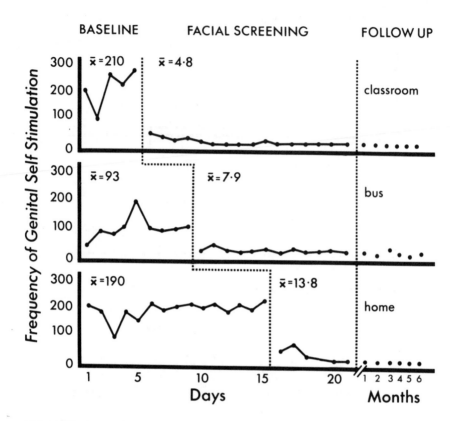

FIG. 13.8. A multiple baseline experiment on three different subjects with trichotillomania. Refer to the text for commentary on the differences between this figure and Fig. 13.7. (Reproduced from Barmann, B.C., & Vitali, D.L. (1982). Facial screening to eliminate trichotillomania in developmentally disabled persons. *Behavior Therapy, 13,* 735–742. Copyright 1982, the Association for the Advancement of Behavior Therapy. Reproduced with permisison of the publisher and author.)

but dependent on a general change in the way in which therapists or attendant staff interact with all subjects, Kazdin (1982) provides a further discussion of this point.

COMPARING MORE THAN ONE TREATMENT WITHIN AN INDIVIDUAL

The experimental designs discussed so far compare an intervention with a suitable baseline control. But clinicians and researchers are often more interested in questions of whether a particular component of treatment is effective, whether one treatment is more effective than another, or with testing theoretical predictions about the impact of certain treatment variables. Single case methods can be extended to meet this challenge but a number of important issues need to be considered.

How many treatments can be compared?

In theory it is possible to investigate an infinite number of treatments but increasing the number of treatments adds demands on the time and ingenuity of the investigator. In general a maximum of two or three treatments can be compared, especially if interaction or joint effects are to be considered (Barrios, 1984).

How quickly can treatments be alternated within an individual?

The rate of change between different treatments depends on several factors:

1. Treatments which take immediate effect can be alternated more rapidly.
2. This is especially true if the treatments produce stable effects with little variation.
3. The third factor concerns the speed at which treatments cease to have an effect once they are withdrawn. Treatments whose effects do not carry over when they are withdrawn are more easily investigated.

It is not necessary for the target variable to return to baseline for multiple comparisons between interventions to be made, neither is a baseline required. For example, Watts (1979) and Teasdale and Fennell (1982) used an experimental design taken from standard group experimental methods. The sequence of treatments was determined by a Latin Square to ensure that each treatment followed every other treatment in a balanced order and that the appropriate number of replications were carried out. It is easy to see how this approach can be used to test general theories on single cases or to test diagnostic formulations. For example, consider an experiment that could be carried out with Mrs S (case study 1) to check the formulation. Mrs S's anxiety ratings to different types of images could be evaluated. Images would vary with respect to the degree of independent decision making and the seriousness of outcome events pending on the wrong decision. Images might include explicit acts of criticism by others. The formulation could then be tested independently of treatment outcome.

Extensions of basic designs

One way of comparing different treatments is to extend the basic A-B-A-B design to include more elements. A second treatment can be included in the design to form the following sequence A-B-A-C-A; this sequence should be replicated within the subject to test the reliability of the changes. In order to control for any confounding due to the order in which the treatments are presented the replication should be in the reverse order, A-C-A-B-A. It is also possible to compare the effectiveness of different treatments using a multiple baseline design by applying the treatments to the different target behaviours or settings. This tactic has not been widely reported in the literature but an example is reported by Clark, Sugrim and Bolton (1982) and some of the limitations discussed by Morley (1994).

Alternating treatments design

In this design a baseline is followed by a phase in which two or more treatments are presented. The order of the treatments is carefully arranged so that they are randomly associated with factors such as the time of day, therapist and any other incidental factors. This follows the standard principle of balancing the experimental treatments with non-experimental factors. After a treatment phase the therapist should be able to select the most powerful treatment and implement it.

Case study 7: Alternating treatments

(Ollendick, Shapiro & Barrett, 1981.) Ollendick and his colleagues compared two treatments for reducing stereotypic behaviour in mentally handicapped children. In each session the children were given an opportunity to engage in simple visual-motor tasks. Physical restraint comprised a verbal warning to stop the behaviour and manually holding the child's hands on the table for 30 seconds. During positive practice the verbal warning was followed by the child being guided through the visual-motor task. No-treatment sessions were also conducted. The results of this experiment for one child are shown in Fig. 13.9. The Figure clearly shows that for this child positive practice was the most effective treatment and this was subsequently introduced in all the sessions.

One feature of case study 7 is that the frequency of sterotypic behaviour was increased under the no-treatment condition. This contrast effect raises an important issue about possible interactions and carry-over effects when multiple treatments are given to one person. Barlow and Hersen (1984) provide an extensive discussion of this issue and suggest that the experimenter should follow three procedural guidelines to ensure that carry-over effects are reduced to a minimum:

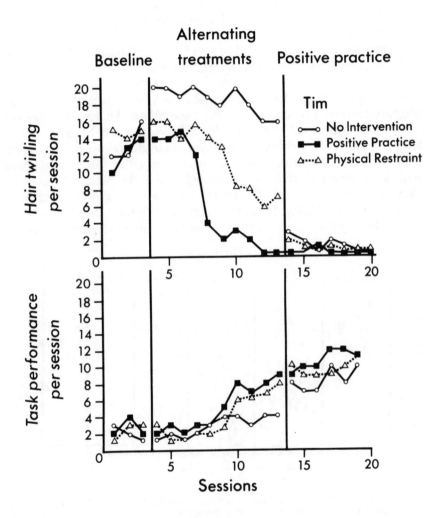

FIG. 13.9. An example of an alternating treatments design used to compare the effectiveness of two treatments to reduce stereotypic behaviour in a mentally retarded boy. The upper panel shows changes in the target behaviour under different treatments. The lower panel shows concurrent changes in the performance of motor tasks during the sessions. This behaviour was not directly reinforced but was tracked to check the hypothesis that stereotypic behaviour interfered with task performance. (Reproduced from Ollendick, T.H., Shapiro, E.S., & Barrett, R.P. (1981). Reducing stereotypic behaviors: an analysis of treatment procedures utilizing an alternating treatments design. *Behavior Therapy, 12,* 570–577. Copyright 1981, by the Association for the Advancement of Behavior Therapy. Reproduced wtih permission of the publisher and author.)

1. Counter-balance the order of treatments.
2. Different treatments should be interspersed by a separating time interval.
3. Rapid alternations should be avoided until the subject has learned to discriminate between the treatments.

Although these guidelines were developed from operant psychology they are relevant to the study of other treatments. Whenever carry-over effects are suspected they should be investigated. Sidman (1960) suggested that the problem can be broached by deliberate manipulation of one of the treatments. If there is a carry over effect this manipulation will be reflected in changes measured under the second treatment. Sidman (1960) called this *functional manipulation* and an example is shown in Fig. 13.10. Higgins Hains and Baer (1989) provide a sophisticated discussion of methods for examining interaction effects.

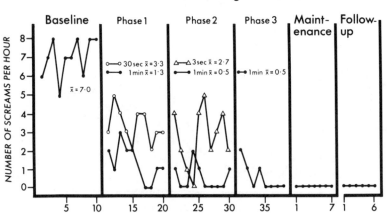

Fig. 13.10. An example of functional manipulation used to check on carry-over effects in an alternating treatments design. The subject was a 2½-year-old normal girl who screamed excessively. During phase 1 facial screening was implemented with two durations, 30 seconds and 1 minute. The 1 minute condition produced the greater suppression. To check whether there was an interference effect the 30 second condition was changed to 3 seconds in phase 2. The 1 minute condition produced the same amount of suppression as in phase 1, suggesting that there was no multiple treatment interference. The authors noted that this interpretation is limited by the very low levels of behaviour under the 1 minute condition (a floor effect). (Reproduced from Singh, N.N., Winton, A.S., & Dawson, M.J. (1982). Suppression of antisocial behavior by facial screening using multiple baseline and alternating treatment designs. *Behavior Therapy, 13*, 511–520. Copyright 1982, the Association for the Advancement of Behavior Therapy. Reproduced with permission of the publisher and author.)

The principle of alternating, or more accurately randomising, different treatments can be incorporated into other experimental designs in order to carry out further checks on threats to the validity of experiments, Figure 13.11 shows some data from an experiment by McKnight et al. (1984) who investigated two treatments for depression for people with different psychological profiles. People with predominantly social skill deficits responded better to a social skills package, whereas those with predominantly irrational cognitions responded better to a cognitive therapy package. This experiment exhibits the relative sophistication and economy of single case methods.

Commentary

The basic single case designs are now well established and their merits and limitations have been articulated and discussed in some detail.

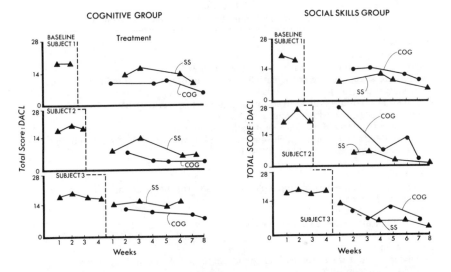

Fig. 13.11. This figure shows the application of an alternating treatments component to a mutliple baseline design. The study investigated the effects of cognitive therapy and social skills training on depressed subjects with either predominantly social or cognitive deficits. A third group with deficits in both domains was also treated but is not shown here. In this figure the outcome measure is a measure of depressed mood. It is clear that the patients' mood improved most when they were treated for their specific deficit. This study illustrates how single case designs can be used to conduct small group experiments. The control built into the single case strategies means that fewer subjects need to be recruited than in a standard groups design. (Reproduced from McKnight D.L., Nelson, R.O., Hayes S.C., & Jarrett, R.B. (1984). Importance of treating individually assessed response classes in the amelioration of depression.. *Behavior Therapy*, *15*, 315–335. Copyright 1984, the Association for the Advancement of Behavior Therapy. Reproduced with permission of the publisher and author.)

Barlow and Hersen (1984) and Kazdin (1982) provide thorough introductions to the designs and the major issues in interpretation of the resultant data. A cardinal feature of single case research is the flexibility of design options. New variations are constantly being devised to meet particular needs (e.g. Higgins Hains & Baer, 1989; Wacker, McMahon, Steege, Berg, Sasso & Melloy, 1990). The main criterion to be considered is whether a design can rule out alternative explanations for the effect one in which one is primarily interested. Table 13.2 outlines some general rules which should be considered when a single-case investigation is planned.

TABLE 13.2
General rules for the conduct of single case experiments

Measures:
    Measure frequently.
    Take measures at different levels (see Figure 13.2)
    Make sure the measures are sensitive to your requirements (individualise them whenever possible).
    Check the reliability and accuracy of measures whenever possible.
    Check on instrumentation changes over time.
    Look for side effects of measurement and intervention.
    Record all external events which seem to be of importance, date them carefully. This will help in the interpretation of the data.

Variability:
    Investigate baseline variability: look for trends in the mean, changes in variance, cyclical changes.
    Control it if you can.
    Smooth it statistically as a last resort.

Interventions:
    Be explicit about the criteria which guide the timing of your intervention:
      1. Baseline stability?
      2. Clinical urgency/reactive intervention?
      3. Statistical & design considerations?
    Specify the intervention:
      1. Content
      2. Duration
      3. Expected temporal impact
      4. Expected magnitude effects
    Make sure that the intervention is enforced long enough to have an effect.
    Monitor the intervention to ensure that it is being carried out (manipulation validity).
    Manipulate the intervention whenever possible to investigate causal effects (reverse or withdraw the intervention).
    Change one variable (aspect of the intervention) at a time.

DISPLAY AND ANALYSIS OF SINGLE CASE DATA

While there is a general consensus about the methodological adequacy of the basic single case designs the analysis of the data remains problematic and the subject of some controversy. Single case data have traditionally been analysed by graphing each data point against time and drawing conclusions by visual inspection. This procedure is understandable when one considers the applied behavioural analysis school from which the experimental designs originate. Baer, an eloquent advocate of ABA philosophy (Baer, 1977, 1988; Parsonson & Baer, 1978, 1992), argues that the thrust of single case research in ABA is to detect effects that are strong, consistent and dependable. He argues that graphical representation and analysis of the data will ensure that only these effects are detected, whereas weak effects which may be statistically significant will be ignored. In statistical terms Baer argues that visual analysis of the data will ensure that Type I errors are minimised (i.e. concluding that there is an effect when there is not), but there is a corresponding increase in Type II errors (failing to detect an effect when it is present).

The application of single case designs to problems, measures and settings markedly different from those found in ABA has resulted in data sets that are much 'messier' than those found in ABA research. Messy data sets are those with conspicuous variability within and between phases, one or more outliers i.e. extreme scores, different trends across phases, and no sharp discontinuities between control (baseline) and treatment phases. The presence of one or more of these features makes it difficult to see changes in the data as a gestalt and real changes in the target behaviour may be obfuscated. One solution to this problem is to use statistical tests to separate reliable changes in some crucial parameter, usually the average of the data, from the inherent variability. There are however a number of problems with many of the statistical tests advocated (see later) and on balance investigators are advised to be cautious in their use of inferential statistics. Nothwithstanding the use of statistics it is of paramount importance that all data is subjected to good visual analysis.

Visual analysis

Good data plots and exploration of these plots play a central role in interpreting and understanding the data. Graphical displays allow one to see the data as a whole, very quickly; this cannot be achieved by reading a set of numbers. Furthermore, most graphical displays are easy to produce and because they can be done by reliable, cheap, portable technology, they are highly flexible and can be used to present data as it is collected. There is, however, a singular paucity of advice on how to present and explore single case data. Kazdin (1982) and Parsonson & Baer (1978) have written introductory guides to graphing data but these were published some time ago and do not reflect more recent thinking about graphical displays, nor do they cover exploratory data analytic techniques, which offer additional tools for the analysis of single case data (Cleveland, 1985; Velleman & Hoaglin, 1981).

Cleveland (1985) has proposed a number of aims for graphical displays. The key components have been summarised by Morley & Adams (1991, p.98) as follows:

(1) Clear vision: make sure that the data stand out and do not let non-data items clutter the presentation. To achieve this Cleveland advises that graphs should be framed on all four sides, this allows data values in the upper right quadrant to be related to the scale values. Only data should appear within the graph frame. Where more than one symbol is used to plot the data, the symbols should be clearly discriminable (see Cleveland, 1985 for details). The axes of the graph should be clearly labelled and appropriate tick marks, pointing outwards, should be inserted.

(2) Clear understanding: graphs should enhance the reader's understanding of the data. Each graph should have an explicit and comprehensive legend. An attempt to do this has been made for the Figures in this chapter.

(3) Scales: choosing appropriate scales for the data is vital. It is best to use scales which encompass the range of the data and allow the data to fill as much of the data frame as possible. Breaks in the scale should be avoided.

(4) General Strategy: graphs are good at condensing a lot of data, but they do require careful study and thought in preparing final versions. Graphing data is likely to be an experimental and iterative process.

Single case data are most frequently presented as relatively unadorned X-Y plots, where the X-axis represents time and the Y-axis is the dependent variable. The data points are usually connected within each phase (baseline, treatment) but break at the point where the experimental conditions change. This point is normally marked by a thin or broken vertical line. Occasionally the mean of each phase may be marked by a line parallel to the X-axis. The overriding merit of this type of display is that all the data are presented. Graphs which use bar charts, the height of which represents only the mean for each phase, are not to be recommended.

In analysing single case data it is necessary to consider several features of the data. Morley & Adams (1991) suggest a variety of techniques which can be used.

1. The central location of each phase. This is frequently represented by the mean but for many single case data sets it is probably more appropriate to use a median estimator as they are resistant to the influence of outliers. A problem with the standard median is that it only takes account of one or two numbers. A 'broadened median' which uses several numbers in the series is to be recommended. It meets the twin goals of being sensitive to a reasonable proportion of the data as well as being resistant to the influence of outliers. Morley & Adams (1991) provide details of its computation.

2. The trend, or shift in the central location of a series of points in time, both within and between phases, should be plotted. Some writers suggest that a linear regression line should be computed and imposed on the graph. This approach has a number of problems. Firstly, it involves some computation, and secondly the calculated slope, b, is susceptible to the influence of outliers. With small data sets a single point may therefore unduly distort the estimation of b. There are two, very similar, methods which can be used to plot linear trend; the split middle technique and the resistant line from three groups. These methods use medians derived from subsets of the data to fix points through which a line may be drawn. They are easy to compute and may be done with published graphs even if the precise data values are not available. The resistant line method also enables the investigator to inspect the data for non-linear trends. Non-linear trends can be examined and displayed in more detail by smoothing the data using a technique which involves calculating and plotting running medians. This method may be useful if the data are very variable. Morley & Adams (1991) provide worked examples of these and other methods for examining trend in the data.

3. Variability in the data, including changes in variation over time, is recognised as a problem in interpreting single case data (e.g. Wampold & Furlong, 1981), but little attention has been given to the question of how to exhibit it and place accurate interpretations on the data. Common methods of displaying variability include the use of range lines, which simply mark the extreme ranges of a set of data, and range bar graphs which show the range of the data around a measure of its central tendency. Morley & Adams (1991) suggested two other methods. The trimmed range is a method

which eliminates the influence of outliers, and the trended range is a method which enhances the display of changes in variation over time.

4. Level, or the change in value between adjacent data points in separate phases. At the time of writing no attention has been given to graphical methods for enhancing the data at the point of transition between phases.

A set of single case data can therefore be expressed in a number of graphical forms in addition to the traditional X-Y plot. Each graph can be constructed to explore different aspects of the data. One method which enables the investigator to look at more than one feature at a time is to draw the basic graph frame, scale and raw data on graph paper in black ink. Clear acetate sheets can be placed over the frame and different aspects of the data can be plotted in distinct colours on separate sheets. Any combination of acetates can then be superimposed to examine the various aspects of the data.

Research on visual analysis.   There is small corpus of empirical work on the interpretation of visual displays and Parsonson & Baer (1992) provide a thorough review of the field. The available data indicate that graphic and statistical analyses do not always agree and there may be systematic biases associated with the observer's prior training in multivariate or visual analytic methods. Most research comparing statistical and visual analysis has used artificial data sets created with known statistical properties. While this controls the displays which observers see, the data is devoid of any contextual information which is always present in clinical and research settings. Whatever the outcome of future research it will still be necessary for investigators to produce good graphical plots and descriptions of the data.

Statistical analysis
Statistical analysis of small sample time series data of the type usually found in clinical psychological research remains a problematic and controversial topic. There is a range of statistical methods available some of which require a sophisticated appreciation of mathematics. Kratochwill and Levin's (1992) edited text *Single-Case Research Design and Analysis*, is an excellent source for many methods. The following section outlines a number of options available to the researcher-clinician.

Evaluating change in 'standard-global' measures.   Figure 13.2 outlined an assessment measurement strategy which included standard-global measures. These are measures, such as the Beck Depression Inventory, whose psychometric properties are established. It is possible to use these measures to evaluate change from pre-/post-intervention. Jacobson and his colleagues (Jacobson & Revenstorf, 1988; Jacobson & Truax, 1991) have suggested criteria for the evaluation of clinically significant changes in psychotherapy. If individuals complete standardised measures in which normative data is available for a non-dysfunctional population and/or a dysfunctional group, Jacobson suggests that there are three criteria by which clinical significance may be operationalised:

a.   The level of functioning after therapy should fall outside the range of the dysfunctional population (more than two standard deviations, in the direction of the normal reference group).
b.   The level of functioning should fall within the range of the non-dysfunctional group.
c.   The level of functioning should place the client closer to the mean of the functional group than the mean of the dysfunctional group.

Statistical approaches to analysing changes in an individual were discussed by Payne and Jones in 1957. Jacobson has applied this analysis to psychotherapy change scores. Jacobson's Reliable Change Index (RCI) (Jacobson & Revenstorf, 1988; Jacobson & Truax, 1991) is a statistical measure of whether the client has improved. The RCI determines whether the observed change is greater than the change which would be expected on the basis of the error in the measure. It is essentially a z score from a normal distribution.

The RCI does not take into account possible effects of regression to the mean. This can be analysed by using the standard error of prediction, if the mean and standard deviation of the normative sample is known. Hsu (1989) provides a clear explanation of this and a table which enables investigators to look up significant changes for a range of changes scores for tests with different test-retest reliabilities. Hsu (1989) also notes that the same approach can be used to estimate whether a deterioration in a client's state is also reliable. While it is probably reasonable to assume that regression to the mean occurs in many measures there are occasions when it does not. Under these conditions application of a correction formula may produce a Type II error, i.e. concluding that a client's scores are unchanged when they have improved (Speer, 1992). Worked examples of these methods are given in Morley (1994), and Hageman and Arrindell (1993) suggest a further refinement of the method.

The use of these statistical criteria is dependent on the availability of appropriate normative data. For some client groups it is questionable whether norms derived from fully functional samples can be meaningfully applied, e.g. it may be inappropriate to apply such norms to people with schizophrenia. Furthermore there are many measures applied to clinical groups for which no normative data are available. The application of Jacobson's clinical criteria and the statistical assessment of such changes must always proceed with due consideration on the part of the investigator.

Evaluating time-series data.   Single case experimental designs specify that many measures of an individual should be taken in time. The sequence of measures is often referred to as a time-series. Experimental and quasi-experimental designs (the A-B design) are interrupted time-series. Statistical analysis of the data may be called for if the effects of interventions are not clearly discernable from the graphical data plots. This might arise when variability and trend in the time-series obfuscates detection of change in the mean or other critical parameter as a result of the intervention. The investigator might also use statistical analysis to confirm and elucidate visual analysis. The use of well known statistical tests, Student's t and the F ratio are generally not recommended in the analysis of time-series data. These tests are predicated on the assumption that the error associated with each score is independent. This assumption is probably violated in single case data sets. Correlated errors will inflate the test statistic considerably. Sharpley and Alavosius (1988) report that even a modest correlation between the errors of 0.3 will inflate a t or F statistic to 136% of its correct value. There is clearly a significant risk of a Type I error in this case.

The question of whether autocorrelated errors are present in typical behavioural data has been hotly debated in recent years. Huitema (1985) claimed that there was little or no evidence of autocorrelation in the published data sets. His position has been challenged and interested readers are referred to Wampold (1988) for detailed coverage. The fundamental issues concern the precision with which autocorrelations can be estimated, and the power of the available statistical techniques; both issues are concerned with the size of the samples available to the investigator. As typical data sets rarely exceed 20 points per phase there is unlikely to be sufficient power in the statistical methods (Busk & Marascuilo, 1992; Huitema & McKean, 1991). The methods of time-series analysis (Gottman, 1981) which rely on accurate identification of appropriate statistical models cannot be sensibly applied to the majority of single case data. Examples of exceptions to this general statement can be found in studies of the psychotherapeutic process where investigators have extensive databases drawn from 100 or more intensive psychotherapy sessions (Fonagy & Moran, 1990, 1994; Jones, Ghannam, Nigg & Dyer, 1993); but see Crosbie (1993).

Randomisation tests do offer a statistical method for analysing single case data sets which is not compromised by the assumptions that underpin the t and F tests, or by the issues of autocorrelation; neither are they dependent on making assumptions about the population from which an individual is drawn. The tests estimate the probability that, for a given set of data points, a more extreme set of scores than the obtained pattern of results would occur if the data were to be rearranged in all possible ways. The major condition to be met by the investigator is that the point at which an intervention is introduced should be selected at random before the start of the experiment. For example, Clements and Hand (1985) conducted an A-B experiment and decided that a minimum of 5 baseline days was necessary and a maximum of 25 was allowable. Within this period an intervention day was selected at random and a total of 44 days of data were collected. The statistical significance of the intervention was computed by calculating the difference in means between successive sets of data representing all the baseline points and all the treatment points that were theoretically possible. (The first difference was between the first 5 days and the last 39 days, the second difference was between the first 6 and last 38 days, and so on up to the first 25 and last 19 days.) Inspection of the resulting mean differences showed that the actual baseline-treatment difference was the third largest of the 21 computed values, giving the probability that this result could be obtained by chance as 3/21, or p = 0.14. Randomisation tests can be applied to the median, an estimate of trend within each phase or virtually any other summary statistic which is reasonable to calculate in the particular case. Hand (1982) provides a clear introduction to the logic of randomisation tests, and more detailed accounts with worked examples for single case data can be found in Busk and Marascuilo (1992), Edgington (1984, 1992), Marascuilo and Busk (1988), and Wampold and Worsham (1986).

CONCLUSIONS

The analysis of single case data is not necessarily an easy process. The writer suggests that the following guidelines represent good practice. (1) Graph the data in several ways so as to display changes in central tendency, trend and variability. (2) Describe the data as you see it supplementing the description with appropriate non-paramentic analyses for each phase of the data (Morley & Adams, 1989). (3) Ask one or more other experienced researcher-clinicians to inspect the data and draw conclusions, i.e. obtain inter-observer agreement. (4) Conduct inferential statistical tests: use randomisation tests if possible and time series analysis if, and only if, there are sufficient data points per phase. At all stages one should be clear about the criteria used to evaluate the data: the maxim that clinical and statistical criteria are different should be kept in mind.

ACKNOWLEDGEMENT

I thank Peter Morley for his help in data collection.

REFERENCES

Baer, D.M. (1977). Perhaps it would be better not to know everything. *Journal of Applied Behavior Analysis, 10*, 167-172.

Baer, D.M. (1988). An autocorrelated commentary on the need for a different debate. *Behavioral Assessment, 10*, 295-298.

Barlow, D.H. & Hersen, M. (1984). *Single Case Experimental Designs*, 2nd edn. New York: Pergamon Press.

Barmann, B.C. & Murray, W.J. (1981). Suppression of inappropriate sexual behavior by facial screening. *Behavior Therapy, 12*, 730-735.

Barmann, B.C. & Vitali, D.L. (1982). Facial screening to eliminate trichotillomania in developmentally disabled persons. *Behavior Therapy, 13*, 735-742.

Barrios, B.A. (1984). Single subject design strategies for examining joint effects: a critical examination. *Behavioral Assessment, 6*, 103-120.

Bernard, M.E., Dennehy, S. & Keefauver, L.W. (1981). Behavioral treatment of excessive coffee and tea drinking: a case study and partial replication. *Behavior Therapy, 12*, 543-548.

Beutler, L.E. & Hamblin, D.L. (1996). Individualised outcome measures of internal change: methodological considerations. *Journal of Consulting and Clinical Psychology, 54*, 48-53.

Busk, P.L. & Marascuilo, L.A. (1992). Statistical analysis in single-case research: issues, procedures, and recommendations, with applications to multiple behaviours. In T.R. Kratochwill & J.R. Levin (eds.) *Single-case research design and analysis: new directions for psychology and education.* Hove, UK: Lawrence Erlbaum Associates Ltd.

Campbell, D.T. & Stanley, J.C. (1966). *Experimental and Quasi-experimental Designs for Research*. Chicago: Rand McNally.

Chadwick, P.D.J. & Lowe, C.F. (1990). Measurement and modification of delusional beliefs. *Journal of Consulting and Clinical Psychology, 58*, 225-232.

Clark, D.A., Sugrim, I. & Bolton, D. (1982). Primary obsessional slowness: a nursing treatment programme with a 13 year old male adolescent. *Behaviour Research and Therapy, 20*, 289-292.

Clements, J.C. & Hand, D.J. (1985). Permutation statistics in single case design. *Behavioural Psychotherapy, 13*, 288-299.

Cleveland, W.S. (1985). *The Elements of Graphing Data*. Monterey, CA: Wadsworth.

Cone, J.D. (1988). Psychometric considerations and the multiple models of behavioral assessment. In A.S. Bellack and M. Hersen (Eds), *Behavioral Assessment* (3rd edition), New York: Pergamon.

Cook, T.D. & Campbell, D.T. (1979). *Quasi-experimentation: Design and Analysis Issues for Field Settings*. Chicago: Rand McNally.

Crosbie, J. (1993). Interrupted time-series analysis with brief single-subject data. *Journal of Consulting and Clinical Psychology, 61*, 966–974.

Edgington, E.S. (1984). Statistics and the single case. In M. Hersen, R.M. Eisler & P.M. Miller (eds.) *Progress in Behavior Modification* Vol. 16. New York: Academic Press

Edgington, E.S. (1992). Nonparametric test for single-case studies. In T.R. Kratochwill & J.R. Levin (Eds.) *Single-case research design and analysis: new directions for psychology and education*. Hillsdale, NJ: Lawrence Erlbaum Associates Inc.

Elashoff, J.D. & Thoresen, C.E. (1978). Choosing a statistical method for analysis of an intensive experiment. In T.R. Kratochwill (Ed), *Single subject research: Strategies for evaluating change*. New York: Academic Press.

Fonagy, P. & Moran, G.S. (1990). Studies on the efficacy of child psychoanalysis. *Journal of Consulting and Clinical Psychology, 58*, 684-695.

Fonagy, P. & Moran, G.S. (1994). Selecting single-case research designs for clinicians. In N. Miller, L. Luborsky, J. Barber, & J. Docherty (eds), *Handbook of psychodynamic research and practice*. New York: Basic Books.

Glass, G.V., Willson, V.L. & Gottman, J.M. (1975). *Design and analysis of time series experiments*. Boulder: Colorado Associated University Press

Gottman, J.M. (1981). *Time-series analysis: A comprehensive introduction for social scientists*. Cambridge: Cambridge University Press

Hageman, W.J.J.M. & Arrindell, W.A. (1993). A further refinement of the reliable change (RC) index by improving the pre-post difference score: introducing the RCID. *Behaviour Research and Therapy, 31*, 693-700.

Hallam, R.S. (1976). A complex view of simple phobias. In H.J. Eysenck (ed.). *Case Studies in Behaviour Therapy*. London: Routledge & Kegan Paul

Hand, D.J. (1982). Statistical tests in experimental psychiatric research. *Psychological Medicine, 12*, 415-421.

Handen, B.L., Apolito, P.M., & Seltzer, G.B. (1984). The use of differential reinforcement of low rates of behavior to decrease repetitive speech in an autistic adolescent. *Journal of Behavior Therapy and Experimental Psychiatry, 15*, 359-364.

Harris, F.N. & Jenson, W.R. (1985). Comparisons of multiple-baseline across persons designs and AB designs with replication: issues and confusions. *Behavioral Assessment, 7*, 121-127.

Hartmann, D.P. (1984). Assessment strategies. In D.H. Barlow & M. Hersen (eds). *Single Case Experimental Designs*. New York: Pergamon Press

Hayes, S.C. (1981). Single case experimental design and empirical clinical practice. *Journal of Consulting and Clinical Psychology, 49*, 193-211.

Hegel, M.T., Ayllon, T., VanderPlate, C., & Spiro-Hawkins, H. (1986). A behavioural procedure for increasing compliance with self-exercise regimens in severely burn-injured patients. *Behaviour Research and Therapy, 24,* 521-528.

Herbst, P.G. (1970). *Behavioural Worlds. The Study of Single Cases.* London: Tavistock Publications.

Higgins Hains, A. & Baer, D.M. (1989). Interaction effects in multielement designs: inevitable, desirable and ignorable. *Journal of Applied Behavior Analysis, 22,* 57-69.

Hilliard, R.B. (1993). Single-case methodology in psychotherapy process and outcome research. *Journal of Consulting and Clinical Psychology, 61,* 373-380.

Hsu, L.M. (1989). Reliable changes in psychotherapy: taking into account regression toward the mean. *Behavioral Assessment, 11,* 459-467.

Huitema, B.E. (1985). Autocorrelation in applied behavior analysis: a myth. *Behavioral Assessment, 7,* 107-118.

Huitema, B.E. & McKean, J.W. (1991). Autocorrelation estimation and inference with small samples. *Psychological Bulletin, 110,* 291-304.

Jacobson, N.S. & Revenstorf, D. (1988). Statistics for assessing the clinical significance of psychotherapy techniques; issues, problems and new developments. *Behavioral Assessment, 10,* 133-145.

Jacobson, N.S. & Truax, P. (1991). Clinical significance: a statistical approach to defining meaningful change in psychotherapy research. *Journal of Abnormal Psychology, 59,* 12-19.

Johnston, J.M. & Pennypacker, H.S. (1980). *Strategies and Tactics of Human Behavioral Research.* Hillsdale, NJ: Lawrence Erlbaum Associates Inc.

Jones, E.E., Ghannam, J., Nigg, N.T., & Dyer, J.E.P. (1993). A paradigm for single-case research: the time series study of a long-term psychotherapy for depression. *Journal of Consulting and Clinical Psychology, 61,* 381-394.

Kazdin, A.E. (1982). *Single case research designs: Methods for clinical and applied settings.* New York: Oxford University Press.

Kazdin, A.E. & Kopel, S.A. (1975). On resolving ambiguities in the multiple-baseline design: Problems and recommendations. *Behaviour Therapy, 6,* 601-608.

Kratochwill, J.R. & Levin, J.R. (eds.) (1992). *Single-case research designs and analysis.* Hove, UK: Lawrence Erlbaum Associates Ltd.

Leff, J.P. & Vaughn, C.E. (1985). *Expressed Emotion in Families: Its Significance for Mental Illness.* New York: Guilford Press.

Lodge, M. (1981). *Magnitude Scaling: Qualitative Measurement of Opinions.* Beverly Hills, CA: Sage Publications.

Mace, F.C. & Lalli, J.S. (1991). Linking descriptive and experimental analyses in the treatment of bizarre speech. *Journal of Applied Behavioral Analysis, 24,* 533-562.

Marascuilo, L.A. & Busk, P.L. (1988). Combining statistics for multiple baseline AB and replicated ABAB designs across subjects. *Behavioral Assessment, 10,* 1-28.

McKnight, D.L., Nelson, R.O., Hayes, S.C., & Jarrett, R.B. (1984). Importance of treating individually assessed response classes in the amelioration of depression. *Behavior Therapy, 15,* 315-335.

Morley, S. (1987). Modification of auditory hallucinations: experimental studies of headphones and earplugs. *Behavioural Psychotherapy, 15,* 240-251.

Morley, S. (1994). Single case methodology in psychological therapy. In S.J.E. Lindsay & G.E. Powell (eds.) *A Handbook of Clinical Adult Psychology* (2nd edition), London: Routledge.

Morley, S. & Adams, M. (1989). Some simple statistical tests for exploring single-case time series data. *British Journal of Clinical Psychology, 28*, 1-18.

Morley, S. & Adams, M. (1991). Graphical analysis of single-case time series data. *British Journal of Clinical Psychology, 30*, 97-115.

Morley, S. & Hassard, A. (1989). The development of a self administered psychophysical scaling method: internal consistency and temporal reliability in chronic pain patients. *Pain, 37*, 33-39.

Ollendick. T.H., Shapiro. E.S., & Barrett. R.P. (1981). Reducing sterotypic behaviors: an analysis of treatment procedures utilizing an alternating treatments design. *Behavior Therapy, 12*, 570-577.

Parry, G., Shapiro, D.A., & Firth, J. (1986). The case of the anxious executive: a study from the research clinic. *British Journal of Medical Psychology, 59*, 221-233.

Parsonson, B.S. & Baer, D.M. (1978). The analysis and presentation of graphic data. In T.R. Kratochwill (ed.) *Single Subject Research: Strategies for Evaluating Change*. New York: Academic Press

Parsonson, B.S. & Baer, D.M. (1992). The visual analysis of data, research into the stimuli controlling it. In T.R. Kratcochwill & J.R. Levin (Eds.) *Single-case research design and analysis: new directions for psychology and education*. Hillsdale, NJ: Lawrence Erlbaum Associates Inc.

Payne, R.W. & Jones, H.G. (1957). Statistics for the investigation of individual cases. *Journal of Clinical Psychology, 13*, 115-121.

Phillips, J.P.N. (1986). Shapiro personal questionnaire and generalised personal questionnaire techniques: a repeated measures individualised outcome measurement. In L.S. Greenberg & W.M. Pinsof (Eds.), *The psychotherapeutic process: a research handbook*. New York: Guilford Press.

Salkovskis, P.M. & Warwick, H.M.C. (1985). Cognitive therapy of obsessive-compulsive disorder: treating treatment failures. *Behavioural Psychotherapy, 13*, 243-255.

Shapiro, M.B. (1961). A method of measuring psychological changes specific to the individual psychiatric patient. *British Journal of Medical Psychology, 34*, 151-155.

Shapiro, M.B. (1975). The single variable approach to assessing the intensity of feelings of depression. *European Journal of Behaviour Analysis and Modification, 2*, 62-70.

Sharpley, C.F. & Alavosius, M.P. (1988). Autocorrelation in behavioral data: an alternative perspective. *Behavioral Assessment, 10*, 243-251.

Sidman, M. (1960). *Tactics of Scientific Research*. New York: Basic Books.

Snyder, J. (1987). Behavioral analysis and treatment of poor diabetic self-care and antisocial behavior: a single-subject experimental study. *Behavior Therapy, 18*, 251-263.

Speer, D.C. (1992). Clinically significant change: Jacobson and Truax (1991) revisited. *Journal of Consulting and Clinical Psychology, 60*, 402-408.

Teasdale, J.D. & Fennell, M.J.V. (1982). Immediate effects on depression of cognitive therapy interviews. *Cognitive Therapy and Research, 6*, 343-353.

Turkat, I.D. & Carlson, C.R. (1984). Data-based versus symptomatic formulation of treatment: the case of a dependent personality. *Journal of Behavior Therapy and Experimental Psychiatry, 15*, 153-160.

Velleman, V.F. & Hoaglin, D.C. (1981). *Applications, Basics, and Computing of Exploratory Data Analysis*. Boston, MA: Duxbury Press

Wacker, D., McMahon, C., Steege, M., Berg, W., Sasso, G., & Melloy, K. (1990). Applications of a sequential alternating treatments design. *Journal of Applied Behavior Analysis, 23,* 333-339.

Wahler, R.G. (1980). The insular mother: her problems in parent child treatment. *Journal of Applied Behavior Analysis, 13,* 207-219.

Wahler, R.G. & Graves, M.G. (1983). Setting events in social networks: ally or enemy in child behavior therapy. *Behavior Therapy, 14,* 19-36.

Wampold, B.E. (ed.) (1988). Special Issue: the autocorrelation debate. *Behavioral Assessment, 10,* no.3.

Wampold, B.E. & Furlong, M.J. (1981). The heuristics of visual inference. *Behavioral Assessment, 3,* 79-92.

Wampold, B.E. & Worsham, N.L. (1986). Randomization tests for multiple baseline designs. *Behavioral Assessment, 8,* 135-143.

Watts, F. (1979). The habituation model of systematic desensitization. *Psychological Bulletin, 86,* 627-637.

Youell, K.J. & McCollough, J. P. (1975). Behavioral treatment of mucous colitis. *Journal of Consulting and Clinical Psychology, 43,* 740-745.

CHAPTER FOURTEEN

Intensive quantitative methods

Paul Alexander   *District Psychology Services,*
St Martin's Hospital, Canterbury

There is no simple definition of intensive quantitative research, but there are a number of key themes which will provide the framework of the chapter. Intensive clinical research aims to look in depth at mental health phenomena and provide meaningful and penetrating analyses, especially of processes of change and interaction. For this purpose it usually employs the rich data base provided by repeated and/or multiple measures.

There are three key features of intensive research that distinguish it from other related methodologies. Firstly, the use of *quantification techniques* identifies a commitment to empirical measurements and statistical analysis of the collected data. This distinguishes it from the qualitative methodologies discussed in Chapter 12. Yet, as Jahoda has commented in connection with one intensive technique, the Interpersonal Perception Method '... quantification need not be limited to insignificant and artificially isolated aspects of psychological phenomena'(Laing, Phillipson & Lee, 1966, p. v). The intensive research tradition shows that quantification techniques are not necessarily reductionistic and impoverishing.

A further aspect of this tradition is the use of *naturalistic* research methods. In this, intensive methods stand in contrast with the experi -mental single-case methods considered in Chapter 13. Naturalistic research permits the study of psychological phenomena without the potentially distorting effects of experimental manipulations. Although one consequence of not applying experimentally based methods is that some naturalistic research is less able to replicate its findings easily.

Naturally occurring data are not necessarily poorly structured. Indeed this methodology has a commitment to the *planned* elicitation of naturally occurring data in order to maximise reliability and validity. For example, the Personal Questionnaire (Shapiro, 1961), which is a self-report measure of symptoms, has been developed with a thorough concern for psychometric issues (Phillips, 1986; Chalkey & Mulhall, 1991). The subject uses the method of paired-comparisons (e.g. 'Does statement A or B best express how anxious you feel?) rather than merely giving a single numerical value ('How anxious are you' rating from 0 to 10). Shapiro's method both reduces response bias and utilises the internal consistency of ratings as a measure of reliability.

The final characteristic is the use of *idiographic* rather than nomothetic data. This reflects the focus upon the intensive study of psychological processes. There are two major problems with group-based research. It is difficult to ensure the homogeneity of subjects on all relevant parameters and these methods can obscure significant individual differences by pooling scores to provide group values. Of course, techniques that have been developed for intensive research, such as the Repertory Grid, can be employed in group-based designs, but such extensions of intensive methods are outside the scope of this chapter.

One important consequence of the focus upon idiographic data is that intensive methodologies rarely, if ever, employ control subjects, and are thus unable to enjoy benefits accruing from control groups—in particular the differentiation between an active treatment and placebo or non-specific factors. This raises the difficulty that many intensive studies assume they are discovering findings unique to the research subject without verifying this assumption. The problem is that, if person-centred measures are being used in the study, the development of a standard form, which would permit controlled comparisons, would breach the central assumptions of such measures. This reflects a methodological tension which individual researchers need to think through in their own particular research contexts. Ryle and Breen (1972a), for example, attempted to integrate both perspectives in their comparison of the Repertory Grid (RG) analyses of neurotic and control subjects, by comparing measures of structure rather than content.

SELF-REPORT AND OBSERVATIONAL MEASURES

Intensive methodologies can employ measures based on either self-report or observational data. These two approaches to measurement partly reflect the different traditions and paradigms of person-centred (or phenomenological) and behavioural psychology. Both have merits and demerits which must carefully be considered in the planning stage of any research study (Nelson, 1981). Self-report measures mainly develop from an introspectionist tradition and emphasise the individual's own account of 'internal events'—their psychological state and processes. Usually these will consist of their perceptions, attitudes or feelings. An individual can also make self-reports about their own behaviour, as in self-monitoring, but such methods derive from behavioural paradigms and will be discussed later. Henceforth in this chapter, for clarity, 'self-report' will be used for phenomenologically derived methods which consider internal experience and 'self-monitoring' for behaviourally derived approaches in which subjects appraise their own overt behaviour. The focus of the perceptions elicited by self-report measures can include other people, the self, abstract roles ('good parent'), ideals ('justice') or inanimate objects and structures (day-hospital or a proposed district addiction service). Typical self-report measures range from unstructured interviews and narrative analyses through to more formalised methods where the subject is provided with a systematised structure but they determine the unique content, e.g. the RG supplies general role-categories to which the subject provides specific named persons. Traditional questionnaires, however, would be seen as self-monitoring measures.

Self-report measures have the advantages of the high personal validity and depth of meaning that flow from subjects expressing their thoughts and feelings in their own words. They are potentially flexible and allow for creative responses; they are essentially ways of approaching the subject material, rather than structured 'tests'. They are also the only possible means of measuring certain clinical problems—e.g. obsessional or paranoid thoughts, sexual or sleeping behaviours. Disadvantages include demonstrating a causal relationship between such covert processes and actual behaviour, and assessing whether such 'introspectionist' data have a reliability and validity lasting beyond a very short time-span. Are a person's self-reports whimsical, fleeting impressions or more lasting and consistent? Self-report methodologies must continually address such issues.

Observational measures focus from the outside upon the subject's behaviour. They are largely derived from behavioural paradigms, which have championed the need for the thorough assessment and monitoring of behavioural change. Craighead, Kazdin and Mahoney (1981), Nelson and Hayes (1986), and Bellack and Hersen (1988) provide good reviews of such assessment and treatment approaches with a wide range of clinical problems. Barlow, Hayes and Nelson (1984), and Bellack and Hersen (1984), focus particularly upon research issues, although only a few of the methods presented could really be considered 'intensive'. Ethological methods are also relevant, as they surpass traditional 'functional analysis' and place even greater emphasis upon detailed observation and description of behaviour—usually in naturalistic situations—and the extension of such approaches to mental health research and developmental psychology is worth noting (Bateson & Hinde, 1976; Snowdon, 1983). A particularly useful discussion of observational and ethological paradigms is provided by Martin and Bateson (1993).

Behavioural psychology stresses its concern with all three systems of behaviour—the motoric (behavioural), physiological, and cognitive. All can be assessed with observational measures but different modes may require varied specific procedures. The majority of observational measures focus upon overt behaviour, but physiological measures (e.g. penile plethysmograph) are gaining in popularity although they are often expensive and time consuming. Furthermore, such measures are rarely appropriate for intensive methodologies. The cognitive mode is mainly assessed by self-monitoring techniques (Ciminero, Nelson & Lipinski, 1977), although other methods do exist (Parks & Hollon, 1988). Typical observational measures include counts of behavioural magnitude, frequency, intensity or duration and the use of ratings or checklists completed by observers. Data can be collected on a continuous or sampling (fixed or randomised) basis. Occasionally it is possible to use indirect measures e.g. tranquilliser prescription as a measure of anxiety.

Observational measures have the advantages of clear operational definition and enhanced reliability, both within and between observers. Assessment can be made in either the clinic or natural environment, the advantage of the former being better control of variables and convenience, whereas the latter provides greater validity. However, there are a number of potential difficulties with such measures. A key requirement is that the unit of observation is meaningful (not too small or too large), but can also be identified reliably. Sometimes, reliability is purchased at the cost of excluding aspects of the broader context that make a unit of observation meaningful. Thus in a study of 'negative verbal interaction', should only single words be rated, or sentences or paragraphs; and should preceding and consequent statements be considered, to provide a context? Should non-verbal qualifiers, which may indicate that the verbal statements are not to be taken seriously, be taken into account—and if so, how? A further issue is that the relevant behaviour has to be adequately sampled to ensure that the important target events occur whilst observations take place. High-frequency behaviours will require reliable sampling procedures whereas low-frequency behaviours may require unrealistically vigilant observers.

The process of taking observational measures often has important implications for both the subject being observed and the observer (Lipinski & Nelson, 1974). Subjects' behaviour may well change significantly with the knowledge that they are being observed ('reactivity'); self-monitoring can also be affected by subjects knowing that their accuracy is being monitored (Nelson, 1981). Similarly, observers' reports can be influenced by a knowledge of the results expected, feedback from the experimenter, and reactivity—awareness that their own performance is being monitored (Haynes & Horn, 1982; Foster, Bell-Dolan & Burge, 1988). One final consideration with observational measures is the need to ensure adequate links between behavioural descriptions and the person's subjective experience.

Particular traditions of research have often used only one class of measurement, apparently failing to see the potential for extending the application of intensive methodologies to other data domains. For example 'studies of structure' (see next section) have largely employed self-report measures to provide structural models of an individual's psychological functioning, whereas 'response' strategies have tended only to use observational measures as a consequence of focusing solely upon overt behaviours as the responses under study. One intention of this chapter is to show that a wider range of application is possible for both these measurement procedures and to illustrate the commonality of methodological issues. A welcome research trend has been the use of a combination of self-report and observational measures, in an attempt to extract maximum benefit from each. Thus Elliott's (1984) 'event-based' phenomenological approach (discussed in detail later) uses behavioural events (observational) to act as cues for the exploration of subjective internal processes.

Intensive methodologies are applicable to a wide range of mental health issues and questions. Historically, many studies have been concerned with psychotherapy process research, but pleasingly investigations are increasingly taking place in other clinical domains. Especially fertile areas may well be medical and health psychology, neuropsychology and 'challenging behaviour'—in its broadest sense. Increased community-based service provision offers further stimulating research opportunities, particularly appropriate for naturalistic research methodologies.

Finally, it is important to consider some more general strategic issues. The more that researchers test out specific, derived hypotheses the more likely they are to provide robust conclusions and the less likely they are to lose direction. This is not to deny the value of clinical 'hunches' in research but to emphasise that these should be translated into clear questions before the research begins. Because intensive methodologies are capable of generating large amounts of data, the researcher can easily become submerged in computer printouts. Without clear research questions the ratio of conclusions to data collected can be poor. Such considerations emphasise the value of a pilot study, wherever possible. Such a pilot study should include data analysis and interpretation as well as anticipating possible difficulties in data collection and the operationalisation of relevant variables.

Researchers need to familiarise themselves with the assumptions about the data and subject pool made by the measuring procedures and to ensure these are not invalidated. This can be particularly pertinent with intensive methodologies which typically use only a small number of subjects and repeated measures, and therefore fail to meet the statistical assumptions of measures developed with large samples of subjects.

TYPES OF DESIGN

This chapter will be organised around a categorisation of intensive designs into four groups, according to the kind of analysis undertaken with the empirical data. This abstract classification will hopefully direct attention to fundamental aspects of the research strategy, and will clarify the range of research questions that can be addressed by each design. In particular, it will become apparent that the most commonly used forms of intensive research are just a sample of those potentially available.

The four categories are (a) comparisons of responses, (b) sequences, (c) studies of structure, and (d) interactions and interexperience. They must be considered as dimensions which overlap at their extremities rather than as mutually exclusive categories, and a number of examples provided will illustrate this. Thus interactive aspects can occur in both responses and sequences designs as well as in interexperience designs. A research strategy will be classified as an 'interaction' when it is assessing mutual influence rather than simply one-way effects. Methodologies in categories (a) and (b) have been used less extensively than those in (c) and (d).

Key dimensions within the categories refer to the number of people, the number of measurement occasions and other significant parameters concerning situational and structural variables (Table 14.1). The majority of the designs in this research tradition are individual based and only one category, that of 'interaction and interexperience', focuses upon the mutual interaction of two or more people. A number of methodologies take serial measures at different points in time in order to explicate change processes but this is not an essential feature of 'intensive' research. Alternative strategies include the comparison of an individual under two different conditions which are not significantly separated in time, or developing structural models of the individual's conceptual world or behaviour.

1. Comparisons of responses

This research strategy compares the responses made by a person in different situations or conditions. Only one variable of the person's behaviour is considered (e.g. extent of stuttering) and the intention is to investigate whether significant associations exist between conditions (e.g. group size) and the response. Many such studies have been carried out in a clinical context but this is not essential and similar research is possible in educational and occupational areas. A good example of this research strategy is Metcalfe's (1956) investigation of an asthmatic patient, which demonstrated a significant relationship between the patient's asthma attacks and meetings with her mother (Table 14.2). The proposed mediating mechanism was that the meetings were negatively emotionally laden and this triggered the underlying somatic vulnerability. The association was demonstrated by a simple frequency count of the asthmatic attacks over an 85-day period under two conditions of the mother's presence or absence. A 2×2 chi-square test revealed a significant correlation.

TABLE 14.1
The four categories of intensive research

Typology	Person	Number of measurement occasions	Other
Responses	1	2 or n	Situational variance
Sequences	1	n	
Structure	1	1 or n	Structural representation
Interaction & interexperience	n	1 or n	

TABLE 14.2
Contact with mother versus asthma attacks

Occurrence of asthma	Days with asthma	Days without asthma
—	15	70
Within 24 hours of being with mother	9 (60%)	14 (20%)
Not in contact with mother for preceding 24 hours	6 (40%)	56 (80%)

Reproduced from Metcalfe (1956) by permission of the British Psychological Society.

Two central methodological issues raised by this research strategy concern the definition of the situation and the definition of the person's responses. It is vital that both can be identified in a reliable and valid manner. The situation requires clear operational description and, wherever possible, discrete onset and offset. Usually situations are defined by direct observation, but self-report measures are possible in principle, e.g. a person could indicate the range of situations in which their obsessional thoughts do or do not occur. Similar issues exist regarding the measurement of the person's responses under different conditions. Observational measures (e.g. checklist of interactional frequency) have high reliability, but self-report measures may tap more relevant variables. Both options are possible and require consideration. Obviously, there will always be a time-lag between the conditions that are being compared, though in many cases this is slight as conditions may be consecutive (e.g. movement from a small to a large group in a day hospital). Furthermore, an ABA design (situation A followed by situation B and then by A again) may be possible to demonstrate clear effects. Sometimes a longer time-scale will be required to demonstrate a clear causal relationship, as in the study by Metcalfe, though this research strategy is not essentially concerned with changes over time.

Studies using the response-comparison methodology often investigate situation-specific behaviour, being concerned with the identification of the conditions under which the behaviour is displayed. The empirical findings are used to provide a theoretical framework to explain the origins and development of the behaviour, and in many cases to suggest future treatment initiatives. Unfortunately for our purposes, a lot of the relevant work, including studies of temper tantrums or self-injurious behaviour, has focused upon effecting change by experimental means, rather than studying the response/situation correlation naturalistically. Such experimental research verifies hypotheses about the causal links maintaining behaviour by observing whether significant changes occur when reinforcement contingencies are altered (e.g. Carr & Newsom, 1985). Methods derived from ethological research are particularly relevant, especially because of their emphasis upon the ecological context of behaviour (Bateson & Hinde, 1976). For example, Esser (1968) describes an observational study, within an ethological perspective, of the interactional behaviour and dominance patterns of schizophrenic patients on a ward.

Generalisability studies also fall into this response-comparison category of research methodologies but their aim is to demonstrate reliability across conditions rather than investigate differences between conditions (see Levy, 1974, for an exposition of the method and some clinical examples). In a study applying generalisability theory to the observation of eating behaviours, Coates and Thoresen (1978) found that reliable measures could be obtained from studying nine variables on three separate occasions. Essentially such studies hope to identify a non-significant difference in the person's response between situations. Many of these studies derive from a treatment context and so may not be fully considered as 'naturalistic', although a tradition of naturalistic observation and assessment of patients does exist in some treatments. The literature on social skills training will provide further examples (e.g. Spence & Shepherd, 1983; Becker & Heimberg, 1988).

2. Sequences

The focus of research methodologies in this category is the investigation of sequences and patterns of responses. This may involve the study of changes over time, but this is not an essential characteristic; a lot of research will solely be concerned with identifying existing—often intricate—response patterns. Such patterns often include regularities in the combination and punctuation of variables, even rhythms.

Clearly, a sequence or pattern can only occur if there are at least two variables under consideration (and often more). This distinguishes these methodologies from those discussed in the previous section, where only a single variable was considered. Furthermore, all methodologies in this category will require that measures of variables are taken on at least two occasions and usually many more times. Concern is upon only a single individual—the study of the covariation of a number of people is discussed later in Section (4).

It is to be expected that the complexity of measurement, analysis and data interpretation will usually increase with the number of variables and occasions of measurement. A number of sophisticated statistical analyses of sequence data have been developed and these will be mentioned later. Developmental studies, which would typically investigate the growth in a child's physical or conceptual skills, could also be classified within this typology, but the intrinsic longitudinal nature of such studies would produce severe constraints on measurement. Research methodologies can employ either self-report or observational measures, but there has been a tendency for observational data to dominate. However Shapiro's (1969) Personal Questionnaire (PQ), which uses self-report data (see later), has made a significant contribution to this area. Furthermore, as discussed by Phillips (1986), the PQ is actually one of a general class of such methodologies.

Within this category there are two slightly different strategies, reflecting attempts to answer differing research questions. The first concerns the sequential embedding of target responses. The behaviours before and after a previously chosen target response are investigated in order to analyse their antecedents/precursors and effects. A common concern would be to identify which behaviours show increased frequency before and after the target event. Relevant examples would be the study of the precipitants and subsequent effects of aggressive or self-injurious behaviour. Research using this strategy has often employed behavioural observational measures, yet the same methods can in principle be applied to thoughts or mood (as 'covert behaviours') as in cognitive psychotherapy, but only if they have discrete onset and offset. The requirement that there be identifiable and reliable onset and offset of key responses is a central methodological constraint of the sequential embedding approach. Naturally, methodologies investigating internal processes would require appropriate self-report measures. A relevant example would be Elliott's (1984) use of his client's mood changes during therapy. Such a strategy is permissible within this tradition as long as the changes in thoughts or mood occur naturally without experimental manipulation.

The second strategy investigates the covariation of two (or more) variables over time (or situation) within a single individual to assess whether they are causally related and if so, what is the pattern of the relationship. Intensive methodologies would be particularly relevant to elucidating such complex patterns. Gershon, Cromer and Klerman (1968) employed repeated observational measures of depression and hostility to see if they were positively or negatively correlated over time. Although, in some patients, they found support for the classic psychodynamic formulation of an inverse correlation between these two variables, other patients revealed a coexistence of manifest hostility and depression. Another example is Chassan's (1979, pp. 231-235) study of a female patient, diagnosed as paranoid schizophrenic. She was interviewed 17 times and on each occasion rated on 20 (observational) items e.g. coherence, affective state, mental state. Analysis of the covariation of items revealed interesting findings, in particular a significant negative correlation between her 'appearance' and her 'orientation for person'. A 2 × 2 contingency table of data from this symptom-pair showed a near-perfect inverse matching—when she had a clear picture of who she was, then her appearance was slovenly. Unfortunately, Chassan fails to identify the meaning of this relationship, but this would ideally be the intention of intensive methodologies. In contrast to the observational data of these two studies, self-report data were employed by Garety (1985) in a PQ study of the covariation of an individual's delusional symptoms. Two patients were independently studied and interest was focused upon monitoring any fluctuation in the intensity and fixity of the self-reported delusions. Both patients completed PQ weekly and three delusional and three control beliefs (e.g. 'the sun will rise tomorrow') were rated on a 5-point scale. Some fluctuation in the strength of the paranoid beliefs was found but the control beliefs remained entirely consistent. Only one patient showed a correlation between medication-intake and weakening of delusional beliefs. One further use of self-report data could be to investigate whether a person's perceptions correlated across different people. Thus, are ratings of 'physical attractiveness' and 'goodness' significantly related? Such a research strategy comes close to issues considered in the later section *Studies of Structure*, particularly when using the Repertory Grid, but can be placed in this present category if it maintains a narrow focus and refrains from a more elaborate structural investigation.

A related research strategy would be the investigation of changes in the covariation of variables. Of special interest would be the study of changes after a significant event, such as psychological therapy, having a baby or vocational training. The PQ has been used by a number of people to study changes during psychological therapy—a task to which it is well suited as it was designed specifically to facilitate repeated measures, often over brief time periods. A dominant theme has concerned the 'immediate improvement effect' in therapy, as rated by the client. Shapiro (1969) reported this effect after behavioural therapy, especially for symptoms of depression and tension. However, Hobson and Shapiro (1970) failed to replicate this when a more psychotherapeutic approach was used. Shapiro and Hobson (1972) found clear PQ 'worsenings' during psychotherapy sessions and went on to suggest that interpretative therapy may produce short-term stress for a client by challenging existing coping mechanisms, but this may provide eventual long-term benefit. This view received mixed support from a study of group psychotherapy by Shapiro, Caplan, Rohde and Watson (1975) as many group members showed variability in PQ scores. However, Tibbles' (1992) RG investigation of the impact on clients of an initial assessment interview for psychodynamic psychotherapy may be more consistent with Shapiro and Hobson (1972). In a study comparing exploratory and prescriptive therapy Parry, Shapiro and Firth (1986) combined repeated PQ scores with the client's perceptions of helpful events in therapy and the therapist's session notes to provide a detailed analysis of the therapeutic process. Two particularly interesting findings were that most symptom change had occurred by session eight, and that different problems changed at different rates in response to different techniques—tension and irritability being influenced by a psychodynamic approach and cognitive/behavioural methods helping concentration and work problems. Greene (1990) used the semantic differential (Osgood, Suci & Tannenbaum, 1957) to explore changes in construal upon two key variables by borderline patients during brief psychodynamic group therapy. The semantic differential is a well-established method in which individual perceptions are rated on 7-point bipolar scales on constructs which relate to three fundamental dimensions—evaluation, potency and activity. Although there are some methodological weaknesses in Greene's study—a small sample size, only one repeated measurement occasion, individual scores were pooled—the results do confirm the hypothesised correlation between increased self esteem of the patients and their decreased use of splitting dynamics within the group.

All of these studies have attempted to look in detail at specific variables within the therapeutic relationship and this approach can be seen as a useful adjunct to more traditional outcome data in under-standing processes of change. The potential of such methods to investigate the effect of therapy on individual variables is large. For example, it may be found that variables that were tightly correlated before therapy have now become more independent, or that variables change at different rates (as indicated by Parry et al.) or in systematic ways. However, one important methodological issue is the need to demonstrate that the study has identified changes in variables and not merely a complex but pre-existing pattern.

The investigation of sequences has produced a group of related, and sophisticated, statistical analyses which essentially test whether items in the sequence are correlated or random. Good descriptions are provided by Everitt and Dunn (1983), Bakeman and Gottman (1986), and Martin and Bateson (1993). Markov analysis (Gottman & Notarius, 1978) is used to assess whether a sequence of events (responses) is ordered or random, and is obtained by comparison of the obtained sequence with an hypothesised random one. A first-order Markov chain is one where the probability of an event C occurring depends only on the immediately preceding event B, whereas in a second-order chain the probability depends on the two preceding events AB. Markov chains can be used to study the responses of a single individual or the correlation between the responses of two people (the latter would fall into category 4).

If times as well as the order of events have been recorded then time series analysis (Gottman, 1981; Morley & Adams, 1991) can be used to provide a description of temporal correlation and interaction (also see Chapter 13). One particular form of time series analysis is Fourier analysis, which was used by Grant, Yager, Sweetwood and Olshen (1982) in a three-year prospective study assessing the correlation between life-events and psychiatric symptoms. Unfortunately, they found no significant results but their study remains methodologically interesting for our purposes. These analyses of sequences are both useful and increasingly popular but they are statistically complex and their assumptions must be fully understood and adhered to in order for the validity of the results to hold. The central methodological parameters for studies of covariation involve ensuring there are sufficient variation of element items (times, people, situations, etc.) and sufficient numbers of observations.

3. Studies of structure

Research methodologies in this category are concerned to develop structural representations—either of a person's conceptual world or of their behaviour. This approach is most commonly associated with phenomenological theories and self-report methods, but potential exists for the development of methods based on behavioural observation. However, phenomenologically derived methods probably tend to be the more complex, time consuming and popular. One of the best examples of this approach is the Repertory Grid (RG) developed by Kelly (1955) and extended more recently by other workers, and a number of examples of RG usage will be provided in this section. Furthermore, it is possible to use PQ ratings (Slater, 1970) or interpersonal perception measures (Childs & Hedges, 1980) as data within a RG analysis.

Generally speaking, researchers using these methods are interested in the way different constituents relate together to form an overall structure. In most cases the structure comprises hierarchically organised components and involves techniques for elucidating these hierarchical arrangements, such as factor analysis. A structural representation of the individual's problem behaviour promotes questions about aetiology, potential for change, or comparison with 'normal' behaviour. Thus Button (1985) has illustrated how the personal meanings provided by anorexic patients help in understanding the development of their condition as well as offering potential therapeutic directions; similarly Ryle and Breen (1972a) demonstrated significant differences between the RG structures of 'normal' and 'neurotic' subjects. The latter tended to see themselves as deviant, very different from their parents and ideal selves, and to make polar judgements. The 'Resistance-to-Change' RG (Fransella & Bannister, 1977) directly assesses the constraints on change in an individual's conceptual structure, by indicating the implication for the total structure of the change of any single construct. This tradition has been expanded by interactive computer programs, such as PEGASUS (Thomas & Shaw, 1977), which permit immediate feedback and 'conversation' about the effects upon a construct system of potential changes—although this, strictly speaking, cannot be considered as naturalistic research.

A second strategy is to measure changes in structure over time. Most often this will be within a treatment context in which behavioural and conceptual change is being sought, but the methodology can also be employed to investigate more naturalistic changes occurring as a consequence of a significant experience such as learning or training. If a longer time-perspective is employed then investigations that may be viewed as more developmentally framed are possible, e.g. changes in self-identity perception by adolescents during their last two years at school. This strategy comes extremely close to the study of covariational change discussed in the previous section when talking of the PQ, and there is potential overlap. The crucial distinction is whether the investigation focuses upon changes in an overall structure, in which case it is rightfully included in this category, or merely the study of a small number of variables. However, this distinction may in some cases be somewhat arbitrary.

In their most complete form these methods assess the person upon multiple items in each of two dimensions (e.g. situations and persons) so that a matrix of correlations can be obtained. Factor analysis (or principal component analysis) of this matrix provides a hierarchical structure demonstrating dimensions that are more centrally important than others. The RG has already been cited as a good example of this approach, and it has fostered numerous relevant studies. Good reviews are provided by Slater, 1976; Fransella and Bannister, 1977; Beail, 1985; and Winter, 1992. The latter is particularly recommended as a comprehensive recent account of the RG and the theoretical framework from which it is derived, personal construct theory. The Q-sort (Stephenson, 1953) can also be included in this category, but would be seen as an inferior method as only two items are considered (self and ideal self) and the dimensions are supplied rather than elicited. The methodology is rarely used today, although Rogers' early research using the Q-sort to study psychotherapy process and outcome was seminal, particularly the confirmation of his hypotheses that clients' self-esteem would increase during successful therapy and that they would come to see themselves in a more 'adjusted' manner (Rogers & Dymond, 1954; Rogers, 1961).

Whereas both the RG and Q-sort are person-centred techniques, structural methodologies using observational data are also possible, although they are rarely employed. The essential requirement would be the development of a matrix of multiple ratings of behaviour in multiple situations. Various aspects of skilled behaviour would seem a good potential area. A person's social skills could be rated upon multiple aspects in multiple situations; or in a rehabilitation context components of work performance could be appraised under various conditions. Analysis of the data matrix might illustrate, for example, that some social skills cluster around an anxiety component and others around an intimacy component, whereas work performance clusters around speed and precision components.

These research strategies provide both conceptual and practical methodological issues. At the practical level it is vital that there is adequate sampling of the relevant domain comprising the matrix, otherwise the findings will be too narrowly based and not representative and generalisable (e.g. a study of a person's 'social world' will consist solely of 'friends and liked people', with a complete absence of disliked people or those viewed ambivalently). Thus it is necessary to ensure a sufficient number and range of elements and constructs. Consideration must be paid to the relative merits of elicited and supplied constructs, and to the statistical assumptions of the rating procedures employed, particularly in terms of the distribution of the scores and scales of measurement. This is particularly salient if factor-analytic procedures are to be employed, as their statistical assumptions must not be breached. The RG literature contains a number of good discussions on these issues (Slater, 1976, 1977; Fransella & Bannister, 1977; Beail, 1985). If observational data are utilised, decisions must be made concerning the number of observers used, the criteria for ratings and the effect upon the subject of being rated (reactivity).

At the conceptual level the central issue for self-report methodologies is to demonstrate a clear link between the conceptual structure derived and the person's actual behaviour. Can the relevant behaviour be understood? Can it be predicted? Often these questions fail to be adequately answered. Observational methodologies suffer the converse difficulties. Although they can predict behavioural performance they largely fail to elucidate the role of the person's perception of the situation.

4. Interaction and interexperience

This last research strategy focuses upon the interpersonal context by investigating the mutual interaction or interexperience of the participants. The element of mutuality differentiates it from those discussed in (1) and (2). Usually studies focus on the dyadic situation but this is not essential, and increased interest in family interaction and therapy has fostered studies of the triadic context (e.g. Scott, Ashworth & Casson, 1970; Scott & Alwyn, 1978; Procter, 1985; Scott, Fagin & Winter, 1993). Furthermore a number of studies of group interaction have consistently been reported over the years (e.g. Smail, 1972; Winter & Trippett, 1977; Koch, 1985; Winter & Gournay, 1987). Methodologies can employ either self-report or observational measures, although the former has been most commonly used; there is an increasing trend for individual studies to employ both. (See next section on the 'events paradigm').

Phenomenologically based methodologies, using self-report techniques, most commonly aim to explicate areas of match and mis-match in the participants' joint construction of the world, and to try to correlate this with aspects of their interaction—usually problems. Essentially this represents a translation of an intrapersonal method, designed for the study of the individual, to the interpersonal context by the comparison of two (or more) individual perspectives. Two good examples of this strategy are Ryle's extension of the RG technique, the Double Dyad Grid (see Ryle, 1985, for a good review), and the interpersonal perception approach discussed later. The elements of the Dyad Grid are relationships rather than people, as in the traditional RG; the Double Dyad Grid requires both partners in a relationship to complete a Dyad Grid independently and these are then compared. Ryle and Breen (1972b) provide an example of the method's use in marital therapy, identifying shared, but problematic, perceptions and projections of the couple.

A slightly different research focus is to investigate the extent to which one member can predict the views or psychological framework of the other. This is often used as an operational definition of empathy and is commonly employed in studies of therapist/client relationship (e.g. Rowe, 1971; Ryle & Lunghi, 1971; Shapiro & Post, 1974; Rowe & Slater, 1976) or marital satisfaction (e.g. Dymond, 1954; Torpy & Measey, 1974; Allen & Thompson, 1984; O'Loughlin, 1989). Rowe (1971) and Ryle and Lunghi (1971), using the RG method, reported that therapists had appreciable insight into their clients' construct systems (correlations between therapist's prediction of client's RG and client's actual RG were 0.32 and 0.50 respectively) but, perhaps more importantly, also identified crucial and systematic misperceptions highly relevant to the therapeutic relationship. Shapiro and Post (1974) found that the major discrepancy between a psychiatrist and patient on PQ ratings was related to the severity with which the symptoms were experienced by the patient, rather than the psychiatrist misunderstanding which symptoms were present. Torpy and Measey (1974), in a study of marriages in which one member was agoraphobic, found a strong correlation between marital satisfaction and accurate prediction of the partner's views, a link commonly found in such studies.

The 'interpersonal perception' approach has typically combined the two preceding strategies by investigating both perceptual match ('agreement') and predictions of partner's views. A spiraliform model is conceptualised in which levels of perception exist, each at a higher level than its predecessor. Although logically there is no limit to the spiral, in practice no methodology considers beyond the third level and some only consider the first two. The dyad A and B, from A's point of view, will have three levels of perspective—the direct perspective (A's view of X [A-X]), the metaperspective (A's view of B's view of X [A-B-X]), and meta-metaperspective (A-B-A-X). Comparison of the direct perspectives of A and B will indicate their agreement (A-X/B-X). Accurate metaperception (A-B-X/B-X) indicates A's understanding of B, whilst accurate usage of the metametaperspective (A-B-A-X/B-A-X), usually termed realisation, indicates A's ability to predict whether B under- stands A or not. Further intrapersonal measures reflecting perceived agreement and feeling understood are also possible, and Alperson (1975) provides a useful mathematical synthesis and description of this general approach.

The best known, and most influential example of this methodology is the Interpersonal Perception Method (IPM) developed by Laing, Phillipson and Lee (1966) within an object-relations framework. Each partner answers 60 descriptions of key relationship issues using three levels of perception, and the dyad is scored in terms of both overall perceptual accuracy and the spirals of agreement, understanding and realisation about each particular issue. In an IPM comparison of disturbed and non-disturbed marriages, Laing et al. found the latter to have significantly more accurate perceptions at all perceptual levels. The same study also illustrated the use of the IPM in an intensive case study of marital therapy. Allen and Thompson (1984) used a form of the IPM to study marital perception and satisfaction. Amongst their sample of 50 normal couples, agreement and feeling understood were the most important determinants of marital satisfaction, rather than higher-order perceptual accuracies. That these findings differ from those of Torpy & Measey (1974) may well be because the previous study investigated marriages containing a partner with psychological difficulties. A related, but inferior, approach to the IPM is the

Interpersonal Perception Technique (IPT) of Drewerey (1969), which in one study indicated that male alcoholic patients were confused about their marital roles and dependency needs (Rae & Drewerey 1972).

Scott, Ashworth and Casson (1970) extended the IPM methodology to the triadic situation with their Family Relations Test (FRT) in their study of families with a schizophrenic child. The patient, their father and mother each made five ratings—their view of themselves, the other two, how the other two see them. The FRT illustrated that families which experienced frequent conflict and hospital admission were characterised by role-conflict, particularly in that the patient saw the parents as being as 'ill' as themselves, thereby apparently invalidating their long-term position at home. Further support for these findings is provided by Scott, Fagin and Winter (1993) in a two-year follow up study of 40 schizophrenic patients and their parents. Procter (1985) developed an interesting methodology in which a common 'family RG' is completed by each family member, permitting an analysis of shared and disparate perceptions which illustrates family dynamics and communication patterns.

Very few studies have employed these methods to assess change over time, yet the potential is vast. Laing et al. (1966) used the IPM to investigate marital therapy, and Childs and Hedges (1980) present a single case study of marital therapy in which IPM data are used as RG elements, and the results employed to shape therapeutic strategy. Alexander (1981) used a development of the IPM to study changes in the client/therapist relationship during psychotherapy, but considerable scope exists for other extensions. Furthermore, the developments started by the FRT and the Family RG can be extended to the four-person situation and beyond, with implications for the study of family and group interaction. The relatively few studies of changes in group perceptions over time have been within the RG tradition and have demonstrated important findings related to group processes which are worth developing (e.g. Fransella & Joyston-Bechal, 1971; Winter & Trippett, 1977; Koch, 1985).

Methodologies employing observational measures study the relationship between the behaviour of two (or more) people. The intention is to identify patterns of behaviour and thus deduce causal relationships (see earlier discussion of Markov chains). For example, in a married couple some behaviours may be positively correlated over time (i.e. behaviour A provokes behaviour B) and others negatively correlated (i.e. turn-taking occurs). Measurement issues concern the definition of the appropriate unit of behaviour and its operational description, together with considerations about the length of time for which subjects should be observed and the effects of being observed (reactivity).

EVENT-BASED PHENOMENOLOGICAL RESEARCH

This final section will look in some detail at 'event-based phenomenological' research, as it provides a good example of a sophisticated and increasingly popular intensive research methodology (of the 'interaction and interexperience' category), and one which is fertile ground for further conceptual and practical development. The major proponent of this research strategy has been Elliott, who (with various co-workers) has been concerned with the investigation of the process of change in psychotherapy by means of significant change events. (See Barkham, 1990, for a concise overview of psychotherapy research). Shapiro's (1989) proposal of a phenomenon-orientated strategy in research in depression is fully compatible with this approach. Elliott's 'discovery orientated approach' (Elliott 1984) has evolved into the 'events paradigm' which is characterised by: (a) focus on clinically significant change events in psychotherapy; (b) simplification by limiting investigation to relatively homogeneous classes of significant event (e.g. insight events); (c) description of therapeutic sequences or 'pathways'—the stages by which clients carry out specific therapeutic tasks within sessions and (d) the development and refinement of 'clinical microtheories' as a research goal (Elliott & Shapiro 1988; pp.141-142).

Elliott's essential research strategy is to identify and describe significant change moments/events in therapy and to link these with the participants' subjective experience, especially the therapist's intention and the effect ('impact') of the therapist's behaviour on the client. Although significant events can be defined by observational measures (change of posture or voice tone, crying, etc.) Elliott has taken them to be those responses reported by the client to be especially helpful or negative (see later). This latter perspective is most in tune with the philosophy of the methodology, in that the participants define the key concerns.

This approach has led to the development of a number of interesting research methods, which are being increasingly combined to provide a comprehensive description of change processes. One intention of this research programme is to be able to suggest therapist intervention tactics that will promote beneficial client changes. Interpersonal Process Recall (IPR) was originated by Kagan but developed extensively by Elliott (1984, 1986). A good introduction to the method is provided by Barker (1985). The essence of IPR is that a videotape of the therapy session is replayed to client and therapist separately in the presence of a trained 'inquirer', to whom they are encouraged to recall their moment-by-moment experience during the session by using the videotape as a cueing device. They can stop the tape whenever they wish and are encouraged to talk about their feelings and thoughts at that moment and their reaction to the other person's behaviour in the therapy session. This is the essence of the 'event-based phenomenological' approach, and may be an attractive method to many investigators because it mirrors the reality of clinical work. IPR can be used non-directively, by allowing the person to stop the tape whenever they wish to explore a personal concern, and this would be especially appropriate for clinical supervision, which is where the method originated. Alternatively IPR can be used in a more systematic manner as a research tool by sampling segments of client/therapist interaction at specific time points during therapy sessions. This is how Elliott has employed the technique, particularly in studying the intentions behind the therapist's responses and the impact felt by the client in terms of both empathy and helpfulness (Elliott, 1979).

Elliott (1984) went on to develop Comprehensive Process Analysis (CPA) as 'a procedure for describing significant change events systematically on a battery of process measures' (p. 254). This is a content analysis in which a transcript of a significant event identified by IPR is categorised on multiple quantitative and qualitative measures assessing five aspects of the therapeutic process (content, action, style, state-experience, and quality). Both client and therapist behaviour is considered and ratings are made by client, therapist and observer. Finally all the measures are integrated in the form of a narrative or comparative analysis across cases. Elliott (1984) illustrates the use of this approach with four different case examples.

The Therapeutic Impact Content Analysis System (TICAS) is an extension of this method (Elliott et al., 1985). By using IPR the client identifies and describes in detail the most helpful and most hindering therapist interventions, which then receive content analysis. Elliott et al. employed 14 categories, derived from pilot data, and proposed these as a good eclectic framework for analysing change processes. They reflect many familiar theoretical constructs (e.g. 'negative therapist reaction'—countertransference; 'understanding'—empathy). In their study TICAS data were used with two different research strategies. The first compared client responses to different therapeutic approaches, and it was found that the dynamic therapy they studied evoked responses of insight and awareness, whereas with cognitive therapy reassurance and insight were most common. The second strategy correlated client response with specific therapist behaviour, by rating the latter on six modes derived from the CPA (question, advisement, reflection, interpretation, reassurance, and self-disclosure). Two general findings emerged: (1) that therapist questions did not help the client feel understood; and (2) therapist self-disclosure enhanced client trust. However, these findings should be seen largely within the context of this particular study and not as being highly generalisable.

Significant factors with both the CPA and TICAS are that they are labour-intensive and time consuming, and may be impractical for anything other than large research studies. To reduce these constraints Elliott and Shapiro (1988) developed Brief Structured Recall (BSR) in which the client is required to identify only the single most helpful event in each session (Llewelyn, Elliott, Shapiro, Hardy & Firth-Cozens, 1988) and to rate this upon a taxonomy of the therapeutic relationship derived from CPA and TICAS. An interesting, more interactive development, is that client and therapist each predict the changes in the client to which the event may lead and these are reviewed after a month. The process remains demanding on time, however, as illustrated by the methodology of the Second Sheffield Psychotherapy Project (Shapiro, Barkham, Hardy & Morrison, 1990) in which BSR is carried out only after the fourth and twelfth sessions.

Elliott's studies and the related Sheffield Psychotherapy Project (Shapiro & Firth-Cozens, 1990) have produced a considerable amount of interesting findings and offer much potential, both in terms of increasing our knowledge of psychotherapy processes and as a methodological model. The events paradigm offers the potential for fine-grained microanalysis of different processes and sequences of client change. One exciting aspect of future research is the prospect of investigating a stage further back in the chain of interaction. Thus, can we identify the client behaviours that 'trigger' the therapist behaviours which the client perceives as being helpful or insight-promoting? However, this will only be addressed more clearly once the assessment procedures become more structured and less time consuming, along the lines of the BSR. However, as indicated earlier, this probably still remains a very demanding research procedure.

A final consideration concerns the reliability and validity of the methods discussed. Barker (1985) raises issues about potential threats to validity arising from forgetting, lack of expressive skills, social desirability and fabrication but considers that overall the IPR has support. Elliot (1986) has reviewed the IPR literature and found evidence for good internal and temporal validity. However, the approach is still in its infancy and will require further sober investigation and consideration of its psychometric properties. This is also true for the content analyses, such as BSR, that have been developed recently and for the underlying strategy of identifying 'helpful' or significant moments within a therapy session.

SUMMARY

Intensive methodologies offer exciting opportunities to understand people in depth by the use of rigorous, yet sensitive, naturalistic research methods. Increasing research interest has been shown in the processes occurring during psychotherapy and it is hoped that important empirical gains will continue. A particularly fertile area appears to be the microanalysis and description of the chain of interaction between the responses of client and therapist. Methods that combine observational and self-report measures, in the manner of Elliott's (1984) 'event-based phenomenology', and which investigate 'significant events' are becoming a dominant paradigm at present. It will be of interest to see how widely used such strategies eventually become, and their consequent influence on clinical theory and practice. However, intensive research should not necessarily be labour-intensive and time consuming, nor be solely concerned with the topic of psychotherapy, and potential exists in many other areas. Two good candidates concern community-based service provision for enduring mental health problems and the investigation of challenging behaviour.

Hopefully, the four typologies detailed here have helped to clarify the central methodological issues in intensive research and this will foster future empirical studies. There are undoubtedly alternative ways in which to conceptualise intensive research (e.g. methodologies employing observational versus self-report measures), but the typology presented appeared to be the most useful. It is important to separate issues concerning research strategy from the more tactical concerns in the precise methods used in the research study, although clearly the two levels influence each other. However, the influence should, in the main, be from the strategic down to the tactical. The typologies presented have tried to focus upon this strategic level to illustrate central constraints and to indicate some areas for future development.

REFERENCES

Alexander, P.T. (1981). *Cognitive Processes in Dyadic Therapy: Client and Therapist Negotiation about the Construction of Reality*. Unpublished PhD Thesis. University of Bristol.

Allen, A. & Thompson, T. (1984). Agreement, understanding, realisation and feeling understood as predictors of communicative satisfaction in marital dyads. *Journal of Marriage and the Family, 46*, 915-921.

Alperson, B.L. (1975). In search of Buber's Ghosts: A calculus for interpersonal phenomenology. *Behavioral Science, 20*, 179-190.

Bakeman, R. & Gottman, J.M. (1986). *Observing Interaction. An Introduction to Sequential Analysis*. Cambridge University Press.

Barker, C.B. (1985). Interpersonal process recall in clinical training and research. In F.N. Watts (ed.) *New Developments in Clinical Psychology*. London: Wiley.

Barkham, M. (1990) Research in individual therapy. In W. Dryden (ed). *Individual Therapy: A Handbook*. Milton Keynes: Open University Press.

Barlow, D.H., Hayes, S.C. & Nelson, R.O. (1984). *The Scientist Practitioner. Research and Accountability in Clinical and Educational Settings*. Boston: Allyn & Bacon.

Bateson, P.P.G. & Hinde, R.A. (eds) (1976). *Growing Points in Ethology*. London: Cambridge University Press.

Beail, N. (ed.) (1985). *Repertory Grid Technique and Personal Constructs: Applications in Clinical and Educational Settings*. London: Croom Helm.

Becker, R.E. & Heimberg, R.G. (1988). Assessment of Social Skills. In A.S. Bellack & M. Hersen (eds.) *Behavioral Assessment. A Practical Handbook*. 3rd Edition. New York: Pergamon.

Bellack, A.S. & Hersen, M. (eds). (1984). *Research Methods in Clinical Psychology*. New York: Pergamon.

Bellack, A.S. & Hersen, M. (1988). *Behavioral Assessment. A Practical Guide*. 3rd Edition. New York: Pergamon.

Button, E. (ed.) (1985). *Personal Construct Theory and Mental Health*. London: Croom Helm.

Carr, E.G.& Newsom, C. (1985). Demand-related tantrums. Conceptualisation and treatment. *Behaviour Modification, 9*, 403-426.

Chalkley, A.J. & Mulhall, D.J. (1991). The PQRSTUV: The Personal Questionnaire Rapid Scaling Technique - 'Ultimate Version'. *British Journal of Clinical Psychology, 30*, 181-183.

Chassan, J.B. (1979). *Research Design in Clinical Psychology and Psychiatry*. 2nd edn. New York: Irvington.

Childs, D. & Hedges, R. (1980). The analysis of interpersonal perceptions as a repertory grid. *British Journal of Medical Psychology, 53*, 127-136.

Ciminero, A.R., Nelson, R. & Lipinski, D.P. (1977). Self monitoring procedures. In A.R. Ciminero, K.S. Calhoun, & H.E. Adams. (eds). *Handbook of Behavioral Assessment*. New York: John Wiley & Sons.

Coates, T.J. & Thoresen, C.E. (1978). Using generalizability theory in behavioral observation. *Behavior Therapy, 9*, 605-613.

Craighead, W.E., Kazdin, A.E. & Mahoney, M.J. (1981). *Behavior Modification: Principles. Issues and Applications*. 2nd edn. Boston: Houghton Miflin.

Drewerey, J. (1969). An interpersonal perception technique. *British Journal of Medical Psychology, 42*, 171-181.

Dymond, R.F. (1954). Interpersonal perception and marital happiness. *Canadian Journal of Psychology, 8*, 164-171.

Elliott, R. (1979). How clients perceive helper behaviors. *Journal of Counseling Psychology, 26*, 285-294.

Elliott, R. (1984). A discovery-oriented approach to significant change events in psychotherapy: interpersonal process recall and comprehensive process analysis. In L.N. Rice & L.S. Greenberg (eds) *Patterns of Change; Intensive Analysis of Psychotherapy Process*. London: Guilford.

Elliot, R. (1986). Interpersonal Process Recall (IPR) as a process research method. In L. Greenberg & W. Pinsof (eds) (1986). *The Psychotherapeutic Process: A Research Handbook*. New York: Guilford.

Elliott, R., James, E., Reimschuessel, C., Cislo, D., & Sack, N. (1985). Significant events and the analysis of immediate therapeutic impact. *Psychotherapy, 22,* 620-630.

Elliott, R. & Shapiro, D.A. (1988) Brief Structured Recall: A more efficient method for studying significant therapy events. *British Journal of Medical Psychology, 61,* 141-153.

Esser, A.H. (1968). Interactional hierarchy and power structure on a psychiatric ward. In S.J. Hutt & C. Hutt (eds). *Behaviour Studies in Psychiatry*. Oxford: Pergamon.

Everitt, B.S. & Dunn, G. (1983). *Advanced methods of data exploration and modelling*. London: Heinemann.

Foster, S.L., Bell-Dolan, D.J., & Burge, D.A. (1988). Behavioral Observation. In A.S. Bellack & M. Hersen (eds). *Behavioral Assessment. A Practical Handbook*. 3rd Edition. New York: Pergamon.

Fransella, F. & Bannister, D. (1977). *A Manual for Repertory Grid Technique*. London: Academic Press.

Fransella, F. & Joyston-Bechal, M.P. (1971). An investigation of conceptual process and pattern change in a psychotherapy group. *British Journal of Psychiatry, 11,* 199-206.

Garety, P. (1985). Delusions: problems in definition and measurement. *British Journal of Medical Psychology, 58,* 25-34.

Gershon, E.S., Cromer, M., & Klerman, G.L. (1968). Hostility and depression. *Psychiatry, 31,* 224-235.

Gottman, J.M. (1981). *Time-Series Analysis: A Comprehensive Introduction for Social Scientists*. Cambridge: Cambridge University Press.

Gottman, J.M. & Notarius. C. (1978). Sequential Analysis of Observational Data Using Markov Chains. In T.R. Kratochwill. (ed). *Single Subject Research. Strategies for Evaluating Change*. New York: Academic Press.

Grant. I., Yager, J., Sweetwood, H.L., & Olshen, R. (1982). Life events and symptoms. Fourier analysis of time series from a three-year prospective inquiry. *Archives of General Psychiatry, 39,* 598-605.

Greene, L.R. (1990). Relationships among sematic differential change measures of splitting, self-fragmentation and object relations in borderline psychopathology. *British Journal of Medical Psychology, 63,* 21-23.

Greenberg, L. & Pinsof, W. (eds). (1986). *The Psychotherapeutic Process: A Research Handbook*. New York: Guilford.

Haynes, S.N. & Horn, W.F. (1982). Reactivity in behavioral observation: A review. *Behavioral Assessment, 4,* 369-386.

Hobson, R.F. & Shapiro, D.A. (1970). The personal questionnaire as a method of assessing change during psychotherapy. *British Journal of Psychiatry, 117,* 623-626.

Kelly, G.A. (1955). *The Psychology of Personal Constructs* vols 1 and 2. New York: Norton.

Koch, H.C.H. (1985). Group Psychotherapy. In E. Button (ed). *Personal Construct Theory and Mental Health*. London: Croom Helm.

Laing, R.D., Phillipson, H., & Lee, A.R. (1966). *Interpersonal Perception*. London: Tavistock.

Levy, P. (1974). Generalizability studies in clinical settings. *British Journal of Social and Clinical Psychology, 13*, 161-172.

Lipinski, D. & Nelson, R.O. (1974). Problems in the use of naturalistic observation as a means of behavioral assessment. *Behavior Therapy, 5*, 341-351.

Llewelyn, S.P., Elliott, R., Shapiro, D.A., Hardy, G., & Firth-Cozens, J. (1988). Client perceptions of significant events in prescriptive and exploratory periods of individual therapy. *British Journal of Clinical Psychology, 27*, 105-114.

Martin, P. & Bateson, P. (1993). *Measuring Behaviour: An Introductory Guide.* 2nd Edition. Cambridge University Press.

Metcalfe, M. (1956). Demonstration of a psychosomatic relationship. *British Journal of Medical Psychology, 29*, 63-66.

Morley, S. & Adams, M. (1991). Graphical analysis of single-case time series data. *British Journal of Clinical Psychology, 30*, 97-115.

Nelson, R.O. (1981). Realistic dependent measures for clinical use. *Journal of Consulting & Clinical Psychology, 49*, 168-182.

Nelson, R.O. & Hayes, S.C. (eds). (1986). *Conceptual foundations of behavioral assessment.* New York: Guilford Press.

O'Loughlin, S. (1989). Use of repertory grids to assess understanding between partners in marital therapy. *International Journal of Personal Construct Psychology, 2*, 143-147.

Osgood, C.E., Suci, G.J., & Tannenbaum, P.H. (1957). *The Measurement of Meaning.* Urbana, Illinois: University of Illinois Press.

Parks, C.W. & Hollon, S.D. (1988). Cognitive Assessment. In A.S. Bellack. & M. Hersen. (eds). *Behavioral Assessment. A Practical Handbook.* 3rd Edition. New York: Pergamon.

Parry, G., Shapiro, D.A., & Firth, J. (1986). The case of the anxious executive: a study from the research clinic. *British Journal of Medical Psychology, 59*, 221-233.

Phillips, J.P.N. (1986). Shapiro Personal Questionnaire and generalised personal questionnaire techniques: A repeated measures individualised outcome measurement. In L.S. Greenberg & W.M. Pinsof (eds). *The Psychotherapeutic Process: A Research Handbook.* New York: Guilford.

Procter, H.G. (1985). Repertory grids in family therapy and research. In N. Beail. (ed). *Repertory Grid Technique and Personal Constructs: Applications in Clinical and Educational Settings.* London: Croom Helm.

Rae, J. & Drewerey, J. (1972). Interpersonal patterns in alcoholic marriages. *British Journal of Psychiatry, 120*, 615-621.

Rice, L.N. & Greenberg, L.S. (eds) (1984). *Patterns of Change; Intensive Analysis of Psychotherapy Process.* London: Guilford.

Rogers, C.R. (1961). *On Becoming a Person.* London: Constable.

Rogers, C.R. & Dymond, R.F. (1954). *Psychotherapy and Personality Change.* Chicago: Chicago University Press.

Rowe. D. (1971). An examination of a psychiatrist's predictions of a patient's constructs. *British Journal of Psychiatry, 118*, 231-244.

Rowe, D. & Slater, P. (1976). Studies of the psychiatrist's insight into the patient's inner world. In P. Slater. (ed). *The Measurement of Interpersonal Space by Grid Technique. Vol 1. Explorations of Intrapersonal Space.* London: Wiley.

Ryle, A.R. (1985). The dyad grid and psychotherapy research. In N. Beail (ed.) *Repertory Grid Technique and Personal Constructs*. London: Croom Helm.

Ryle, A.R. & Breen, D. (1972a). Some differences in the personal constructs of neurotic and normal subjects. *British Journal of Psychiatry, 120*, 483-489.

Ryle, A.R. & Breen, D. (1972b). The use of the double dyad grid in the clinical setting. *British Journal of Medical Psychology, 45*, 383-389.

Ryle, A.R. & Lunghi, M. (1971). A therapist's prediction of a patient's dyad grid. *British Journal of Psychiatry, 118*, 555-560.

Scott, R.D. & Alwyn, S. (1978). Patient - parent relationships and the course and outcome of schizophrenia. *British Journal of Medical Psychology, 51*, 343-355.

Scott, R.D., Ashworth, P.L., & Casson, P.D. (1970). Violation of parental role structure and outcome in schizophrenia. *Social Science & Medicine, 4*,41-64.

Scott, R.D., Fagin, L., & Winter, D. (1993). The importance of the Role of the Patient in the Outcome of Schizophrenia. *British Journal of Psychiatry, 163*, 62-68.

Shapiro, D.A. & Hobson, R.F. (1972). Change in psychotherapy: a single case study. *Psychological Medicine, 2*, 312-317.

Shapiro, D.A., Caplan, H.L., Rohde, P.D., & Watson, J.P. (1975). Personal Questionnaire changes and their correlates in a psychotherapy group. *British Journal of Medical Psychology, 48*, 207-215.

Shapiro, D.A., Barkham, M., Hardy, G.E., & Morrison, L.A. (1990). The Second Sheffield Psychotherapy Project: Rationale, design and preliminary outcome data. *British Journal of Medical Psychology, 63*, 97-108.

Shapiro, D.A. & Firth-Cozens, J. (1990) Two-Year Follow-up of the Sheffield Psychotherapy Project. *British Journal of Psychiatry, 157*, 389-391.

Shapiro, M.B. (1961). A method of measuring changes specific to the individual psychiatric patient. *British Journal of Medical Psychology, M*, 151-155.

Shapiro, M.B. (1969). Short-term improvements in the symptoms of affective disorder. *British Journal of Social and Clinical Psychology, 8*, 187-188.

Shapiro, M.B. (1989). A phenomenon-orientated strategy in depression research. *British Journal of Clinical Psychology, 28*, 289-306.

Shapiro, M.B. & Post, F. (1974). Comparison of self-ratings of psychiatric patients with ratings made by a psychiatrist. *British Journal of Psychiatry, 125*, 36-41.

Slater, P. (1970). Personal questionnaire data treated as a form of repertory grid. *British Journal of Social and Clinical Psychology, 9*, 357-370.

Slater, P. (ed.) (1976). *The Measurement of lntrapersonal Space by Grid Technique. Vol. 1. Explorations of Intrapersonal Space*. London: Wiley.

Slater, P. (ed.) (1977). *The Measurement of Intrapersonal Space by Grid Technique. Vol. 2. Dimensions of Intrapersonal Space*. London: Wiley.

Smail, D.J. (1972). A grid measure of empathy in a therapeutic group. *British Journal of Medical Psychology, 45*, 165-169.

Snowdon, C.T. (1983). Ethology, comparative psychology and animal behavior. *Annual Review of Psychology, 34*, 63-94.

Spence, S. & Shepherd, G. (1983). *Developments in Social Skills Training*. London: Academic Press.

Stephenson, W. (1953). *The Study of Behaviour: Q-Technique and its Methodology*. University of Chicago Press.

Thomas, L.F. & Shaw, M.L.G. (1977). *PEGASUS Manual*. Brunel University. Centre for the Study of Human Learning.

Tibbles, P.N. (1992). Changes in depression and personal construing following assessment for dynamic psychotherapy. *British Journal of Medical Psychology, 65*, 9-15.

Torpy, D. & Measey, L.G. (1974). Marital interaction in agoraphobia. *Journal of Clinical Psychology, 30*, 351-354.

Winter, D.A. (1992). *Personal Construct Psychology in Clinical Practice: Theory, Research and Clinical Applications*. London: Routledge.

Winter, D.A. & Gournay, K. (1987). Constriction and construction in agoraphobia. *British Journal of Medical Psychology, 60*, 233-244.

Winter, D.A. & Trippett, C.J. (1977). Serial change in group psychotherapy. *British Journal of Medical Psychology, 50*, 341-347.

CHAPTER FIFTEEN

Studying people in their social settings

Jim Orford *School of Psychology, University of Birmingham*

THE NEED TO STUDY PEOPLE IN THEIR SOCIAL SETTINGS

Those who wish to study people as social beings face a paradox. On the one hand behavioural and mental health research appears to be most rigorously scientific when it controls and simplifies the phenomena to be studied. To do this people are often studied under laboratory or 'test' conditions and study is often concentrated on certain properties or functions of individual people without reference to their social environments. To do research with people in their social settings, on the other hand, it is necessary to leave the security of that familiar kind of research and venture out into territory where nothing seems controlled or controllable and where all is complexity and interdependence. The intending researcher of people-in-settings may very reasonably ask whether science is possible at all under those circumstances. I hope to convince the reader of this chapter that it is.

I am inclined to think, though, that the complexity referred to in the previous paragraph is responsible for stopping a lot of practitioners from embarking on research at all. They deal in their professional lives with complexity; but the research designs and methods they are familiar with seem not to be able to do justice to it. One practitioner-researcher, for example, may wish to study how families can best cope with mental ill-health or a chronic physical condition. But the number of families that it would be feasible to study in sufficient depth might be modest and in practice the structures of available families would probably vary greatly, hence introducing a number of confounding variables such as family size, one versus two parents, and stage of the family life cycle. Furthermore none of the existing standard measures of ways of coping with stress, or of family cohesion or family atmosphere might seem quite appropriate. Another intending researcher may wish to evaluate an innovative form of group therapy for incest 'survivors': but it may be thought premature to assess outcome because the method is so new and comparatively untried, while the process is fast-moving and difficult to capture. Others may want to study stress and 'burn-out' among nurses working in a hospital intensive care unit or in a residential establishment for people with learning difficulties, but there are so many variables: a nurse's age and length of service, extent of post-qualification training, the nurse's home circumstances and demands, staffing levels in the unit, quality of supervision, availability of support from other nurses, and so on *ad infinitum*. Another prospective researcher may want to study the ways in which a hospital ward and a community team combine to provide a service for people with severe mental disorder, or the ways in which a voluntary organisation and a health service team work together to provide a service for people with drug problems. In planning service delivery, answers to these questions may be more important than answers to questions to do with the precise treatment methods used by the collaborating agencies, but researching complex treatment systems may appear to present formidable problems.

THE PRINCIPLE OF INTERACTIONISM

The researcher who tackles one of these issues is working at the interface between individual people and the social settings or systems of which they are part. Interactionism provides a good guiding principle for research of this kind and this is captured in Lewin's (1951) famous equation, $B = f(P,E)$, or 'Behaviour is a joint function of person and environment and their interaction'. Whether the setting is the family, a therapeutic group, a treatment unit, or a complex treatment delivery system, the principle is that the behaviour (or experience or development) of people who occupy the setting as members, clients, or workers, is influenced by properties and processes that belong to the setting, in interaction with characteristics of the individual people themselves.

This principle may seem self-evident to many readers, but it has generally been ignored in behavioural and mental health research which has tended, under the dominant influence of a bio-medical approach, to focus exclusively on the personal or individual determinants of behaviour and health (Heller, 1989; Orford, 1992). This individualistic bias is gradually being challenged by a psycho-social perspective and ultimately will be replaced, it is to be hoped, by a more complete bio-psycho-social model. The challenge is coming from a number of directions. Epidemiological research, for example, is showing how macro-level social factors such as socio-economic status and the equitability of the distribution of wealth in a population affect health outcomes such as rates of death due to heart disease (Wilkinson, 1992). On a more 'micro' level, research in the social psychology of health is showing, among many other things, that decision-making autonomy at work is associated with good employee physical and mental health (Parkes, 1989). In both cases personal-individual factors, such as smoking and general beliefs about the controllability of events, are also relevant. Instances like these, which illustrate the general principle of social-individual interaction, abound in the behavioural and mental health field.

People-in-settings research should have something to say, therefore, about the behaviour or experience of individual participants and also something about the properties of their settings or systems. Because of the individualistic bias in behavioural and mental health research in the past, it is more likely that the E part of the equation will cause the researcher difficulty. There are numerous detailed personality and attitude theories and scales at the individual level, but there exists much less to draw on when trying to conceptualise and assess relevant aspects of people's social environments. Often we have to be content with little more than what Bronfenbrenner (1988) has termed a 'social address'. For example we may know little more than that a family is of a particular size or particular social class or ethnic background. What we need to know is, more precisely, what it is about the environment of the family so categorised that interacts with characteristics of family members to produce an effect on behaviour, experience or development.

Along with a number of important social behaviour theorists we can conceive of the social environment as existing on a number of different levels. One of these theorists is Barker who made extensive use of the notion of a 'behaviour setting'. According to Barker (1968, p.17) behaviour settings were, '... stable extra-individual units with great coercive power over the behaviour that occurs within them'. Although he was principally interested in small-scale behaviour settings such as school classes, shops, offices, and meeting rooms, Baker recognised that there were systems within systems related to one another in a hierarchy of authority and influence. For example an individual class was part of a larger system consisting of a school as a whole, and the latter in turn was part of the school system controlled by a Board at the level of the town or county. The same would be true of the hierarchical relationship between an individual health service unit, such as a community mental health centre, a hospital ward, or a group home, and the larger community service or hospital of which it is a part, and, higher still, the regional or national policy-making and planning system that influences the local service.

Bronfenbrenner (1979) also used the analogy of nested assemblies of systems within systems, extending, as Table 15.1 shows, from micro-level systems such as home, school, or treatment unit, to macro-level systems consisting of the wider pattern of prevailing ideas and norms common to the whole community. The two intermediate levels are particularly interesting because they represent powerful but less obvious ways in which the social environment can affect the experience of individuals. The mesosystem had an especially important part to play in Bronfenbrenner's own theory of development. His central idea here was that human development would be positively enhanced if two micro-level settings in which a developing person was involved (e.g. home and school for a young child) were strongly and positively linked rather than weakly or negatively related. The exo-level captures his insight that aspects of the social environment might be crucially important for individuals, even though the latter might have no personal, first-hand knowledge of the settings concerned. The influence of people's places of work on the psychological well-being of other members of their families is a good example.

TABLE 1
Systems at four levels (based on Bronfenbrenner, 1979)

Micro-level	Systems of which the individual person has direct experience on a regular basis, e.g. home, school, work group, club.
Meso-level	System consisting of two or more of a person's micro-level systems and the links between them, eg. home–school, hospital–patient's family, mother's family–father's family after separation.
Exo-level	Systems that influence the person and the person's micro- and meso-level systems, but which the person has no direct experience of him/herself, e.g. a school governing body, a parent's place of work, the county transport department.
Macro-level	Systems on a larger scale that determine the prevailing ideology and the social structure within which the individual person and his/her micro-, meso-, and exo-level systems operate, e.g. current rate of unemployment, other conditions of the labour market, gender roles in society.

Good research on people-in-their-settings needs, therefore, to provide some kind of link between the behaviour or experience of individual people and some aspect of social settings or systems. The models described by Barker and Bronfenbrenner by no means exhaust the ways in which we can think about the social environment, but they do provide a useful starting point. In attempting this kind of research it is useful to ask oneself (1) what characteristics of social settings or systems are being studied and at what level, and (2) what ideas are being tested about how these characteristics interact with and influence the lives of the individual actors involved. In the remainder of this chapter we shall see how a number of researchers have approached this difficult task of carrying out research that is truly about people, their social settings, and the links between the two.

SOME EXAMPLES OF PEOPLE-IN-SETTINGS RESEARCH

The following examples have been chosen to illustrate how (i) theory, (ii) research design, and (iii) research methods, can be used to serve the aim of carrying out research that does justice to the principle of interactionism.

Theory

It is generally the case that research is more satisfactory if it is solidly anchored in good theory. Otherwise there are dangers of 'reinventing the wheel' and, particularly given the nature of people-in-settings research, of feeling quite adrift and overcome by the complexity of it all. It can also give a greater sense of satisfaction to be able to contribute to the testing and development of theory while producing findings that are relevant to the problem immediately to hand. Thereby one is really being a 'scientist-practitioner'.

A good example of theory-derived behaviour-setting research was Barker and Gump's (1964) comparison of large and small high schools. They were interested in testing a prediction derived from responsibility theory (originally termed 'manning' theory) that in settings where there are relatively few individuals compared to the number of roles that have to be performed (settings that are relatively underoccupied or 'undermanned' in the original terminology) there would be greater opportunity and felt pressure for individuals to take on roles and positions of greater involvement or responsibility. As predicted, pupils in small schools were found to participate in a greater range of behaviour settings, and were twice as often active performers in those settings. For example they were more likely to be active performers in team sports, in artistic pursuits, or in task-oriented roles. This study also provided a good illustration of the way in which a characteristic of a behaviour setting can interact with individual characteristics: size of school made the greatest difference to children from lower socio-economic status homes and those with lower IQs, who tended to be the ones without roles in the larger schools where there were fewer roles available per pupil.

This is an interesting example for a number of reasons. For one thing, it was like a lot of the best research, elegantly simple in conception. The research question could be simply stated: Are pupils in smaller schools more involved in school than those in larger schools? It also had the distinct advantage that one of the principal variables—size of school—was no trouble to assess. It also had the great strength that the question was derived from a theory of how people behave in different types of settings. Hence a positive finding strengthened the general theory as well as providing results of interest to school planners, teachers, pupils, and parents. Indeed the theory of active engagement in responsible and valued roles is of very wide applicability in the psychology of health and development (O'Donnell,1980).

A second study illustrating the use of a theoretical concept—autonomy among staff of a human service organisation in this case—was that conducted by Tizard (1975) on staff behaviour in 13 residential nurseries. All were intended to be run on 'family group care' lines with groups of six children each, with their own rooms and personal nursing staff, but in practice there were marked differences in the degree to which nursing staff were truly autonomous in providing child care for their groups. On the basis of their observations in the nurseries, Tizard and her colleagues categorised nurseries on the basis of unit autonomy. At one extreme were nurseries with low nurse autonomy, effectively run centrally by the matrons (Tizard, 1975, p.106):

> Decisions were made on an entirely routine basis or else referred to the matron. Each day was strictly time-tabled, the matron would make frequent inspections of each group, and freedom of the nurse and child was very limited. The children were moved through the day 'en bloc' ... The nurse had little more autonomy than the children, e.g. she would have to ask permission to take the children for a walk or to turn on the television set.

At the other extreme were nurseries characterised by high nurse autonomy (ibid, p.107):

The staff were responsible for shopping, cooking, making excursions with the children and arranging their own day. The children could move freely about the house and garden and the staff rarely referred a decision to the matron ... The nurse's role, in fact, approximated more closely to that of a foster-mother. Since she could plan her own day and was not under constant surveillance she could treat the children more flexibly.

It was predicted, and found, that the more autonomous staff would spend more time talking to the children in their care, and more time playing, reading, and giving information to them. What is more, children in units with more independent nursing staff had higher scores on tests of verbal comprehension. Here, then, we have a study that begins to unravel some of the complexities of people in their settings. We see nurses being influenced in their work by the authority systems governing their work settings, and we see them in turn 'passing on' some of this influence to the children. There is even evidence consistent with the expectation that the effects of this social process will be evident in the measured verbal abilities of the children. Note, however, that this study must have involved a lot of very careful and detailed observation of both nurse autonomy and nurse–child interaction, not to mention a lot of preliminary work in negotiating researcher access to a range of nursery units. One price that is paid for doing such detailed work in small social systems is the corresponding smallness of N (the number of 'units' in the analysis i.e. 13 in this case). In this study, for example, it turned out that nurse autonomy was probably correlated with a relatively favourable staff-to-child ratio. The latter could, therefore, have been the more important variable and the numbers were far too small to tease this out statistically. The great gain of this kind of work, on the other hand, is the possibility of explicating complex social processes, which, with additional research may build to a richer understanding of person–settings interaction and its effects on relevant human behaviour and mental health.

The third and final study to be described in this section is of particular interest to the present author, not only because of its subject matter, but also because of the theory on which it was based. Bennett, Wolin, Reiss, and Teitelbaum (1987) set out to examine one possible environmental mechanism that might explain why the offspring of parents with alcohol problems are around twice as likely as other people to experience such problems themselves as adults. Their work focused on family rituals— especially family dinner times and holidays—and the theory that if these were not well preserved in the family of origin then it would be difficult for the offspring to recreate a sound family tradition in their own adult families. The sample of married offspring of parents with drinking problems was recruited from both treatment agencies and newspaper advertisements. Offspring and spouse were separately interviewed with a focus on family life as a child, and were then interviewed together focusing on present family life. The main variables to do with family of origin rituals, their maintenance in the face of parental drinking problems, and their transmission into the lives of the new families were coded according to a detailed instruction manual. Sons of fathers with drinking problems were found to be the most likely to show 'transmission' of drinking problems into adulthood, but after allowing for this risk factor, protective factors were found to include: whether dinner rituals remained 'distinctive' (i.e. minimally altered) in the family of origin even during the parent's heaviest drinking years; whether the spouse's family of origin included dinner rituals at a high level; and whether there had been a high level of 'planfullness' or 'deliberateness' on the part of offspring and spouse in choosing to follow the family ritual of one or other family of origin.

The Bennett et al. study, as well as being soundly based on theory and taking great pains in the recruitment of an appropriate sample, also provides an example of the use of semi-structured interviews to obtain data about social processes, and we shall turn to it again in the section on research methods.

Research design

Settling on a design that enables the research question(s) to be answered with a reasonable degree of confidence is one of the hardest aspects of doing research. Because of constraints of time, resources, availability of participants, etc., it is always tempting to settle for a design that cannot logically answer the question posed (e.g. omitting to include a control group when the question under investigation clearly calls for one). To put it another way, there are always potential 'threats' to the validity of the answers or conclusions reached at the end, and the object of the process of choosing a suitable design at the outset is to reduce those threats to a minimum (Campbell & Stanley, 1963). Note that the object is not to eliminate these threats altogether: there are always constraints in doing research and there is never a perfect design. All research designs have some weaknesses.

People-in-settings research poses more design problems than most. Experimental designs are difficult to achieve. But as we shall see they are not impossible and a range of quasi-experimental designs are also available. Furthermore this kind of research does lend itself to lateral thinking about design, and there is now a wide variety of allowable designs to choose from. The following examples illustrate: the use of experimental design; quasi-experimental design; large sample survey design; an ecological, area study; intensive, small N research; and use of the case study approach. Each has been used to investigate some aspect of the relationship between people and their settings.

An experiment in increased decision-making

Jackson's (1983) study of nurses, clerical workers, and technicians working in a hospital out-patient department is one that succeeded in manipulating participation in decision-making within an experimental design. The hospital had brought in new regulations requiring regular and frequent staff meetings, and half the out-patient units were chosen at random to start immediately by holding at least two meetings a month from then on. Three and six months later, role conflict, role ambiguity, and emotional strain were all lower in those units that had made the change, and perceived influence was greater. Based on the multivariate statistical technique know as 'path analysis' (which consists of a series of multiple regression analyses) Jackson concluded that the process whereby increased participation might be having an effect was of the kind shown in Fig. 15.1.

Evaluating a crisis intervention service

Although random assignment is rarely practical when doing people-in-settings research, a wide variety of quasi-experimental designs are possible, each of which offers a measure of control and hence some protection against threats to the validity of conclusions. One of the most powerful of such designs of use for evaluating a service intervention within a complex service delivery system, is an 'interrupted time series with non-equivalent comparison group' design (Campbell & Stanley, 1963). Figure 15.2 shows the major findings from a study of a mental health crisis intervention project that employed exactly such a design. A principal aim was to reduce psychiatric hospital admissions, and the results of using this research design give good grounds for concluding that this had been achieved. By plotting admissions for three-month intervals starting two years before the project started and continuing for another three years thereafter (the 'interrupted time series' element) it was possible to show (both by visual inspection of the Figure and by using appropriate statistics that showed a significant change in the slope of the plot after the start of the project) that a reduction in admissions had occurred in the area (or 'sub-zone' as they called it) covered by the new project. Confidence in the conclusions is much strengthened, however, by the plotting of data from a 'comparison' area. The latter was chosen to be as similar as possible to the

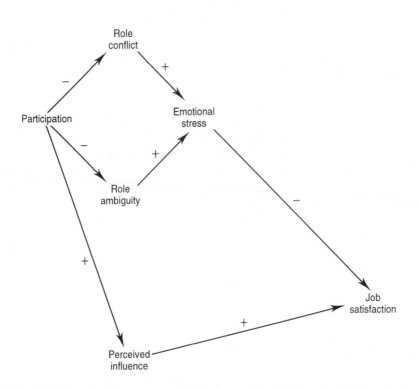

FIG. 15.1. Causal pathways suggested by the results of Jackson's (1983) study of participation in decision-making.

experimental area in terms of demographic characteristics and overall health care policies, and data were collected over the same period of time. There was an absence of significant change in hospital admissions for the comparison area.

Studying the effects of women's employment on mental health

Most research on people-in-settings, however, does not employ an experimental or quasi-experimental design. There are many other possibilities, depending on the research question, and they vary in many respects. In terms of N, or sample size, for example, they vary from large N sample surveys to N=1 case studies. Rosenfield (1989), for example, used data from three existing survey data sets (with a total N of over 1000) in the USA to study rates of anxiety and depression in different groups of women depending on whether or not they were employed outside the home, level of earned income, whether they had children at home, and whether they described employment as creating greater

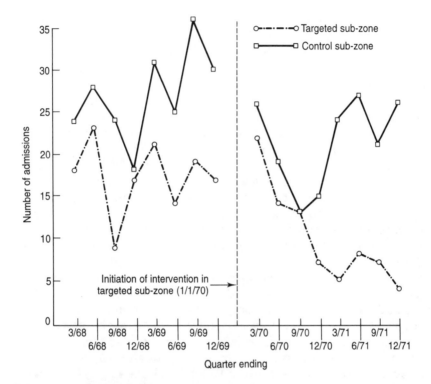

FIG. 15.2. Use of time-series analysis with comparison group, showing the effect of introducing a crisis intervention service. Reproduced by permission from Delaney, Seidman, and Willis, 1978.

demands on them. Rosenfield was able to show that anxiety and depression rates were only low for women with outside employment (which had been predicted by many people on the grounds that this would equalise women's and men's power resources) when earned income was similar to men's, and when outside work did not produce extra burden. Of particular interest here is the link between the two social settings of home and work. It is difficult enough for research to grapple with the complexities of single social systems or settings, but there is increasing recognition that the lives of individuals are affected not just by social settings in isolation but by two or more settings in combination; whether they create complementary or contradictory demands and opportunities for individuals, and whether they are connected and in what ways. This important idea corresponds to Bronfenbrenner's meso-level system.

Rosenfield (1992) has since extended this research, finding evidence from the same survey data that husbands' levels of anxiety or depression are relatively high when their wives are in outside employment, but only if their income relative to their wives is decreased as a result and their share of domestic work increased. This can be seen as an example of the working of Bronfenbrenner's exo-level system in so far as aspects of women's work settings (such as negotiations of pay) are seen to have an impact on the husbands' mental health even though the husbands may have no direct experience of or influence on those settings.

The strengths and weaknesses of the type of research carried out by Rosenfield are complementary to those of some of the smaller N research projects described later. A large N is necessary in order to construct categories based on even as few as three or four variables in order to have sufficient statistical power to test with any confidence an hypothesis that the categories differ in terms of variables such as anxiety or depression. Survey methodology with forced-choice responses for relatively quick analysis is almost certainly necessary. Indeed Rosenfield's ingenuity in using existing survey data sets is to be admired; it may often be possible to negotiate the use of other researchers' data and sometimes data sets are available to researchers nationally (e.g. the National Census, and data from national cohorts such as the National Child Development Study). An inevitable weakness of this kind of research, however, is bound to be the relative superficiality of some of the measures. For example in Rosenfield's research the measure of division of housework was based on a single item asking whether it was the responsibility of the respondent primarily, was shared, or was primarily the responsibility of someone else.

The causes of childhood road accidents

A study that also used a largish N but gathering data in a very different way was that conducted by Bagley (1992) into the social and personal correlates of child pedestrian and bicycle injuries. He carried out an 'ecological' analysis by examining the records of 400 such injuries at the accident and emergency department of the main hospital in one English town, in order to study the areas of the town in which the child victims lived. He found that children who had had such accidents were distributed very unevenly across the 100 or so enumeration districts into which the town could be divided, there being particular clusters of accidents in a central city area characterised by cheap, low-quality housing, and in a pre-war edge-of-town estate of poor quality with public housing close to a busy main road, with many poor families and high rates of delinquency. Regression analyses showed that characteristics of the enumeration districts that accounted for much of the variation in accident rates included: amount of traffic flow in the area between 3 and 5m; the distance a child had to travel to find a protected play-space;

proportion of families in Classes IV or V (according to the Registrar General's classification system); population per acre; juvenile crime rate; and rate of referral to child psychiatric clinics. This exercise in itself demonstrates the creative use of available documents and records which are often neglected by mental health researchers who feel they need to collect new data of their own.

Bagley went further, however, and set out to test the idea that some of the same factors might discriminate those children who did and did not have accidents *within* the high-risk districts. This is important, as it is mistaken to assume that the same factors that differentiate high- from low-risk areas also discriminate high- from low-risk individuals (this common assumption is often referred to as 'the ecological fallacy'). Bagley asked teachers in three primary schools in the central city high-risk area to identify children who had experienced such accidents, and they were then compared on a number of variables with randomly selected children matched for sex and school class. This analysis also found that Class IV and V and living somewhere that involved crossing a busy street to school or play-space differentiated accident and no-accident children, but other significant factors suggested that some children might be individually 'accident prone'. For example, accident children were more likely to have been involved with police or social agencies, and to have been involved in other types of accident, had lower scores on a standardised measure of verbal reasoning, and were rated by teachers as having more emotional and behavioural problems on a standardised measure. Taken together, then, the two parts of this exemplary study begin to unravel the combined environmental and individual factors that put certain children at more than average risk of accidents.

Living with families: An intensive study

At the other end of the scale, at least in terms of N, are intensive studies of small numbers of people-in-settings (see also Chapter 14). A particularly interesting example is Vetere and Gale's (1987) study of nine families who had had contact with a clinic for the treatment of childhood psychological difficulties. They chose a highly innovative and intensive design that involved the researcher living with a family in the latter's own home for a period of four to seven days. Needless to say this was very demanding on the researcher who, according to Vetere and Gale (1987, p.90) '... rose with them [the family] in the morning and retired once they had gone to bed. Throughout the day the family was tracked within the house and garden, on shopping trips, outings, religious meetings, and social calls'. The researchers naturally did not follow family members into places where it would have been too intrusive, and did not normally go with them to work or school. No notes were taken in front of the family, and each hour the researcher retreated to somewhere private to record observations into a dictaphone. Complete transcripts of the recorded notes were produced. Notes were to be descriptive rather than interpretive as the following short extract illustrates (ibid, pp.136–137):

> Tom (father) went upstairs to have a bath and I went into the kitchen to watch Sal (mother) prepare the evening meal. Pete (elder son) joined us. We were having plaice for tea and Sal was frying it. Pete said he didn't like fish and wanted something done separately. Sal expressed surprise at the fact that he didn't like it but Pete insisted with a very tired air that she knew that he didn't like fish. John (younger son) popped his head round the door and said he would be having fish for tea as he quite liked it.

Space can not begin to do justice to the results of this exciting piece of research. Suffice it to say that these data, supplemented with the results of special procedures such as repertory grids completed by two members of the same family, were analysed in a variety of ways, some highly statistical (e.g. coding social behaviours according to a modified Interaction Process Analysis coding scheme, and examining contingencies between one social act and the next) and others much more interpretive. The following is a short extract from the latter type of analysis of material from the same family, using 'distance-regulation' theory as the framework (ibid. p.136):

> The father's involvement in the external world extends beyond normal working hours. His associates are males and women are not welcome in their company. This distance from the home is complemented by boundaries within the home ... Affective tone between husband and wife and elder son is negative. Mother still clings to her own mother and has not freed herself for a full relationship with her spouse. Power is vested in the elder son who makes many day-to-day decisions.

The participant observer method used by Vetere and Gale is quite new to behavioural and mental health research and is still comparatively rare, but it shows how a bold step can be taken to design research in such a way that data are produced that could not possibly be obtained with more conventional research designs.

A case study of the life and death of one hospital

The last design to be illustrated in this section is the single 'case study', a form of research that Bromley (1986), for one, views as fundamental to the human sciences. He believes it has been neglected and has acquired a poor reputation in the behavioural and mental health field partly because in the past many single 'case histories' have adopted a less than rigorous approach to the use of evidence. Case studies take many forms but the one chosen here is a book-length account of one private psychiatric hospital in the USA which opened in 1950 and closed a mere 10 years later (Stotland & Kobler, 1965).

The account of the life and death of this one institution was the product of a collaboration between a deeply involved 'insider' (Kobler) who joined the hospital staff as Chief Clinical Psychologist, and a Social Psychologist (Stotland) who started to work with Kobler on a study of a suicide 'epidemic' that occurred at the hospital during the year before it closed. The research developed into a complete history of the hospital based on interviews with 83 people and an analysis of nursing notes rescued from destruction at the eleventh hour. Not all case studies are on this scale of course and it is impossible to summarise the results in a few words. Among the major themes that appear in the book, however, are two that recur here and in other case studies of naturally occurring organisational change. One is the constant interaction between the contribution of powerful individuals (charismatic leaders in the form of Medical Directors or Board members figure large in the account, as do individuals cast in the role of destructive influences) and the structure and functioning of the institution itself (the power of the Board containing founder members of strong psychoanalytical persuasion was one such factor). A second theme is the negative spiralling of events leading to eventual crisis and disaster. A detailed case study like this one of an organisation, or one built around the experiences of an individual person, a family, or a group, can provide an illumination of individual and social processes that complements the findings of research based on larger numbers and statistical findings. Both kinds of research are legitimate and both are necessary.

Research methods

Research 'methods' here refers to the particular procedures whereby key concepts or variables are operationalised. This might include a specified set of instructions for coding a feature of interpersonal interaction (as in the Interaction Process Analysis used by Vetere & Gale, 1987) or a standard set of questionnaire items for assessing the perceived 'atmosphere' or 'climate' of a setting according to individuals who participate in it (as in the various scales developed by Moos, e.g. 1974, for assessing the perceived atmosphere of hospital wards, community-oriented treatment programmes, and families). In the case of people-in-settings research we are looking especially for ways of operationalising concepts that truly integrate settings and the individuals that inhabit them. We are particularly interested in variables that are not simply the properties of individual people nor simply properties of their settings, but which are genuinely people-in-setting variables.

A variety of research methods have already been described in the previous sections in the course of examining theories and designs. The further examples that follow illustrate: the detailed study of interactions recorded on video; structured questioning on a topic such as social support; and the use of semi-structured interviews analysed quantitatively or qualitatively.

Women's assertiveness in work team meetings

A study that was carried out while the researcher was a postgraduate student sought to examine responses to women's assertive behaviour at work (Corner, 1993). Weekly business meetings of a small number of multi-disciplinary teams working in the mental health or mental handicap fields served as the settings in which assertiveness, or lack of it, was to be observed. A small number of such meetings were videotaped in their entirety. The recordings were examined in minute detail and an edited tape plus a transcription were made containing sequences of interaction that contained assertive utterances. Two or three weeks after such a meeting each participant was individually interviewed using a procedure known as Interpersonal Process Recall (IPR; Kagan, 1984). This involved showing the interviewee key sections of the tape with accompanying passages of transcript, and asking a number of standard but open-ended questions about how the interviewees construed what was occurring and how they had felt at different points during the interaction that had occurred. Replies were coded according to, among other things, the types of attributions that were made to explain why assertiveness had or had not occurred. Corner found that women team members were often conscious of not speaking up in meetings and they were much more likely to attribute not speaking up to 'internal' reasons (e.g. 'lack confidence'; 'not strong enough') than were men, who were more likely to make 'external' attributions (e.g 'lack of time'; 'others don't allow me the opportunity'). Regarding the reactions that women elicited from others when they were assertive, previous research has been inconsistent, some research finding that women's assertiveness produced a more negative response than did men's, other research failing to find this effect. Corner hypothesised that it might depend on the type of assertiveness displayed: 'simple' or unqualified assertion on the part of women might be badly received, whereas 'empathic' assertion (i.e. assertive utterances qualified by explanations or statements implying appreciation of how the recipient felt, etc.) might be well received. For men there would be no difference. There was an effect in the data but not exactly the one Corner had expected. Whereas other team members responded in a rather similar way to simple and empathic assertion by women, men's simple assertion was better received than men's empathic assertion which was often responded to in a hostile way.

In this research the methods of videotaping naturally occurring interaction plus the subsequent IPR interviews paid dividends, but both were time consuming to put into effect and produced data that were complicated and time consuming to analyse. Arranging for video-recording to be done in the natural 'field' setting of a health team's office rather than in the laboratory, was itself no easy matter, and several participants felt that their behaviour had been affected to some extent by the presence of the camera.

Comparing the social support networks of psychiatric and medical patients

Research on social support is exemplified by Tolsdorf's (1976) comparison of the social support networks of 10 psychiatric patients (all with diagnoses of 'schizophrenia') and 10 medical patients. Social support has become a topic of great interest in health research in recent years and there exists a variety of methods for approaching it. There are, for example, a variety of longer and shorter structured interview procedures for assessing the availability and/or perceived adequacy of a person's social support (e.g. Henderson et al., 1980; Power, Champion, & Aris, 1988). Tolsdorf, however, employed the structural network approach involving a listing of all the individuals in a focal person's network (they had to be known by name, to have an ongoing personal relationship of some kind with the focal person, and some contact at least once a year). Questions were then asked about 'content areas' involved in relationships with each member of the network (whether they were linked by reason of being primary kin, secondary kin, friend, economic ties, recreational interests, etc.), what functions a member of the network served for and medical patient groups. The networks of the former had lower 'relationship density'; they had fewer 'multiplex' relationships; contained a higher proportion of kinship members and linkages; and more 'functional indegree', less 'functional outdegree', and a higher proportion of 'asymmetric relationships'.

TABLE 15.2
Social network variables (based on Tolsdorf, 1976)

Structure	Content	Function
Size The number of people included in the network	*Relationship density* Average number of content areas per relationship	*Functional indegree* Number of functions served for the focal person
	Multiplex relationships Number of relationships containing more than one content area	*Functional outdegree* Number of functions served by the focal person
Adjacency density The number of relationships between people in the network as a proportion of those possible	*Kinship members* Number of focal person's links that are with kin	*Asymmetric relationships* Number of relationships with functions given and received imbalanced
	Kinship links Number of all network links that are accounted for by kin	*Functional people* Number of people giving emotional support, advice, or feedback

Using less structured interviews

The Tolsdorf study represents one way of obtaining data about people-in-settings on the basis of interviews with individual informants: in this case the questions were quite highly structured and the means of converting the replies into results quite mathematical and mechanical. Individual interviews are very often used in people-in-settings research but the styles of interview and ways of using the data vary greatly. The Bennett et al. (1987) research, described earlier, provides a contrast with the Tolsdorf study, because questions were less structured and replies were open-ended and later coded by the researchers. But for the interview data to be used in this way it is essential that the variables (e.g. 'distinctiveness of dinner time ritual' in the Bennett et al. research) be very clearly conceptualised and precisely defined. Even though Bennett et al. paid great attention to this kind of detail, inter-rater reliability coefficients were sometimes quite modest (in the range 0.4–0.6).

Although the Bennett et al. method of carefully coding certain pre-defined constructs (either as simply present or absent, or using a rating scale of degree of severity) is one way of using semi-structured interview data to do person-in-settings research, it is by no means the only one. One alternative is to make a count of the number of times certain kinds of remark are made by an interviewee. This is the method that has been used for assessing degree of 'criticism' expressed by a close relative (mother, wife, etc.) when interviewed about a recently hospitalised or recently diagnosed psychiatrically ill family member. Along with 'emotional over-involvement', which is rated from the interview recording and transcript using the same kind of method used by Bennett et al., the number of critical remarks made by the relative is used to arrive at a categorisation of the family as high or low on 'expressed emotion' (e.g. Kuipers & Bebbington, 1988). For purposes of this research, what constitutes a 'critical remark', is very carefully defined. Non-verbal components of an utterance, including tone of voice, change of speaking rate, and emphasis, are as important as verbal aspects; hence tape-recordings of the interview are essential. This use of interview material therefore has an observational flavour to it: it is not just what a person says that gives an indication of social events that may be occurring at home, but also how often certain things are said, and how they are said. The expressed emotion line of research has undoubtedly been very successful, partly because of its clear operational definitions, and partly because of its consistent success in predicting relapse on the basis of high family-expressed emotion.

The experiences of close relatives of people with drinking or drug problems

Although the foregoing may be thought of as different ways of obtaining quantitative data from the open-ended material generated by semi-structured interviews, the qualitative research approach provides a contrasting way of using such material that does not necessarily involve assigning numerical values (Henwood & Pigeon, 1992; Stiles, 1993; Chapter 12 in the present volume). Research currently being conducted by the present author and colleagues illustrates one way in which this can be done (Orford et al., 1992). We are interested in exploring the experiences of close relatives of people with drinking or drug problems, how and why they cope and react in certain ways, and how these ways of coping are related to their personal experiences and social positions, and to their own health. Ninety families have been so far recruited, like Bennett et al. via both agencies and advertising. Semi-structured interviews are held with one close relative in each family and in sub-samples interviews are also held with second relatives, the problem alcohol or drug users, and with other family members in a joint family meeting. Interviews are lengthy, averaging four to five hours. It often comes as a surprise to those who are not familiar with this sort of research that interviewees can tolerate such long interviews, which are often, but not always, conducted in a single session. Most researchers who have worked in this field, however, know that people can usually tolerate, indeed welcome, the opportunity to talk at length about family problems. In fact it is the interviewers who experience the greater difficulty! In our research they are required to make detailed notes at the time including exact quotations from the interviewee, to check their notes over within 24 hours of conducting the interview, and to prepare a detailed written report within a few days. These reports average around 15 word-processed, single-spaced pages of text which then form the material for analysis.

To cut a long story short, we are looking in the analysis for recurring themes, for detailed understanding and examples of the social events or processes underlying these themes, and possible links between them. Once provisional themes have been identified, the process of conducting qualitative analysis in this way is much aided by use of one of a number of programmes available for PCs—the one we use is Textbase Alpha. Themes are given code names, and codes are assigned to passages of text which may be of any length and which may overlap. The programme can print out a whole interview with all codes shown in the margin, and can collate and print out all examples of a certain code from one or more interviews.

One of the codes being used in our present research for example, is COPCON which signifies 'controlling coping' on the part of a relative. As a result of collecting numerous instances of COPCON (four instances taken from two interviews are shown in Table 15.3) we are now able to document in considerable detail a variety of sub-types of controlling efforts (e.g. keeping a careful watch on the user; putting friends off; making a rule about drinking or drug taking at home), the explanations relatives give for trying to control (e.g. to cut down the user's consumption; the relative felt the user and the situation were out of control; concern over the user's safety), and what relatives believe to be some of the consequences of trying to control (which are largely negative, e.g. the user resists attempts to control; it leads to confrontations which upset the relative).

Would-be researchers should never embark on qualitative research of this kind in order to escape the rigours of quantification and statistics, as qualitative research is equally if not more demanding! Novice qualitative researchers often find it particularly daunting when faced with their data in the form of many pages of text and no very clear directions about how to proceed. The process of organising such data is a creative and partly subjective one, and at that stage it is very useful to have extended meetings with research colleagues or other interested parties in order to read over and think creatively about the data and how they can be coded.

The example of our own research just described is that of a comparatively large and externally funded piece of research, but there

TABLE 15.3
Computer-sorted instances of Controlling Coping from two interviews

Print from UK1 of copcon: 114–126
At times it seems her father could be and is violent towards her mother. Verbal violence occurs regularly and physical violence has occurred several times in the past year. At times *F* has verbally intervened in the past but it has made things worse. *F* feels that if she does intervene physically things could turn nasty.

Print from UK1 of copcon: 274–281
F has tried a couple of strategies to reduce her father's drinking. She has both tried to put her father's friends off by telling them not to come round so often and she has also tried to put her father off going out with his friends, whom she feels have an effect on her father's drinking. Putting off her father's friends did initially have a small effect, but it wasn't long-term only temporary. She achieved this by saying her father wasn't in when his friends rang up.

Print from UK2 of copcon: 57–67
About this time *F* realised that he (husband) was drinking small bottles of whiskey as she kept finding them. At this stage she thought he may have a problem with drinking and so she bought a house with the idea that he would stop drinking because he couldn't afford it.

Print from UK2 of copcon: 84–90
At times *F* would go out and when she came back he wasn't there. She said she knew something was wrong when he wasn't in, because he never went out. She used to go out and look for him and many a time found him wandering the streets.

F = Family member being interviewed

are now a number of examples of dissertations successfully completed as part of clinical psychology training, based in each case on between six and twelve lengthy semi-structured interviews. For example Goodbody (1988) interviewed women caring at home for relatives who were dependent by reason of chronic illness or handicap of some kind. She deliberately chose a number of families that between them were experiencing a range of different illnesses and handicaps in order to study what might be common among the backgrounds and experiences of women carers. Titley (1990) interviewed women who were involuntarily infertile and who had been trying unsuccessfully to conceive for a number of years. Both projects produced tentative but detailed models of the social psychological processes involved based on a small number of first-hand accounts. Indeed qualitative research is probably best adapted to this 'inductive', or theory-building, phase of the scientific process rather than to the more 'deductive' or hypothesis testing phase. There are those, however, who argue that, with larger data sets and the use of 'theoretical sampling' (i.e. recruiting participants according to theory rather than aiming for representativeness), qualitative data can be used to test as well as generate theory (Strauss & Corbin, 1990).

Three classic studies

Let us finish with three pieces of research, each of which was a large ambitious study that has rightly become a classic. Beginning researchers will be lucky to be associated with such a project, but we can all at least admire them, take heart from them, and seek to copy aspects of their designs and methods. Each manages in a different way to go a long way towards doing full justice to Lewin's famous equation by really studying the interaction of person and social environment.

Socially redesigning a mental hospital ward

The first, reported by Fairweather (1964), involved the random assignment of psychiatric patients to one or other of two hospital wards that were physically almost identical. One was run on traditional lines with much staff control, whereas the other was organised on 'small group' lines. Patients on the latter ward were given a great deal of decision-making autonomy. They were organised into small groups which were responsible for welcoming new patients, assigning and carrying out tasks, and even advising on fellow patients' progress and ultimate discharge date. The difference in patients' behaviour on the two wards was dramatic. Behaviour was time-sampled by having an observer walk through each ward at random intervals, noting and coding the behaviour of each patient. Patients were more likely to be observed talking to each other on the small group ward, and the more demanding or complex the category of social behaviour the greater the difference. For example the number of times three or more patients were found interacting together was exceedingly small on the traditional ward but considerably greater on the small group ward. On the former ward patients were often asleep or inactive, and incidents of 'pathological behaviour' such as hallucinating were common. These categories were much reduced on the small group ward, and when pathological behaviour did occur it was met with concern rather than indifference. Patients on the small group ward were also much more lively and participative in ward meetings. Two groups of staff were involved in this experiment and they switched wards halfway through the study. Both sets of staff spoke more during traditional ward meetings, but both rated more positively their experiences while working on the small group ward. Finally small group ward patients spent significantly fewer days in hospital.

This study also noted the individual contribution in the form of differences in social behaviour according to diagnosis. Patients with non-psychotic diagnoses were most socially active and those with psychotic diagnoses who had periods of hospitalisation totalling more than four years were the least active. Nevertheless for all patient groups there was greater social activity on the small group ward.

The importance of social climate in secondary schools

The second of our three 'classics' is a study carried out by Rutter and his colleagues (Rutter, Maughan, Mortimore, & Ouston, 1979) on the social climate of 12 inner-city London secondary schools. The research involved record searches, interviews with school staff, pupil questionnaires, and systematic observation of classes. Four outcome criteria were employed: school attendance, pupil behaviour, delinquency record, and exam results. There were large differences between schools in terms of these outcomes and these were associated with variables at a number of levels. At the individual level there were correlations with pupils' verbal reasoning scores and with emotional and conduct problems. At the family level there were correlations with occupational status of the main breadwinner. At the level of school climate—the principal focus of the research—there were correlations with the balance of rewards over punishments, between the behaviour criterion and the percentage of pupils named in assembly for work done, between exam results and amount of pupils' work displayed on the walls, between attendance and prizes for sporting achievements, and between both behaviour and exam results and the percentage of pupils who had taken special responsibilities such as form captain or homework monitor (in line, it may be noted, with predictions from responsibility theory). At the staff system level, examination results correlated with the existence of checks on whether teachers were setting homework. At the 'ecological' level there were correlations between both delinquency and exam results and a categorisation of the areas in which pupils lived ('advantageous', 'middling', or 'disadvantageous') based on a number of variables similar to those used in Bagley's analysis of child accidents. School climate ceased to be a significant correlate of attendance and delinquency once these ecological influences had been statistically controlled, but it remained significant for exam results and pupil behaviour.

The effects on children of economic hardship

The final study to be described is part of a series of studies of parents who were living in Berkeley, California at the time of the economic depression between the two World Wars, and of their children and grandchildren. The findings of Elder and Caspi (1988) were that the mental health of some children was adversely affected by the economic hardship experienced by their families during these years. Whether or not a child was so affected depended on a complex interplay of factors including the child's sex and age at the time of economic hardship, the personal stability of the child's father, and the strength of the father and mother's marital bond. Financial loss to the family was important for the child's adjustment but only if it increased the probability of arbitrary parenting by fathers. As Elder and Caspi put it (1988, p.39), 'As long as discipline is consistently applied, children seemed to be highly resilient under a wide variety of parental styles ...'. Adding further complexity to the picture, it was boys who were in their early childhood when their families were adversely affected economically who were the most affected. The suggestion from the data is that this result may be traceable to the fact that boys lost more in terms of closeness to their fathers without compensation in their relationships to their mothers, whereas young girls lost less in terms of their relationships with their fathers and developed stronger ties with their mothers. Children who were older were less at risk. Indeed there was evidence that for some their mental health may have benefited as a consequence of increased pressure to take on useful adult roles, either inside the home (more often for girls) or outside it (mostly boys).

CONCLUSIONS

I hope the illustrations of research given in this chapter will have inspired intending researchers to believe that it is possible to study the complexity presented by people in their social settings. As in all research it is important to start out with a clear research question (or two at most). In the case of people-in-settings research this should ask in some way about how Person (P) and Environment (E) interact to influence the behaviour, experience, or development of people who occupy that setting.

A research design and research methods then need to be chosen that are appropriate for providing some sort of answer to that question(s). This is a critical stage and it calls for being bold! Don't settle too easily for a safe but weak design or for well-known but weak methods. The range to choose from is vast, particularly now that the field is opening up to designs and methods from the social sciences, such as case study and qualitative research. People-in-settings are inherently complex and we need all the imagination and lateral thinking at our disposal to explore them. Persuade your supervisor to support you in taking a risk!

REFERENCES

Bagley, C. (1992). The urban environment and child pedestrian and bicycle injuries: Interaction of ecological and personality characteristics. *Journal of Community and Applied Social Psychology, 2,* 281-290.

Barker, R. (1968). *Ecological psychology: Concepts and methods for studying the environment of human behavior.* Stanford, CA: Stanford University Press.

Barker, R. & Gump, P. (Eds.) (1964). *Big school, small school.* Stanford, CA: Stanford University Press.

Bennett, L., Wolin, S., Reiss, D., & Teitelbaum, M. (1987). Couples at risk for transmission of alcoholism: Protective influences. *Family Process, 26,* 111-129.

Bromley, D. (1986). *The case-study method in psychology and related disciplines.* Chichester, UK: Wiley.

Bronfenbrenner, U. (1979). *The ecology of human development: Experiments by nature and design.* Cambridge, MA: Harvard University Press.

Bronfenbrenner, U. (1988). Interacting systems in human development. Research paradigms: Present and future. In N. Bolger, A. Caspi, G. Downey, & M. Moorehouse (Eds.), *Persons in context: Developmental processes.* Cambridge: Cambridge University Press.

Campbell, D. & Stanley, J. (1963). Experimental and quasi-experimental designs for research on teaching. In N. Gage (Ed.), *Handbook of research on teaching,* Chicago: Rand McNally.

Corner, A. (1993). *Circumplex models: Theory, methodology and practice.* Unpublished PhD thesis, University of Exeter.

Delaney, J., Seidman, E., & Willis, G. (1978). Crisis intervention and the prevention of institutionalisation. *American Journal of Community Psychology, 6,* 33-45.

Elder, G. & Caspi, A. (1988). Economic stress in lives: Developmental perspectives. *Journal of Social Issues, 44,* 25-45.

Fairweather, G. (Ed.) (1964). *Social psychology in treating mental illness.* New York: Wiley.

Goodbody, L. (1988). Unpublished MSc dissertation, University of Exeter.

Heller, K. (1989). The return to community. *American Journal of Community Psychology, 1,* 71-76.

Henderson, S., Bryne, D., Duncan-Jones, P., Scott, R., & Adcock, S. (1980). Social relationships, adversity and neurosis: A study of associations in a general population sample. *British Journal of Psychiatry, 136,* 574-583.

Henwood, K. & Pigeon, N. (1992). Qualitative research and psychological theorizing. *British Journal of Psychology, 83,* 97-111.

Jackson, S. (1983). Participation in decision making as a strategy for reducing job related strain. *Journal of Applied Psychology, 68,* 3-19.

Kagan, N. (1984). Interpersonal process recall: Basic methods and recent research. In D. Larsen (Ed.), *Teaching psychological skills.* Monterey, CA: Brooks/Coles.

Kuipers, L. & Bebbington, P. (1988). Expressed emotion research in schizophrenia: Theoretical and clinical implications. *Psychological Medicine, 18,* 893-909.

Lewin, K. (1951). *Field theory in social science.* New York: Harper.

Moos, R. (1974). *Evaluating treatment environments: A social ecological approach.* New York: Wiley.

O'Donnell, C. (1980). Environmental design and the prevention of psychological problems. In P. Feldman & J. Orford (Eds.), *Psychological problems: The social context*. Chichester, UK: Wiley.

Orford, J. (1992). *Community psychology: Theory and practice*. Chichester, UK: Wiley.

Orford, J., Rigby, K., Miller, T., Tod, A., Bennett, G., & Velleman, R. (1992). Ways of coping with excessive drug use in the family: A provisional typology based on the accounts of 50 close relatives. *Journal of Community and Applied Social Psychology, 2*, 163-184.

Parkes, K. (1989). Personal control in an occupational context. In A. Steptoe & A. Appels (Eds.), *Stress, personal control and health*. Chichester, UK: Wiley.

Power, M., Champion, L., & Aris, S. (1988). The development of a measure of social support: The significant others (SOS) scale. *British Journal of Clinical Psychology, 27*, 349-358.

Rosenfield, S. (1989). The effects of women's employment: Personal control and sex differences in mental health. *Journal of Health and Social Behavior, 30*,77-91.

Rosenfield, S. (1992). The costs of sharing: Wives' employment and husbands' mental health. *Journal of Health and Social Behavior, 33*, 213-225.

Rutter, M., Maughan, B., Mortimore, P., & Ouston, J. (1979). *Fifteen thousand hours*. London: Open Books.

Stiles, W. (1993). Quality control in qualitative research. *Clinical Psychology Review, 13*, 593-618.

Stotland, E. & Kobler, A. (1965). *Life and death of a mental hospital*. Seattle: University of Washington press.

Strauss, A. & Corbin, J. (1990). *Basics of qualitative research: Grounded theory procedures and techniques*. Newbury Park, CA: Sage.

Titley, M. (1990). Unpublished MSc dissertation, University of Exeter.

Tizard, B. (1975). In J. Tizard, I. Sinclair, & R. Clarke (Eds.), *Varieties of residential experience* London: Routledge & Kegan Paul.

Tolsdorf, C. (1976). Social networks, support and coping: An exploratory study. *Family Process, 15*, 407-417.

Vetere, A.& Gale, A. (1987). *Ecological studies of family life*. Chichester, UK: Wiley.

Wilkinson, R. (1992). Income distribution and life expectancy. *British Medical Journal, 304*, 165-168.

CHAPTER SIXTEEN

Epidemiological and survey methods

David J. Cooke *Glasgow Caledonian University*
and Douglas Inch Centre, Glasgow

Epidemiological methods are, by necessity, different from those adopted in the confines of the laboratory or in carefully controlled clinical trials. Epidemiological data are dirty; samples are rarely complete, independent variables are difficult to control, confounding factors may abound.

The principles and methods of epidemiology are wide ranging yet this chapter must be brief. Because of this constraint, this chapter will only provide a glimpse of some of the basic concepts, the basic techniques, and indeed, some of the basic problems in epidemiology.

Five facets of epidemiology will be considered. Firstly, what is epidemiology and what value and relevance does it have for the research-minded clinician? Secondly, what experimental designs can be applied in epidemiological research? Thirdly, how are suitable measures chosen or developed? Fourthly, having obtained results, how can they be analysed to the greatest effect? Fifthly, what practical problems might be encountered in carrying out epidemiological research and how might these problems be resolved?

WHAT IS EPIDEMIOLOGY?

A good place to begin is to consider the question, what is epidemiology? Leighton (1979, p. 235), perhaps the doyen of psychiatric epidemiology, described it as follows: 'Epidemiology is not only concerned with population rates of illness, but also with detecting factors which are associated with their origin, course and outcome.'

On the most basic level epidemiology is concerned with questions such as how many cases of senile dementia are there in the general population, or how many new cases of depression occur each year? Thus, epidemiology is about detecting and counting cases of disorder or illness.

Leighton's quote indicates that epidemiology goes beyond these simple counting activities. Epidemiologists are concerned with aetiological factors and factors that may ameliorate conditions. Thus epidemiologists will ask questions such as do life events cause depression, do social support networks protect individuals from the effects of stress, does the diet contribute to coronary heart disease and will exercise provide protection against coronary heart disease?

It is thus clear that epidemiology is a broad subject which deals not only with the distribution of illness but also with the causes of illness.

WHY IS EPIDEMIOLOGY IMPORTANT?

Why should the topic be of interest to those working in the field of mental health? There are three important reasons; the first relates to service planning, the second and third relate to our understanding of disorders.

The planning of health services is facilitated by estimating the level of need and demand. The case identification and counting functions of epidemiology can provide the necessary estimates. For example, in the Isle of Wight study neuropsychiatric disorders were studied amongst 2000 school age children (Rutter et al., 1970). Over 6% of the children were found to require treatment or advice, and indeed, 2% were identified as suffering from severe psychiatric disturbance. Only 0.7% of the sample were receiving formal treatment or advice and, therefore, the health care services were providing support for only 10% of the cases of need.

Epidemiological research may not only describe the overall level of need but also it may identify those in greatest need. The work of Brown & Harris (1978a), for example, suggested that the risk of depression is highest amongst working-class women with young children. It could be argued that in times of limited resources, those resources that are available should be mobilised to assist this group.

Thus in principle epidemiological information should be of value to health care planners; unfortunately, in practice little of this information is used. Kreitman (1980, p. 41) described the reality with force: 'The policies advanced by the Department of Health and Social Security and the Scottish Home and Health Departments emerge as pronouncements which scorn the aid of data.'

The second reason to carry out epidemiological research relates to improving our understanding of disease and disorder. Patients studied in hospital and clinics may not make the best subjects. Shepherd, Cooper, Brown and Kalton (1966) showed that only 5% of GP patients with 'conspicuous psychiatric morbidity' were referred for psychiatric consultation. Not only do such patients comprise a small proportion of all those who are disordered or disturbed. but also, they are non-representative. Fahy (1974a, b, 1975) in a series of studies, demonstrated that powerful selective factors operate. For example, of individuals with the same moderate degree of depression, men were much more likely to be referred to a psychiatrist than women.

Goldberg and Huxley (1980) argued that community cases have to pass through four filters before they receive psychiatric in-patient care (Fig. 16.1).

A variety of factors influence transition through each filter; few of these factors are related to symptomatology. Goldberg and Huxley (1980) indicated that referral from the primary care level to the psychiatric services is influenced by the GP's confidence in managing psychiatric problems, his or her attitude towards psychiatrists, the quality and availability of psychiatric services, the attitude of the patient and his or her family towards receiving psychiatric care as well as the presenting symptoms. Thus psychiatric patients are not representative of all those who are disordered: they are the small proportion who have elected or have been selected to become patients. Goldberg and Huxley (1980) argued that of every 250 community cases only six receive psychiatric in-patient care.

This is important because aetiological arguments based on such subjects can be misleading: Ingham and Miller (1976) argued that mythologies have developed about the causes of physical disease when only patients are studied. For example, epidemiological studies of iron deficiency and anaemia demonstrated the lack of a clear association whereas studies of patients had suggested its presence. Epidemiological studies have the advantage of having greater generality.

What other advantages accrue from the study of non-biased samples? Leighton (1979, p. 237) argued that 'Data generated from people in their natural habitat often contains much that is not found in clinics.' Epidemiologists who study people in their natural habitat may detect new types or new syndromes of disturbance. A community study of depression in Glasgow yielded four types of depression which, while showing certain similarities to psychiatric types of depression, also showed marked differences (Cooke, 1980a).

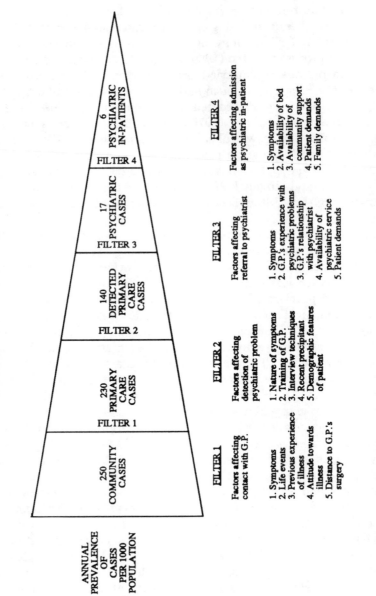

FIG. 16.1 Factors affecting the selection and detection of psychiatric cases. (After Goldberg & Huxley, 1980).

More importantly, if we study people in their natural habitat, then it may be possible to clarify the association between disturbance and other factors and, indeed, between disturbance and potential aetiological factors. Paykel et al. (1969) demonstrated that 'undesirable' events and 'exit' events had a more powerful impact on depression than did events in general. Bebbington, Tennant and Hurry (1981) and Cooke (1981) have demonstrated, in community studies, that life events are associated with neurotic depression but not associated with other forms of depression. Thus the associations between potential causes (e.g. life events) and particular disorders (i.e. neurotic depression) can be clarified using unbiased samples.

My third and final plea in favour of epidemiological studies is that it may be valuable to study people who are not ill or not disturbed. Psychologists are trained to study all forms of behaviour, not just disturbed behaviour. If we base our theories and procedures merely on those who are suffering from psychological disturbance or maladaptive behaviour, we will be less able to identify or evaluate those psychological mechanisms that may lead to the amelioration of problems. It has been argued that an expert on drowning may not be the best person to teach someone to swim. By studying people with no apparent mental illness or behavioural disturbance it may be possible to specify which aspects of their social support network, their lifestyle or their habitual cognitive processes lead them to avoid such difficulties. Having described what epidemiology is and why it should be of interest to the clinician, I will now examine some of the methods used.

THE DESIGN OF EPIDEMIOLOGICAL STUDIES

Epidemiological studies are designed to count cases of disorder but, more importantly, they are designed to assess associations between risk factors and disorders. How can these associations be determined? Studies are often classified by the manner in which subjects are selected—for example, case-control studies versus cohorts studies—and in terms of the time period considered, for example, retrospective studies, prospective studies and cross-sectional studies. Inferences regarding the association between risk factors and disorder are tied to these two dimensions of design.

Case-control studies versus cohort studies

In case-control studies, perhaps more correctly, case-comparison studies, the cases' exposure to risk is compared with that of the controls. In a case-control study the investigator may select cases from one of a variety of sources; from cases diagnosed in the community, from cases diagnosed in a hospital or cases referred to a particular clinic. Controls may be obtained from one or more sources including non-cases from a community sample, patients in hospital who do not have the disorder or any related disorder, or relatives or associates of the cases. Case-control studies are cheaper and less difficult to carry out than cohort studies. Unfortunately, the fundamental problem underlying case-control methodology is that it is not possible to determine what proportion of the total population is represented by either the cases or the controls. Thus the relative frequency of exposure amongst the cases and the controls is not necessarily the same as that in the population of origin.

This is not a problem in cohort studies as the relative frequency of exposure is known. Cohort studies are of two types. In the first type, subjects are grouped in terms of whether they have been exposed to the putative cause. The relative frequency of cases in those exposed, as compared with those who were not exposed, is determined. In the second type, a representative sample of a population is obtained and the subjects are divided into cases and non-cases using standardised techniques.

In both types of cohort design it is possible to determine what proportion of the total population is represented by the cases and the controls: thus it is possible to determine accurately the importance of any risk factor.

Firmer conclusions can be made about the relationship between exposure and a disorder using a cohort design as compared with a case-control design. Cohort studies are frequently used to increase the accuracy of findings obtained with case-control studies. As an example of this process, MacMahon and Pugh (1970) indicated that, in the research on smoking and lung cancer, some 15 case-control studies were published before the first cohort study became available. Unfortunately, when the frequency of a disorder is low, very large cohorts are required if stable estimates of the rate of a disorder and its association with risk factors are to be obtained.

Retrospective, prospective and cross-sectional studies

Time is the second dimension used to describe common epidemiological designs. Designs are either retrospective, prospective or cross-sectional in form.

In retrospective studies the investigator looks back from apparent effects at preceding causes. In studies of depression the investigator may look at life events or social support over the previous 12 months (e.g. Brown & Harris, 1978a; Miller & Ingham, 1979), in physical diseases, such as lung cancer, smoking habits over 20 years may be assessed (Doll & Hill, 1952).

In prospective studies the investigator identifies putative causes at one time point and follows the subjects to determine who becomes disordered and who does not. In addition, recovery can be examined. With depression this time interval may be 12 months or more (Brown, Craig & Harris, 1985; Surtees, Sashidharan & Dean, 1986). With physical disorders, such as lung cancer, the time period may be 20 years or more (Doll & Peto, 1976).

In cross-sectional studies, the investigator measures cause and effect occurring at the same point of time.

These different designs have their own particular advantages and disadvantages. These are outlined in Table 16.1

The major advantages of a retrospective study are that they are relatively cheap to carry out because comparatively small numbers of subjects are interviewed on only one occasion. This has the concomitant advantage that results are obtained quickly. Retrospective studies are most efficient when used to study rare disorders because it is possible to compare all cases of the rare disorder with suitable controls. However,

TABLE 16.1
Advantages and disadvantages of three common epidemiological designs

Type of study	Advantages		Disadvantages	
Retrospective	1.	Cost comparatively low	1.	Estimates of risk less accurate
	2	Results are obtained quickly		
	3.	Efficient when considering rare diseases	2.	Recall may cause distortion
	4.	Small samples are required		
Prospective	1.	Less bias—information is recorded before outcome is known	1.	Cost comparatively high— large samples observed over long periods
	2.	Efficient when considering rare risk factors	2.	Delay between selection of subjects and the development of disorder
	3.	Multiple outcomes can be studied	3.	Inefficient when considering rare diseases
			4.	Periodic examination of subject may influence outcome
Cross-sectional	1.	Low cost	1.	Estimates of risk less accurate
	2.	Results are obtained quickly		
	3.	Useful in studies of sub-clinical conditions where records are unlikely to exist	2.	Cannot be used to establish the time sequence between putative cause and effect

there are disadvantages with this type of study. Estimates of risk are less accurate. Also, when dealing with subject recall there may be significant distortion of recall through the active re-organisation of memory (Bartlett, 1932). Where medical records are used, there are problems of inaccurate or incomplete recording.

The advantages of prospective studies mirror the disadvantages of retrospective studies. Information obtained in prospective studies is less likely to be biased because it is recorded before the investigator knows about the onset of the disorder. Prospective studies are particularly efficient when examining risk factors which are unusual in the population because all cases of exposure can be studied. Thus it would be an appropriate design for studying people exposed to high levels of radiation.

Despite these distinct advantages, prospective studies have distinct disadvantages. The cost is comparatively high because it is necessary to study large numbers of subjects over long periods of time. The very nature of the design results in there being a considerable delay in results becoming available because of the delay between the selection of subjects and the development of the disorder. Prospective studies are particularly inefficient when rare diseases are being considered because large samples are required if a sufficient number of cases is to be identified. This problem can be overcome by selecting a sample in which there is likely to be a high inception rate for new disorders. The study of Brown et al. (1985) is a good example of this approach. On the basis of their previous work, they decided to select a sample of working-class women with one child at home. By doing this they ensured a high inception rate of new disorders in the period under which the study was carried out. A final difficulty with prospective studies is that periodic examination of subjects may affect the outcome of the study. This is particularly true in studies of psychological disorders where investigators may adopt, or may be manoeuvred into, a counselling role.

The final type of study is the cross-sectional study. Cross-sectional studies have the distinct advantage that they are quick and relatively inexpensive to carry out. They are particularly useful when an investigator is taking a preliminary look at a problem or when he or she is investigating sub-clinical conditions where reliable records are unlikely to exist. Unfortunately, cross-sectional studies suffer from the significant disadvantage that they cannot be used to establish the temporal relationship between a putative cause and a putative effect. Thus they cannot be used to evaluate causal mechanisms. For example, an investigator may study the serum cholesterol levels of subjects with coronary heart disease and compare these levels with those obtained in subjects without coronary heart disease. In general, there would be an elevation in those with coronary heart disease. It is only possible, however, to make the causal inference that elevated serum cholesterol level leads to coronary heart disease when it is demonstrated that there is an increased rate of coronary heart disease in those people whose serum cholesterol level was elevated on a previous occasion. Cross-sectional studies, therefore, can only provide suggestive evidence. They are of little value in epidemiological research which attempts to make aetiological statements.

SELECTING MEASUREMENT PROCEDURES

The investigator has chosen a design to suit his or her purpose and resources. The next step is to decide how to measure the constructs that may be of importance.

Epidemiological measurement techniques have proliferated and developed in the last decade. It could be argued that concern with method has eclipsed concern for substantive results.

There are two broad options in the acquisition of a measuring instrument; the investigator can use an instrument that is already developed or can develop his or her own. The selection of an instrument 'off the shelf' has many advantages. It is efficient in terms of time and in terms of development costs. Developed instruments are generally buttressed by evidence of reliability and validity; the investigator can thus be more certain of the results. Results obtained with such an instrument are easier to communicate. This may have the concomitant and not inconsiderable advantage that editors are more likely to publish the findings of the study.

Instruments have been developed to measure a wide range of characteristics from psychiatric symptoms (e.g. PSE-Wing, Nixon, Mann & Left, 1977) and social support (e.g. Henderson et al., 1980), through life events (Brown & Harris, 1978a) and hassles (Dohrenwend & Shrout, 1985), to demographic factors (Atkinson, 1971), vulnerable self-esteem (Mollon & Parry, 1984) and coping behaviour (Miller et al., 1985).

Developing an instrument has obvious attractions for the 'hero innovator', but in addition it may be necessary if suitable instruments are not available to tap the domains that are of interest in a particular study. Further, many of the standardised instruments are based on evidence obtained from psychiatric cases. As noted earlier, the form and nature of psychiatric disorder in the general population may well differ from that in the population in which the measures were originally developed.

In choosing between developing and selecting an instrument, the investigator has to make a series of decisions which relate to time, cost, validity and suitability of particular measures. Whatever strategy is adopted, there are certain features of instruments that are desirable in any epidemiological study: there are certain questions that the investigator should ask about all instruments.

Is the instrument reliable?

If an instrument is unreliable it cannot measure variation across subjects or variation within subjects across time. Error will swamp true scores or true changes. The acceptable level of reliability depends on the purpose of the research. In basic explorative research it is often wasteful to choose instruments or develop instruments with reliability beyond 0.80 (Nunnally, 1967). Very little attenuation of associations will occur at this level of reliability and to increase reliability beyond this may require very lengthy procedures.

How can reliability be best achieved? In general, with qualitative social psychological information such as life event schedules or social adjustment scales, interviews fare rather better than rating scales (Cooke, 1985). This is probably true for most domains of interest in psychological epidemiology. Yager, Grant, Sweetwood and Gerst (1981, p. 347) indicated why this might be the case: 'Interviews are likely to increase the subject's motivation and involvement, clarifying ambiguous meaning of items and result in more accurate time framing of event answers.' It was once thought that self-report questionnaires were more 'scientific' because experimenter effects were less likely. However, the advantages of interviews as outlined by Yager et al. (1981) outweigh this disadvantage. If the researcher is developing an instrument, interview schedules will probably give the most reliable and valid information.

What is being measured?

This question underpins the problems of construct validity: that is, which constructs are operationalised by our instruments? (Cook & Campbell, 1979). This is important for practical research and for theoretical understanding. From a practical point of view if constructs are clearly specified then it is easier to communicate and discuss results. From a theoretical point of view, clear constructs can enhance our understanding of processes. These two points can be illustrated using the construct of 'depression'.

Weckowitz (1973) indicated that the term 'depression' can denote three distinct constructs; a normal affective state, a symptom or a diagnostic entity. Confusion arises if the construct of 'depression' is not clearly specified. Miller and Ingham (1979) and Brown and Harris

(1978a) examined the effects of life events on 'depression'. Miller and Ingham used 'depression' to describe depressed mood; Brown and Harris used 'depression' to describe a diagnostic entity that not only included depressed mood but also a wide range of symptoms from irritability to retardation, diurnal variation and weight loss. These investigators are talking about different constructs, different processes and, indeed, different experiences. If we wish to understand the processes or experiences we must be clear about which construct is being used.

The problem of construct validity exists whether 'off the shelf' or tailor-made instruments are used. Cook and Campbell (1979) argued that there are two broad strategies that can be used to enhance construct validity, namely, careful pre-experimental specification of constructs and careful data analysis.

In the pre-experimental phase it is necessary to define what is and what is not characteristic of each core construct. For example, it may be necessary to distinguish among life events, social support, symptoms and personality factors. If these distinctions are not made then spurious relationships may arise because two apparently distinct measures are really measuring the same construct. A concrete example may clarify this point. Weissman and Paykel (1974) reported a significant relationship between social adjustment and depression in depressed women. Examination of their social adjustment scale reveals that many of the items relate to primary symptoms of depression: for example, guilt, worry, resentment, distress, and disinterest in sexual contact. Their social adjustment construct appears to be an amalgam of symptoms and social adjustment variables. Therefore, use of their instrument in an unmodified form obscures rather than clarifies the link between depression and social adjustment. How can construct validity be improved? Derogatis, Klerman and Lipman (1972) and Ni Bhrolchain (1979) argued that clarity is increased when constructs are defined in restrictive terms. Thus 'depression' is best defined in terms of signs and symptoms and not in terms of correlated, but conceptually distinct, features such as demographic, personality and social adjustment variables.

Even if each construct domain is described in clear and restrictive terms, several constructs may be necessary to describe any domain in a satisfactory manner. In the symptom domain there may be reactive and endogenous depression, social support may be instrumental or expressive, life events may be exits or entrances. Thus even with restricted definitions all these domains may still be too heterogeneous. Fortunately, careful analysis can come to the rescue in this situation.

Techniques such as factor analysis, principal component analysis, latent trait analysis can be useful. These techniques specify constructs by grouping related items or symptoms and distinguishes these from unrelated items or symptoms. Thus domains of interest can be refined: symptoms can be amalgamated into discrete syndromes, different types of social support can be described. The value of these techniques will be described in more detail in the section on data analysis.

In selecting or in developing an instrument it is essential that the investigator is clear about which constructs are being measured by each instrument.

Categorical or dimensional measures?

A final and fundamental decision, perhaps dilemma, faced by the investigator is whether the disorder should be measured in terms of cases of disorder or in terms of the degree of the disorder; that is, as a category or as a dimension. This is partly an epistemological decision dependent on how the disorder is viewed; however, it is a decision that has practical implications. Traditionally, in psychiatric epidemiology, respondents have been divided into cases and non-cases: cases represent people with symptoms similar to patients observed in psychiatric clinics, all other people are non-cases. This approach has both advantages and disadvantages. On the positive side, measures of 'caseness' provide a metric which clinicians can use to understand the nature of the disorder being described, health administrators can use to estimate the number of people who require services, and statisticians can use to calculate measures of incidence, prevalence and risk. Thus, caseness measures have practical value.

On the negative side, caseness measures are of less value when aetiological analysis is desired. There are three specific disadvantages. Firstly, caseness measures are generally developed on the small and biased group of individuals who squeeze through the four filters that separate the community from the psychiatric ward (see earlier). This has two consequences. The syndromes of the psychiatric ward may not exist in the community. In addition, the instruments, while being reliable for rating severe levels of symptomatology, may be less reliable at lesser intensities. If caseness measures are developed they must be developed for use with community cases.

Secondly, caseness measures are frequently dimensions of disorder that have been split arbitrarily into 'case' and 'non-case' levels. Brown, Ni Bhrolchain and Harris (1975, p. 229) confirmed that the division may be arbitrary: 'There is evidently an arbitrary element in choosing a cut off point between a case and a borderline (case).' In aetiological analysis this is important; the decision of 'what is a case?' can radically affect the putative relationship amongst risk factors and caseness. Patterns of results may change depending on the cut-off points selected (Cooke, 1980b).

Thirdly, dichotomising information into cases can result in a substantial loss of information. Statistical power suffers. Larger samples are required to demonstrate the same effect.

To summarise, the concept of a case has been described as '... a chimera existing only in the mind of the investigator' (Copland, 1981, p. 11). It is a chimera with practical value in the description of the rate of a disorder; it has less value for aetiological epidemiology.

In conclusion, decisions about which instruments should be used are complex. These decisions depend on the nature of the questions being asked and the availability of suitable measures.

ANALYSIS OF INFORMATION

The fieldwork is complete, the questionnaires are coded and the information is safely stored in the local computer. How should this information be analysed? Epidemiological information can be analysed in a variety of ways, from the simple to the complex. The mode of analysis adopted depends on the quality of the information available and the purpose of the study. We will start by looking at some simple descriptive statistics and move on to statistics that provide a more comprehensive insight into the information obtained.

Rates of disorder

The counting of cases is the fundamental feature of descriptive epidemiology. The number of cases is most often expressed as a rate. The simple rate of a disorder can be defined as:

$$\frac{\text{Number of disorders in a specific period}}{\substack{\text{Population at risk of disorder} \\ \text{in a specific period}}} \times C$$

where C typically equals 1000 or 100,000.

This simple rate provides a clear description of the probability of a disorder within this population during a specific time period. Normally, two different types of rates are used: rates of prevalence and rates of incidence.

Prevalence can be defined as the number of cases of a disorder during a period or interval divided by the total population. If the period is short (e.g. a day or a week) then the rate is described as point prevalence. If the period is longer, typically a year, then the rate is described as period prevalence. Thus, for example, an investigator may describe the number of cases of schizophrenia which may be observed in a year or the number of cases of depression observed during one week. Prevalence is a comparatively simple measure to derive because the investigator does not have to determine when the disorder started: identifying the start of a disorder can be difficult particularly with mild psychological difficulties (Cranach, Eberlein, & Holl, 1981). Prevalence is an important measure as it can be of practical value in the planning of services and the level of manpower and workload. It is of less value in aetiological studies because the investigator has no information about the relationship between potential causes and the onset of the disorder.

By way of contrast, incidence rates are of value in aetiological epidemiology. A comparison of incidence rates across groups that have been differentially exposed to risk makes it possible to identify which risk factors are important. Incidence can be defined as:

$$\frac{\text{Number of new cases of a disorder in a specific period}}{\text{Population at risk over a period of time}} \times C$$

where C typically equals 1000 or 100,000,

The numerator is usually the number of people who have had a disorder, and thus this measure indicates the probability that an individual will get the disorder during a fixed period. With frequent or episodic disorders, such as depression or the common cold, the numerator may be the number of episodes of disorder. This measure of incidence will describe the average number of episodes of depression or the common cold experienced per head of population.

The denominator in the incidence equation may have to be adjusted or corrected. Generally, the denominator is the population at risk; however, with fairly frequent disorders, such as psychological disorders, cases of disorder should be excluded from the denominator. If this correction is not made then the precision of the estimate will be diminished.

Simple rates of prevalence and incidence are easy to calculate and they accurately summarise the findings of a particular study. They suffer from the significant disadvantage that they are influenced by the nature and structure of the population studied. With disorders, such as depression, which are firmly tied to demographic features such as age, sex and socio-economic status, crude rates of incidence or prevalence can distort or mislead. For example, the rate of depression is generally twice as high amongst women as amongst men (Weissman & Klerman, 1977).

If the investigator compares crude incidence rates across two populations then the rates may differ merely because the ratio of males to females differs across the two populations. It is necessary, therefore, to move from crude rates to *specific* or *adjusted* rates.

Specific incidence or prevalence rates are those derived, not for the total population, but rather for some sub-group of the population. Typically specific rates are derived for different demographic groups such as young and old, males and females, and middle class and working class. Specific rates can be used to identify those at greatest risk; thus these specific rates can be of value both for the planning of services and for promoting the understanding of a disorder.

Adjusted rates are used to provide a summary of the information derived from one population to facilitate comparison of information derived from another population. These rates are adjusted or standardised to take account of the differences in the demographic structure of different populations. There are two broad approaches to the calculation of adjusted rates, the direct method and the indirect method. Using the direct method the sex-specific rates in the two populations to be compared are adjusted to a 'standard' population of known sex ratio. In the indirect method the sex specific rates of the smallest or most unstable population is adjusted to the larger, and usually more stable, population (see Mausner & Kramer, 1985, for technical details).

Rates provide a simple and valuable description of the distribution of disorders. While rates are of interest, epidemiologists are generally more interested in the nature and strength of the relationship between risk factors and disorders. Approaches to this problem will now be considered.

Relationships between risk and disorder

How can the significance or importance of a particular risk factor be estimated? Many researchers are still content to report the statistical significance of results. It is a statistical cliche, yet a cliche worth repeating, that statistical significance tells us little about the size of an association. Hays (1963, p. 204) expressed this point clearly: 'Virtually any study can be made to show significant results if one uses enough subjects, regardless of how nonsensical the context may be.' If we depend on statistical significance we do not know if the effect of the risk factor is significant yet trivial; or, indeed, significant yet nonsensical.

Psychologists and other research workers have tried to measure importance using measures such as variance explained. This is a seductive approach: unfortunately, it has pitfalls. It is enlightening to consider what variance explained actually indicates and an example from the field of cancer epidemiology may provide the clearest idea of its applicability. Epidemiological evidence indicates that smoking has a powerful effect on the incidence of lung cancer. The variance explained in the incidence of lung cancer by cigarette smoking, in one major study, is only 0.003% (Doll & Peto, 1976). Thus one of the most accepted epidemiological findings does not look convincing if the variance explained statistic is used as a measure. This apparent anomaly arises because variance-explained measures the accuracy with which it can be predicted that an individual smoker will develop lung cancer, it does not measure the overall impact of smoking. Although few non-smokers develop lung cancer, it is also the case that most smokers do not develop the disease. This point may be clearer if it is illustrated graphically (Fig. 16.2).

By careful calculation two graphs of hypothetical research findings on the association between life events and symptoms have been derived,

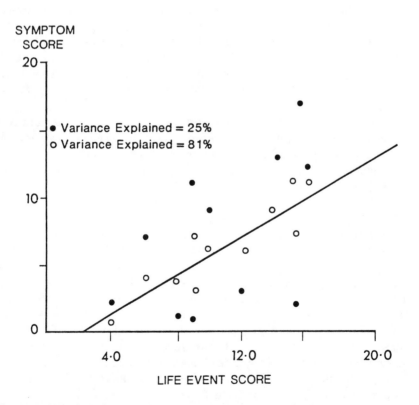

FIG. 16.2. Hypothetical results showing two distributions with identical slopes but with different amounts of variance explained.

with the same slope but with different correlations. Thus the overall magnitude of the effect is the same, though the level of variance explained is very different in the two distributions. In one distribution we can accurately predict an individual's symptom score from his or her life event score, in the other case this can be done with much less accuracy. The proportion of total variance explained, therefore, is not a good measure of the importance of a risk factor.

If this measure is inadequate, what other measures can be used? Epidemiologists have a plethora of measures. Murphy (1983) listed nine measures including positive predictive value, prior odds of disease, specificity and relative risk. Other epidemiological indices include attributable risk, attributable risk per cent and population attributable risk per cent.

Two of these measures, namely relative risk and population attributable risk per cent, are of particular value in the estimation of the importance of risk factors.

Relative risks can be defined as the ratio of the rate of disorder amongst those who have been exposed to a risk factor to the rate of disorder amongst those who have not been exposed (McMahon & Pugh, 1970). It can be calculated as shown in Table 16.2.

The concept underlying relative risk may be easier to grasp if we return to the example of smoking and lung cancer already used. The rate of cases of lung cancer among those who smoke 20 cigarettes a day has been estimated to be 32 times the rate amongst non-smokers. The relative risk is thus 32. Therefore, if an individual smokes 20 cigarettes a day, on average, the risk of lung cancer is 32 times that of a non-smoker. A high relative risk tends to increase the plausibility of a causal hypothesis.

Relative risk is a valuable measure for experts; however, it is of less value for the general clinician who merely requires some notion of the

TABLE 16.2
Calculation of relative risk

		Case	Non-case
Exposure to risk factor	Yes	a	b
	No	c	d

Cohort studies

Relative risk = $\dfrac{a(c + d)}{c(a = b)}$

Case-control studies

Relative risk = $\dfrac{ad}{bc}$

power of an effect. To interpret relative risk one really needs to know what is a 'big' relative risk and this depends on the disorder being studied and the base risk of the disorder. Despite this minor drawback relative risk can be of a considerable value in the interpretation of epidemiological information.

Population attributable risk per cent, by way of contrast, does provide an immediate sense of the importance of a risk factor. Population attributable risk per cent can be defined as the maximum proportion of cases of a disorder in the population as a whole that can be directly attributed to the experience of a risk factor. This index can be calculated as shown in Table 16.3.

The value of this measure can be illustrated by returning to the example of smoking and lung cancer. It has been estimated that up to 86% of the deaths through lung cancer can be attributed to smoking (Doll & Peto, 1976). If all smokers stopped, then up to 86% of the cases of lung cancer would disappear. This is a measure that clinicians and health care planners can grasp instantly; this is the number of people who have a disorder because of their exposure to a particular risk.

Recent reviews of the life event and depression literature (Cooke & Hole, 1983; Cooke, 1986) have demonstrated the utility of these two indices. Relative risks were found to range from 2.6 to 6.8. Compared with the relative risks for heavy smoking and lung cancer these risks are comparatively modest; however, in the context of epidemiological studies as a whole they are significant and suggestive of a causal association. With female subjects anything between 37% and 69% of cases of depression could be attributed to the effect of stressful life events. These two measures, therefore, provide a simple yet valuable indication of the importance of risk factors. Moreover, these indices can be used to tackle two other problems of analysis in epidemiology—the problem of specificity and the problem of synergy.

TABLE 16.3
Calculation of population attributable risk per cent

		Case	Non-case
Exposure to risk factor	Yes	a	b
	No	c	d

Cohort studies

$$PAR\% = \frac{ad - bc}{(a + c)(c + d)} \cdot 100$$

Case-control studies

$$PAR\% = \frac{ad - bc}{(a + c)d} \cdot 100$$

Assessing specificity

A central idea in epidemiological research is the notion of specificity. Following Susser (1973), specificity may be regarded as the extent to which one variable can be used to predict another. An example from the smoking literature may illustrate the importance of specificity (Fig. 16.3).

In the early studies on smoking and disease Doll and Hill (1952) found relationships between all forms of smoking and death due to all causes. The relative risk, however, was comparatively small (i.e. 1.3). To enhance specificity Doll and Hill refined the domain of potential causes by excluding cigar smoking and pipe smoking and examined deaths through all causes following cigarette smoking. The relative risk was increased to a modest 1.7. They then refined the effect side of the equation by ignoring all forms of death apart from lung cancer and they found a substantial relative risk, a risk of 32. Doll and Hill established that cigarette smoking had a specific effect on lung cancer.

Specificity does two things. Firstly, specificity increases the plausibility of a causal relationship. Secondly, specificity helps the investigator exclude irrelevancies, irrelevancies of risk and irrelevancies of disorder. This is as true of psychological data as it is of lung cancer data. In the life event field, Paykel and his colleagues found that undesirable events and events that entailed the loss of someone important had greater causal impact than events in general (Paykel et al., 1969). Refining the other side of the equation, Cooke (1981) and Bebbington et al. (1981) showed that life events influenced neurotic or anxiety depression but not other forms of depression. Comparison of relative risks allows the investigator to evaluate the specificity of an effect.

Simple or synergistic effects

Relative risk and population attributable risk per cent can be used to examine the influence that more than one risk factor may have on the rate of a disorder. In simple terms, two risk factors may independently

Smoking	Relative risk	Disorder
Cigarettes, pipe, cigar smoking	1.3	Death from all causes
Cigarette smoking	1.7	Death from all causes
Cigarette smoking	32	Death from lung cancer

FIG. 16.3. The specificity of the relationship between types of smoking and disease.

produce proportional increases in the risk of a disorder or their concatenation may produce a disproportionate or synergistic increase in the risk of a disorder. For example, serum cholesterol level and smoking may independently affect the risk of coronary heart disease. Thus measures to reduce cholesterol and measures to reduce smoking would both decrease the risk of coronary heart disease in proportion to their relative risks. By way of contrast, consumption of alcohol and smoking are thought to have a synergistic effect on the risk of oesophageal cancer (Tuyns, Pequignot & Jensen, 1977). Thus the risk of oesophageal cancer for the non-smoking drinker is slightly elevated, the risk for a smoking non-drinker is slightly elevated but the risk for someone who smokes and drinks is dramatically increased.

The presence or absence of synergy is important both from the point of view of prevention and from the point of view of understanding the nature of a disorder. In the synergistic case prevention is comparatively easy because removal of one risk factor, e.g. smoking, dramatically reduces the risk of oesophageal cancer. In the non-synergistic case removal of one risk factor only reduces the risk of heart disease partially. Theoretically, the synergistic relationship implies that there is a biological interaction between smoking and alcohol which leads to oesophageal cancer. This suggests avenues that should be explored to identify the physical mechanisms underpinning the disease. In the absence of synergy it is less likely that biological interaction is present.

Synergy may be important in psychological epidemiology. In the recent British literature there has been a considerable preoccupation with the interpretation of the ways in which two risk factors may affect the risk of psychological disturbance (Tennant & Bebbington, 1978; Brown & Harris, 1978b; Everitt & Smith, 1979). Rutter (1981) has argued that this is a rather pointless controversy since any conclusion about synergy must depend on the statistical model that is assumed to underlie the relationship. By examining the appropriate relative risks it is possible to determine whether risks are additive or synergistic in nature. To illustrate this point two examples from the literature on life events will be considered (Table 16.4).

The first results (Table 16.4a) are taken from a study in which the effects of life events and housing problems on the rate of depression were examined (Paykel, Emms, Fletcher & Rassaby, 1980). The relative risk for each of the four cells are tabulated. The risk when the subject has housing problems is three times more than when she does not have housing problems. The risk when she has experienced recent life events is nine times more, while the risk when she has both life events and housing problems is just less than twelve. Given rounding error, this suggests that the effects are additive. If a synergistic effect was present,

TABLE 16.4

(a) Relative risks illustrating an additive interaction between two risk factors with regard to their effect on puerperal depression. Data from Paykel et al. (1980)

		Life events	
		No	Yes
Housing problems	Yes	4.23	11.46
	No	1.00	10.31

(b) Table of relative risks illustrating a multiplicative interaction between two risk factors with regard to their effect on depression.
Data from Parry and Shapiro (1985)

		Life events	
		No	Yes
Lack of instrumental support	Yes	2.40	4.56
	No	1.00	1.90

the relative risk for combined risks would be over 40. The second example comes from a study by Parry and Shapiro (1986) in which the occurrence of depression was examined in relation to life events and to the level of expressive social support (Table 16.4b).

In this example, the relative risk for those who lack instrumental social support is 2.4, for those who have experienced recent life events 1.9 and for those with both risk factors the relative risk is 4.64. The product of the individual risks is 4.56. It would appear, therefore, that the appropriate model in this instance is synergistic rather than additive. Thus people with poor social support are apparently at considerable risk when they experience a life event. This has important clinical and theoretical implications as it suggests that by improving an individual's social support we may reduce the impact of life events. Life events may be difficult to prevent: social support can be enhanced.

More complex methods of analysis

The forms of analysis just described are useful when the investigator is examining the association between one or two risk factors and a disorder. In more complex situations, where the investigator wishes to determine how a larger set of variables affects a disorder, it is necessary to use multivariate statistics. The form the analysis takes depends on the questions to be answered.

In the space available, it would be impossible to provide a detailed account of the application of these techniques, however, each of the procedures will be described briefly and examples of their application will be given (Table 16.5).

Discriminant function analysis is a technique for refining categories of people or patients. Ni Bhrolchain, Brown and Harris (1979) applied discriminant function analysis to refine the distinction between cases of neurotic and psychotic depression. All symptoms of depression were analysed to find out which ones distinguish between cases of neurotic and psychotic depression. The best combination of discriminating symptoms was derived and cases were re-assigned to the neurotic or psychotic group on the basis of scores estimated from the discriminant function. Sharper categories were thereby achieved and individual patients were allocated to the groups with greater reliability.

Principal component analysis and *factor analysis* are techniques that are designed to divide variables into groups which are interrelated and distinguish them from other groups of variables (Eysenck, 1953). These are valuable techniques because they exclude irrelevancies from measures, they generate more reliable variables (Armor, 1969) and may enhance construct validity.

TABLE 16.5
The function of more complex statistical techniques

Procedure	Question to be answered
Discriminant function analysis	Which variables best discriminate two or more groups of people from each other? How well can these different groups be separated?
Principal component analysis and factor analysis	Which variables are correlated with each other and distinct from other variables? How may a large number of variables be expressed in terms of a smaller number of factors or constructs?
Multiple regression analysis	Which combination of independent variables predict the dependent variable (usually a continuous measure of disorder)? What are the relative contributions of the independent variables to prediction?
Log-linear analysis	Which combination of independent variables (usually dichotomous risk factors) predict the dependent variables (usually a dichotomous 'caseness' measure)?
Mathematical models	What is the pattern of effects which influence the dependent variable? What is the overall size of the multiple effect? What change would occur in the dependent variable if the level of independent variables is changed? What assumptions underpin the putative causal associations?

Cooke (1980a) applied principal component analysis to symptom data collected in a community study. Four components or syndromes of depression emerged and were labelled 'anxiety depression', 'cognitive depression', 'vegetative depression' and 'classic endogenous depression'. This slimming down of the symptom domain allowed the demonstration of specificity in that only 'anxiety depression' was found to be associated with stressful life events (Cooke, 1981). The construct validity of the association between life events and 'anxiety depression' was thereby enhanced.

Multiple regression analysis is a technique that estimates how well a set of independent variables such as demographic factors, social support variables and measures of stress can predict the level of a dependent variable such as depression. It is a valuable technique because the relative importance of risk factors or other variables can be estimated and, also, the overall accuracy of the prediction can be estimated. Paykel et al. (1980) applied this technique to predict puerperal depression. They demonstrated that five variables—namely undesirable life events, age, previous history of psychiatric disorder, post-partum blues and marital difficulties—in combination predicted 40% of the variance in puerperal depression. Each variable contributed a similar amount to the prediction. Thus the investigators could evaluate the relative importance of these variables and determine how much variability had yet to be explained.

Log-linear analysis is a technique akin to multiple regression analysis. However, it is generally used with discrete rather than continuous variables. Dichotomous risk factors are used to predict dichotomous measures of disorder.

The final set of procedures to be considered are *mathematical models*. Mathematical models have been used extensively in the social sciences (e.g. Wold & Jureen, 1953; Blalock, 1964; Werts & Linn, 1970). They are designed to provide over-simplified analogues of reality by describing a limited number of variables and their interrelationships.

Mathematical models have three major advantages when they are applied to the analysis of survey data. Firstly, as Dunn (1981) indicated, their application may provide a more complete understanding of results by providing a detailed explanation of the pattern of the results. Mathematical models can be used to assess the pattern of effects in complex multivariable situations. As an example of this approach Duncan-Jones (1986) was able to distinguish long-term causes of anxiety and depression such as hereditary and childhood experiences from short-term causes such as stressful life events. In addition, he was able to demonstrate the relative importance of these two types of causes. His model suggested that long-term causes were three times as important as short-term causes. This has important implications for the treatment of such disorder.

The second advantage of mathematical models is that they provide an analogue to reality and thus changes can be predicted using the model. Dunn and Skuse (1981) used a mathematical model to describe the pattern of depression found in a general practice. Using this model they were able to predict the recovery rate of patients with chronic depression and also to predict the incidence rate of new episodes of depression from past contacts at the general practice surgery.

The third, and perhaps most important, advantage of a mathematical model is that it constrains the investigator to make explicit non-ambiguous statements regarding theoretical constructs and presumed causal mechanisms. By being forced to make his or her model explicit the investigator may highlight unwarranted assumptions (Blalock, 1964; Dunn, 1981).

These multivariate techniques are valuable; however, their application can be fraught with difficulties. Considerable technical expertise is required if results obtained are to be sensible. Most investigators will require expert guidance on the application of these techniques, if they are to avoid the trap of 'garbage in, garbage out'.

PRACTICAL PROBLEMS IN THE ORGANISATION OF EPIDEMIOLOGICAL RESEARCH

The final section of this chapter considers what is perhaps the most important hurdle faced by any epidemiologist, namely, organising the fieldwork. The major problems in fieldwork can be eased by the proper training of interviewers and by the careful control and monitoring of interview information as it is collected.

Training interviewers

Training is fundamental. Most research interviewers will not have interviewed before, and if they have interviewed before, then their approach and techniques may not be those that you have chosen to use in your study.

The first task in training is to teach the details of the interview schedule and the interview procedure. Consistency in the phrasing of questioning and the application of anchor points is vital at the beginning of the project. There will be plenty of time for definitions to drift as the project proceeds! Video role-play is desirable. This gives trainees confidence and it allows the investigator to ensure the appropriate application of anchor points and interview techniques. Once interviewers have learned the basics of the interview then they must be taught the pace, tone and style of questions to be used. If the approach adopted calls for semi-structured interviewing then the interviewers need to be taught such skills as reflection and prompting by the presentation of balanced alternatives.

Piloting the interview in the population of interest can reap benefits. The interviewers will develop their skills in locating the target person, they will learn how to reduce the refusal rate and they will gain confidence in using the interview procedures. Particular problems in the form of questions can be identified and resolved before the main study begins.

Quality control

The second major hurdle faced by the investigator is that of keeping control of the information as it is received. Epidemiological studies generate large amounts of information; questionnaires are usually long and samples are usually large. Information can be degraded by non-contacts or refusals, inadequate coding and even by the falsification of data. If these problems are not minimised then the validity of the study can be threatened.

Simple steps can be taken to limit these problems. Non-contacts occur when, despite all efforts, the specified individual cannot be located and interviewed. This can be a problem because non-contacts may systematically bias a sample. For example, individuals working away from home, perhaps on the North Sea oil rigs, differ significantly from those living at home. Individuals with alcohol problems may be more difficult to contact because they are more often in public houses than others. Non-contacts, therefore, can bias results. To counter this problem it is established practice that six attempts should be made to contact the individual, at different times of the day and of the week, before they are designated as a non-contact.

Refusers can have an equally damaging effect on the validity of the study. Anxious or depressed individuals may be less likely to co-operate because of their symptoms and thus, a systematic bias enters the study. Refusals are more difficult to combat than non-contacts because people have an absolute right not to be coerced into giving personal information. Fortunately, few people are totally unwilling to co-operate with a study if: (a) they are provided with a proper explanation of its purpose; (b) they are reassured that information given will be confidential; and (c) it is demonstrated to them, by way of appropriate identification, that a bona fide organisation is carrying out the study. If the subject is showing only minor reluctance then a pleasant, reassuring and quietly persistent approach on the part of the interviewer can often pay dividends.

Once the interview schedule is returned to the research office it is important that a clerical officer checks immediately that the schedule is filled in completely. Often in the depth of an interview, the interviewer will forget to complete a section of the schedule, If they are reminded immediately they can often provide the missing information.

Traditionally, information from interviews is transferred to a computer coding sheet. This information is then typed onto computer files. During transfer of information errors inevitably creep in. It is sensible, therefore, to reduce the possibility of error by reducing the number of times information is transferred. If the interview schedule is appropriately coded, with computer columns down the righthand margin, then information can be directly transferred (Fig. 16.4). As a bonus, an extra clerical task is also avoided.

Card No. $\boxed{0}$ $\boxed{1}$
         1 2

1. Referral code   ☐ ☐ ☐
            3 4 5

2. Sex
    1 — Male   ☐
    2 — Female   6

3. Age
What age were you on your last birthday?   ☐ ☐
            7 8

4. Household composition
How many people live here regularly who are cared for by the same ☐ ☐
person as yourself?   9 10

5. Marital status
Are you single, married, or widowed?
    1 — single
    2 — married
    3 — divorced   ☐
    4 — separated   11
    5 — widowed
    6 — remarried

6. Employment caregory
Were you in paid employment at the time of the offence?
    1 — yes and over 30 hrs/week
    2 — yes and under 30 hrs/week
    3 — unemployed for 3 months or less
    4 — unemployed for 6 months or less   ☐
    5 — unemployed for 1 year or less   12
    6 — unemployed for 3 years or less
    7 — unemployed for 5 years or less
    8 — unemployed for more than 5 years

FIG. 16.4. Illustration of interview schedule pre-coded for direct entry onto a computer.

A further problem that any investigator should be aware of is the possibility that interviewers will fabricate interviews. Interviewing can be unpleasant and tedious. An interviewer may be expected to traipse the streets on cold and windy evenings and, indeed, by the time they have asked the same questions a hundred times their interest may begin to wane. The temptation to fake is always present. To prevent this the investigator should make the interviewer aware that he or she is conscious of the problem. The procedure that is commonly used is to contact a random sample of subjects who have been interviewed to determine whether the interview actually took place.

The field of epidemiology is complex but rewarding. Many of the theoretical problems confronted by psychologists in clinical settings can only be tackled through the application of epidemiological methods. The identification of coping and adaptive mechanisms is one of several advantages of the epidemiological approach. In addition, epidemiological information can be of considerable value in the planning and development of services. The complexities of the inherent methodological problem should not deter the clinician from taking an interest in this illuminating and valuable field.

ACKNOWLEDGEMENTS

I thank Patrick Miller and David Hole for their helpful comments on an earlier draft. In addition, I would like to thank Mrs Rowena Cook for preparing the manuscript with such care.

REFERENCES

Armor, D.J. (1969). Theta reliability and factor scaling. *Sociological Methodology, 2*, 17-50.

Atkinson, J. (1971). *A Handbook for Interviewers: A Manual for Social Survey Interviewing Practice and Procedures on Structured Interviewing*. 2nd edn. HMSO: Social Survey Division.

Bartlett, F.C. (1932). *Remembering*. Cambridge University Press.

Bebbington, P., Tennant, C. & Hurry, J. (1981). Adversity and the nature of psychiatric disorder in the community. *Journal of Affective Disorders, 3*, 345-366.

Blalock, H.M. (1964). *Causal Inferences in Non-experimental Research*. The University of North Carolina Press.

Brown, G.W., Craig, T.K.J. & Harris, T.O. (1985). Depression: distress or disease? Some epidemiological considerations. *British Journal of Psychiatry, 147*, 612-622.

Brown, G.W. & Harris, T.O. (1978a). *Social Origins of Depression: A Study of Psychiatric Disorder in Women*. London: Tavistock.

Brown, G.W. & Harris, T.O. (1987b). Social origins of depression: A reply. *Psychological Medicine, 8,* 577-588.

Brown, G.W., Ni Bhrolchain, M. & Harris, T.O. (1975). Social class and psychiatric disturbance among women in an urban population. *Sociology, 9,* 225-254.

Cook, T.D. & Campbell, D.T. (1979). *Quasi-experimentation, Design and Analysis Issues for Field Settings*. Chicago: Rand McNally College Publishing Company.

Cooke, D.J. (1980a). The structure of depression found in the general population. *Psychological Medicine, 10,* 455-463.

Cooke, D.J. (1980b). Causal modelling with contingency tables. *British Journal of Psychiatry, 137,* 582-584.

Cooke, D.J. (1981). Life events and syndromes of depression in the general population. *Social Psychiatry, 16,* 181-186.

Cooke, D.J. (1985). The reliability of a brief life event interview. *Journal of Psychosomatic Research, 29,* 361-365.

Cooke, D.J. (1986). The significance of life events as a cause of psychological and physical disorder. In B. Cooper (ed.) *Psychiatric Epidemiology: Process and Prospects*. London: Croom Helm.

Cooke, D.J. & Hole, D. (1983). The aetiological importance of stressful life events. *British Journal of Psychiatry, 143,* 397-400.

Copland, J. (1981). What is a case? A case for what? In J.K. Wing, P.E. Bebbington, & L.N. Robins, (eds) *What is a Case? The Problem of Definition in Psychiatric Community Surveys*. London: Grant McIntyre.

Cranach, M., Von. Eberlein, R. & Holl, B. (1981). The concept of onset in psychiatry. In J.K. Wing, P.E. Bebbington, & L.N. Robins (eds.) *What is a Case? The Problem of Definition in Psychiatric Community Surveys*. London: Grant McIntyre.

Derogatis, L.R., Klerman, G.R. & Lipman, R.S. (1972). Anxiety states and depressive neurosis: issues on nosological discrimination. *Journal of Nervous and Mental Disease, 155,* 392-403.

Dohrenwend, B.P. & Shrout, P.E. (1985). 'Hassles' in the conceptualisation and measurement of life stress variables. *American Psychologist, 20,* 780-785.

Doll, R. & Hill, A.B. (1952). A study of the aetiology of carcinoma of the lung. *British Medical Journal, ii,* 1271-1286.

Doll, R. & Peto, R. (1976). Mortality in relation to smoking: 20 years observations on male British doctors. *British Medical Journal, ii,* 1525-1536.

Duncan-Jones, P. (1986). Modelling the aetiology of neurosis: long-term and short-term factors. In B. Cooper (ed.) *Psychiatric Epidemiology: Progress and Prospects*. London: Croom Helm.

Dunn, G. (1981). The role of linear models in psychiatric epidemiology. *Psychological Medicine, 11,* 179-184.

Dunn, G. & Skuse, D. (1981). The natural history of depression and general practice: Stochastic models. *Psychological Medicine, 11,* 755-764.

Everitt, B.S. & Smith, A.M.R. (1979). Interactions in contingency tables: a brief discussion of alternative definitions. *Psychological Medicine, 9,* 581-583.

Eysenck, H.J. (1953). The logical basis of factor analysis. *American Psychologist, 8,* 105-114.

Fahy, T.J. (1974a). Pathways of specialist referral of depressed patients from general practice. *British Journal of Psychiatry, 124,* 231-239.

Fahy, T.J. (1974b). Depression in hospital and in general practice: a direct clinical comparison. *British Journal of Psychiatry, 124,* 240-242.

Fahy, T.J. (1975). Some problems of method in the study of depression in general practice. *Cambridge Medical Publications, 82,* 82-89.

Goldberg, D. & Huxley, P. (1980). *Mental Illness in The Community: The Pathway to Psychiatric Care.* London: Tavistock Publications.

Hays, L.W. (1963). *Statistics.* London: Holt, Rinehart and Winston.

Henderson, S., Byrne, O.G., Duncan-Jones, P., Scott, R. & Adcock, S. (1980). Social relationships. adversity and neurosis: A study of associations in a general population sample. *British Journal of Psychiatry, 136,* 574-583.

Ingham, J.G. & Miller, P.McC. (1976). The concept of prevalence applied to psychiatric disorders and symptoms. *Psychological Medicine, 6,* 217-225.

Kreitman, N. (1980). Epidemiological Psychiatry: the present and the future. In M. Lader (ed.) *Priorities in Psychiatric Research.* Chichester: John Wiley & Sons.

Leighton, A.H. (1979). Research directions in psychiatric epidemiology. *Psychological Medicine, 9,* 234-247.

MacMahon, B. & Pugh, T.F. (1970). *Epidemiology: Principles and Methods.* Boston: Little, Brown & Company.

Mausner, J.F. & Kramer, S. (1985). *Epidemiology, An Introductory Text.* Philadelphia: W.B. Saunders.

Miller, P.McC. & Ingham, J.G. (1979). Reflections on the life-event-to-illness link with some preliminary findings. In I.G. Sarason & C.D. Spielberger (eds.) *Stress and Anxiety.* Vol 6. New York: John Wiley.

Miller, P.McC., Surtees, P. G., Kreitman, N., Ingham, J., & Sashidharan, S.P. (1985). Maladaptive coping responses to stress: a study of illness inception. *Journal of Nervous and Mental Disease, 173,* 707-716.

Mollon, P. & Parry, G. (1984). The fragile self: narcissistic disturbance and the protective function of depression. *British Journal of Medical Psychology, 57,* 137-146.

Murphy, J.R. (1983). The relationship of relative risk and positive predictive value two by two tables. *American Journal of Epidemiology, 117,* 86-89.

Ni Bhrolchain, M. (1979). Psychotic and neurotic depression: I. Some points of method. *British Journal of Psychiatry, 134,* 87-93.

Ni Bhrolchain, M., Brown, G.W. & Harris, T.O. (1979). Psychotic and neurotic depression: 2. Clinical characteristics. *British Journal of Psychiatry, 134,* 94-107.

Nunnally, J.C. (1967). *Psychometric Theory.* New York: McGraw Hill Book Company.

Parry, G. & Shapiro, D.A. (1986). Social support and life events in working class women: stress buffering or independent effects? *Archives of General Psychiatry, 43,* 315-323.

Paykel, E.S., Emms, E.M., Fletcher, J., & Rassaby, E.S. (1980). Life events and social support in puerperal depression. *British Journal of Psychiatry, 136,* 339-346.

Paykel, E.S., Myres, J.K., Dienelt, M.N., Klerman, G.L., Lindenthai, J.J., & Pepper, M.P. (1969). Life events and depression: a controlled study. *Archives of General Psychiatry, 21,* 753-760.

Rutter, M. (1981). Stress, coping and development: some issues and some questions. *Journal of Child Psychology and Psychiatry, 22,* 323-356.

Rutter, M., Tizard, J., Yule, W., Graham, P., & Whitmore, K. (1976). Research reports: Isle of Wight studies 1964-1974. *Psychological Medicine, 6,* 313-332.

Shepherd, M., Cooper, B., Brown, A.C., & Kalton, G.W. (1966). *Psychiatric illness in General Practice.* Oxford University Press.

Surtees, P., Sashidharan, S.P., & Dean, C. (1986). Affective disorder amongst women in the general population: a longitudinal study. *British Journal of Psychiatry, 148,* 176-186.

Susser, M. (1973). *Causal Thinking in the Health Sciences.* New York: Oxford University Press.

Tennant, C. & Bebbington, P. (1978). The social causation of depression: A critique of the work of Brown and his colleagues. *Psychological Medicine, 8,* 565-575.

Tuyns, A., Pequignot, G., & Jensen, O.M. (1977). *Annual Report.* Lyons: International Agency for Research on Cancer.

Weckowicz, T. (1973). A multidimensional theory of depression. In A. Boyle (ed.) *Multivariate Analysis and Psychological Theory.* London: Academic Press.

Weissman, M.M. & Klerman, G.L. (1977). Sex differences and the epidemiology of depression. *Archives of General Psychiatry, 34,* 98-111.

Weissman, M.M. & Paykel, E.S. (1974). *The Depressed Woman: A Study of Social Relationships.* Chicago: University of Chicago Press.

Werts, C.E. & Linn, R.L. (1970). Path analysis: psychological examples. *Psychological Bulletin, 74,* 193-212.

Wing, J.K.. Nixon, J.M., Mann, S.A., & Leff, J. P. (1977). Reliability of the P.S.E. (ninth edition) used in a population study. *Psychological Medicine, 7,* 505-516.

Wold, H. & Jureen, L. (1953). *Demand Analysis: A Study in Econometrics.* New York: Wiley.

Yager, J., Grant, I., Sweetwood, H.L., & Gerst, M. (1981). Life event reports by psychiatric patients, non-patients, and their partners. *Archives of General Psychiatry, 38,* 343-347.

CHAPTER SEVENTEEN

Research in service planning

Geoff Shepherd   *The Sainsbury Centre, London*

An interest in collecting data rarely intrudes into the process of planning or evaluating services. Most professionals in the health service seem to presume to know already without any data, not only what services are required, but also how they are currently functioning. To question either often seems pointless and faintly tedious. Yet the role of the sceptic is an important one. Of course, I am not suggesting that anyone who provides services can stand completely outside their prejudices and take a truly 'objective' view of what is going on. However, they can at least try to put their prejudices alongside their data and attempt to clarify to what extent the one has permeated the other. They can also remind people of the true nature and extent of the difficulties when these blatantly contradict the plans and proposals that are being put forward. There is a natural tendency to be drawn to easy (and cheap) solutions to what are complex personal and social problems, and when this happens someone has to nudge the planners and politicians with a little reality.

This is particularly important given the dramatic changes that have occurred—and that will continue to occur—in the overall pattern of psychiatric services. The need for intelligent and realistic advice has never been greater and the problems of running a dispersed, multi-agency, multi-site service have yet to be really faced. Planners and administrators have been under pressure to close hospitals, but under less pressure to develop a comprehensive and co-ordinated network of alternatives in the community. Where specific residential or community projects have been set up, a whole new set of problems with regard to research methods and evaluative techniques has arisen.

There are thus two distinct kinds of planning and evaluation exercises: the one is concerned with planning and evaluation at the level of *overall service development,* while the other is concerned with planning and evaluation at the level of *specific projects.* These will now be discussed separately. Most of the examples I will use are drawn from the field of adult mental health, particularly the care and rehabilitation of those with long-term social and psychiatric disorders, since this is the group with whom I am most familiar. However, there are some general implications for service planning and evaluation with other client groups—e.g. the elderly and the mentally handicapped—and I hope that these will also emerge.

RESEARCH AND PLANNING OVERALL SERVICE DEVELOPMENTS

This section will be concerned with the planning and evaluation of a complete service or network of facilities, such as in the rundown of a large mental hospital or the creation of a new district service. Three principal questions will be considered:

1. What is the estimated overall magnitude of the population requiring this service? *How many?*
2. What is the nature and range of facilities that are likely to be required? *What kind of service?*
3. Once in place, how will the new service be monitored and evaluated? *How do we tell if it is working?*

How many?

The problem of accurately identifying the overall numbers of people to require a particular kind of service is a daunting one. If we are simply concerned with the existing population of a mental hospital and the task is re-provision of services on another site (or sites), it should be relatively easy to obtain an estimate of the numbers (e.g. Levene, Donaldson & Brandon, 1985). However, such simple 'head-counts' run into difficulties if the population under study is not clearly defined. Apart from specifying obvious parameters as age, length of stay, etc., more complex 'boundary problems' may arise. For example, do you include people from the existing catchment area of the hospital, or only those from the catchment area as planned in the future? Boundary problems of this kind mean that plans from other districts may need to be taken into account.

But the fundamental difficulty with cross-sectional survey data is that they tell you little about the *dynamics* in the population under study. For planning purposes it is these dynamics that are often the most important. Thus, you need to know not only how many people require services now, but also how many are likely to require services in 'x' years time. Making these predictions constitutes one of the most difficult aspects of planning and it has led to some of the most celebrated blunders. The most famous of these is probably the prediction about future bed numbers made by Tooth and Brooke (1961). These were based upon existing trends in hospital populations which had begun to fall rapidly after the 1959 Mental Health Act following the introduction of more 'open-door' policies and the widespread use of new neuropeptic drugs. Using these data Tooth and Brooke predicted that there would be no long-stay patients left in mental hospitals by the mid-1970s. These predictions were based on an extrapolation from current practice which is only valid where conditions are stable, or where the factors affecting accumulation or rundown are clearly understood (preferably both). This was obviously not the case regarding mental hospitals 20 years ago and it is still not the case today.

Recent surveys of mental hospital populations indicate that the age of the population is gradually increasing (Bewley, Bland, Mechen & Walch, 1981; Early & Nicholas, 1977; 1981). This is understandable given the correlation of age and disability, and the tendency to discharge the less disabled patients first. Most authors conclude from this that the rate of rundown in existing long-stay populations is likely to decrease assuming that there is no dramatic increase in the availability of alternative accommodation for disabled elderly people in the community. The rundown of the existing old long-stay population will then depend largely upon their mortality. This in turn will depend upon the precise characteristics of the population under consideration. Since each hospital has its own unique history and each has been influenced by a unique set of factors, the age composition of its residents and their rates of decline will vary depending upon specific local circumstances. This is reflected in the variation of mortality rates from study to study (although in nearly all cases the rates among psychiatric patients tend to be 2-3 times higher than comparable 'normal' controls). What is really required is therefore a specific modelling exercise for each population as described, for example by Moore (1985).

As indicated, this kind of projection also assumes that rates of decline through other mechanisms (e.g. discharge to alternatives in the community) will remain relatively stable and this may prove to be incorrect. For example, in the UK there has recently been a massive increase in private nursing homes for the elderly (House of Commons,

1985) which has been brought about mainly through the increased availability of funding (DHSS benefits) combined with local factors. If any of these parameters were to change suddenly, particularly the availability of funding, then clearly the predictions would alter. Exactly the same kind of arguments can be made with regard to the *accumulation* of 'new' long-stay inpatients (NLS) in the future. In the UK the annual incidence of NLS varies quite considerably from region to region with a median of around 3-4 per 100,000 per year (Jennings, 1982). This produces widespread differences in prevalence as illustrated in Table 17.1.

Once again, variation is explicable partly by local factors, e.g. demography (rural versus urban); existence of an active rehabilitation service; availability of alternative places in the community; and partly by national policies to shorten lengths of admission and not to rely on the mental hospitals to provide long-term care, Such factors also contribute to the heterogeneity of the population concerned. (Thus, in some places the NLS will constitute only the most severely disabled people who cannot manage outside the hospital, whereas in other places the mix may be rather different.) Variations in prevalence of this kind underline the need to understand how the total service system operates and how one kind of service element may 'substitute' for another.

In epidemiological terms, the categorisation 'new long-stay' refers to service use, not to the distribution of a specific kind of disorder. Data on service use are therefore not the same as traditional epidemiological data. Thus if one particular kind of service can be substituted for another (e.g. beds in private nursing homes for beds in hospital) then the

TABLE 17.1
Number of hospital beds for 'new' long-stay inpatients per 100,000 total population occupied in seven Register areas (1981)

Area	No. of beds occupied for between 1 and 5 years
Camberwell	56
Salford	58
Cardiff	46
Nottingham	38
Southampton	37
Oxford	16
Worcester	20

Adapted from Wing (1984).

apparent 'prevalence' of the disorder will decrease. Of course, the true prevalence has not changed, it has simply shifted from one place to another in the overall system. If service usage is confused with true prevalence in this way, then it may create the illusion that the service is being more effective when, in fact, it is not. As an example, in the United States it has been estimated that between 1969 and 1973 the resident population of nursing homes (aged 65 and over) with chronic mental disorders increased by more than 100% and over the same time similar residents in state hospitals decreased by 30-40% (Goldman, 1983). 'De-institutionalisation' can therefore become 'trans-institutionalisation'.

Of course, estimating the true prevalence of a disorder is extremely complex (see Chapter 16) but it may be useful to have some basic epidemiological facts at your fingertips. For example, cross-cultural studies of the prevalence of schizophrenia suggests that most populations contain around 1 in 200 persons with the disorder (Warner, 1985). This stands in marked contrast to the one-year period prevalence for total recognisable psychiatric disorder in the community which has been estimated at around 250/1000, of which 230 present to General Practitioners, who recognise 140, and refer on to psychiatrists just 17. The number at risk of admission per year is 6 per 1000 (Goldberg & Huxley, 1980). Of course, these kinds of figures are subject to local variation, and having some idea of the local factors may help to apply appropriate 'multipliers' to give some estimate of overall numbers.

In trying to plan services for total populations, we also come up against the fundamental problem of defining who psychiatric services are for. Are there not many people 'out there' who never come into contact with services, but who also have psychological needs? The answer is probably 'yes', but we would do well to be cautious about just how far we intend to open the 'floodgates' to them. As Goldberg and Huxley's figures remind us, for every person referred to a psychiatrist there are likely to be another eight who continue to be cared for by their GPs (and another five whom the GP does not even recognise as cases). Furthermore, it is generally the most severe disorders who pass the 'filters' most easily and enter the system.

Richman and Barry (1985) suggest that the concept of 'unmet need' is often a myth perpetuated by those who wish to justify the diversion of resources from existing services, rather than devoting them to the correction of existing problems in the delivery of care. They also comment upon the associated tendency to 'medicalise' problems of everyday life, and the professional neglect of those with the most serious disorders in favour of better functioning individuals on the edge of what would normally be regarded as 'patienthood'. One needs to be careful, therefore, when attempting to define the magnitude of the problem to take qualitative, as well as quantative, factors into account. The apparently simple question, 'How many?' thus turns out to be a difficult one to answer. Getting accurate figures on population sizes, and especially making accurate predictions about future needs, is not easy. But approximate figures, particularly if they are based on local data, are certainly better than no figures at all (and also probably better than attempts to extrapolate from inappropriate national norms).

It is also important that some of the factors that are liable to influence the size of the error are clearly identified and that an attempt is made to allow for them. One must always be on guard against the tendency to employ overoptimistic assumptions and to underestimate need. Everybody wants to believe that demand for health services in the future will be less than it is today, but as yet this has never happened. In purely pragmatic terms, there may also be an advantage in erring on the side of overgenerous resource allocation since at least it allows for redeployment. You cannot redeploy resources that you have not got.

What kind of service?

There are essentially two approaches to defining service needs. These may be characterised respectively as *service-led* and *client-led*. Service-led planning attempts to create a comprehensive range of services based on a 'shopping list' of service elements. These are then deployed according to some set of general national norms. Service needs are thus defined according to an overall concept of what would constitute a comprehensive range of provisions. In the USA, the National Institute of Mental Health has attempted to provide such a model (Stroul, 1984, 1986), and in the UK MIND's Manifesto *Common Concern* (MIND, 1983) provides a similar list of facilities which health districts might wish to consider in their planning of services. Part of this list is reproduced in Table 17.2.

Various DHSS planning documents can then be used to provide guidelines as to the levels of provision required for each different kind of facility, for example:

Service element	Norms from DHSS (1975; 1985)
Acute beds in general hospitals	30-50/100,000
Short-stay hostels	15-24/100,000
Long-stay hostels	4-6/100,000
Day hospitals (excluding in-patients)	30/100,000
Day centres	60/100,000
Day hospitals (psychogeriatric)	30/100,000

TABLE 17.2
Services for chronic mental illness (taken from MIND, 1983)

Rehabilitation and resettlement team
Social services area teams
   either generic social work for a defined local population or specialist social work
   arranged in client groups
Occupational therapy department with ADL
Hospital rehabilitation unit or wards
Progressive hospital accommodation—
   cubicles, single rooms, group living, flats, rehabilitation homes within hospitals

Day hospitals: special arrangements for chronic mental illness

Day centres: provided by local authority

Local authority old persons' homes

Sheltered lodging scheme: landlady groups

Supervised accommodation:
   1. Run by District Council
   2. Run by voluntary associations, e.g. MIND, housing associations

Halfway homes, run by, e.g. Richmond Fellowship

Hospital hostels: the experimental schemes

Mental illness hostels
   1. Residential
   2. Assessment and crisis
   3. Rehabilitation

Special hostels: run by, e.g. St Dismas, the Cyrenians

Rehabilitation houses

Sheltered housing: warden supervised

Very sheltered housing:
   1. Warden supervised and with augmented home care services
   2. Managed jointly by social services and housing departments

Independent housing: special housing schemes and housing associations

Industrial therapy (graded work)

Sheltered work:
   1. Local authority
   2. Voluntary bodies, e.g. Psychiatric Rehabilitation Association
   3. Department of Employment
   4. Industrial rehabilitation units
   5. Industrial therapy organisations
   6. Enclave working

Social rehabilitation groups—literacy, social skills, domestic management

Joint health and social services resettlement scheme

This may sound crude and mechanistic, but it is how much planning is done and it does have some merits. At the very least, it should ensure that basic, minimum levels of provision are met. For example, if a survey of local available services is completed and this is compared with the guidelines, then certain deficiencies may be highlighted. Are there sufficient (or too many) acute beds? Are there both short- and long-stay hostel places? How many? Where are they situated in relation to the populations in need? Is there a day hospital facility? Are there adequate day-care provisions for long-term support day centres? What do they provide? Is there a balance of work-orientated day care and social support? etc. This identification of gaps in service provision can be very useful and may assist in the creation of a more comprehensive system. Of course, it does not solve the problem of priorities. It may also ignore the specificity of local conditions highlighted earlier and it can place too great an emphasis on quantitative aspects of provisions at the expense of more subtle considerations about the qualitative nature of services. (The question should not be how many hostels/day centres, etc. do we need, but what *kind* of services do we require to meet an individual's needs?) Despite these reservations, normative planning should not be rejected out of hand.

The alternative approach starts from the opposite end, i.e. it purports to be 'client-led'. It can be sub-divided into a *'deductive'* model in which service needs are deduced from a general set of principles or axioms and an *'inductive'* model in which services are constructed on the basis of a detailed consideration of individual clients' needs.

The 'deductive' model usually starts by defining service needs according to certain basic axioms. Thus, the principles of 'normalisation' provide an overall conceptual framework within which a range of services may be planned and evaluated (O'Brien & Tyne, 1981). The use of 'socially valued means', the attempts to reduce stigmatisation, the avoidance of age inappropriate activities, etc., provide broad parameters within which service developments may proceed. Normalisation theory has also developed systematic methods to assess individual clients and to evaluate services according to specific criteria, e.g. the 'PASS' system (Wolfensberger & Glenn, 1975). These ideas provide a conceptual framework for directing service developments and perhaps it is the need for such an overall framework in relation to the run-down of large institutions that partly accounts for their recent popularity.

Normalisation theory is not, of course, the only set of principles that can be used to provide a rationale for service developments. Other principles may be gleaned from the work of researchers like Leona Bachrach (1980) and Stein and Test (1978; 1985). Based on an analysis of the social functions served by institutions and the practical experiences of setting up a community service, they identify two central principles:

1. The service system should be adequate to ensure that the individual's unmet needs are met, i.e. the system should be sufficient to ensure that each individual gets the amount and type of each service required.
2. The service system should not meet needs the person is able to meet him/herself, i.e. a comprehensive mental health service must assume responsibility for those aspects of an individual's functioning which have, for whatever reason, broken down. On the other hand, it must preserve and support those aspects that are still intact.

These principles, together with ideas like accessibility, quality of care, comprehensiveness, continuity, and the importance of co-ordination, can then be used to provide a framework for the strategic planning of services, e.g. Cambridge Health Authority (1984). It must be recognised that such general principles can lead to problems of interpretation in particular instances. For example, what do you do if you want to build a service on the principles of normalisation and clients' expressed choice is for segregated facilities? The interpretation of such general principles in specific instances may therefore require additional expertise.

On the other hand, the 'inductive' model begins with a detailed assessment of individual clients' needs. This often supplements statements of general principles and may be achieved in a number of ways. The most common is probably to use a standardised rating scale such as REHAB (Baker & Hall, 1983) or the CAPE (Clifton Assessment Procedure for the Elderly; Pattie & Gilleard, 1979). Some illustrative data collected using the CAPE are shown in Table 17.3.

They suggest that the numbers of patients who are likely to be able to function in relatively unsupervised accommodation is fairly small (around 25 per cent). The majority appear to need levels of supervision at least analagous to Part III homes for the elderly. Of course, these proportions will vary in different hospitals, dependent upon their own unique history of rehabilitation services. They should also not be seen as strictly *predictive* of behaviour across settings. Given all that we know concerning the specificity of behaviour, results like these are probably best regarded simply as an indication of the numbers in specific sub-groups who are currently functioning at a particular criterion level. They should certainly not be used to predict the 'potential' of individuals. That can only be done by the careful process of assessment, treatment and review, which lies at the heart of good clinical practice.

TABLE 17.3
CAPE scores for 130 long-stay patients at Fulbourn Hospital (1983)

CAPE dependency levels	No.	(%)
A. *No impairment: independent elderly,* comparable to those living without support in the community.	11	(8)
B. *Mild impairment: low dependency,* likely to include those needing some support in the community,. warden-supervised accommodation and the better residents in residential accommodation.	22	(17)
C. *Moderate impairment: medium dependency,* people functioning on this level are likely to need residential care or considerable support and help if at home.	44	(35)
D. *Marked impairment: high dependency,* it is within this category that there is greatest overlap between those in social services accommodation and those in hospital care.	37	(28)
E. *Severe impairment: maximum dependency,* this level is seen most often in psycho-geriatric wards, and the people who remain in the community homes/EMI hostels often present considerable problems to staff in terms of their demands on staff time.	16	(12)

Mean age 63 years (range 30–85)

Mean length of admission: 21 years (range 1–54 y)

Survey data of this kind also have other limitations. Although such scales may be reliable, their content validity may still be questioned. The items they contain may have been selected carefully, but our knowledge about what contributes most critically to functioning in the community is still very imperfect and there is no guarantee that these scales necessarily tap the most important dimensions. For example, Kingsley, McAusland and Towell (1985) argue that the social networks of long-stay patients should be considered as just as important as their instrumental or social abilities. Similarly, clients' own wishes and ambitions need to be assessed and standardised rating scales are usually not very adequate for this purpose. An alternative approach is to ask staff to judge directly patients' suitability for various kinds of residential or day facilities. A recent example of this approach is the Bexley Hospital Patients' Needs Survey (Clifford & Szyndler, 1986). In this study all the patients who had been in Bexley Hospital for more than one year were rated on a number of scales covering the amount of supervision required to perform a range of basic living skills (shopping, cooking, personal hygiene, etc.). Staff were then asked to make recommendations concerning the most suitable type of accommodation and day programme. Some of these data are shown in Tables 17.4 and 17.5.

Rather like the CAPE data shown earlier, these results suggest that the majority of these residents are judged to require fairly highly supervised residential accommodation (over 70% with 24 hour cover) and fairly low pressure day programmes. Clifford and Szyndler present other data to support the validity of these judgements and they also report some attempts to get the patients to express their preferences. (Only 37% expressed a clear preference, and of these 40% wished to remain in hospital.) One therefore has to weigh up the advantages of developing new questionnaires and a new format for recording staff judgements when relatively quick and easy standard instruments like the CAPE and the REHAB scales already exist which appear to serve very similar purposes. There is also the danger that staff judgements, even if reliable, will lack validity and will be contaminated through over-influence of the institutional setting, or lack of knowledge of the alternatives.

What about asking the patients directly? We noted earlier that this can be difficult. In the Bexley survey less than 40% expressed a clear preference. Similarly, in Mann and Cree's (1976) study of new long-stay patients only 60% expressed a definite preference. (In both cases, it is interesting that just under half expressed a preference to remain in

TABLE 17.4
Recommended accommodation

	No.	(%)
Independent living	2	(0.7)
With family	2	(0.7)
Independent group home	1	(0.4)
Supported group home	14	(5.1)
Rehabilitation unit	23	(8.4)
Low-staffed home	30	(10.9)
High-staffed home (24 hour cover)	102	(37.1)
Very sheltered nursing home	87	(31.6)
Other	14	(5.1)
Total	275	(100)

From Clifford and Szyndler (1986).

TABLE 17.5
Recommended programme of day activities

	No.	(%)
Maintenance—low pressure low expectation. Some training in self-care and daily living skills.	162	(58.9)
Maintenance 'plus'—low pressure, but with greater emphasis on training and higher expectations of independence	59	(21.4)
Socialisation—strong emphasis on development and maintenance of self-care skills. Social activities/ sheltered work encouraged.	37	(13.5)
Socialisation 'plus'—as above, but strong emphasis on social integration. High-level sheltered work/Adult Education/Paid employment.	12	(4.4)
Follow-up only	5	(1.8)
Totals	275	(100)

From Clifford and Szyndler (1986).

hospital.) However, MacCarthy, Benson and Brewin (1986) report a study where a group of disabled long-term patients in the community gave very clear and consistent views as to what they saw as being problematic and difficult in their lives and what they wanted help with. Needless to say their perceptions and priorities were sometimes very different from the staff who were looking after them. Obtaining reliable information from patients, particularly some of the most disabled long-stay is difficult, but it may be possible. It is clearly worth the effort,

A final source of information to consider when assessing service needs are the patients' close family and relatives. It is only fairly recently that relatives' views have been considered important in the care and management of adult psychiatric patients. For too long they were simply blamed rather than being seen as a resource (Kuipers & Bebbington, 1985). As an example of their value in service planning Creer, Sturt and Wykes (1982) report the results of interviews with a sample of 52 relatives of long-term patients (mainly schizophrenic) living in the community; 34 said they would like some additional or modified service. These suggestions are shown in Table 17.6.

Interestingly, there is a relatively high priority attached to day care, short-term admission, additional social work help (financial assistance?) and greater involvement with hospital staff. The relatives did not seem to be requesting additional social activities, domiciliary or home-help. These results have clear service implications.

TABLE 17.6
Additional services desired by relatives

Service desired by relative*	No. of patients	(%)
Day care, employment rehabilitation, sheltered work, etc. to suit patient's specialised needs	8	(15)
A break (includes holiday for patient to give relative a rest)	7	(13)
Social worker	7	(13)
More inclusion by hospital staff, or opportunity to speak to patient's doctor	7	(13)
Change in some aspect of patient's current night-care setting	7	(13)
Money and material help	5	(10)
Change in some aspect of patient's day-care setting	5	(10)
Domiciliary psychiatric services (e.g. community nurse)	4	(8)
Alternative residential care or sheltered accommodation for patient	4	(8)
More responsive emergency services	4	(8)
Re-housing	4	(8)
Social activities for patient	3	(6)
Home help	1	(2)

*34 relatives (65% of those interviewed) wanted some change in services currently provided and/or some additional help; the number of patients totals in excess of 34 as many desired more than one change

From Creer et al. (1982).

Thus we have looked at a number of methods to assess service needs and it is clear that no one approach is sufficient on its own. Each has advantages and disadvantages and we need to be aware of their strengths and limitations. Ultimately the definition of 'need' is usually ideological, i.e. it is not based on empirical knowledge about how a particular kind of service provision will lead to a specific outcome. So, how can the 'process' of care be more closely examined?

How well is it working?

At a technical level the best tool for service evaluation is probably the case register. This is a data-linkage system, usually computerised, which records an individual's contacts with the services. Case registers are usually restricted to psychiatric services and only operate with regard to the population of a given geographical area. (For a good introduction to the use of case registers in monitoring and evaluation, see Walsh, 1985.) A number of different types of contact may be recorded and cross-referenced (e.g. out-patient attendances, day attendances, in-patient admissions, see Wooff, Freeman & Fryers, 1983). Because case registers can monitor specific kinds of contacts they may also be used to study particular groups of patients. They may then be used as a sampling frame for more in-depth investigations e.g. Sturt, Wykes and Creer's (1982) study of 'high-contact' users in Camberwell.

Case registers are thus the most sophisticated device available for evaluating the impact of new service developments. However, they are also time consuming and expensive to set up and maintain and they provide only quantitative information about service use. They cannot tell you anything about the *quality* of service being provided or anything very meaningful about outcome. In these days of micro-computers, the trend is therefore to employ much smaller, more specific information systems (e.g. Gibbons, 1986). These 'mini' systems can provide qualitative as well as quantitative information and enable one to keep a track of individual care plans, review dates, case management responsibilities, etc., as well as monitoring contacts with the service by a specific client group (in this case schizophrenia). They are thus valuable not only as a research tool, but also for direct practical and clinical purposes.

Of course, fairly simple 'book-keeping' data may be collected without sophisticated systems providing that someone is willing to help develop a suitable data sheet and supply the motivation for its completion. For example, the development of day services in a particular district can be monitored with a simple form which each unit completes on a three-monthly, or six-monthly basis, covering:

1. Number of new clients referred.
2. Sources of referral.
3. Number accepted from each source.
4. Number currently attending.
5. Number leaving over the specified time period.
6. Changes in activities/programme offered.
7. Changes in staffing.
8. Any other developments.

Regular sharing of this kind of information between units can also help the service develop in an integrated and co-ordinated fashion.

RESEARCH AND PLANNING SPECIFIC PROJECTS

I will now turn to research regarding specific projects and consider how we can answer questions such as:

1. Is the project meeting its aims?
2. What is the quality of care being provided?
3. Does the project fit into the overall aims of the service?

Is the project meeting its aims?

In order to answer this question, there must be a clear initial statement of aims. Usually, this takes the form of an 'operational policy', and this should describe such features as:

1. General aims and objectives.
2. Details of client groups to be served (including selection criteria).
3. Location.
4. Staffing.
5. Internal management arrangements.
6. Lengths of stay.
7. How aims and objectives will be achieved (details of treatment programme).
8. External management structure (who supervises?).
9. Methods of evaluation.

The purpose of an operational policy is to define, in as detailed a way as possible, the overall aims and objectives of the unit. An alternative to a formal Operational Policy is simply to try to define the nature of the service to be provided. For example, Anthony, Cohen and Farkas (1982) have attempted to 'operationalise' the necessary ingredients of a rehabilitation programme (Table 17.7). It is obviously important, if the effectiveness of the project is to be monitored, that this kind of clear operationalisation of aims is achieved.

What is the quality of care being provided?

'Quality of care' (QOC) can be defined at a number of different levels (Shepherd, 1984; Lavender, 1985). First, we need to consider the physical structure of the facility. Ever since institutions were built we have been concerned with the most suitable environment in which to offer care, though concepts of what is suitable have changed very much over time. The standards outlined by the Welsh Office in their Appendix

TABLE 17.7
The essential ingredients of a psychiatric rehabilitation programme

Ingredient	Examples of how observed
1. Functional assessment of client skills in relation to environmental demand	1. Client records show a listing of client skill strengths and deficits in relation to environmental demands; strengths and deficits are behaviourally defined and indicate client's present and needed level of functioning
2. Client involvement in the rehabilitation assessment and intervention	2. Record forms have places for client signoff and comments; percentage of clients who actually sign off; sample of audiotapes of client interviews indicate client understanding of *what* programme is doing and *why*
3. Systematic individual client rehabilitation plan	3. Written or taped examples of objective, behavioural, step-by-step client plans; a central 'bank' of available rehabilitation curricula; client records specify on which plans client is working
4. Direct teaching of skills to clients	4. Practitioners can identify the skills they are capable of teaching, describe the teaching process, and demonstrate their teaching techniques. Programme's daily calendar reflects blocks of time devoted to skill training
5. Environmental assessment and modification	5. Practitioners can describe characteristics of client's environment to which client is being rehabilitated and how the environment may be modified to support the client's skills level. Functional assessment should have assessed unique environmental demands
6. Follow-up of clients in their real-life environment	6. Client records indicate a monitoring plan and descriptions of monitoring results; audiotapes of practitioner and feedback sessions; record-keeping forms provide spaces for changes in the intervention plan. Percentage of clients whose plans have changed; number of appointments for 'follow-along' services
7. A rehabilitation team approach	7. Team members can verbally describe each client's observable goals and the responsibilities of each team member in relation to those goals (may refer to client's records for this information)
8. A rehabilitation referral procedure	8. Client records indicate referral letters requesting specific outcomes by specific dates; telephone referrals demonstrate these same rehabilitation referral ingredients
9. Evaluation of observable outcomes and utilisation of evaluation results	9. Agency records show the pooled outcome data for all clients; agency directors can verbally describe their setting's most significant client outcome
10. Consumer involvement in policy and planning	10. Administrators can list the number of joint meetings with consumers; consumer ratings of satisfaction with the rehabilitation programme

From Anthony et al. (1982).

to the Nodder Report (DHSS, 1979) and by the DHSS in *Home Life* (Centre for Policy on Ageing, 1984) provide useful guidelines. However, one cannot equate quality of care with the adequacy of the physical environment. Like other aspects of QOC a good physical environment offers a necessary, but not sufficient, condition for a good quality of care.

The second level at which quality of care may be evaluated concerns the 'process' of care, i.e. the organisation and management practices within the unit and how these are reflected in the amount and nature of staff-client interactions.

Organisation and management practices may be analysed in a number of different ways. For example, Norma Raynes and her colleagues tried to operationalise Golfman's concept of the 'total institution' (Golfman, 1961). They developed instruments to measure organisation and management practices along four dimensions: rigidity of routine, block treatment, depersonalisation, and staff-patient distance (King, Raynes & Tizard, 1971). More recently they have included staffs' perceptions of their involvement in the running of the unit as an important variable (Raynes, Pratt & Roses, 1979). Raynes' ideas have been used by Shepherd and Richardson (1979) and Garety and Morris (1984) to study management practices in day and residential settings for the care of long-term patients. These studies showed considerable variation in the extent to which such settings are organised to meet the needs of individual clients. There also seemed to be a correlation between client-orientated management practices and levels of staff-client interaction. Where organisation and management practices were more client-orientated, staff were likely to interact with clients more frequently and in a more positive way. Both client-centred management practices and high levels of positive staff-client interaction seemed to be correlated with perceived staff involvement in decision-making.

An alternative way of looking at management practices is the Hospital-Hostel Practices Profile (HHPP) developed by Wykes, Sturt and Creer (1982). This assesses the restrictiveness versus permissiveness of the environment based on ideas first set out by Wing and Brown (1970) and later used by Hewett, Ryan and Wing (1975) and Ryan (1979). It surveys practices under a number of headings, e.g. restrictions on activity (bedtimes, rising times, etc.), personal possessions, meals and snacks, health and hygiene, care of rooms, and contact with services (GP, hairdresser, etc.). Wykes et al., report results from a number of day and residential units, and the HHPP provides a useful way of assessing 'restrictiveness', particularly in residential settings. However, it measures many of the same dimensions tapped by the scales of King et al. (1971) and there is little to choose between them. Perhaps there may be slightly more comparative data available for the HHPP at present. The similarity of these measures is illustrated by Wykes' (1982) study of the hospital hostel which also figured in the study by Garety and Morris (1984). Wykes found that the hostel ward was significantly less restrictive on the HHPP than comparable hospital wards; furthermore, staff considered many more of the residents' problems as requiring intervention. This is consistent with the resident orientation identified by Garety and Morris.

The final level on which QOC may be considered concerns the outcome of care, i.e. the actual functioning of the clients themselves. A good physical environment, with client-orientated management and relatively 'permissive' practices, should facilitate high levels of positive staff-client interaction which in turn should be reflected in good outcomes with high levels of functioning. So, how may these be evaluated? Once again, client functioning has a number of different aspects and each of these needs to be considered separately. First, there is 'objective' functioning as assessed by rating scales or by other methods of direct observation. Choice of appropriate measures will depend upon a number of specific criteria such as the aims of the unit, the amount of training required, length and sophistication of the instrument, etc.

In general, it is probably best to concentrate on one or two fairly simple measures which reflect the fundamental aims and objectives of the project. For example, the simple time-budget measure used in the Wykes (1982) study showed how hostel-ward residents spent less time doing nothing compared with residents living in a traditional hospital ward. Similarly, evaluation using instruments like the REHAB 'General Behaviour' scores, and Wykes and Sturt's (1986) 'Social Behaviour Schedule', provide good overall indications of observer-rated functioning. Client satisfaction is another important measure, although, as we saw earlier, it may be difficult to obtain valid assessments. Relatives' satisfaction might also be considered, particularly where new services are being developed that place additional responsibilities on the relatives. Finally, the importance of staff attitudes should not be forgotten. All new projects depend upon the enthusiasm and commitment of staff and their expressed satisfaction, whether measured directly or indirectly (through sickness, absenteeism, etc.) is crucial.

Thus, quality of care is a complex construct. It cannot be defined by a single measurement and its various aspects may have to be given different weights in different settings. The central question when assessing QOC remains an understanding of the process whereby features of the care provided have a direct influence on the outcomes obtained.

Does the project fit into the overall aims of the service?

This takes us back to the interface between the overall services and the operation of a new development. Those groups who have an overall responsibility (Health Care Planning Teams, Joint Development Teams, etc.) clearly do not require large amounts of detailed information as to what is happening in every specific project, but they do require some information to ensure that new developments are staying within the strategy outlined in the original plan. One way to achieve this is for the overall planning team to set up a number of working sub-groups each with responsibility for a particular area of service development (e.g. day care, accommodation, sheltered work, crisis and emergency, etc.) If they establish regular reviews with written reports to the 'parent' planning team then they can monitor progress in each of the sub-groups.

RESEARCH DESIGNS

We have seen repeatedly how the problems of evaluation hinge around identifying relationships between particular facets of the service and the various outcomes. Unravelling such causal questions is the task of research designs. This topic is fully discussed elsewhere in this book but it may be worth making one or two comments here.

The starting point for any evaluation must be the formulation of a clear question about the relationship between two variables or sets of variables. Hopefully, the measures reviewed in this chapter give plenty of scope for the operational definition of specific dependent and independent variables. What one then has to do is explore their causal relationship. The traditional tool for investigating causal relationships in psychology has been the random controlled trial. However, for various reasons (small numbers, difficulties in matching, ethical problems, etc.) such designs may not be so useful in a service context. Here, different kinds of 'quasi-experiments' (Cook & Campbell, 1979) may be preferable. These do not employ conventional control groups, but rely instead on 'single case' studies, where control is obtained by using an extended set of baseline observations on a single subject (or unit). These kinds of single-subject, pre-post, designs can be very useful in service evaluation (e.g. in case registers, see Wing & Hailey, 1972). In small-scale studies, even simple pre-post evaluations can be useful. For example, Figs 17.1 and 17.2 show changes in the REHAB scores of two groups of old long-stay residents following transfer from a traditional ward to supported houses in the hospital grounds.

Although strictly speaking one cannot conclude that transfer 'caused' the improvements (because of the lack of adequate baseline data) the

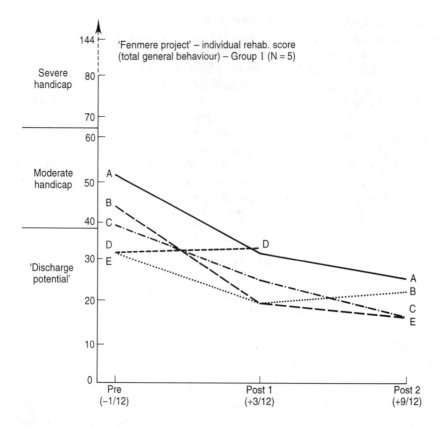

FIG. 17.1. Fenmere Project—individual rehabilitation scores for total general behaviour. Group I (five subjects).

trends are nevertheless interesting. They suggest a number of more specific hypotheses. For example, why did group I apparently show a steady trend towards improvement (with one exception) while group II only began improving some time after they had been transferred? Was it because group I were better prepared? Was it due to differences in staff? Was it due to differences between the groups? (Group I were generally of a high level of functioning at the beginning.) Was it a 'floor' effect on the measure? Why did one patient in group II show such a marked deterioration in functioning? Does this suggest that there are some old long-stay residents for whom this kind of small-scale domestic setting is not suitable? The answers to these questions need not trouble us here; the point is that such simple, uncontrolled evaluations can generate a number of useful ideas which can then be followed up in more rigorous, carefully controlled designs.

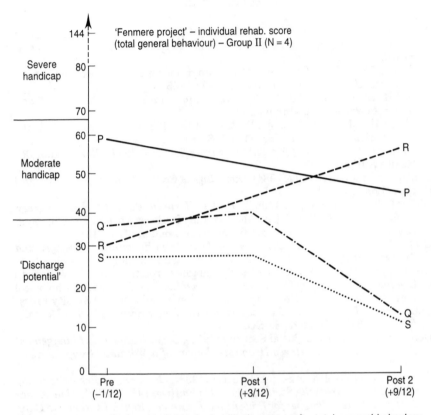

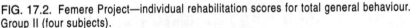

FIG. 17.2. Femere Project—individual rehabilitation scores for total general behaviour. Group II (four subjects).

CONCLUSIONS

I have tried in this chapter to cover the basic research issues relating to service planning and evaluation, both at the level of overall service development and in connection with specific projects. Services are difficult things to do research on, they are multi-dimensional, they are complicated and they are elusive, always 'on the move'. Research methods must therefore not only be subtle and sophisticated, they must also be dynamic and capable of adapting to the changing characteristics of the clients and the changing perceptions of their needs. They must also be responsive to a changing social and economic climate. Empirical data can only capture a tiny fragment of this complex reality, but the challenge of trying to provide some kind of scientific basis for service development remains one of the most interesting—and potentially valuable—contributions that the social scientist can make.

REFERENCES

Anthony, W.A., Cohen, M.R., & Farkas, M. (1982). A Psychiatric Rehabilitation Treatment Program: Can I Recognize One If I See One? *Community Mental Health Journal, 18*, 83-95.

Bachrach, L.L. (1980). Overview: Model programs for chronic mental patients. *American Journal of Psychiatry, 137*, 1023-1031.

Baker, R. & Hall, J.N. (1983). *REHAB: Rehabilitation Evaluation Hall and Baker*. Aberdeen: Vine Publishing.

Bewley, T.H., Bland, M., Mechen, D., & Walch, E. (1981). New Chronic Patients. *British Medical Journal, 283*, 1161-1164.

Cambridge Health Authority (1984). *Strategic Plan 1984-1994*. Cambridge Health Authority, UK.

Centre for Policy on Ageing (1984). *Home Life: A Code of Practice for Residential Care*. London: CPA.

Clifford, P. & Szyndler, J. (1986). *Bexley Hospital Patients' Needs Survey*. Available from National Unit for Psychiatric Research and Development. Lewisham Hospital, Lewisham High Street, London SE13 6LH.

Cook, T.D. & Campbell, D.T. (1979). *Quasi-experimentation—Design and Analysis Issues for Field Settings*. Chicago: Rand McNally.

Creer, C., Sturt, E., & Wykes, T. (1982). The role of relatives. In J.K. Wing (ed.) *Long-term Community Care: Experience in a London Borough*. Psychological Medicine Monograph, Supplement 2. London: Cambridge University Press.

Department of Health & Social Security (1975). *Better Services for the Mentally Ill*. Cmnd.6233. London: HMSO.

Department of Health & Social Security (1979). *Organisation and Management Problems of Mental Illness Hospitals: Report of a Working Group*. London: DHSS.

Department of Health & Social Security (1985). *Government Response to the Second Report from the Social Services Committee. 1985-1985 Session. Annex 1. Mental Illness: Policies for Prevention, Treatment, Rehabilitation and Care*. Cmnd.9674. London: HMSO.

Early, D.F. & Nicholas, M. (1977). Dissolution of the Mental Hospital: Fifteen Years On. *British Journal of Psychiatry, 130*, 117-122.

Early, D.F. & Nicholas, M. (1981). Two decades of change: Glenside Hospital population surveys 1960-80. *British Medical Journal, 282*, 1446-1449.

Garety, P.A. & Morris, I. (1984). A new unit for long-stay psychiatric patients: organisation. attitudes and quality of care. *Psychological Medicine, 14*, 183-192.

Gibbons, J. (1986). *Co-ordinated Aftercare for Schizophrenia: The Community Care Information Unit*. University Department of Psychiatry. Royal South Hants. Hospital, Southampton S09 4PE, UK.

Golfmann, E. (1962). *Asylums: Essays on the Social Situation of Mental Patients and Other Inmates*. New York: Anchor Books, Doubleday.

Goldberg, D. & Huxley, P. (1980). *Mental Illness in the Community*. London: Tavistock Publications.

Goldman, H.H. (1983). The demography of deinstitutionalisation. In L.L. Bachtach (ed.) *Deinstitutionalisation*. San Francisco: Jossey Bass.

Hewett, S., Ryan, P., & Wing, J.K. (1975). Living without the mental hospitals. *Journal of Social Policy, 4*, 391-404.

House of Commons (1985). *Second Report from the Social Services Committee: Community Care with Special Reference to Adult Mentally Ill and Mentally Handicapped People*. London: HMSO.

Jennings, C. (1982). *Statistics from Eight Psychiatric Case Registers in Great Britain 1976-1981*. Southampton Psychiatric Case Register, Knowle Hospital, Hants PO17 5NA, UK.

King, R., Raynes, N., & Tizard, J. (1971). *Patterns of Residential Care*. London: Routledge & Kegan Paul.

Kingsley, S., McAusland, T., & Towell, D. (1985). *Managing Psychiatric Services in Transition: Designing the Arrangements for Moving People from Large Hospitals into Local Services*. London: Kings Fund Centre.

Kuipers, L. & Bebbington, P. (1985). Relatives as a Resource in the Management of Functional Illness. *British Journal of Psychiatry, 147*, 465-470.

Lavender, A. (1985). Quality of care and staff practices in long-stay settings. In F.N. Watts (ed.) *New Developments in Clinical Psychology*. Chichester, UK: The British Psychological Society/Wiley.

Levene, L.S., Donaldson, L.J., & Brandon, S. (1985). How likely is it that a district health authority can close its large mental hospitals? *British Journal of Psychiatry, 147*, 150-155.

MacCarthy, B., Benson, J., & Brewin, C.R. (1986). Task motivation and problem appraisal in long-term psychiatric patients. *Psychological Medicine, 16*, 431-438.

Mann, S.A. & Cree, W. (1976). 'New' long-stay psychiatric patients: a national sample survey of fifteen mental hospitals in England and Wales 1972/3. *Psychological Medicine, 6*, 603-616.

MIND (1983). *Common Concern*. London: MIND Publications.

Moore, A.J. (1985). *Long-stay Psychiatric Rehabilitation Bed Requirements in Cambridge: A Planning Model*. Unpublished MFCM Thesis, Cambridge Health Authority, UK.

O'Brien, J. & Tyne, A. (1981). *The Principle of Normalisation: A Foundation for Effective Services*. London: Campaign for Mental Health.

Pattie, A.H. & Gilleard, C.J. (1979). *Clifton Assessment Procedures for the Elderly (CAPE)*. Windsor: NFER-Nelson.

Raynes, N., Pratt, M., & Roses, S. (1979). *Organisational Structure and The Care of the Mentally Handicapped*. London: Croom Helm.

Richman, A. & Barry, A. (1985). More and More is Less and Less: The Myth of Massive Psychiatric Need. *British Journal of Psychiatry, 146*, 164-168.

Ryan, P. (1979). Residential care for the mentally disabled. In J.K. Wing & R. Ilsen (eds.) *Community Care for the Mentally Disabled*. London: Oxford University Press.

Shepherd, G. (1984). Quality of Care. In *Institutional Care and Rehabilitation*. Chapter 4. London: Longmans.

Shepherd, G. & Richardson, A. (1979). Organisation and Interaction in Psychiatric Day Centres. *Psychological Medicine, 9*, 573-579.

Stein, L.I. & Test, M.A. (1978). An alternative to mental hospital treatment. In L.I. Stein & M.A. Test (eds.) *Alternatives to Mental Hospital Treatment*. New York: Plenum Press.

Stein, L.I. & Test, M.A. (eds.) (1985). *The Training in Community Living Model: A Decade of Experience*. San Francisco: Jossey-Bass Inc.

Stroul, B.A. (1984). *Toward Community Support Systems for the Mentally Disabled: The NIMH Communitv Support Program*. Available from the Center for Rehabilitation Research and Training in Mental Health, Boston University, Boston, Mass.

Stroul, B.A. (1986). *Models of Community Support Services: Approaches to Helping Persons with Long-term Mental Illness*. Available from the Center for Rehabilitation Research and Training in Mental Health, Boston University, Boston, Mass.

Sturt, E., Wykes, T. & Creer, C. (1982). Demographic. social and clinical characteristics of the sample. In J.K. Wing (ed.) *Long-term Community Care: Experience in a London Borough*. Psychological Medicine Monograph Supplement, 2. Cambridge University Press.

Tooth, G.C. & Brooke, E. (1961). Trends in the Mental Hospital Population and their effect on Future Planning. *Lancet, i*, 710-713.

Walsh, D. (1985). Case registers for monitoring treatment outcome in chronic functional psychoses. In T. Helgason (ed.) *The Long-term Treatment of Functional Psychoses*. London: Cambridge University Press.

Warner, R. (1985). *Recovery from Schizophrenia*. London: Routledge & Kegan Paul.

Wing, J.K. & Brown, G.W. (1970). *Institutional and Schizophrenia: A Comparative Study of Three Mental Hospitals, 1960-1968*. London: Cambridge University Press.

Wing, J.K. & Hailey, A. (eds.) (1972). *Evaluation, a Community Psychiatric Service: The Camberwell Register, 1964-1971*. London: Oxford University Press.

Wolfensberger, W. & Glenn, L. (1975). *Program Analysis of Service Systems*. 3rd edn. Toronto: National Institute of Mental Retardation.

Wooff, K., Freeman, H.L., & Fryers, T. (1983). Psychiatric service use in Salford: A comparison of point-prevalence ratios 1968 and 1978. *British Journal of Psychiatry, 142*, 588-597.

Wykes, T. (1982). A hostel-ward for 'new' long-stay patients: an evaluative study of 'a ward in a house'. In J.K. Wing (ed.). *Long-term Community Care: Experience in a London Borough*. Psychological Medicine Monograph Supplement, 2. Cambridge University Press.

Wykes, T. & Sturt, E. (1986). The measurement of social behaviour in psychiatric patients: An assessment of the reliability and validity of the SBS schedule. *British Journal of Psychiatry, 148*, 1-11.

Wykes, T., Sturt, E., & Creer, C. (1982). Practices of day and residential units in relation to the social behaviour of attenders. In J.K. Wing (ed.) *Long-term Community Care: Experience in a London Borough*. Psychological Medicine Monograph Supplement, 2. Cambridge University Press.

CHAPTER EIGHTEEN

Service evaluation and audit methods

Glenys Parry *Sheffield Consulting and Clinical Psychologists, Community Health Sheffield*

INTRODUCTION

One of the most widespread applications of research skills and methods is in evaluating or auditing services. This type of research differs from basic scientific research. When undertaking to evaluate or audit a service or an aspect of a service, we adapt and use methods, measurement principles, measures, designs, and statistical techniques from basic behavioural and mental health research, but our purpose is different. Audit and evaluation are intended to improve clinical practice and services, to monitor and justify the use of resources, and to inform decision making, rather than to build theory and improve understanding by addressing scientific questions. Even applied research is not primarily driven by the immediate needs of service funders, managers and clinicians. Evaluation and audit are examples of *applicable* rather than applied research. Milne (1987) compiles a Table to summarise these differences (See Table 18.1).

TABLE 18.1

Factor	Basic Research	Evaluative Research
1. Purpose of research	To build theories and improve understanding	To make decisions and improve programmes
2. Applicablity of findings	Widely applicable	Results only directly relevant to same programme and setting
3. Value of research	To establish 'truth'	To improve worth of programme
4. Measurement	Standardised instruments: rigorous control; scientific standards essential (e.g. randomisation)	Ragbag of measuring tools; control very difficult to achieve; scientific standards desirable
5. Topics	Anything	Socially important phenomena
6. Judgement	Eschewed	Integral
7. Research consumers	Secondary, not identified	Primary
8. Politics	An improper consideration	A necessary and important consideration
9. Replicability	Important hallmark	Neither important nor possible
10. Setting	Not treated as significant; highly controlled	Essential aspect; control very limited
11. Publication	Major academic goal of research	Uncommon and secondary

Reproduced with permission from Milne, D. (1987) *Evaluating Mental Health Practice: Methods and Applications.* London: Croom Helm

DIFFERENCES BETWEEN RESEARCH AND AUDIT: THE EXAMPLE OF PSYCHOTHERAPY TREATMENT RESEARCH

One example within the mental health field that illustrates these distinctions is the contrast between psychotherapy treatment research and therapists' clinical audit or psychotherapy service evaluation.

Psychotherapy treatment research addresses fundamental scientific questions about the nature of psychological change, factors that influence psychotherapeutic outcome, and the processes by which this takes place. In terms of the four types of validity outlined by Cook and Campbell (1979), psychotherapy treatment research designs aim to eliminate threats to statistical conclusion, and internal and construct validity (see Shapiro, Chapter 10). In doing so, they must necessarily sacrifice external validity or generalisability. The very features that make the results scientifically convincing limit their applicability; randomisation, homogeneous samples, 'pure' manualised treatments, and extensive measurement procedures. There are a number of circumstances where clinical realism is fatal to the first three forms of validity and treatment researchers, quite understandably, prefer to sacrifice external validity. The service evaluator, on the other hand, must ensure that the results primarily have external validity. The evaluative researcher selects methods that have utility in solving practical problems and providing information needed for making funding and service delivery decisions. The service auditor strives to gather data that lead directly to maintaining standards and improving services, without addressing theoretical questions. There are ways in which some data of scientific interest can be gleaned 'on the back of' evaluation projects and indeed, the two activities complement each other. However, the fundamental tension between the two should not be underestimated.

For example, randomisation is held to be the best protection against systematic pre-treatment differences but has a number of difficulties, particularly with small sample sizes (Hsu, 1989; Kraemer, 1981) and often post-hoc statistical correction for bias is required, such as the use of residual gain scores. The effect of pre-measures is removed from the variance of the post measures, and the analysis of the remaining variance is free of contamination by this or any set of covariates that may be partialled out. But as Tuchfeld (1979) points out, these attempts to reconcile non-random differences by statistical manipulation are trying to treat groups 'as if' they were equal prior to the occurrence of some event or process—but the evaluative researcher is often most interested in what the pre-intervention differences are and the real effects of the intervention as delivered. The example is given of controlling statistically for atmospheric pressure, and finding that the Himalayan and the Catskill mountain ranges turn out to be equal in average height.

A more fundamental criticism of the randomised controlled trial is made by Brewin and Bradley (1989) who argue that where patients have a preference for one form of treatment over another, the bias introduced by differential consent, participation, or attrition is considerable although in many research reports, invisible. They recommend greater use of designs that allow patient choice. Their argument is highly applicable to psychotherapy research where patients often have well expressed preferences for treatment types, indeed are often seeking a particular approach, and where clinical assessors routinely make treatment-of-choice decisions.

Heterogeneity in patient samples is a threat to statistical conclusion validity and hence selection criteria are rather stringent, often excluding those patients with complex or multiple needs who are frequently referred to psychotherapy services. Treatment integrity, where standardised manualised treatments are delivered, is also vital to statistical conclusion validity but rarely are such treatments used in clinical practice. Indeed, many clinicians argue that the essence of good practice, in whichever therapy mode, lies in building a formulation of each case which then dictates the treatment plan and hence allows techniques to be responsive to the needs of the individual patient (Ryle, 1990). The extensive measurement procedures and multiple assessments required by researchers have considerable impact on the therapy itself (Firth, Shapiro, & Parry, 1986) and are again unrepresentative of the service context where such levels of measurement are unacceptably costly and intrusive.

The weaknesses of psychotherapy research in relation to external validity are therefore severe and lead to an incomplete or misleading picture, specifically by masking naturally occurring interactions between variables in complex service systems. However, problematic external validity is not the only reason psychotherapy research is limited in its usefulness to service practitioners and planners. Outcome research has been opaque with regard to the processes by which therapeutic outcomes are achieved. Therapies used in research have sometimes been unrecognisable to clinicians. Another widespread practice has been to rely on statistical significance to estimate effectiveness although it is possible to reject the null hypothesis in a group comparison and still obtain clinically trivial results.

Psychotherapy researchers themselves have been acutely aware of these issues and recent developments in psychotherapy research promise to overcome some of these difficulties. There has been renewed interest in the analysis of psychotherapy process; the new paradigm uses meaningful sequences of therapy events within their context (Rice & Greenberg, 1984; Safran, McMain, Crocker, & Murray, 1990). Intensive process analysis is yielding clinically relevant data on unconscious processes and psychodynamic mechanisms in therapy (Horowitz & Stinson, 1991; Luborsky & Crits-Cristoph, 1990). More researchers are now adopting methods of estimating the clinical significance of measured changes (Jacobson & Truax, 1991). There is an explicit commitment to developing more clinically relevant research methods (Newman & Howard, 1991). Shapiro (this volume, Chapter 10) points out that there is no perfect outcome study and that choice of research design is 'a creative compromise based upon explicit under-standing of the implications of the choice made.' Psychotherapy and other mental health researchers legitimately ask different questions from those of service planners and policymakers. It is inappropriate to expect behavioural and mental health research to provide all the information needed for planning, commissioning and improving services.

DIFFERENCES BETWEEN AUDIT AND EVALUATION

Although clinical audit and service evaluation share the purpose of improving services and informing policy or planning decisions, there are differences between them. The two can be distinguished in terms of the perspective from which they are undertaken and the scale of the project. In simple terms, audit is practitioner based, conducted by oneself and one's peers, to review systematically and critically the quality of clinical care. The process involves developing standards of practice and gathering information about how well the service meets these in order to improve the service. Data gathering in itself, for example on levels of service activity, does not constitute an audit, without the element of enquiring how one can improve the quality of service (Crombie, Davies, Abraham, & Florey, 1993). Evaluation, on the other hand, stands back from the operational detail of the service somewhat, giving more of an outside perspective. Evaluation may be undertaken by evaluative researchers who are not part of the service, and indeed, may not themselves be clinical practitioners.

Audit is, ideally, a short cycle affair, where an aspect of the service or of clinical practice can be identified, monitored, and reflected back to service practitioners relatively quickly to allow changes in practice to be implemented and the effects of the changes to be examined. For example, Firth-Cozens (1993) describes a descriptive and outcome audit in a psychiatric day hospital. In addition to basic socio-demographic information and descriptive data about treatment, a general measure of symptoms was administered and a criterion was agreed for clinical improvement (one standard deviation from the intake mean). This allowed the staff of the day hospital to examine more critically the characteristics of those patients who were not meeting the criterion, finding that they were the older women and those who had been sexually abused. These findings allowed the staff to introduce more appropriate services for these two groups, to provide different training for some staff, and to plan a more coherent approach across the District to the needs of these patients. Thus the audit loop was closed and ideally the audit would be continued, in order to establish that improvements in effectiveness were actually achieved.

Service evaluation tends to be planned on a larger and longer scale, examining the impact of a new service or a redesigned service delivery system. For example, in a service evaluation conducted by Conway, Melzer, and Hale (1994) after people with schizophrenia in an inner London health district were found to have high levels of psychotic symptomatology and social disability but very low levels of supported housing and structured day activity, a new way of delivering services was devised. Community mental health nurses were redeployed to target their efforts with this patient group and new community teams implemented a case management system. The effects of these service improvements were assessed by studying the progress of a cohort of 51 patients over three years, interviewing them before and after the new service design. This evaluation was able to show that psychiatric symptomatology was reduced considerably but that improvements in social functioning did not follow. It can be expected that the form of service *evaluation* of which this is a good example will have broader generalisability than the first example of a clinical *audit*.

APPROACHES TO EVALUATION AND AUDIT

A number of different methods of evaluating and improving services have been developed, including service evaluation, operational research, clinical audit, service audit, quality assurance, and total quality management.

Service evaluation arose in the US during the 1960s and 70s in response to concerns about the cost and effectiveness of Federal human service programmes (Attkisson, Hargreaves, Horowitz, & Sorensen, 1978) and has been defined as 'the systematic application of social research procedures in assessing the conceptualization and design, implementation and utility of social intervention programs' (Rossi & Freeman, 1982; p.20). In contrast to quality assurance programmes, trained external evaluators investigate a service or project and report to the 'stakeholders'. In practice, service evaluation has tended to be less concerned with process and more with outcomes (Green & Attkisson, 1984).

Service evaluation has the advantages of relative skill and objectivity but is not a routine part of the service and there may be problems with implementing changes as a result of such feedback. For example, in the US, Federal funding of Community Mental Health Centres in the 1960s and 70s was accompanied by the requirement that the impact of the centres be evaluated. However, it was widely reported that despite massive investment, this mandatory evaluation failed to improve services (Windle, 1979) and that the evaluation results did not influence decision making, and failed to lead to better cost-effectiveness or to provide more equitable services. There is considerable current investment in England in health care evaluation through the NHS Research and Development programme (Department of Health, 1991, 1994). The funding is tightly linked to Government priorities for targeted gains in the population's health but there is no reason to believe that the long-standing problem has been resolved, of planning and service design decisions being under-influenced by the results of evaluative research (Wurzburg, 1979).

Operational research methods evolved as a management tool in improving cost-effectiveness of programmes by constructing mathematical models based on organisational prototypes and manipulating these to provide a solution to problems under study (Hillier & Lieberman, 1974). They have been advocated in mental health evaluation (Fox & Kuldau, 1968) and psychotherapy service evaluation (Yates, 1980). These methods link structure, process, and outcome in service systems, for example, to minimise treatment delays and underutilisation or to find the quickest or least costly route through the network of mental health providers. However, although the prototypes are easily understood, the technical details of applying the mathematical models have precluded their use by the non-specialist in routine service delivery.

Medical audit has been defined as 'the systematic, critical analysis of the quality of medical care, including the procedures used for diagnosis and treatment, the use of resources and the resulting outcome and quality of life for the patient' (Department of Health, 1989). This definition is all-encompassing, but in practice frequently refers to professional self-monitoring, based on peer review of the care process, often using retrospective study of case notes. This form of quality monitoring in medicine was formalised in the UK with the introduction of the NHS reforms and has since been extended to non-medical professions (Normand, 1991). In the US, medical audit has been embodied in legislation since 1972 and some of the difficulties encountered there may emerge in the UK. For example, peer review is open to bias (Horrobin, 1982); the appropriation of confidential audit notes in negligence litigation reduces compliance (Charlton, 1983); and costs of the professional audit system in relation to demonstrable benefits become problematic (Fulchiero et al., 1980). In addition to these problems, the usefulness of single-profession audit is limited in mental health services that are provided by inter-disciplinary cooperation. For this reason, *clinical audit*, where all participating professions collaborate to examine multidisciplinary care protocols, is now preferred by those funding audit in the UK health system.

The term *service audit* can be used to refer to self-monitoring methods which are not confined to a single profession but which aim to describe service process and outcome. This is therefore a form of service evaluation, but is undertaken by practitioners as a routine aspect of service delivery. It has great utility for mental health services that are delivered by therapists from a number of professional backgrounds.

McDonald, Marks, and Blizard (1988) present an excellent example of service audit from a behaviour therapy service provided as part of a training programme for nurse therapists. Results are reported from a series of 1384 patients treated by 41 trainees over 8 years using descriptors of the patient population, the treatments given, and problem-centred outcome measures. The routine monitoring of symptom severity and outcome of treatment can be successfully computerised to allow assessment of overall service performance (Bullmore, Joyce, Marks, & Connolly, 1992).

Quality assurance is a form of audit that monitors the process by which therapy is delivered, setting standards for performance and inspecting whether or not they are achieved (Lalonde, 1982). Ideally practitioners themselves choose the criteria for judging service quality, define the norms for good care, set specific standards of performance, and monitor adherence to these, using a 'quality circle' (Mohr & Mohr, 1983). Inevitably, process standards that are easy to monitor (such as waiting time from referral to first appointment) tend to take precedence over those that are more difficult (e.g. aspects of therapist in-session behaviour).

Total Quality Management (TQM) is based on a management-led commitment to continual improvements in quality by improving existing processes and devising new and better processes (Collard, 1989; Juran, 1988). It assumes that poor quality arises from bad systems not bad people. This moves away from a 'standards and inspection' model towards creating an organisational climate where people are enthusiastic to identify deficiencies in quality and to work together to rectify them (Smith, 1990). A number of problem-solving tools have been identified in this regard.

In tackling an audit or evaluation task, these methods are often best combined. They all serve the principle of service practitioners or service planners reflecting on practice to learn from experience, embodied in the concepts of the reflective practitioner (Schon, 1983), the learning organisation (Garratt, 1987) and the self-evaluating organisation (Wildavsky, 1972).

EVALUATION FRAMEWORKS

When designing a service evaluation or an audit endeavour, it is useful to work within a framework, to understand the different aspects of the service that can be the focus of the evaluation, depending on its dominant purpose. The general distinction between service structure, process, and outcomes is a useful one and the framework describing these, presented by Donabedian (1980), is one that has overarching applicability. Service structure includes such factors as appointment systems, equipment, patient case notes, buildings, and so on. Process relates to treatment procedures, communication, the sequence of steps experienced by clients, whereas outcome refers to such matters as clinical outcomes, cost efficiency, quality of life, or patient satisfaction.

An excellent example of a list of process topics for audit in a psychotherapy service is provided by Fonagy and Higgitt (1989) and reproduced in Table 18.2.

The act of evaluation implies appraisal against some predetermined criterion of a good service. The importance of clarity over service goals cannot be overemphasised, and indeed one of the practical difficulties for evaluative researchers is discovering what the objectives of a service or a programme actually are, as they are rarely made fully explicit. There are a number of criteria on which a service can be judged successful. Maxwell's (1984) six dimensions—relevance (appropriateness), equity, accessibility, acceptability, effectiveness, and efficiency—provide a useful framework for setting targets and evaluating whether they are met.

Firth-Cozens (1993) has combined Donabedian's factors with a version of Maxwell's framework to form a matrix which provides a useful tool in choosing audit topics. Table 18.3 shows examples of potential audit topics in community mental health services, located within the matrix.

EVALUATION AND AUDIT TECHNIQUES

Taking each of the criteria of successful services given by Maxwell (1984), I shall discuss a range of methods and techniques useful in service audit and evaluative research.

Service relevance or appropriateness

This criterion addresses the extent to which the service provided is matched to the particular needs of the recipients. A service could be of high quality and efficient but be inappropriate for those receiving it.

Service providers are often limited in the extent to which they can evaluate relevance. If criteria for excluding people from the service have been locally agreed (for example, minimum levels of symptomatology, no prior treatment in primary care), adherence to these can be monitored. Regular audit of those patients with negative outcomes can

TABLE 18.2
Some example items in the clinical audit of psychotherapy

Items	Examples of audit measures
Speed of dealing with referrals	Time
Availability of a range of therapeutic approaches	Review of the range of treatment
Depth and quality of initial assessment	Review of assessment summaries by board of experts
Clarity of diagnosis and formulation and treatment plan	Review of case records in order to produce fresh formulation
Handling of untreated cases	Review of the nature and quality of advice offered to patients not taken on for psychotherapy
Type and length of treatment	Review of case records by experts
Quality of records	Review of treatment session summaries
Level of training of those offering the treatment	Review of curriculum vitae of therapists
Level of supervision provided	Review of frequency of supervision sessions
Adequacy of liaison with primary care	Review of the appropriateness of medication to psychotherapeutic goals
Unnecessary disruptions to patients' treatments	Review of frequency of treatments disrupted by therapist departure
Management of handovers	Detailed review of six randomly selected cases where therapist changed
Management of crisis situations	Expert review of all patients who required admission
Frequency of negative response to therapy	Detailed review of all attempted suicides and suicides
Regular review system	Frequency of reviews and their detail
Follow up arrangements	Frequency of follow up and depth of follow up arranged

Reprinted with permission from Fonagy, P. & Higgit, A. (1989) Evaluating the performance of departments of psychotherapy. *Psychoanalytic Psychotherapy, 4,* 121–153.

also indicate groups to whom a service is being provided inappropriately. However, this leaves a danger of a self-perpetuating process whereby patients are only referred for the specific things the service can offer, and these patients appear to be having their needs met, while at the same time there are many other people whose requirements are being ignored. The way to tackle this is to measure population needs in the district or catchment area and to compare these with the referred population. Although this is the specified role of Health Authorities in

TABLE 18.3

	Structure	Process	Outcome
Equity & access	Availability of psychotherapy service. Day hospital relief for carers. Standards set for level of community staff. Conditions in community homes	Minority languages catered for in terms of interpreters, bilingual professional. Waiting times for assessment, outpatients Patients' Charter.	Does DNA rate reduce when interpreters available?
Acceptability & responsiveness	Patient satisfaction with wards, community homes, access to senior staff. Are the services offered reflecting patient needs?	Patient & carer's satisfaction with communication, responsiveness to needs, frequency of appointments etc.	Was outcome acceptable in terms of quality of life, satisfaction, family dynamics etc.?
Appropriateness	Do we have appropriately trained staff for the patients we see? Survey of security arrangement of rooms used by psychiatrists to assess emergency referrals. Conditions of consulting rooms.	Are our physical investigations appropriate? Are we giving CBT, psychotherapy, OT, play therapy, group therapy etc. when appropriate? Are particular patient groups seeing appropriate levels and types of professional? Are patients receiving appropriate psychometric testing, OT & nursing assessment?	Does drop out reduce when appropriate assessment is conducted?
Communication	Are our notes maintained in an acceptable manner? Do we have easy access to information for patients? Are our confidentiality procedures adequate?	Do letters to GPs have sufficient information? Are our communications to each member of the team acceptable? Do we make it clear to patients'relatives the treatment options that are possible/available?	Is outcome communicated sufficiently well to patients/relatives, GPs and other community staff?
Continuity	Where continuity of care is not possible, are notes maintained to ensure similar care?	Do patients have continuity of care from one person where that is called for? Follow-up of patients referred from general hospital to addiction unit.	Is there continuity in aftercare? Respite care.
Effectiveness	Are wards/hostels etc. sufficiently clean?	Is alcohol/drug dependency 'absent' at each appointment? Are we maintaining patient compliance in drug therapy? Are community patients competent in necessary life skills? Is our proportion of bedsores meeting national standards?	Are our outcomes in short-term therapy as good as they should be? What are our long-term outcomes for substance abuse, truancy, carers' health, marital discord, sexual abuse, independence etc.? Is our relapse/readmission rating meeting our standards?
Efficiency	Procedure for reducing non-attendance is being followed	Are tests, procedures, seclusions, drugs, therapies given only when indicated? Time spent travelling.	Is the length of therapy no longer than is necessary according to research?

the UK, in practice, both those commissioning and those providing services need to cooperate in estimating service relevance.

Rossi and Freeman (1982) give an equation to estimate the coverage of a service, which expresses the number of people in need to whom the service is given as a proportion of the total number in need within the population, then adjusts for the proportion of those receiving service who are not in need of it.

In using these estimators, the definition of who 'needs' a mental health service is vital. Brewin et al. (1987) address this problem usefully in relation to the continuing community care of people with mental health disabilities, with a system of defining and identifying met and unmet need in relation to individuals. When identifying population needs, Siegel, Attkisson, & Carson (1978) emphasise the importance of using a variety of information sources from different organisational levels at different points in time. Methods of estimating population needs and service coverage include epidemiological estimates (Wing, 1994), community surveys (Weiss, 1975), social indicators (Bell, Nguyen, Warheit, & Buhl, 1978), and key informants (NIMH, 1976).

Service equity

A service is inequitable if people in need of it are unwarrantedly excluded from it, on the basis of sociodemographic variables that are irrelevant to their capacity to benefit from it. For example, factors that have been shown to unfairly influence whether or not psychotherapy service is received include age, race, and socio-economic status (Garfield, 1986; Lorion & Felner, 1986). This commonly occurs because referral and assessment patterns have developed inequitably without anyone being aware of the fact. In order to obtain a crude indicator of equity a service can regularly monitor a cohort of referred patients on these characteristics and compare this with expected referral profiles, based on epidemiological data and the socio-demography of the catchment area. It will be clear that evaluation of service equity is closely, and sometimes problematically, linked to service relevance. Services that are appropriately targeted will necessarily exclude some patients whose needs would not be met by that service, but it is important to continue to address the question of whether such exclusions are equitable.

Service accessibility

Blocks to access include the geographical location of the service, long waiting lists, and the referral practices of the service 'gatekeepers'. Published research offers little information about accessibility of services, but it can be monitored by tracking the geographical distribution of referred patients and by comparing referral rates of the potential gatekeepers, such as General Practitioners.

Service acceptability and measurement of user satisfaction

Acceptability is the criterion closest to the Total Quality Management directive of 'meeting customer requirements'. In delivering a consumer-oriented service, it is vital to find methods of legitimating the user's viewpoint on service delivery issues and obtaining genuinely discriminating data.

Over the last 20 years there have been appreciable developments in the measurement of user satisfaction. The service user's perspective has become increasingly valued and the importance of using these views in auditing and evaluating services is now unchallenged. It is possible to trace a profound change in emphasis over this period, where the user's views were once seen as making only a marginal contribution to the evaluation of services, to a position which asserts that meeting users' requirements is a fundamental definition of service quality and enhancing service acceptability a fundamental goal of audit. Larsen, Attkisson, Hargreaves, and Nguyen (1979) make the point that there is an ethical requirement for publicly funded services to take client satisfaction into account, as they have virtually no financial incentive to satisfy the client or to involve the client in the evaluative process.

Satisfaction is a complex concept and can be understood as a product of at least three elements—the 'objective' quality of the service, the individual's preferences, and the individual's expectancies. Differences in user satisfaction between services or within the same service over time, could reflect any combination of these (Ware, Snyder, Wright, & Davies, 1983).

Measures of satisfaction are commonly self-completed questionnaires. In developing the Client Satisfaction Questionnaire (CSQ, 1979), Larsen et al. have helped to bring some standardisation to what had previously been a hotch potch of poorly designed and psychometrically inadequate homegrown measures. This is an 8-item scale derived from 45 items on the basis of high loadings on the unrotated first factor in a factor analysis, and high inter-item and item–total correlations. It has been widely used and adapted, showing good internal consistency and acceptable validity.

One major difficulty in practice is overestimation of user satisfaction. There are at least four reasons why this happens (Kalman, 1983). First, there is a problem persuading the dissatisfied users, who tend to drop out of treatment early, or to have had unsuccessful treatments, to fill in and return questionnaires. For those who do fill in the questionaire, there are pressures to conform with the expectation that the service was helpful and a tendency to an 'agreement' response set. If the patients are dependent on the treatment facility now or in the future it is particularly difficult for them to express negative views. Some questionnaires used to measure acceptability tend to be insensitive to dissatisfaction, leading to ceiling effects and positively skewed distributions.

There have been a number of solutions proposed to these difficulties (Larsen et al., 1979; Lebow, 1982). First, given that the purpose of audit is to identify areas ripe for improvement, it is helpful to focus on *dissatisfaction* data, for example by identifying subgroups of dissatisfied clients within a service, or aspects of the service with which users are less satisfied. One can then compare results over time when new aspects of service or improvements in service are introduced. This overcomes another problem, the lack of meaningful comparisons in satisfaction data. The figure of, say, 5% of users not satisfied, means very little on its own. It is difficult to compare with results from other services because of differences in method, timing of measurement, case mix, and so on. On the other hand, the figure is more meaningful if we know that before a planned service improvement was implemented, 10% of users were dissatisfied .

Sources of distortion in responses, particularly acquiescence, social desirability, and reactivity, can be reduced by using independent data collectors, taking care to guarantee anonymity, to explain that the assessment evaluates the service not the clients, that the analysis focuses on group data, and providing reassurance about the use to which the data will be put.

Another useful approach is to relate satisfaction to client expectations, exploring whether the service disappointed or exceeded these, and hence gaining insight into possible inappropriate expectations. This can suggest improvements in how the service is presented to potential users.

A common strategy is to triangulate measures so that one is not dependent solely on questionnaire data. Behavioural measures include drop out rates, or whether people actually do recommend the service to others (rather than saying they would do so). A further suggestion, rarely implemented, has been to take the Goal Attainment Scaling method (Kiresuk & Lund, 1978; see later) and to use it specifically to agree the domains and scaling of satisfaction measurement between the user and their mental health professional (Bornstein & Rychtarik, 1983). This has the considerable advantages of all idiographic measures, which are their sensitivity to personal meanings, preferences, and expectations, but shares their disadvantages of higher cost and effort with loss of parsimony and comparability. The idiographic approach can complement service-wide standard measurement, and is justified where aspects of services valued by users are different from the priorities of service providers and managers, and individual preferences for service features vary considerably. Given the cost and complexity of negotiating individual goals, other methods of giving the user perspective salience can be considered, for example, establishing a panel of users or ex-users willing to be involved with service audit.

The specific problem of low response rates to questionnaires can be tackled in an evaluation study by pre-selecting a sample of the clinic or service population which is representative but small enough to manage an intensive follow-up effort, including tracking people to new addresses, making multiple attempts to contact them, and so on.

Despite these difficulties, some broad conclusions about user satisfaction can be drawn. Not surprisingly, mutual agreed termination of treatment gives the highest satisfaction. Demographic characteristics have not generally been found to be good predictors, although some services have poorer satisfaction ratings from ethnic minority clients. Some client groups are consistently less satisfied with services, including drug abusers, suicidal clients, psychotic clients, and those with enduring mental health problems (Lebow, 1982). User preferences between treatments are not well understood (Yeaton & Sechrest, 1981) although some treatments are by their nature likely to be less acceptable, for example, phobic patients dislike aversive imaginal or in vivo behavioural treatments. It is possible some treatments of high efficacy have low acceptability, thus reducing their clinical effectiveness. The search for ways to make such treatments more acceptable to users therefore becomes a high priority.

In summary, there are great benefits for service audit in routinely including a simple, low-cost measure of service acceptability with adequate psychometric properties (Attkisson & Zwick, 1982; Budman & Springer, 1987; Lebow & Newman, 1987) although there is a problem of blandly uninformative results when high proportions of those questioned report themselves as 'satisfied'. For this reason, services that are committed to taking users' views seriously should focus on discovering and eliminating sources of patient dissatisfaction with the service.

Service effectiveness and outcome evaluation
Although user satisfaction is higher where treatment has been effective, it would in theory be possible to provide a mental health service that is cost-efficient and acceptable to patients and referrers—prompt, reliable, accessible, courteous, timely, and informative—but which does not provide the most effective treatments in terms of good mental health

outcomes. Unless outcomes are routinely monitored, practitioners receive no objective feedback and ineffective practice can continue without reflection.

Choice of outcome measures depends on the level of the evaluation or the purpose of the audit. There is certainly no shortage of candidates; Lambert and Hill (1994) report that one survey found a total of 1410 outcome measures in a review of outcome research in 20 selected journals from 1983 to 1988. However, more than half of these were used in only one study. A much smaller pool of instruments is used repeatedly. They suggest that the most commonly used instruments in psychotherapy outcome research are the State-Trait Anxiety Inventory (STAI); the Beck Depression Inventory (BDI); the Symptom Checklist-90 (SCL-90); the Locke-Wallace Marital Adjustment Inventory; and the Minnesota Multiphasic Personality Inventory (MMPI). Although frequently used in research, the MMPI is too long and user-hostile to be suitable for audit and service evaluation, but the others are functional. Clinical practitioners seek to use measures that can be incorporated easily into the process of client contact (Nelson, 1981). Many of the instruments developed in psychiatric research are short and unintrusive enough to be suitable (Thompson, 1989).

Fonagy and Higgitt (1989), in relation to the evaluation of psychotherapy services, argue strongly for broadening the base of outcome measurement from the over-reliance on paper and pencil questionnaires. They favour sophisticated structured interview self-report methods combined with therapist-rated observable change and social indicators, such as service utilisation, court appearances, and school attendance. They see little merit in using ratings from independent 'experts' or patient's relatives.

Measures that are suitable for tracking change in psychotherapy patients are often not suitable for measuring the effectiveness of services for people with severe, enduring mental health problems. The problem of selecting rating scales for evaluating these services has been addressed by Green and Gracely (1987). They subjected seven brief rating scales to a weighted multi-attribute utility analysis (Edwards, Guttentag, & Snapper, 1975). The weightings emphasised the criteria of group relevance, objective referents, good psychometrics, and being widely understood, with low cost and clinical usefulness close behind. On this basis they found that two scales were much better than the others. The Level of Functioning scale (Newman, 1980; Newman et al., 1983) contains 10 levels that describe patients who vary in functioning from total dependence to needing no mental health service contact, with 20–50-word descriptions covering four areas of functioning: self-care, social, vocational, and stress tolerance. This measure was most useful clinically, better able to identify treatment processes, and easier to explain to many audiences. The Role Functioning Scale (McPheeters, 1984) contains four subscales, three of which were selected: working productivity, independent living, and extended social network relationships. These were anchored with seven 15–25-word descriptions summing to get a measure of global role functioning. This appeared to raters to be more relevant to people with enduring mental illness than the Level of Functioning scale, by addressing role functioning. Green and Gracely conclude that the choice of either scale can be defended but that any measure should be evaluated on a pilot basis in the setting where it will be used.

An outcome that is often seen as particularly relevant to people with severe, longstanding mental illnesses is their quality of life. For example, Lehman (1983) reports a survey of 278 Los Angeles 'board & care' home residents on personal characteristics, objective quality of life indicators (living situation, family, social relations, leisure, finances, law-safety, work, health), and the same domains assessed subjectively. As objective quality of life indicators have only modest relationships with life satisfaction in the general population, this model emphasises subjective quality of life.

The search for a practical set of instruments for measuring outcomes in different mental health services continues; a recent UK research initiative from the Mental Health Foundation calls for proposals to develop a core battery of measures suitable for evaluating psychotherapy services, and the Department of Health in England is sponsoring the development of outcome scales for community mental health services (Wing, Curtis, & Beevor, 1994).

The type of measure one chooses will depend on whether the service as a whole is to be evaluated or whether one is more interested in auditing the change processes in homogeneous subgroups of clients. To evaluate the whole service, outcomes are monitored using nomothetic multitrait measures of global outcomes (for example, of symptomatology, difficulties in personal relationships). Nested within this, nomothetic unitrait measures of specific outcomes (e.g. eating disorder or obsessional compulsive disorder) or idiographic measures (e.g. personal questionnaires, repertory grids) can be used. The principles and practice of these forms of outcome measurement are described elsewhere in this volume and will not be covered further here.

When data from a standardised measure are obtained on a clinic population over a period of time, it is possible to obtain a picture of service performance by plotting intake, end of therapy, and follow-up scores in the way described by Jacobson and Truax (1991). They graph the intake scores against the end of therapy scores, giving a scatterplot where the diagonal line represents no change; scores below the line represent improvement, and those above the line deterioration (see Fig. 18.1). A reliable change index is calculated in terms of the standard error of measurement of the instrument and is represented by the dotted lines above and below the no-change diagonal. The horizontal lines represent one and two standard deviations from the intake mean. As a rule of thumb, when someone's score has moved to a point more than one standard deviation from the clinic mean, they can be seen to have improved, and when two standard deviations, to have recovered (Jacobson, Follette, & Revenstorf, 1984). The clinical significance of change can be estimated more precisely when there are normative data available on inpatient, outpatient, and non-clinical populations, as, for example, there are for the SCL-90 and the BDI. The horizontal lines are then drawn to represent cutoffs between adjacent distributions; e.g. between mildly and moderately symptomatic and between moderately and severely symptomatic.

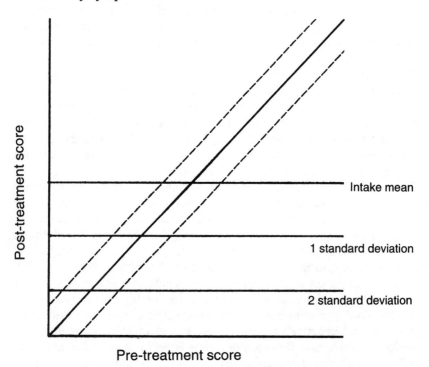

FIG. 18.1. Scatterplot of intake scores against end of therapy scores. Adapted from Jacobson and Truax, 1991.

Where there are consistent negative correlations between admission scores and change scores, it is possible that the statistical phenomenon of regression to the mean is leading one to overestimate improvement rates. One way to correct this is to use the Edwards-Nunnally method which introduces an adjustment, the estimated true score, that is substituted for the initial scores (Nunnally, 1967). The confidence interval of two standard errors of measurement is then centred on the estimated true admission scores and subsequent scores are compared; improvement, no improvement, no change, or deterioration assigned according to whether a score falls above, within, or below the confidence interval.

Speer (1994) used this method in a cohort of 92 anxious and depressed clients, finding an improvement rate of 51% and a deterioration rate of 5%. Speer argues that the traditional language of mental health outcome research has alienated decision makers and has failed to influence them. For example, most service purchasers or managers find it hard to understand what it means to say 'the average psychotherapy client is better off at the end of treatment than 80% of untreated people with a similar problem'. By using standard improvement and deterioration rates, decision and policy makers are given more comprehensible information. Of course, this begs the question of whether mental health providers want to place simple, end-of-treatment improvement rates in the hands of decision makers. Some would argue that this is dangerously inadequate as a basis for purchasing services.

In contrast to these approaches, which judge success in terms of the end-of-therapy scores moving towards the distribution of non-clinical population scores, practitioners point out that what would be a disappointing outcome for one patient could represent an extraordinary achievement for another (Strupp, 1986). Goal attainment scaling (Kiresuk & Lund, 1978) overcomes this problem by establishing criteria for success for each individual patient separately. For each client, a number of domains are established where improvements are expected from treatment. For each domain, five levels of outcome are described in terms that are observable and verifiable, so that, for example, what would be an excellent, good, or poor outcome is spelled out and agreed with the client. Despite methodological flaws and limitations (Calsyn & Davidson, 1978; Cytrynbaum, Ginath, Birdwell, & Brant, 1979), this remains an instructive way for clinicians and clients to test the impact of their therapeutic work against their own predictions.

Service efficiency and economic evaluation

Efficiency maximises service output for a given input: improving efficiency increases therapeutic activity for the same costs or maintains throughput at a lower cost. Routine examination of the management of referral flow, waiting lists, assessment processes, and length of intervention can reveal striking examples of inefficient practice within a service, some of which are very simply remedied once the feedback has been received.

From the perspective of those allocating resources, efficiency is clearly vital, but clinicians are hostile to improving efficiency at the cost of service quality or effectiveness. Cost effectiveness is therefore a more useful concept than cost efficiency. Here one is aiming to obtain better outcomes for a given cost, or the same outcomes for a lower cost.

As well as the distinction between cost efficiency and cost effectiveness, health economists discuss cost utility and cost benefit. Briefly stated, cost-utility analysis expands the concept of effectiveness to estimate the quality of life remaining to the individual in comparing different treatments. It has been criticised for using a technical and opaque procedure to mask the fact that these resource allocations are matters of social values and political debate (Carr-Hill, 1991). Cost-benefit analysis measures costs and outcomes in the same units (usually monetary) and attempts to compare broader social benefits of treatments (Johannesson & Jönsson, 1991). The true conceptual distinctions between these approaches have probably been overstated (Phelps & Mushlin, 1991).

A number of methods have been developed to estimate cost effectiveness in psychotherapy services (Yates, 1980; Yates & Newman, 1980) but in practice there are considerable technical problems, for example in specifying what should be included in costs and how broadly to interpret outcomes (Sorensen & Grove, 1978; Weinstein, 1990). However, service evaluation can include simple estimates of cost effectiveness without entering into complex technical procedures (Siegert & Yates, 1980). Newman and Howard (1986, p.186) state that 'the most pervasive myth within the clinical community is that costs are the business of business and not a clinical concern'. Every therapy given has an opportunity cost; for example, by undertaking a 100-session therapy, the opportunity to give five people 20-session therapies is lost. Newman and Howard introduce the clinically meaningful concept of 'therapeutic effort' which can be assessed as part of service evaluation. This includes three components; the dosage of each element of treatment, the extent to which it restricts the patient's life, and the cumulative costs in human and material resources.

EVALUATION IN CONTEXT

In reviewing the dimensions on which mental health services can be evaluated, and the range of techniques available, it is easy to pluck service evaluation out of its context. This section attempts to redress this by briefly discussing the organisational, strategic, and systemic background to these activities.

Most service evaluation and audit is undertaken for complex reasons, attempting to balance the goals of the different players in the health care system; funders, providers, policy makers, and consumers. Effectiveness, efficiency, and acceptability are potentially contradictory in terms of the goals of these stakeholders. Vuori (1982, p.5) rightly reminds us that 'evaluation is by definition a value-laden activity, and must be acknowledged to be so, thus suggesting the need to take all relevant parties' views into consideration'. A systemic appreciation of the role of service evaluation is therefore very helpful. One such approach to service evaluation is described by Campbell, Steenbarger, Smith, and Stucky (1982). They begin by acknowledging that there are multiple perspectives on the evaluation question and give a relativistic, perspectival interpretation of results. The evaluation issues are reformulated in terms of all the systems involved and their paths of influence. This model is highly appropriate to mental health service evaluation. Many carefully designed evaluations have failed because of the neglect of this principle, for example where external evaluators meet with implacable organisational resistance or where an enthusiastic but naïve service manager finds their best efforts to monitor team performance subtly sabotaged by unwilling staff. Hardy (1994) advises on how to make the evaluation more likely to be successful by ensuring it is consistent with the underlying goals and values of the host organisation.

Service evaluations are commissioned by many different interests. In the UK, this includes Department of Health policymakers and executives; local health authorities and their public health departments; hospitals and community services and their service managers; senior clinicians and clinical directors; charities, voluntary organisations, and user groups. The unexpressed reasons for the commission are as important to understand as the formal brief. If one only paid attention to the latter, one might believe that it was all in order to improve the quality of care, to ensure accountability and the right use of public money, or to gain understanding of services and innovation in providing them. Other, less explicit, reasons for commissioning an evaluation could include the post hoc justification of an unpopular managerial decision, the search for rescue when a service is in trouble, a substitute for committing revenue to a service, or a desire to have a 'quick fix' for an intractable organisational problem.

Service evaluation projects do not always have the impact the evaluators expect on management or provider behaviour. At times, this is simply because one has misread the commissioners' true purposes, but it is often because insufficient care has been taken to ensure that service staff and managers feel that they have ownership of the project. If this is not achieved, there will be no commitment to implementing changes on the basis of evaluation results. These issues point to the importance of using exploratory, naturalistic designs, developing political as well as evaluation skills, and aiming for congruence of project content, context, and process with organisational goals. The other common mistake is to fail to leave enough time for presenting and disseminating results. When planning the evaluation it is always tempting to cut down on time at the end for writing up, as this adds to the cost of the work without apparently adding much value. Even if one is not working within an explicit action research paradigm, it is very wasteful of all the resources and effort used in the evaluation if the results are not properly communicated and given the best possible opportunity to influence practice.

REFERENCES

Attkisson, C.C., Hargreaves, W.A., Horowitz, M.J., & Sorensen, J.E. (1978). *Evaluation of Human Service Programs.* New York: Academic Press.

Attkisson, C.C. & Zwick, R. (1982). The Client Satisfaction Questionnaire: psychometric properties and correlations with service utilization and psychotherapy outcome. *Evaluation and Program Planning, 5,* 233-237.

Bell, R.A., Nguyen, T.D., Warheit, G.J., & Buhl, J.M. (1978). Service utilization, social indicator and citizen survey approaches to human service need assessment. In C.C. Attkisson, W.A. Hargreaves, M.J. Horowitz, & J.E. Sorensen, (Eds.), *Evaluation of Human Service Programs.* New York: Academic Press.

Bornstein, P.H. & Rychtarik, R.G. (1983). Consumer satisfaction in adult behaviour therapy: Procedures, problems and future perspectives. *Behaviour Therapy, 14,* 191-208.

Brewin, C.R. & Bradley, C. (1989). Patient preferences and randomised clinical trials. *British Medical Journal, 299,* 313-5

Brewin, C.R., Wing, J.K., Mangen, S.P., Brugha, T.S., & MacCarthy, B. (1987). Principles and practice of measuring needs in the long-term mentally ill: the MRC needs for care assessment. *Psychological Medicine, 17,* 971-981.

Budman, S.H. & Springer, T. (1987). Treatment delay, outcome and satisfaction in time-limited group and individual psychotherapy. *Professional Psychology: Research and Practice, 18,* 647-649.

Bullmore, E., Joyce, H., Marks, I.M., & Connolly, J. (1992). A computerised quality assurance system (QAS) on a general psychiatric ward: Towards efficient clinical audit. *Journal of Mental Health, 1*, 257-263.

Calsyn, R. & Davidson, W. (1978). Do we really want a program evaluation strategy based on individual goals? *Community Mental Health Journal, 14*, 300-308.

Campbell, D.E., Steenbarger, B.N., Smith, T.W., & Stucky, R.J. (1982). An ecological systems approach to evaluation. *Evaluation Review, 6*, 625-648.

Carr-Hill, R.A. (1991). Allocating resources to health care: is the QALY (Quality Adjusted Life Year) a technical solution to a political problem? *International Journal of Health Services, 21*, 351-363

Charlton, S.S. (1983). Lack of protection for confidentiality of peer review records in court. *Australian Clinical Review, 10*, 29-30.

Collard, R. (1989). *Total Quality: Success Through People*. Harrogate: Institute of Personnel Management.

Conway, A.S., Melzer, D., & Hale, A.S. (1994). The outcome of targeting community mental health services: evidence from the West Lambeth schizophrenia cohort. *British Medical Journal, 308*, 627-630.

Cook, T.D. & Campbell, D.T. (1979). *Quasi-experimentation: Design and Analysis for Field Settings*. Chicago: Rand McNally.

Crombie, I.K., Davies, H.T.O., Abraham, S.C.S., & Florey, C. Du V. (1993). *The Audit Handbook: Improving Health Care Through Clinical Audit*. Chichester, UK: Wiley.

Cytrynbaum, S.Y., Ginath, Y., Birdwell, J., & Brant, L. (1979). Goal attainment scaling: a critical review. *Evaluation Quarterly, 3*, 5-40.

Department of Health (1989). *Medical Audit. Working Paper 6 of Working For Patients*. London: HMSO.

Department of Health (1991). *Research for Health. A research and development strategy for the NHS*. London: HMSO.

Department of Health (1994). *Supporting Research and Development in the NHS*. A report to the Minister for Health by a Research & Development Task Force chaired by Professor Anthony Culyer. London: HMSO

Donabedian, A. (1980). Basic approaches to assessment. Chapter 3 in *The Definition of Quality and Approaches to its Assessment*. Ann Arbor MI: Health Administration Press.

Edwards, W., Guttentag, M., & Snapper, K. (1975). A decision-theoretic approach to evaluation research. In E.L. Struening & M. Guttentag (Eds.), *Handbook of Evaluation Research* (Vol 1) Beverly Hills, CA; Sage Publications.

Firth, J., Shapiro, D.A., & Parry, G. (1986). The impact of research on the practice of psychotherapy. *British Journal of Psychotherapy, 2*, 169-179.

Firth-Cozens, J. (1993). *Audit in Mental Health Services*. Hove, UK: Lawrence Erlbaum Associates Ltd.

Fonagy, P. & Higgitt, A. (1989). Evaluating the performance of departments of psychotherapy. *Psychoanalytic Psychotherapy, 4*, 121-153.

Fox, P.D. & Kuldau, M. (1968). Expanding the framework for mental health program evaluation. *Archives of General Psychiatry, 19*, 538-544.

Fulchiero, A., Miller, S., Foler, C.R., Ballantine, H.T., & Amorosino, C.S. (1980). Can the PRSOs be cost effective? *New England Journal of Medicine, 299*, 574-580.

Garfield, S.L. (1986). Research on client variables in psychotherapy. In S.L. Garfield & A.E. Bergin (Eds.), *Handbook of Psychotherapy and Behaviour Change* (3rd edn) New York: Wiley.

Garrett, B. (1987). *The Learning Organisation and the Need for Directors who Think*. London: Fontana.

Green, R.S. & Attkisson, C.C. (1984). Quality assurance and program evaluation. *American Behavioural Scientist, 27*, 552-582.

Green, R.S & Gracely, E.J. (1987). Selecting a rating scale for evaluating services to the chronically mentally ill. *Community Mental Health Journal, 23*, 91-102.

Hardy, G. (1994). Organizational factors. In M. Aveline & D.A. Shapiro (Eds.), *Research Foundations for Psychotherapy Practice*, Chichester, UK: Wiley.

Hillier, F.S. & Lieberman, G.J. (1974). *Operations Research*. San Francisco: Holden-Day.

Horowitz, M.J. & Stinson, C. (1991). University of California, San Francisco Center for the Study of Neuroses. Program on conscious and unconscious mental processes. In L.E. Beutler & M. Crago (Eds.), *Psychotherapy Research: An International Review of Programmatic Studies*.Washington: American Psychological Association.

Horrobin, D.F. (1982). Peer review: a philosophically faulty concept which is proving disastrous for science. *Behavioural and Brain Sciences, 5*, 217-218.

Hsu, L.M. (1989). Random sampling, randomization and equivalence of contrasted groups in psychotherapy outcome research. *Journal of Consulting and Clinical Psychology, 57*, 131-137.

Jacobson, N.S., Follette, W.C., & Revenstorf, D. (1984). Psychotherapy outcome research. Methods for reporting variability and evaluating clinical significance. *Behavior Therapy, 15*, 336-352.

Jacobson, N.S. & Truax, P. (1991). Clinical significance: a statistical approach to defining meaningful change in psychotherapy research. *Journal of Consulting and Clinical Psychology, 59*, 12-19.

Johannesson, M. & Jönsson, B. (1991). Economic evaluation in health care: Is there a role for cost-benefit analysis? *Health Policy, 17*, 1-23.

Juran, J.M. (1988). *Juran on Planning for Quality*. New York: The Free Press.

Kalman, T.P. (1983). An overview of patient satisfaction with psychiatric treatment. *Hospital and Community Psychiatry, 34*, 48-54.

Kiresuk, T.J. & Lund, S.H. (1978). Goal attainment scaling. In C.C. Attkisson, W.A. Hargreaves, M.J. Horowitz, & J.E. Sorensen (Eds.), *Evaluation of Human Service Programs*. New York: Academic Press.

Kraemer, H.C. (1981). Coping strategies in psychiatric clinical research. *Journal of Consulting and Clinical Psychology, 49*, 309-319.

Lalonde, B.I.D. (1982). Quality assurance. In M.J. Austin & W.E. Hershey (Eds.), *Handbook on Mental Health Administration*. San Francisco: Jossey-Bass.

Lambert, M.J. & Hill, C.E. (1994). Assessing psychotherapy outcomes and processes. In A.E. Bergin & S.L. Garfield (Eds.), *Handbook of Psychotherapy and Behavior Change*. (4th Edn.) New York: Wiley.

Larsen, D.L., Attkisson, C.C., Hargreaves, W.A., & Nguyen, T.D. (1979). Assessment of client/patient satisfaction: Development of a general scale. *Evaluation and Program Planning, 2*, 197-207.

Lebow, J. (1982). Consumer satisfaction with mental health treatment. *Psychological Bulletin, 91*, 244-259.

Lebow, J.L. & Newman, F.L. (1987). The utilization of simple measures in mental health program evaluation. *Evaluation and Program Planning, 10*, 189-190.

Lehman, A.F. (1983). The well-being of chronic mental patients: Assessing their Quality of Life. *Archives of General Psychiatry, 40*, 369-373.

Lorion, R.P. & Felner, R.D. (1986). Research on psychotherapy with the disadvantaged. In S.L. Garfield & A.E. Bergin (Eds.), *Handbook of Psychotherapy and Behaviour Change* (3rd edn) New York: Wiley.

Luborsky, L. & Crits-Cristoph, P. (eds) (1990). *Understanding Transference: The Core Conflictual Relationship Theme Method*. New York: Basic Books.

Maxwell, R.J. (1984). Quality assessment in health. *British Medical Journal, 288*, 1470-1472.

McDonald, R., Marks, I.M., & Blizard, R. (1988). Quality assurance of outcome in mental health care: a model for routine use in clinical settings. *Health Trends, 20*, 111-114.

McPheeters, H.L. (1984). Statewide mental health outcome evaluation: A perspective of two southern states. *Community Mental Health Journal, 20*, 44-55.

Milne, D. (1987). *Evaluating Mental Health Practice: Methods and Applications*. London: Croom Helm.

Mohr, W.L. & Mohr, H. (1983). *Quality Circles*. Reading, MA: Addison Wesley,

Nelson, R.O. (1981). Realistic dependent measures for clinical use. *Journal of Consulting and Clinical Psychology, 49*, 168-182.

Newman, F.L. (1980). Strengths, uses and problems of global scales as an evaluation instrument. *Evaluation and Program Planning, 3*, 257-268

Newman, F.L., Heverly, M.A., Rosen, M., Kopta, S.M., & Bedell, R. (1983). Influences on internal evaluation data dependability: Clinicians as a source of variance. In A.J. Love (Ed.), *Developing effective internal evaluation: Vol 20 New Directions for Program Evaluation*. San Francisco: Jossey Bass Inc.

Newman, F.L., & Howard, K.I. (1986). Therapeutic effort, treatment outcome and national health policy. *Amercian Psychologist, 41*, 181-187.

Newman, F.L. & Howard, K.I. (1991). Introduction to the special section on seeking new clinical research methods. *Journal of Consulting and Clinical Psychology, 59*, 8-11.

NIMH (National Institute for Mental Health) (1976). *A Working Manual of Simple Program Evaluation Techniques for Community Mental Health Centers*. Washington, DC: Government Printing Office.

Normand, C. (1991). *Clinical Audit in Professions Allied to Medicine and Related Therapy Professions: Report to the Department of Health*. Belfast: Health and Health Care Research Unit, Queens University.

Nunnally, J.C. (1967). *Psychometric Theory*. New York: McGraw Hill.

Phelps, C.E. & Mushlin, A.I. (1991). On the (near) equivalence of cost-effectiveness and cost-benefit analysis. *International Journal of Technology Assessment in Health Care, 7*, 12-21.

Rice, L.N. & Greenberg, L.S. (1984). The new research paradigm. In L.N. Rice & L.S. Greenberg (Eds.), *Patterns of Change: Intensive Analysis of Psychotherapy Process*. New York: Guilford Press.

Rossi, M.H. & Freeman, H.E. (1982). *Evaluation: A Systematic Approach*. (2nd edn.) Beverly Hills, CA: Sage Publications.

Ryle, A. (1990). Treating patients with personality disorders. In *Cognitive Analytic Therapy: Active Participation in Change*. Chichester, UK: Wiley.

Safran, J.D., McMain, S., Crocker, P., & Murray, P. (1990). Therapeutic alliance rupture as a therapy event for empirical investigation. *Psychotherapy, 27,* 154-165.

Schon, D.A. (1983). *The Reflective Practitioner*. London: Temple Smith.

Siegel, L.M., Attkisson, C.C., & Carson, L.G. (1978). Need identification and program planning in the community context. In C.C. Attkisson, W.A. Hargreaves, M.J. Horowitz, & J.E. Sorensen, (Eds.), *Evaluation of Human Service Programs*. New York: Academic Press.

Siegert, F.A. & Yates, B.T. (1980). Behavioural child-management cost effectiveness: A comparison of individual in-office, individual in-home and group delivery systems for behavioural child management. *Evaluation and the Health Professions, 3,* 123-152.

Smith, R. (1990). Medicine's need for kaizen; putting quality first. *British Medical Journal, 301,* 679-680.

Sorensen, J.E. & Grove, H.D. (1978). Using cost-outcome and cost-effectiveness analyses for improved program management and accountability. In C.C. Attkisson, W.A. Hargreaves, M.J. Horowitz, & J.E. Sorensen (Eds.), *Evaluation of Human Service Programs*. New York: Academic Press.

Speer, D.C. (1994). Can treatment research inform decision makers? Nonexperimental method issues and examples among older outpatients. *Journal of Consulting and Clinical Psychology, 62,* 560-568.

Strupp, H.H. (1986). Psychotherapy. Research, practice and public policy (how to avoid dead ends). *American Psychologist, 41,* 120-130.

Thompson, C. (Ed.) (1989). *The Instruments of Psychiatric Research*. Chichester, UK: Wiley.

Tuchfeld, B.S. (1979). Some approaches to assessing change. In L. Datta & R. Perloff (Eds.), *Improving Evaluations*. Beverly Hills/London: Sage Publications.

Vuori, H.Y. (1982). *Quality assurance of health services: concepts and methodologies. Public Health in Europe 16*. Copenhagen: World Health Organisation.

Ware, J.E., Snyder, M.K., Wright, W.R., & Davies, A.R. (1983). Defining and measuring patient satisfaction with medical care. *Evaluation and Program Planning, 6,* 247-263.

Weinstein, M.C. (1990). Principles of cost-effective resource allocation in health care organisations. *International Journal of Technology Assessment in Health Care, 6,* 93-103.

Weiss, A.T. (1975). The consumer model of assessing community health needs. *Evaluation, 2,* 71-73.

Wildavsky, A. (1972). The self-evaluating organisation. *Public Administration Review, 32,* 509-520.

Windle, C. (1979). Searching for the JND in mental health. In L. Datta & R. Perloff (Eds.), *Improving Evaluations*. Beverly Hills/London: Sage Publications.

Wing, J.K. (1994). Mental Illness. In *Needs Assessment*. London: Routledge.

Wing, J.K., Curtis, R., & Beevor, A. (1994). Health of the nation: Measuring mental health outcomes. *Psychiatric Bulletin, 18,* 690-691.

Wurzburg, G. (1979). What limits the impact of evaluations on Federal policy? In L. Datta & R. Perloff (Eds.), *Improving Evaluations*. Beverly Hills/London: Sage Publications.

Yates, B. (1980). *Improving Effectiveness and Reducing Costs in Mental Health*. Springfield, IL: Thomas

Yates, B. & Newman, F.L. (1980). Approaches to cost-effectiveness analysis and cost-benefit analysis in psychotherapy. In G.R. Vandenbos (Ed.), *Psychotherapy: Practice, Research, Policy*. Beverley Hills, CA: Sage.

Yeaton, W. & Sechrest, L. (1981). Critical dimensions in the choice and maintenance of successful treatments: Strength, integrity and effectiveness. *Journal of Consulting and Clinical Psychology, 49*, 156-167.

Author Index

Subject Index